冨樫義博

"IF I COULD BE REINCARNATED AS ANYONE, WHO WOULD I BE" PART 3: A PSYCHIC. A REALLY STRONG ONE. MY POWERS MANIFEST IN MY SENIOR YEAR OF HIGH SCHOOL AFTER I FAIL THE EXAMS FOR A TOP COLLEGE. USING MY POWERS OF TELEPATHY, PSYCHOKINESIS, AND TELEPORTATION, I COMMIT A MULTITUDE OF EVIL ACTS, BUT I STOP AFTER MEETING A GIRL WITH PRECOGNITION WHO GOES TO MY CRAM SCHOOL, AND WE FALL IN LOVE. (MAN, I'M AN IDIOT.) AFTER THE GIRL'S PRECOG POWERS WARN US THAT SOME BIG-TIME COUNTRY'S INTELLIGENCE DIVISION IS COMING TO THREATEN OUR LIVES, WE ESCAPE FROM THEIR ASSASSINS AND BEGIN WHAT WILL BECOME A DAILY ROUTINE OF ESCAPE AND MORTAL COMBAT. WE ARE STILL IN HIDING IN SOME UNDISCLOSED LOCATION TODAY.

—YOSHIHIRO TOGASHI, 1991

Born in 1966, Yoshihiro Togashi won the prestigious Tezuka Award for new manga artists at the age of 20. He debuted in Japan's WEEKLY SHONEN JUMP magazine in 1988 with the romantic comedy manga TENDE SHOWARU CUPID. His hit comic YU YU HAKUSHO ran in SHONEN JUMP from 1990 to 1994. Togashi's other manga include I'M NOT AFRAID OF WOLVES!, LEVEL E, and HUNTER X HUNTER. He and his wife, SAILOR MOON creator Naoko Takeuchi, have a son.

YUYU HAKUSHO VOL. 3
The SHONEN JUMP Graphic Novel Edition

This graphic novel contains material that was originally published in English in **SHONEN JUMP** #9-12.

STORY AND ART BY
YOSHIHIRO TOGASHI

English Adaptation/Gary Leach
Translation/Lillian Olsen
Touch-Up Art & Lettering/Cynthia Dobson and Bill Schuch
Graphics & Cover Design/Sean Lee
Senior Editor/Jason Thompson
Graphic Novel Editor/Shaenon K. Garrity

Associate Managing Editor/Albert Totten
Managing Editor/Annette Roman
Production Manager/Noboru Watanabe
Editor in Chief/Hyoe Narita
Sr. Director, Licensing and Acquisitions/Rika Inouye
V.P. of Marketing/Liza Coppola
V.P. of Strategic Development/Yumi Hoashi
Publisher/Seiji Horibuchi

PARENTAL ADVISORY
YUYU HAKUSHO is rated "T" for teens. It may contain violence, language, alcohol or tobacco usage, or suggestive situations. It is recommended for ages 13 and up.

Printed in Canada.

Published by VIZ, LLC
P.O. Box 77010 • San Francisco, CA 94107

SHONEN JUMP Graphic Novel Edition
10 9 8 7 6 5 4 3 2 1
First printing, January 2004

www.viz.com

THE WORLD'S
MOST POPULAR MANGA

GRAPHIC NOVEL
www.shonenjump.com

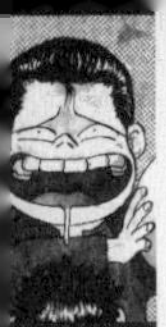

SHONEN JUMP GRAPHIC NOVEL

YuYu HAKUSHO™

Vol.3
IN THE FLESH

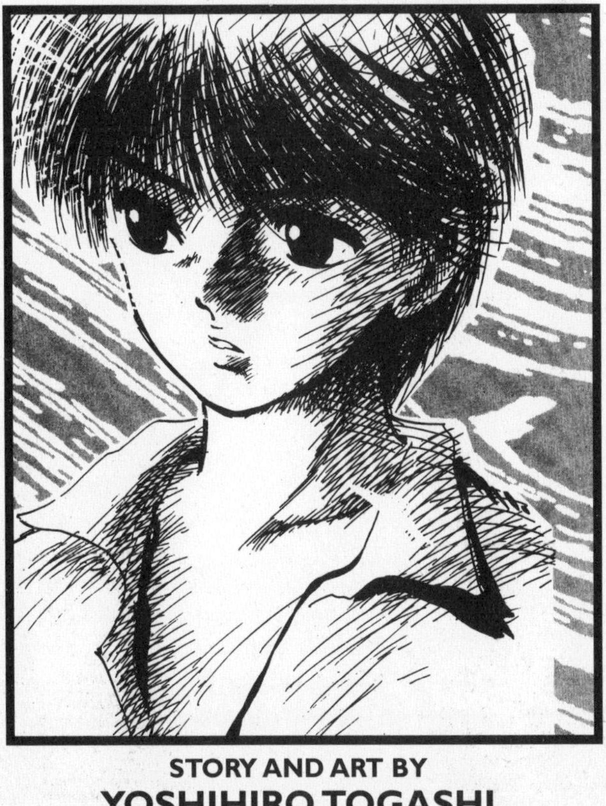

STORY AND ART BY
YOSHIHIRO TOGASHI

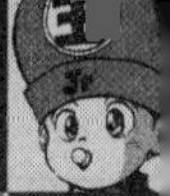

THE STORY SO FAR...

When surly street punk Yusuke Urameshi died in an unexpected act of self-sacrifice, the Underworld decided to give him a second chance. After weeks of trials in the afterlife, Yusuke has returned to his body and to life. But the Underworld isn't through with him yet. As Yusuke resumes his old life of junior-high delinquency, his contacts in the spirit world prepare to introduce him to a whole new career...

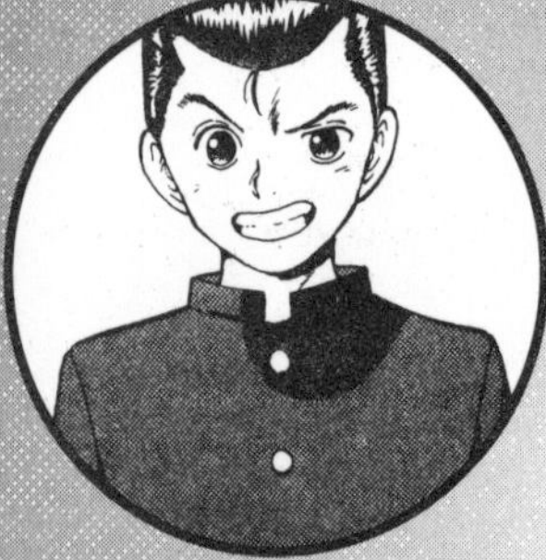

YUSUKE URAMESHI 浦飯幽助
The toughest student at Sarayashiki Junior High - until his untimely death. Now he's finally rejoined the world of the living.

ぼたん BOTAN
The ferrywoman of the Sanzu River (the River Styx in Western mythology), Botan guided Yusuke through his trials in the afterlife.

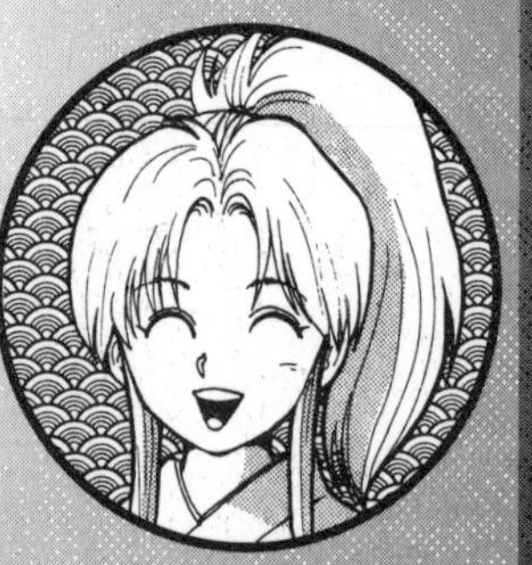

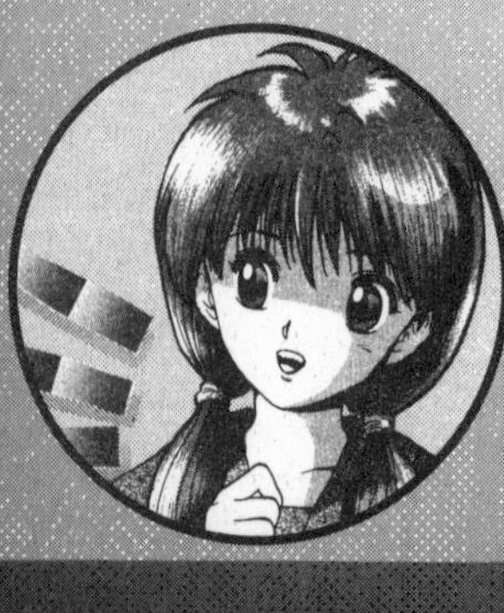

KEIKO YUKIMURA 雪村螢子
Yusuke's childhood friend. She cared for his comatose body while he was dead and delivered the kiss that returned him to life.

コエンマ KOENMA

The son of King Enma, lord of the Underworld. He runs the spirit world while his father is away.

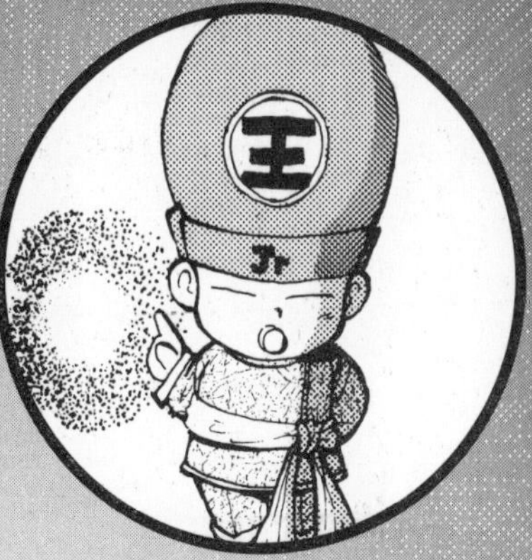

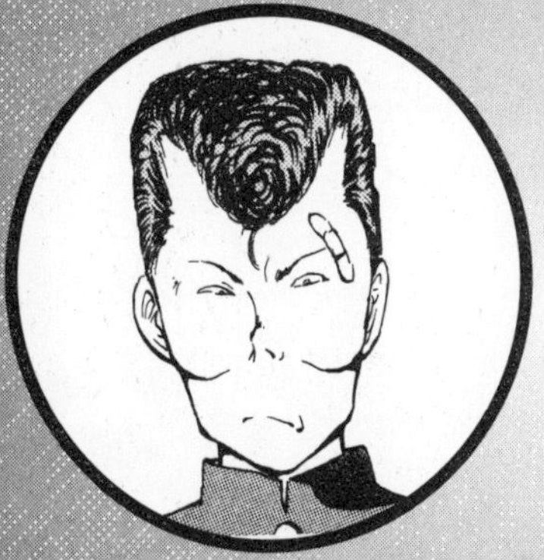

KUWABARA 桑原

Another Sarayashiki delinquent, and Yusuke's chief rival. An encounter with the ghostly Yusuke awakened untapped psychic powers within him.

浦飯温子 ATSUKO URAMESHI

Yusuke's loving but flaky mom, who's better at partying than looking after her delinquent son.

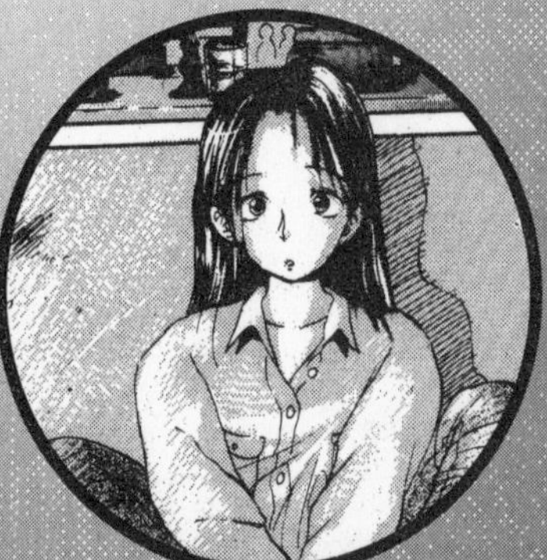

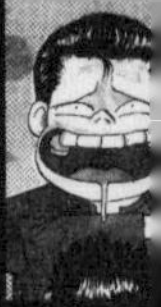

YU YU HAKUSHO VOLUME 3 IN THE FLESH

CONTENTS

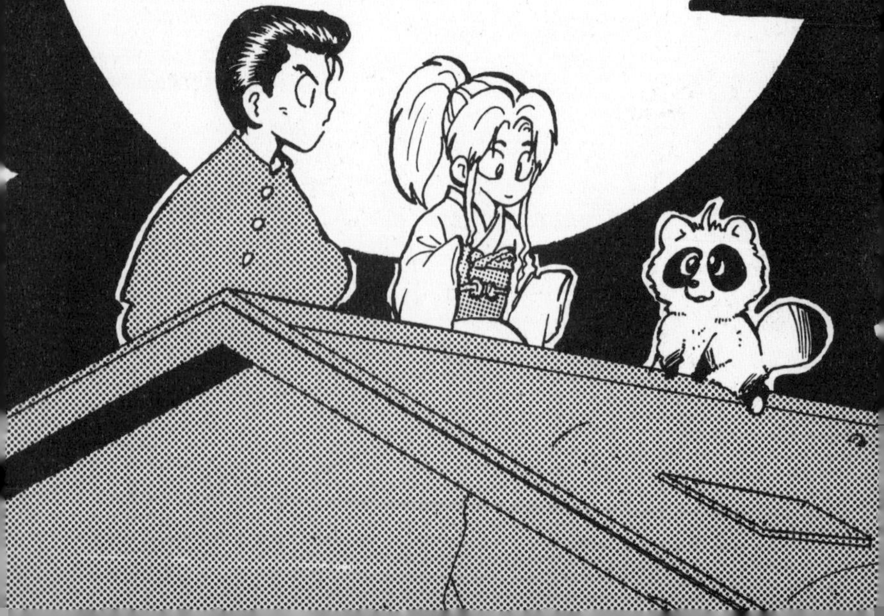

READ THIS WAY

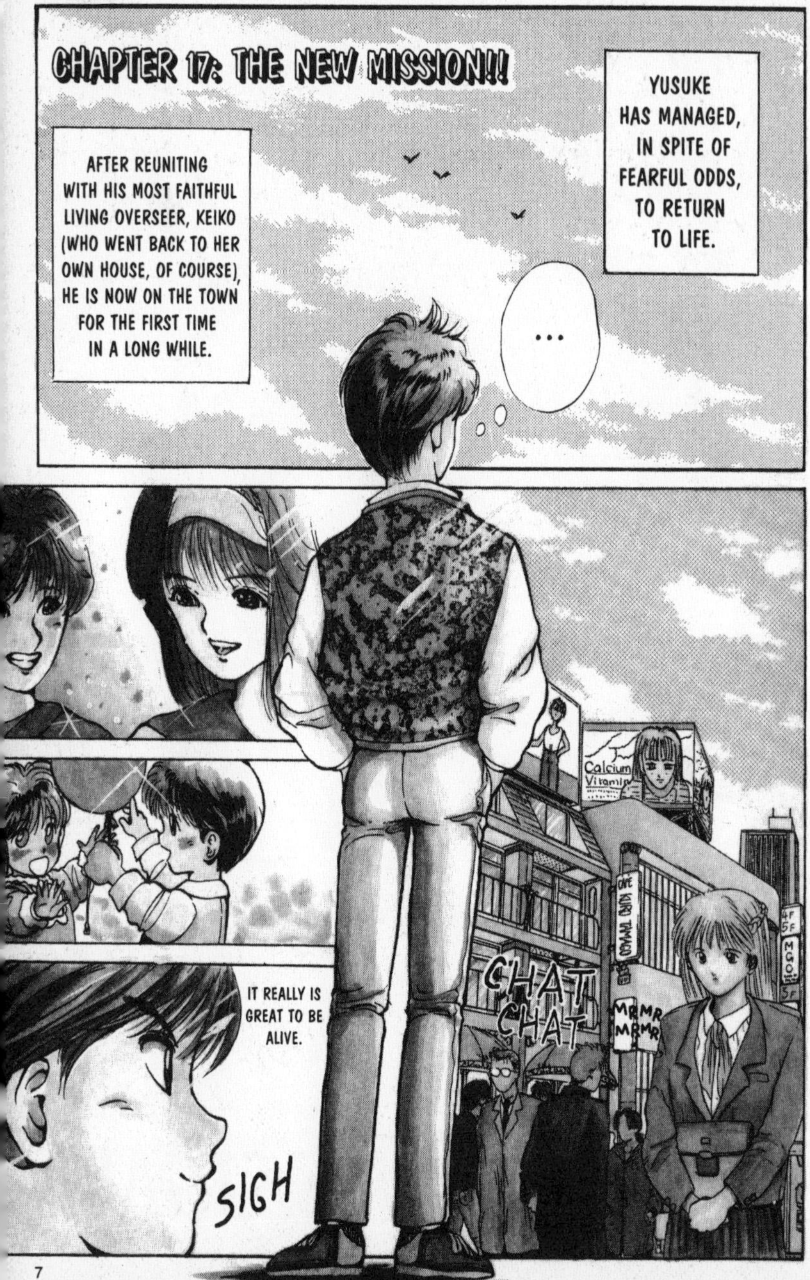
CHAPTER 17: THE NEW MISSION!!
YUSUKE HAS MANAGED, IN SPITE OF FEARFUL ODDS, TO RETURN TO LIFE.
AFTER REUNITING WITH HIS MOST FAITHFUL LIVING OVERSEER, KEIKO (WHO WENT BACK TO HER OWN HOUSE, OF COURSE), HE IS NOW ON THE TOWN FOR THE FIRST TIME IN A LONG WHILE.
...
Calcium
CHAT CHAT
MR MR MR MR
IT REALLY IS GREAT TO BE ALIVE.
SIGH

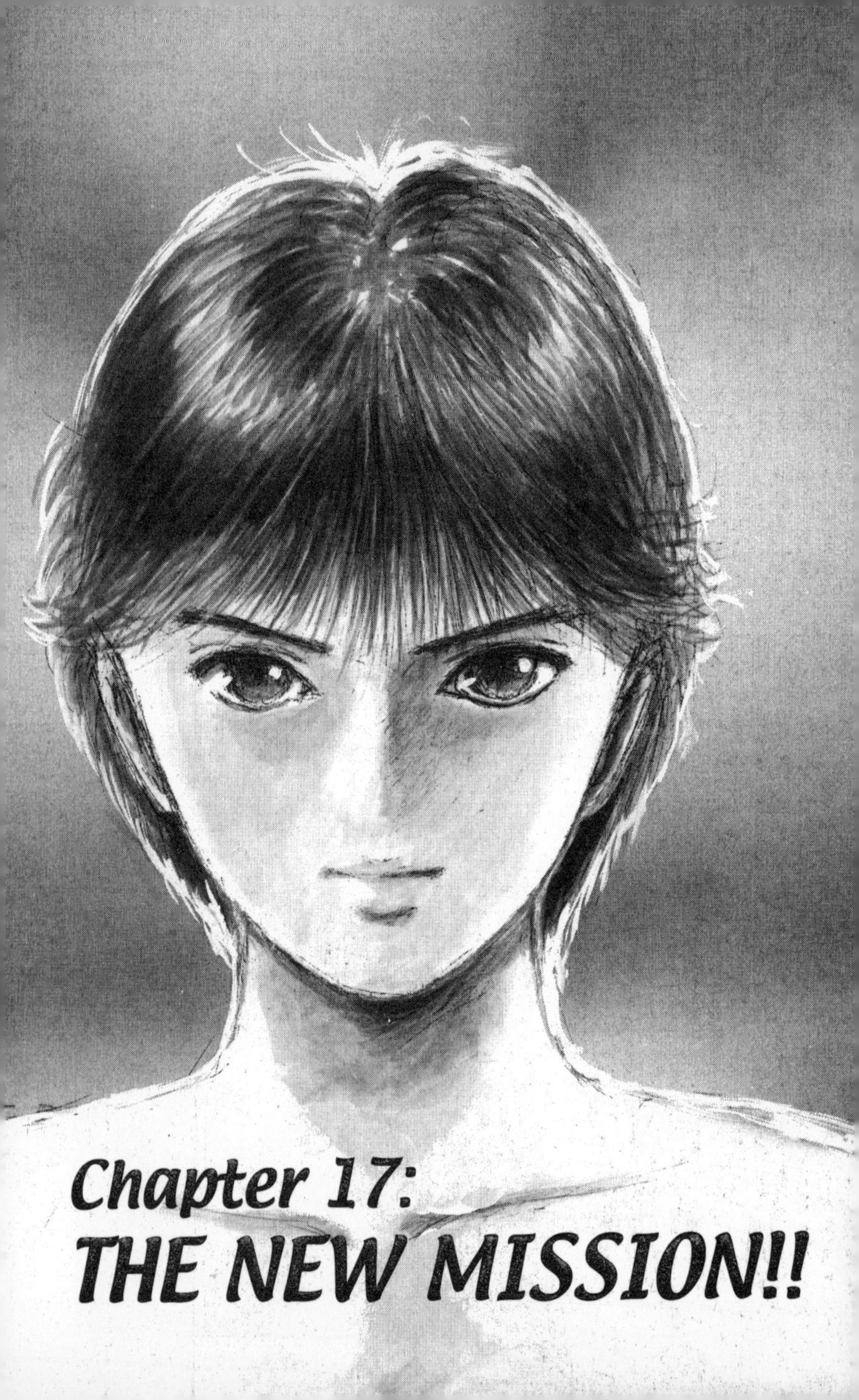

Chapter 17: THE NEW MISSION!!

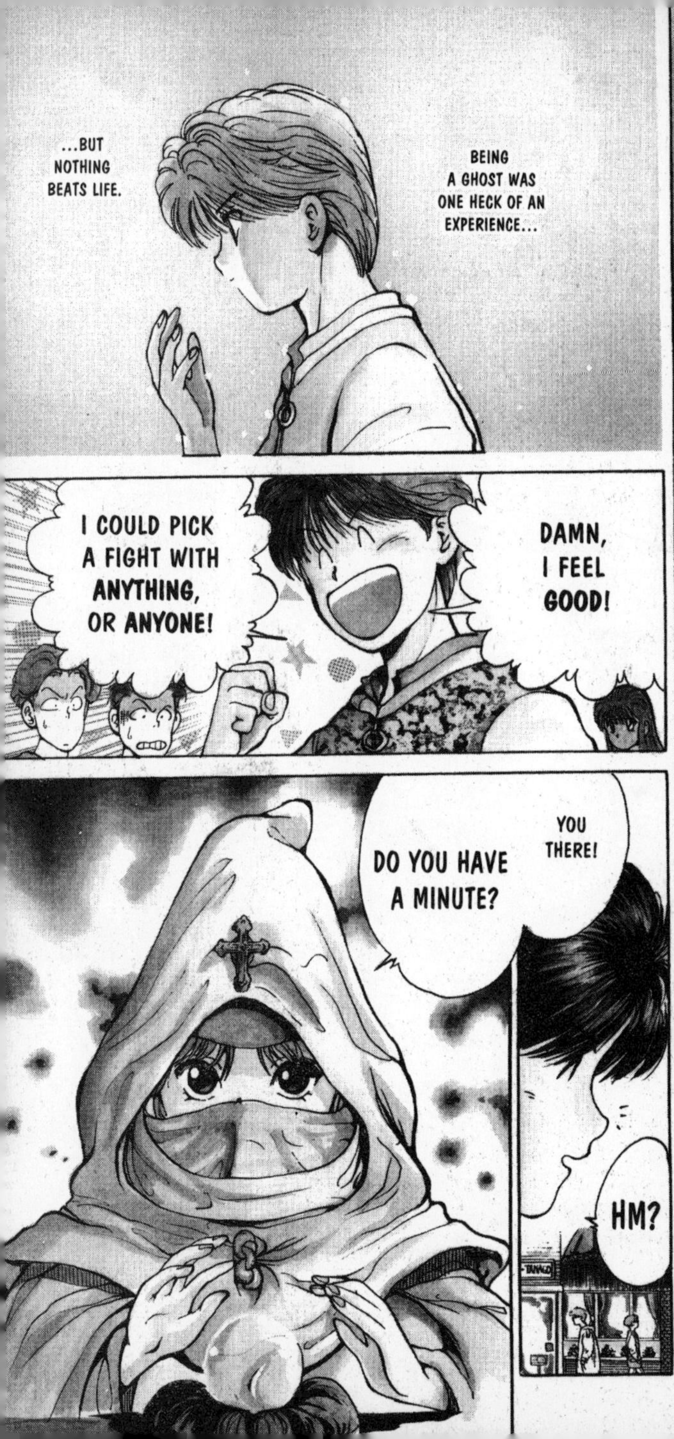
BEING A GHOST WAS ONE HECK OF AN EXPERIENCE...
...BUT NOTHING BEATS LIFE.
DAMN, I FEEL GOOD!
I COULD PICK A FIGHT WITH ANYTHING, OR ANYONE!
YOU THERE!
DO YOU HAVE A MINUTE?
HM?

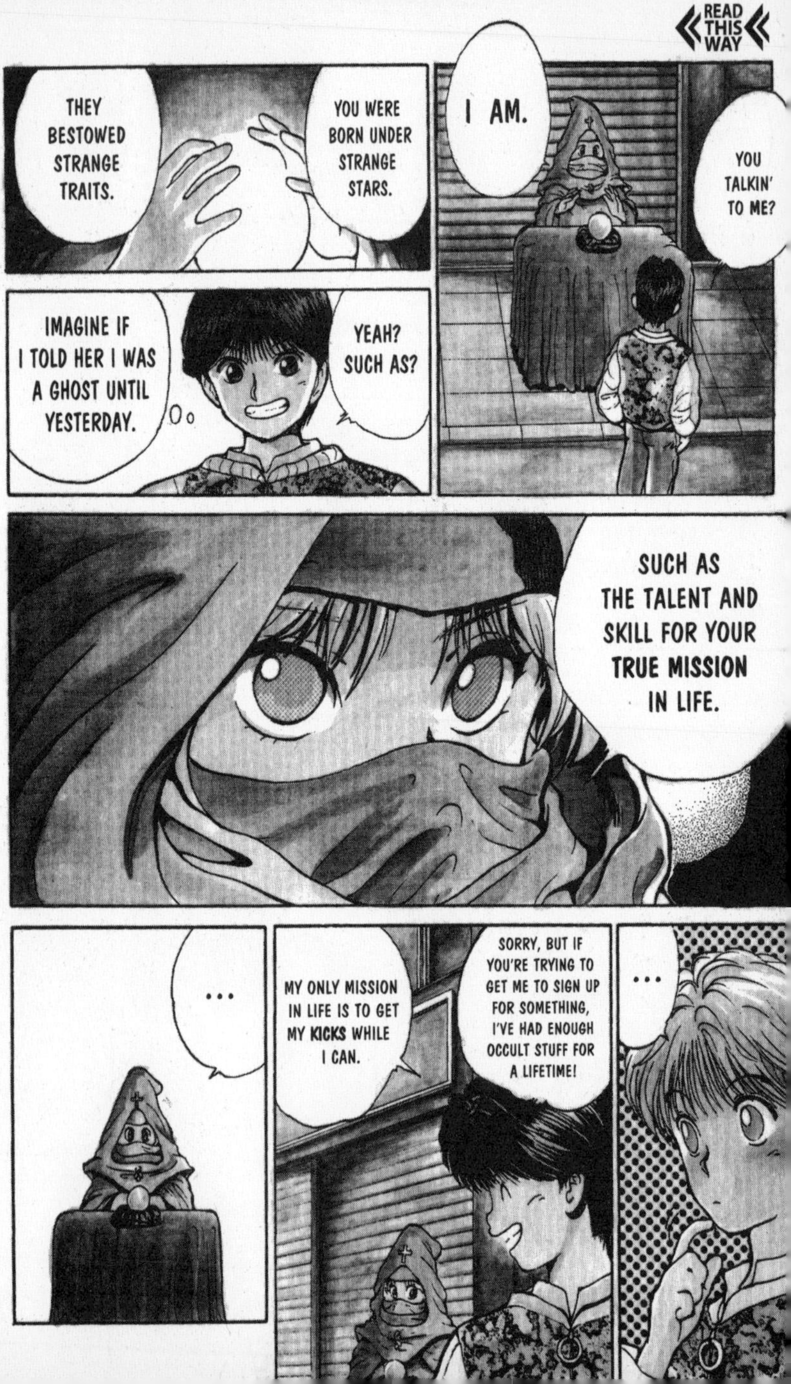
READ THIS WAY
YOU TALKIN' TO ME?
I AM.
YOU WERE BORN UNDER STRANGE STARS.
THEY BESTOWED STRANGE TRAITS.
YEAH? SUCH AS?
IMAGINE IF I TOLD HER I WAS A GHOST UNTIL YESTERDAY.
SUCH AS THE TALENT AND SKILL FOR YOUR TRUE MISSION IN LIFE.
...
SORRY, BUT IF YOU'RE TRYING TO GET ME TO SIGN UP FOR SOMETHING, I'VE HAD ENOUGH OCCULT STUFF FOR A LIFETIME!
MY ONLY MISSION IN LIFE IS TO GET MY KICKS WHILE I CAN.
...

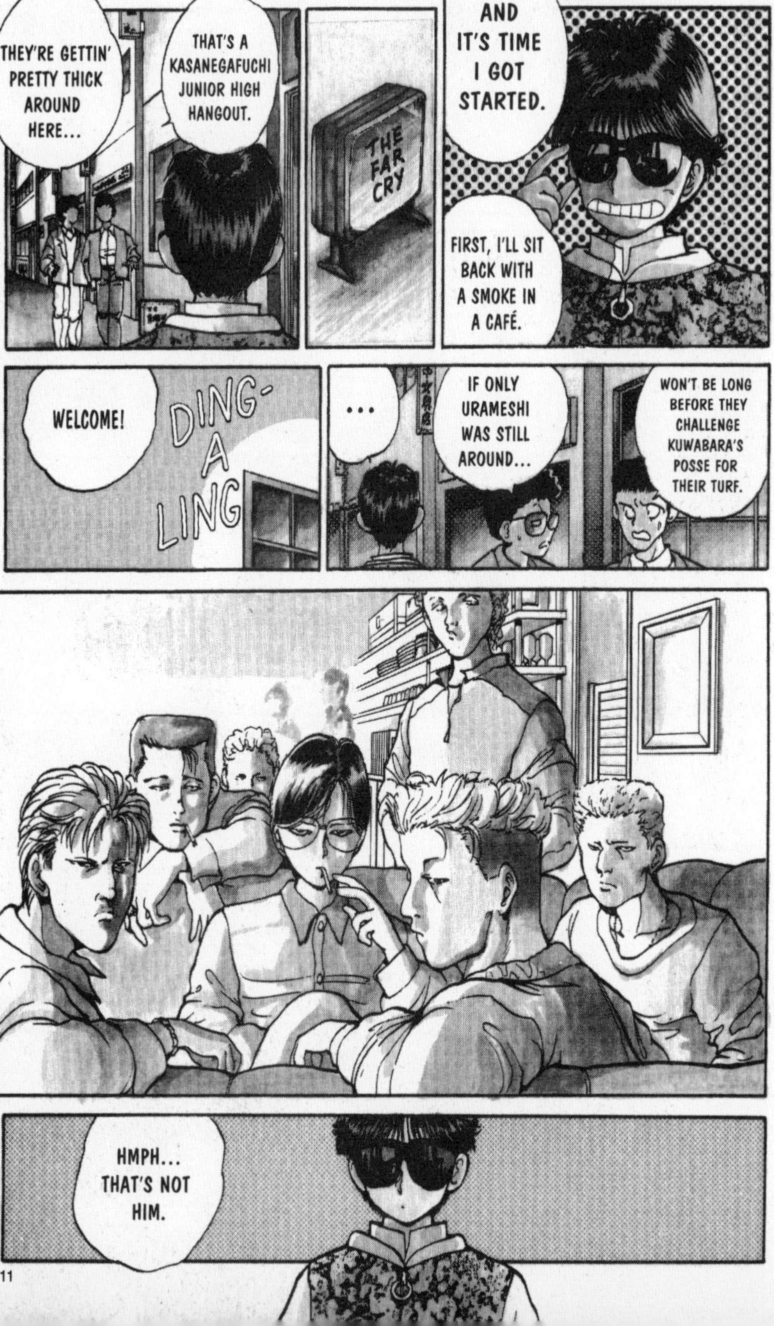
AND IT'S TIME I GOT STARTED.
FIRST, I'LL SIT BACK WITH A SMOKE IN A CAFÉ.
THE FAR CRY
THAT'S A KASANEGAFUCHI JUNIOR HIGH HANGOUT.
THEY'RE GETTIN' PRETTY THICK AROUND HERE...
WON'T BE LONG BEFORE THEY CHALLENGE KUWABARA'S POSSE FOR THEIR TURF.
IF ONLY URAMESHI WAS STILL AROUND...
...
DING-A-LING
WELCOME!
HMPH... THAT'S NOT HIM.

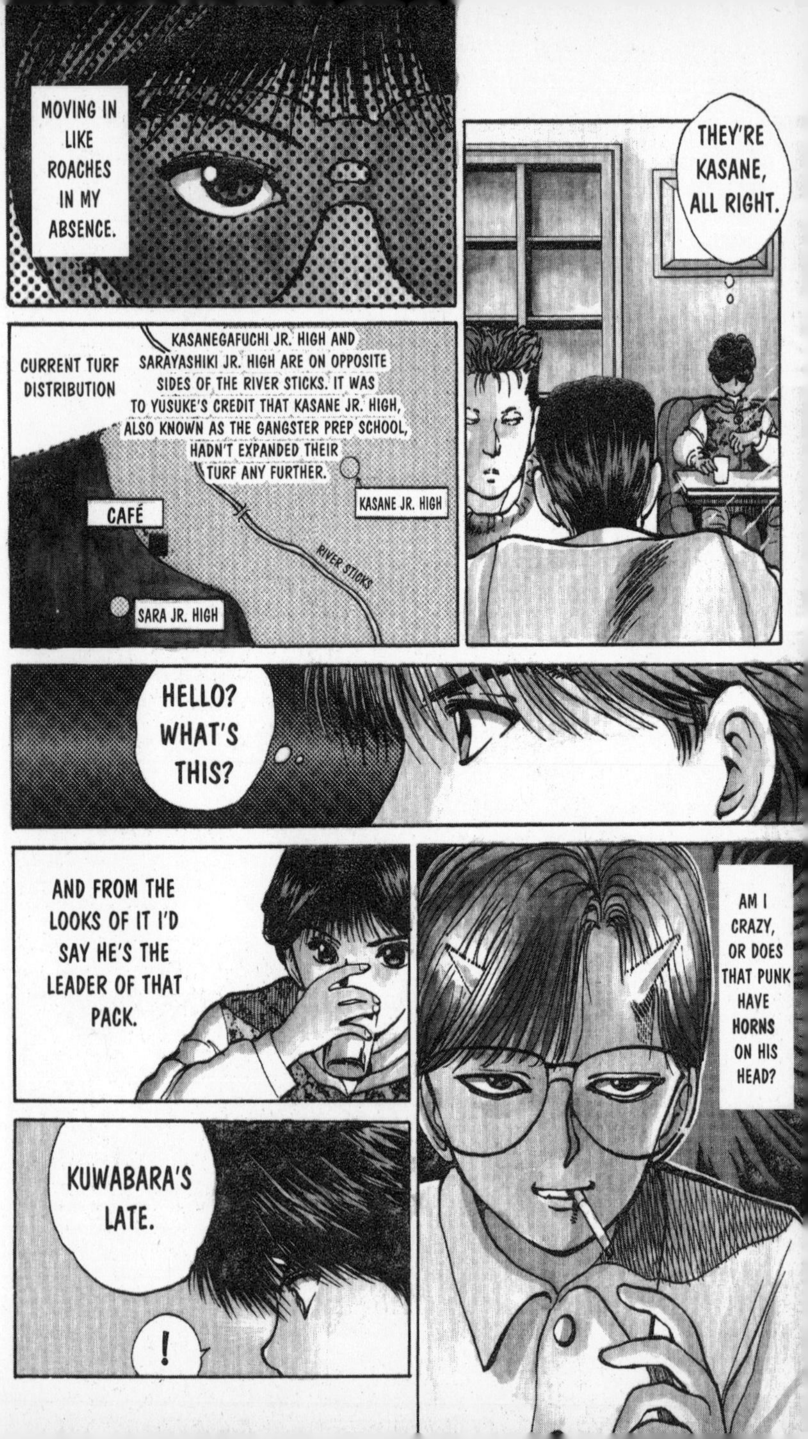
THEY'RE KASANE, ALL RIGHT.
MOVING IN LIKE ROACHES IN MY ABSENCE.
CURRENT TURF DISTRIBUTION
KASANEGAFUCHI JR. HIGH AND SARAYASHIKI JR. HIGH ARE ON OPPOSITE SIDES OF THE RIVER STICKS. IT WAS TO YUSUKE'S CREDIT THAT KASANE JR. HIGH, ALSO KNOWN AS THE GANGSTER PREP SCHOOL, HADN'T EXPANDED THEIR TURF ANY FURTHER.
KASANE JR. HIGH
CAFÉ
RIVER STICKS
SARA JR. HIGH
HELLO? WHAT'S THIS?
AM I CRAZY, OR DOES THAT PUNK HAVE HORNS ON HIS HEAD?
AND FROM THE LOOKS OF IT I'D SAY HE'S THE LEADER OF THAT PACK.
KUWABARA'S LATE.
!

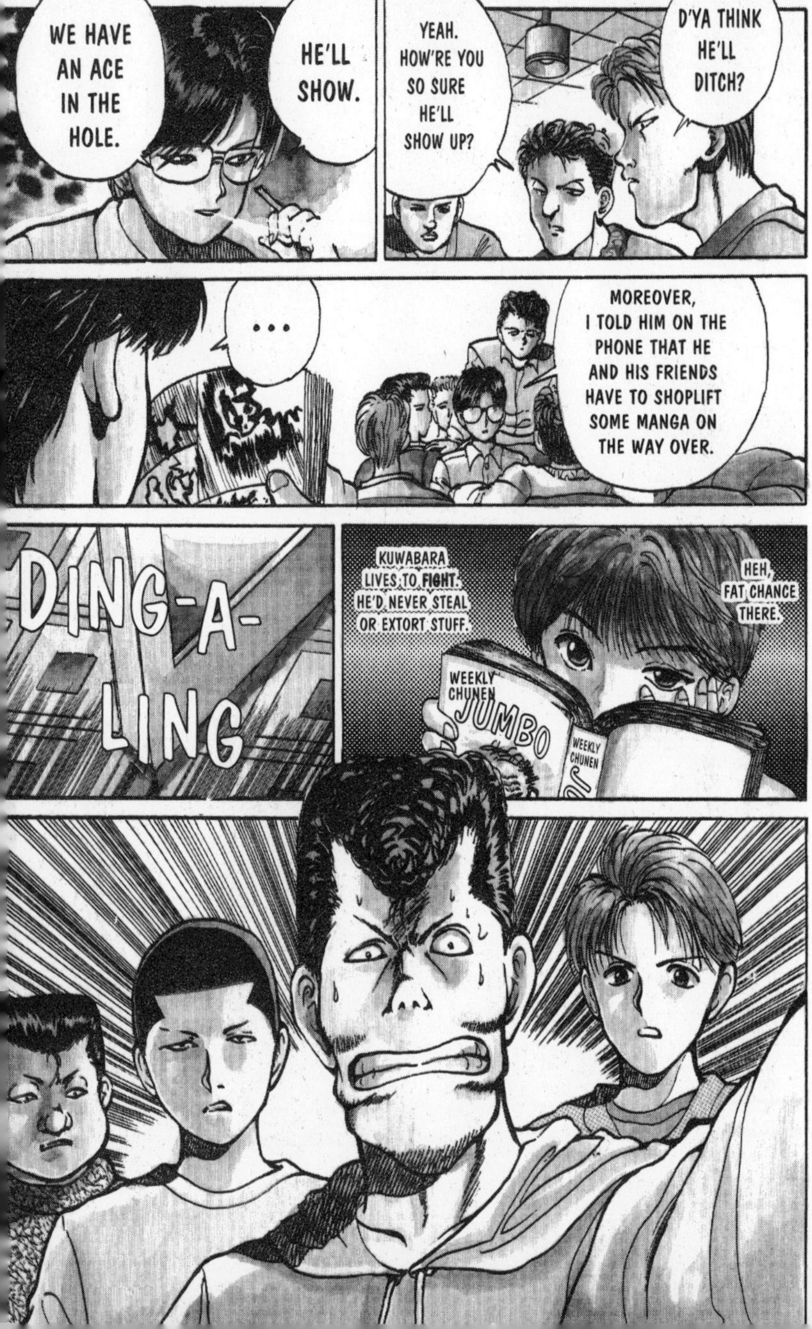
D'YA THINK HE'LL DITCH?
YEAH. HOW'RE YOU SO SURE HE'LL SHOW UP?
HE'LL SHOW.
WE HAVE AN ACE IN THE HOLE.
MOREOVER, I TOLD HIM ON THE PHONE THAT HE AND HIS FRIENDS HAVE TO SHOPLIFT SOME MANGA ON THE WAY OVER.
...
HEH, FAT CHANCE THERE.
KUWABARA LIVES TO FIGHT. HE'D NEVER STEAL OR EXTORT STUFF.
WEEKLY CHUNEN JUMBO
WEEKLY CHUNEN
DING-A-LING

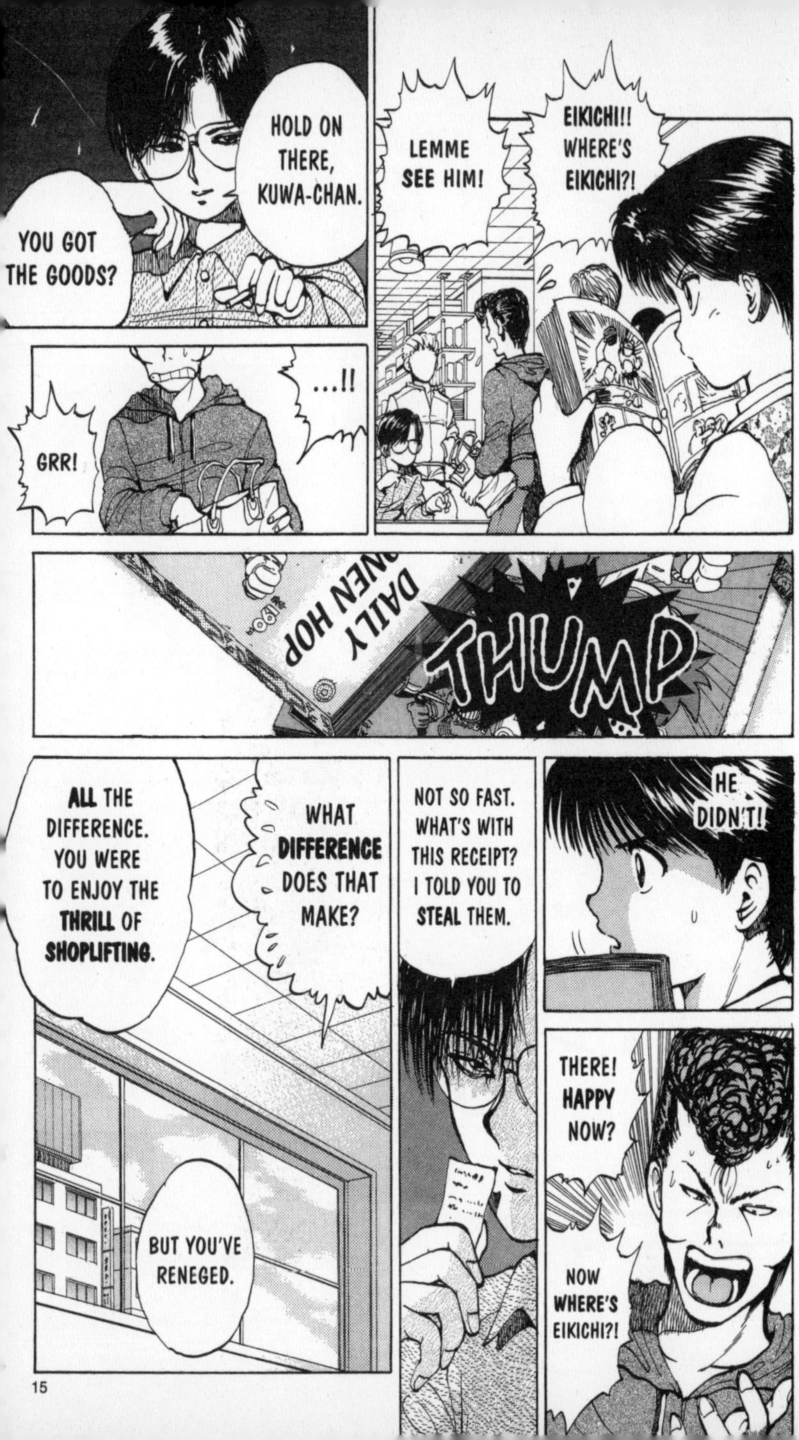
EIKICHI!! WHERE'S EIKICHI?!
LEMME SEE HIM!
HOLD ON THERE, KUWA-CHAN.
YOU GOT THE GOODS?
...!!
GRR!
THUMP
DAILY
NEN HOP
HE DIDN'T!
THERE! HAPPY NOW?
NOW WHERE'S EIKICHI?!
NOT SO FAST. WHAT'S WITH THIS RECEIPT? I TOLD YOU TO STEAL THEM.
WHAT DIFFERENCE DOES THAT MAKE?
ALL THE DIFFERENCE. YOU WERE TO ENJOY THE THRILL OF SHOPLIFTING.
BUT YOU'VE RENEGED.

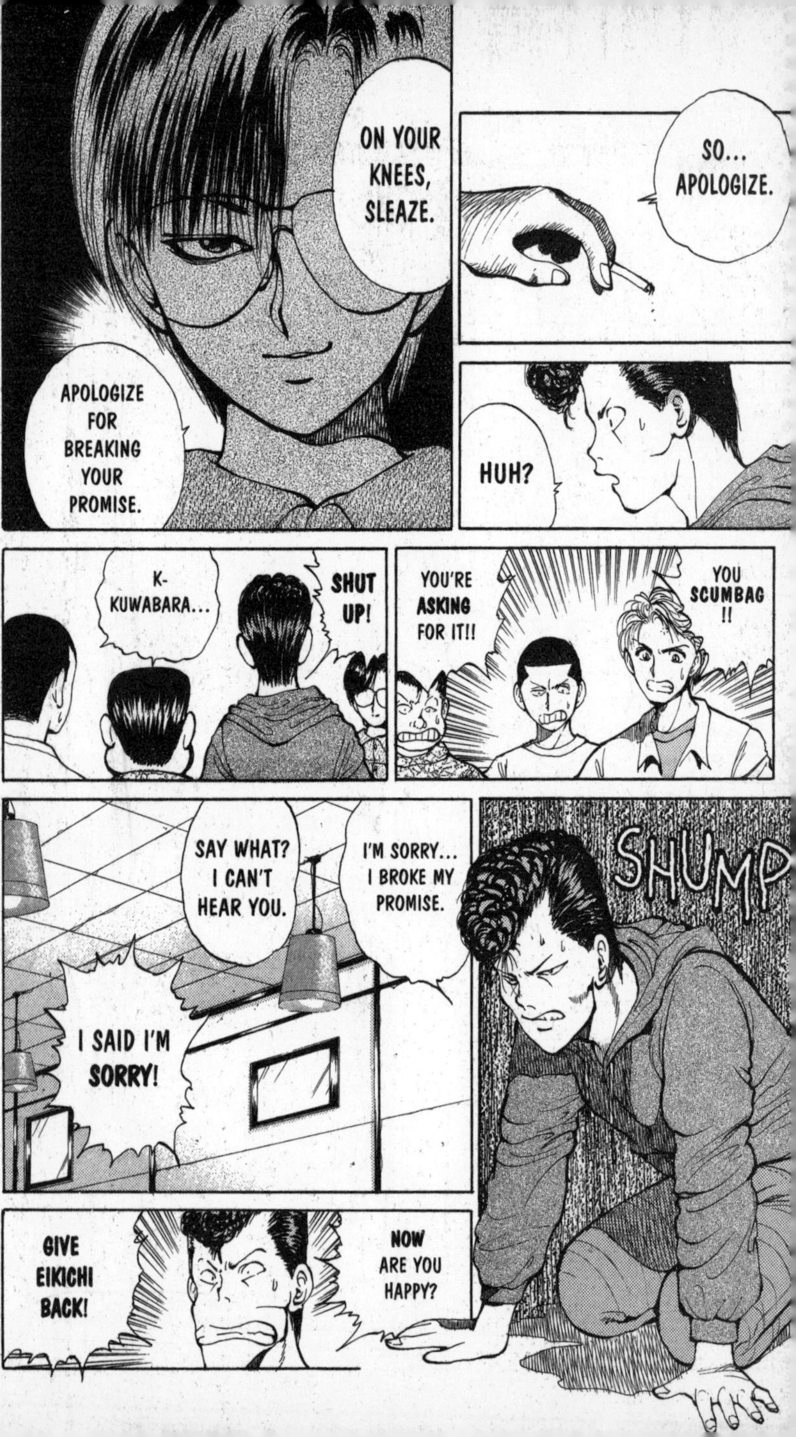
SO... APOLOGIZE.
HUH?
ON YOUR KNEES, SLEAZE.
APOLOGIZE FOR BREAKING YOUR PROMISE.
YOU SCUMBAG!!
YOU'RE ASKING FOR IT!!
SHUT UP!
K-KUWABARA...
SHUMP
I'M SORRY... I BROKE MY PROMISE.
SAY WHAT? I CAN'T HEAR YOU.
I SAID I'M SORRY!
NOW ARE YOU HAPPY?
GIVE EIKICHI BACK!

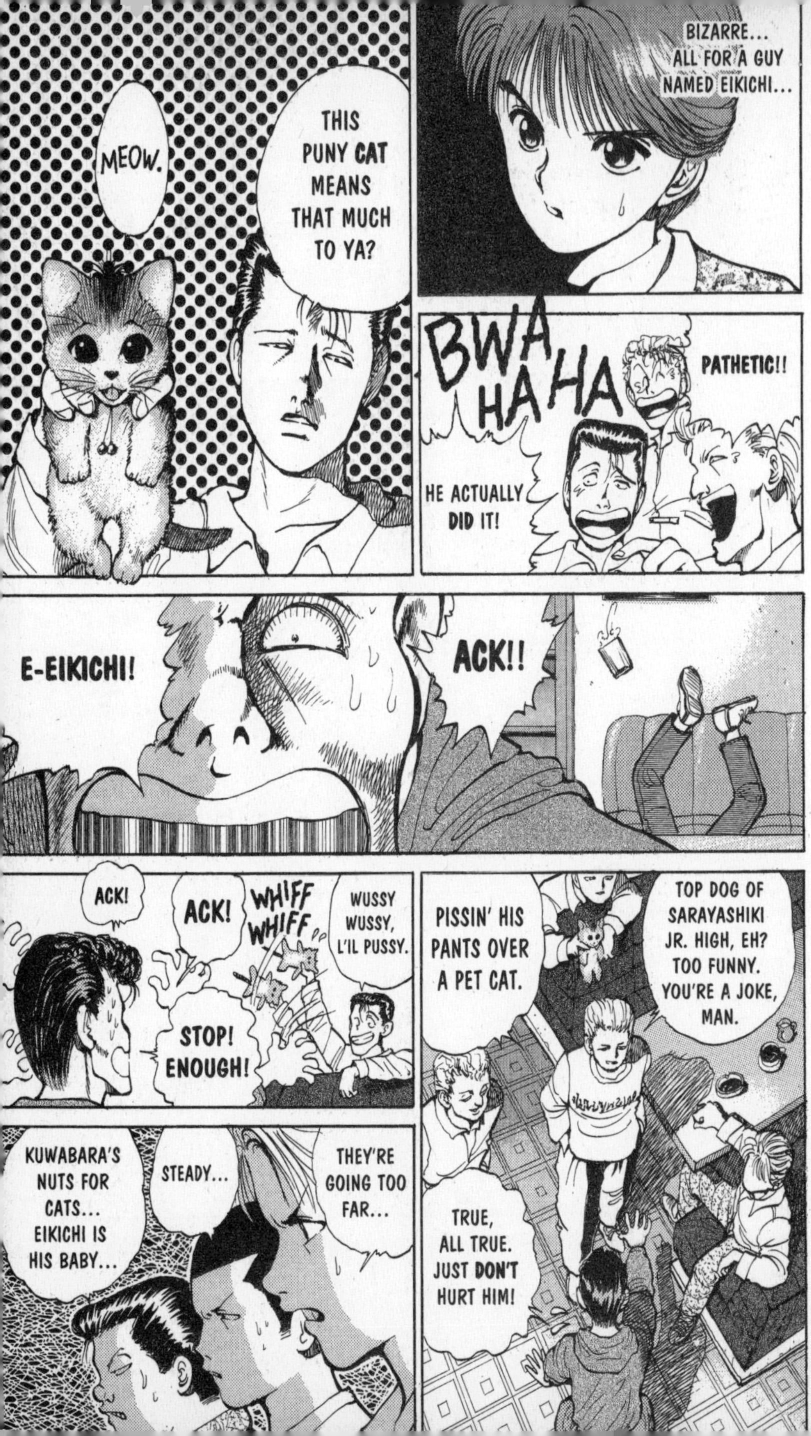
BIZARRE... ALL FOR A GUY NAMED EIKICHI...
BWA HA HA
PATHETIC!!
HE ACTUALLY DID IT!
THIS PUNY CAT MEANS THAT MUCH TO YA?
MEOW.
ACK!!
E-EIKICHI!
TOP DOG OF SARAYASHIKI JR. HIGH, EH? TOO FUNNY. YOU'RE A JOKE, MAN.
PISSIN' HIS PANTS OVER A PET CAT.
TRUE, ALL TRUE. JUST DON'T HURT HIM!
WUSSY WUSSY, L'IL PUSSY.
WHIFF WHIFF
ACK!
ACK!
STOP! ENOUGH!
THEY'RE GOING TOO FAR...
STEADY...
KUWABARA'S NUTS FOR CATS... EIKICHI IS HIS BABY...

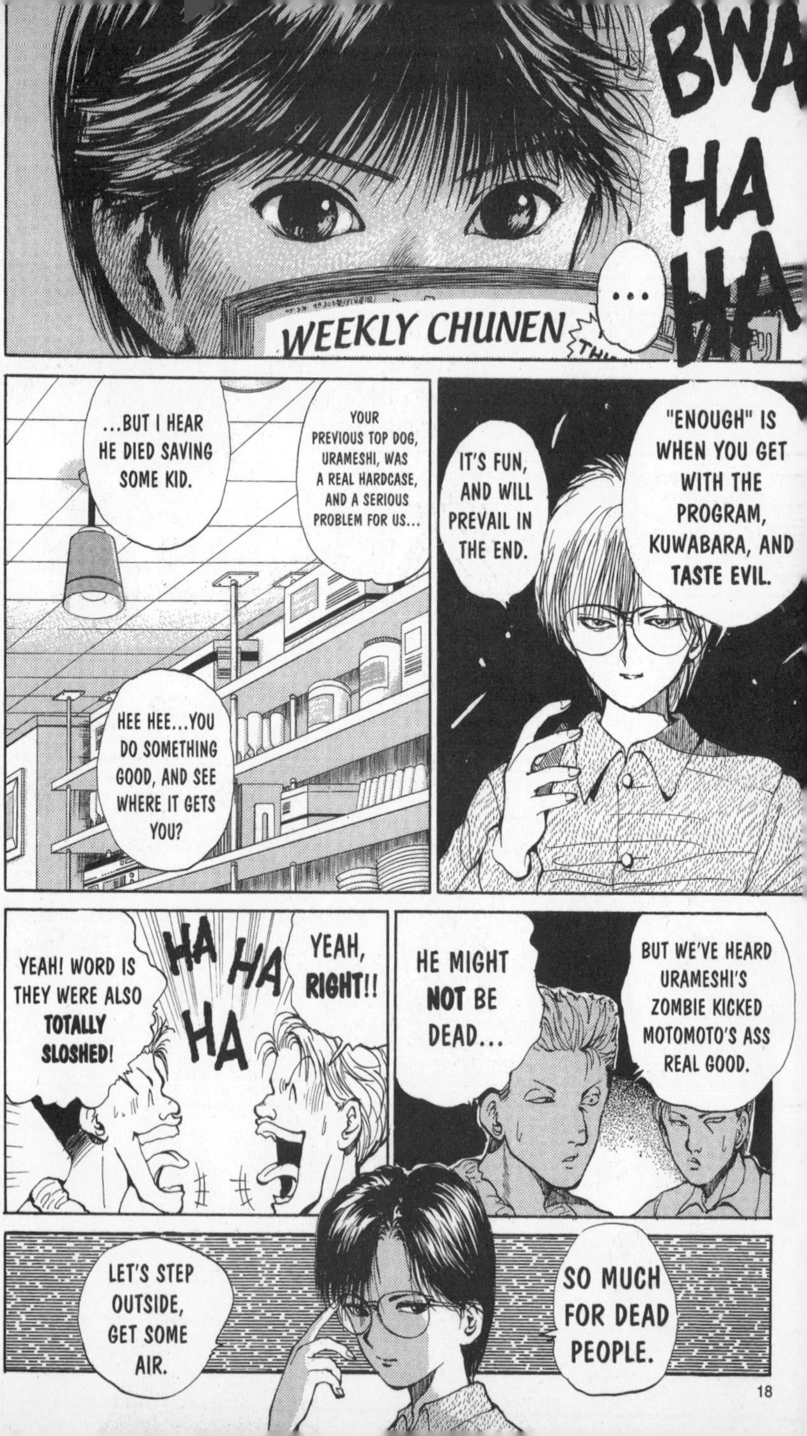
BWA HA HA HA
...
WEEKLY CHUNEN
"ENOUGH" IS WHEN YOU GET WITH THE PROGRAM, KUWABARA, AND TASTE EVIL.
IT'S FUN, AND WILL PREVAIL IN THE END.
YOUR PREVIOUS TOP DOG, URAMESHI, WAS A REAL HARDCASE, AND A SERIOUS PROBLEM FOR US...
...BUT I HEAR HE DIED SAVING SOME KID.
HEE HEE...YOU DO SOMETHING GOOD, AND SEE WHERE IT GETS YOU?
BUT WE'VE HEARD URAMESHI'S ZOMBIE KICKED MOTOMOTO'S ASS REAL GOOD.
HE MIGHT **NOT** BE DEAD...
YEAH, **RIGHT!!**
HA HA HA
YEAH! WORD IS THEY WERE ALSO **TOTALLY SLOSHED!**
SO MUCH FOR DEAD PEOPLE.
LET'S STEP OUTSIDE, GET SOME AIR.

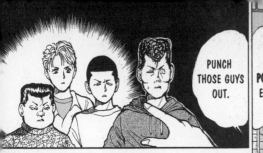

I'VE HAD IT WITH BEIN' JERKED AROUND!
MAKE YOUR POINT AND GIVE EIKICHI BACK!!
OK, LAST ORDER.
PUNCH THOSE GUYS OUT.
THEY'VE BEEN GIVING ME "THE LOOK" THE WHOLE TIME.
POUND 'EM TILL I SAY ENOUGH!
ONE... TWO...GO!
MEW
...
I...
...WON'T DO THAT!
SWUSH

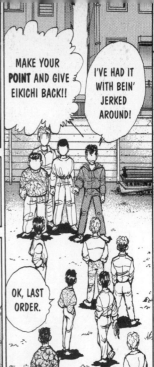

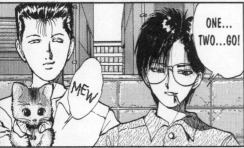

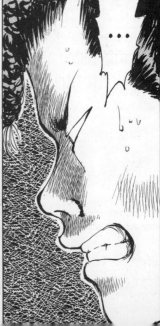

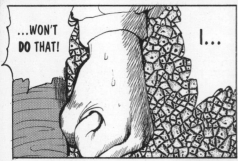

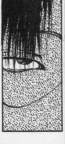

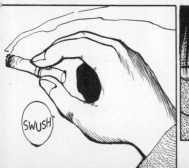

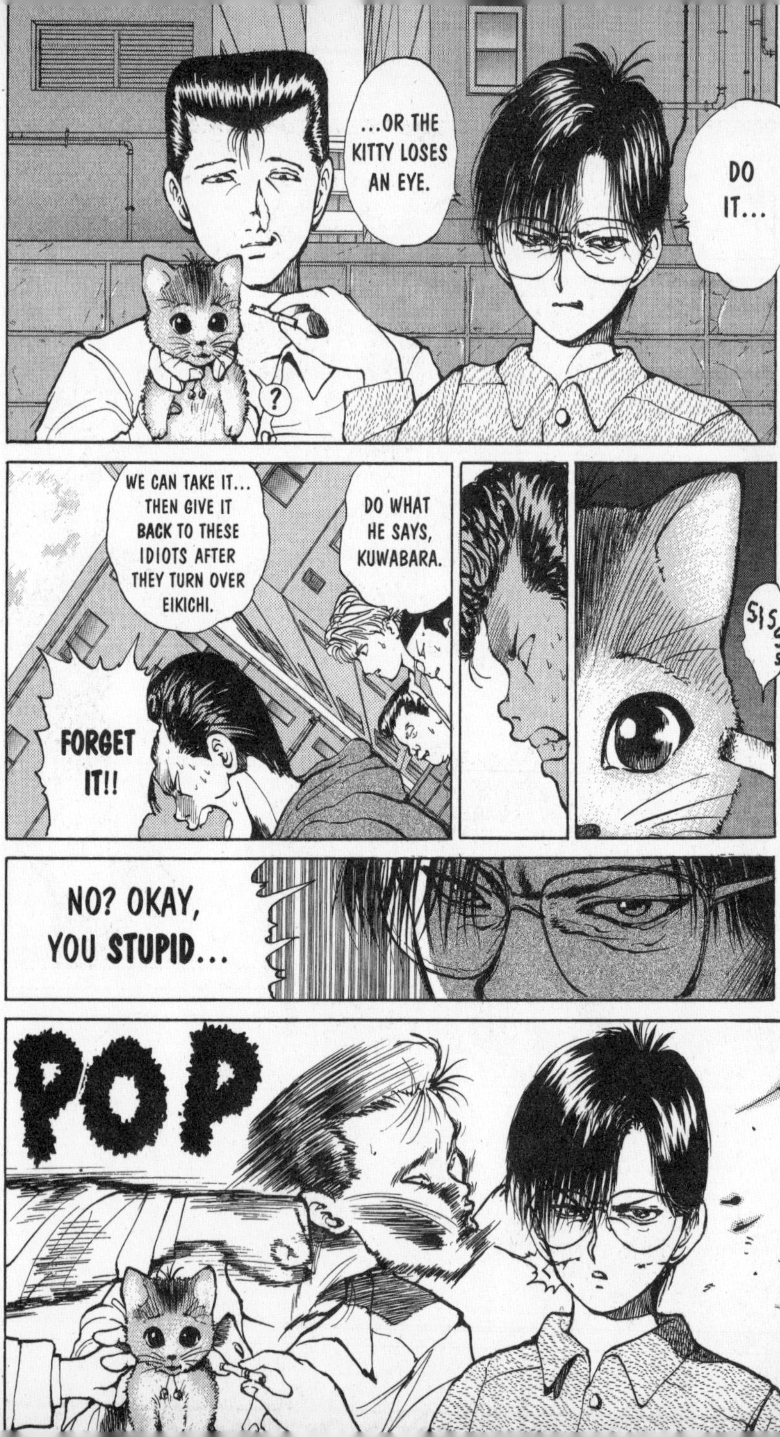
DO IT...
...OR THE KITTY LOSES AN EYE.
SISSS
DO WHAT HE SAYS, KUWABARA.
WE CAN TAKE IT... THEN GIVE IT BACK TO THESE IDIOTS AFTER THEY TURN OVER EIKICHI.
FORGET IT!!
NO? OKAY, YOU STUPID...
POP

READ THIS WAY

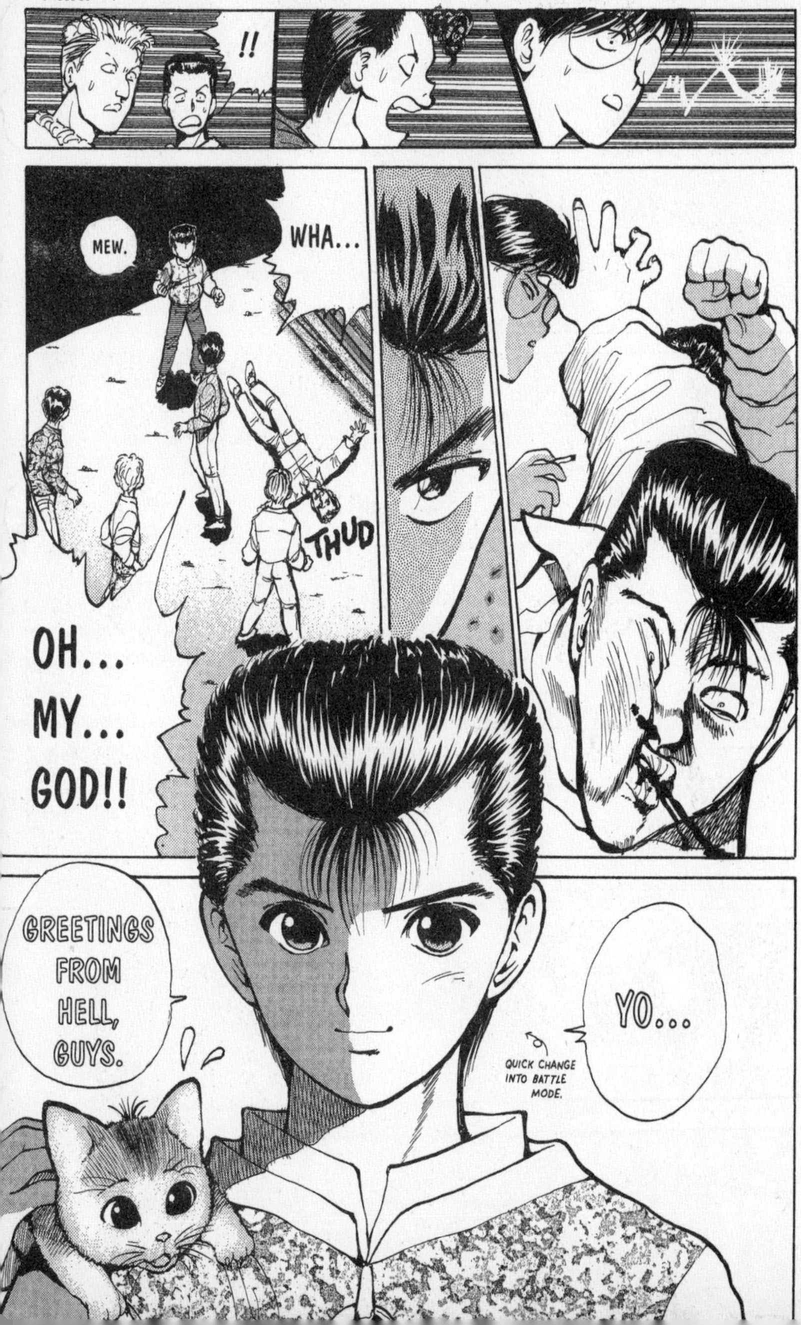
!!
WHA...
MEW.
THUD
OH... MY... GOD!!
YO...
QUICK CHANGE INTO BATTLE MODE.
GREETINGS FROM HELL, GUYS.

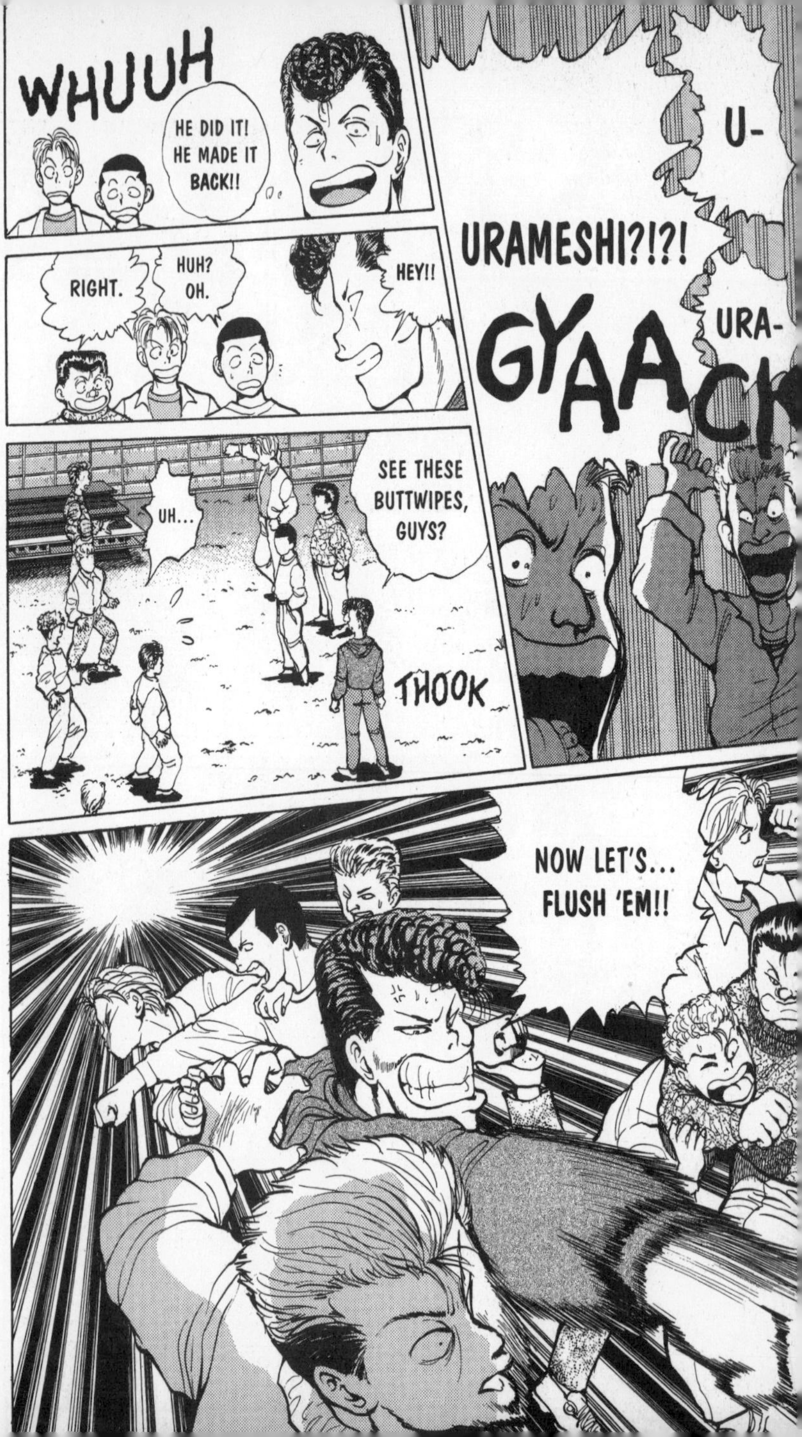
U-
URAMESHI?!?!
URA-
GYAACK
WHUUH
HE DID IT! HE MADE IT BACK!!
HEY!!
HUH? OH.
RIGHT.
SEE THESE BUTTWIPES, GUYS?
UH...
THOOK
NOW LET'S... FLUSH 'EM!!

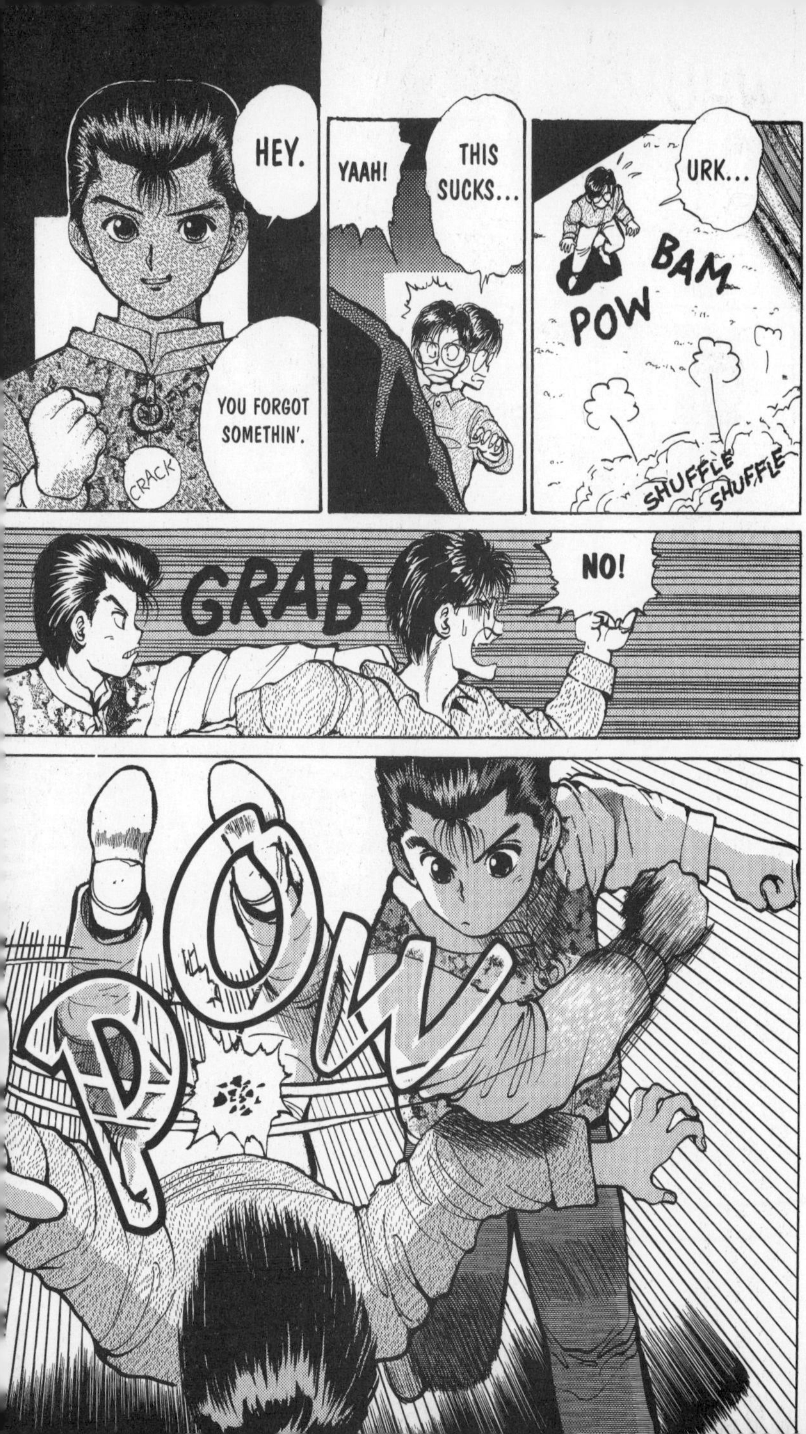
URK...
BAM
POW
SHUFFLE SHUFFLE
THIS SUCKS...
YAAH!
HEY.
YOU FORGOT SOMETHIN'.
CRACK
NO!
GRAB
POW

READ THIS WAY

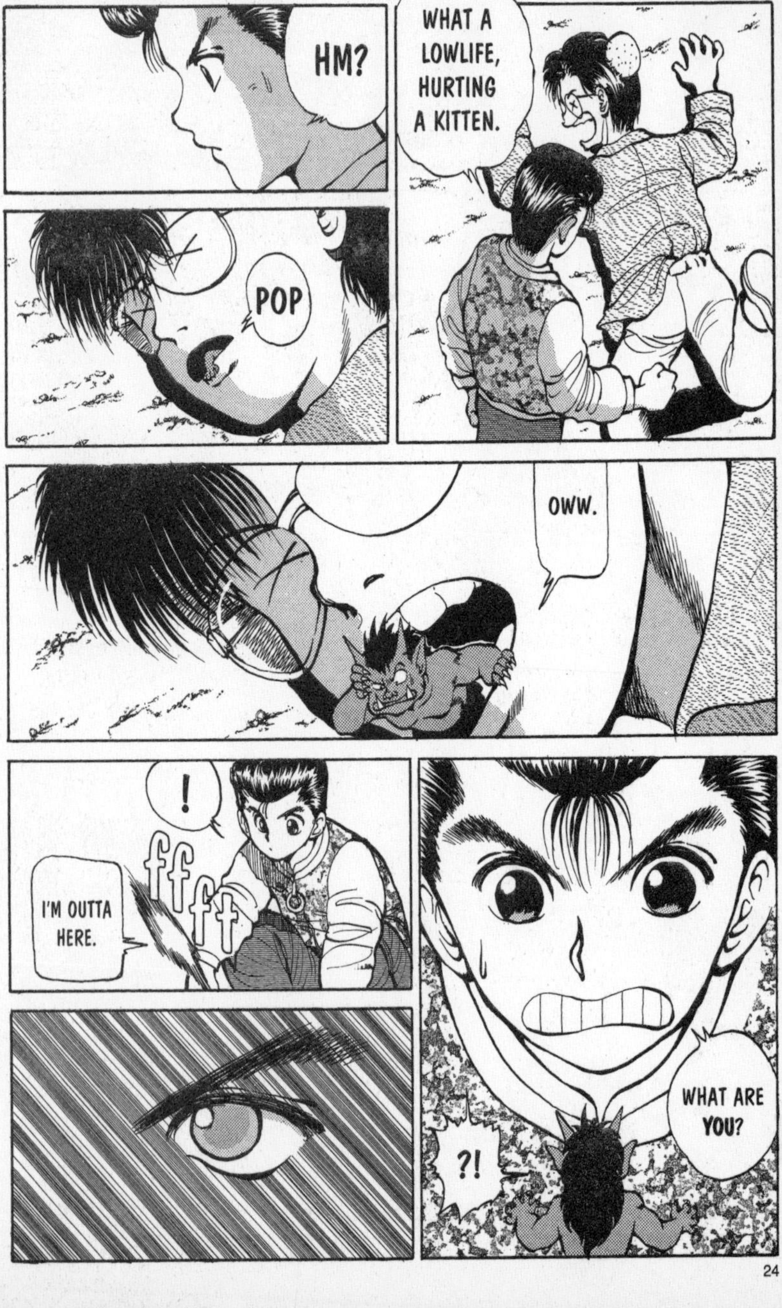

WHAT A LOWLIFE, HURTING A KITTEN.
HM?
POP
OWW.
WHAT ARE YOU?
?!
!
ffff
I'M OUTTA HERE.

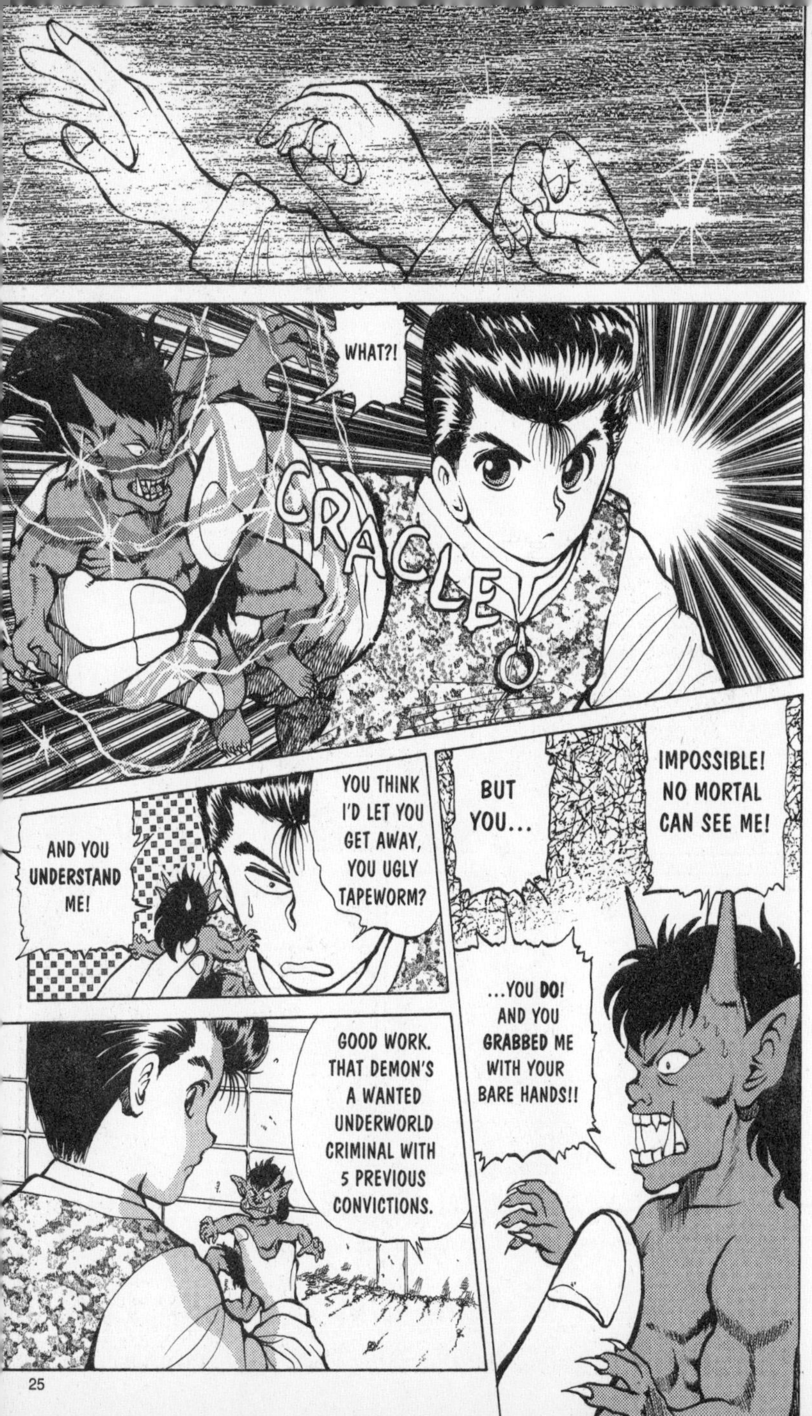
WHAT?!
CRACLE
IMPOSSIBLE! NO MORTAL CAN SEE ME!
BUT YOU...
...YOU DO! AND YOU GRABBED ME WITH YOUR BARE HANDS!!
YOU THINK I'D LET YOU GET AWAY, YOU UGLY TAPEWORM?
AND YOU UNDERSTAND ME!
GOOD WORK. THAT DEMON'S A WANTED UNDERWORLD CRIMINAL WITH 5 PREVIOUS CONVICTIONS.

READ THIS WAY

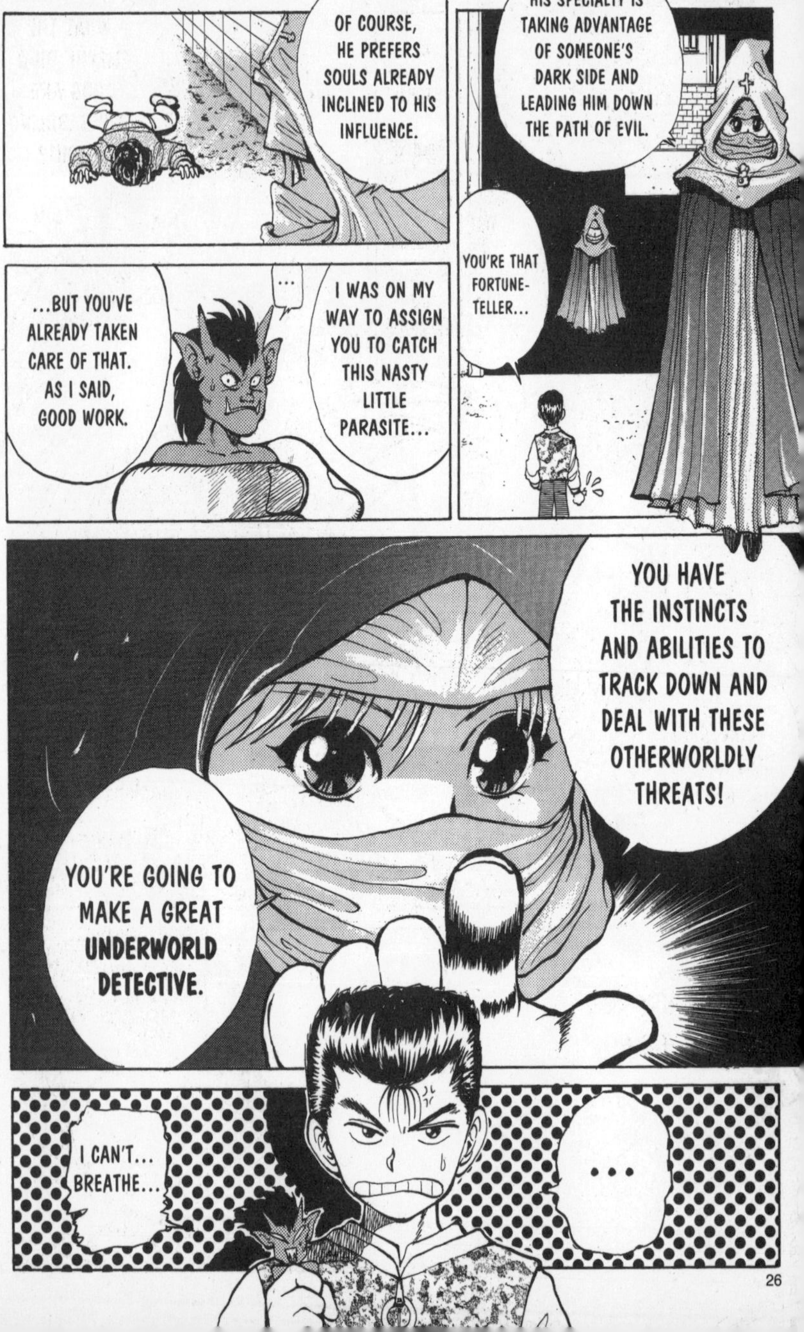
HIS SPECIALTY IS TAKING ADVANTAGE OF SOMEONE'S DARK SIDE AND LEADING HIM DOWN THE PATH OF EVIL.
YOU'RE THAT FORTUNE-TELLER...
OF COURSE, HE PREFERS SOULS ALREADY INCLINED TO HIS INFLUENCE.
I WAS ON MY WAY TO ASSIGN YOU TO CATCH THIS NASTY LITTLE PARASITE...
...
...BUT YOU'VE ALREADY TAKEN CARE OF THAT. AS I SAID, GOOD WORK.
YOU HAVE THE INSTINCTS AND ABILITIES TO TRACK DOWN AND DEAL WITH THESE OTHERWORLDLY THREATS!
YOU'RE GOING TO MAKE A GREAT **UNDERWORLD DETECTIVE**.
...
I CAN'T... BREATHE...

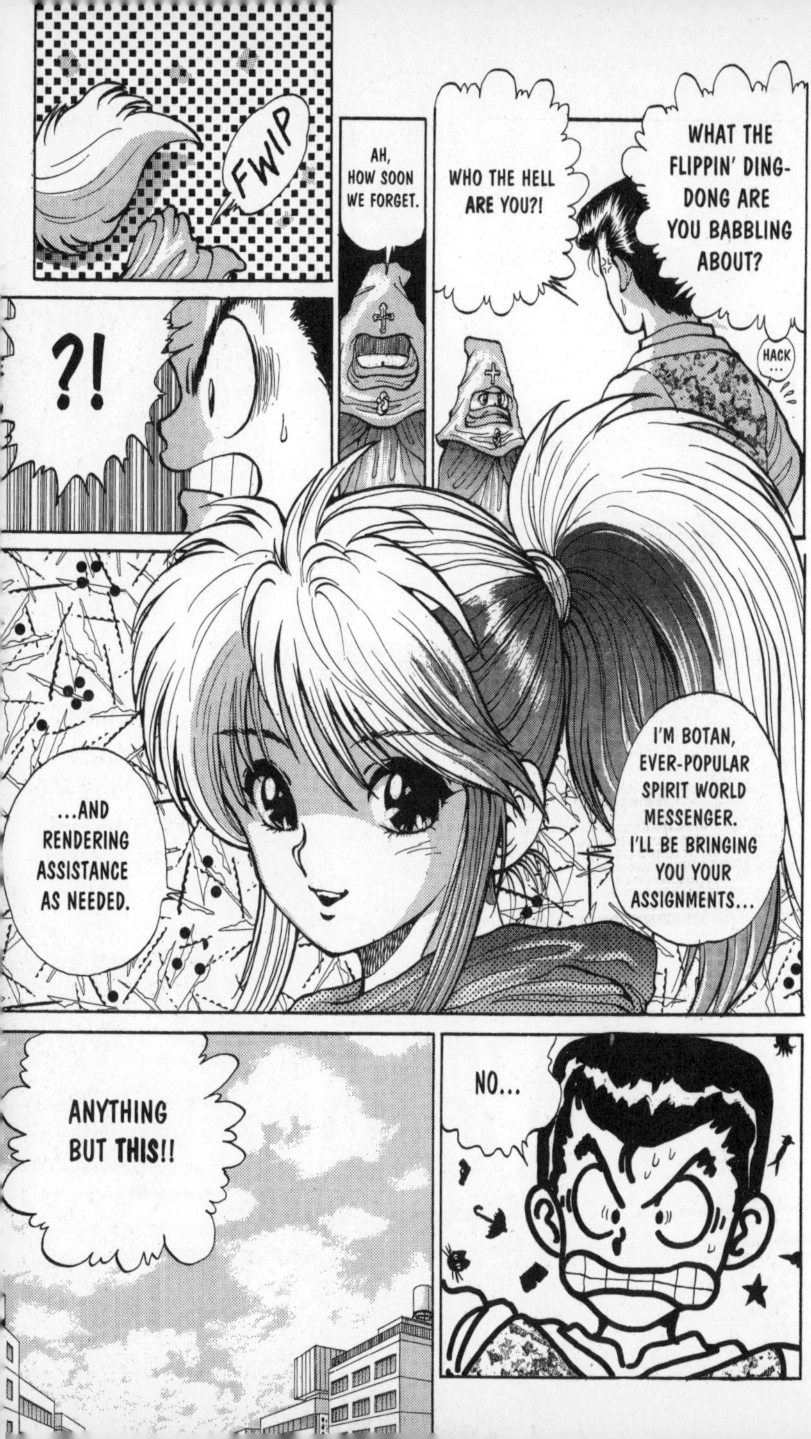
WHAT THE FLIPPIN' DING-DONG ARE YOU BABBLING ABOUT?
HACK...
WHO THE HELL ARE YOU?!
AH, HOW SOON WE FORGET.
FWIP
?!
I'M BOTAN, EVER-POPULAR SPIRIT WORLD MESSENGER. I'LL BE BRINGING YOU YOUR ASSIGNMENTS...
...AND RENDERING ASSISTANCE AS NEEDED.
NO...
ANYTHING BUT THIS!!

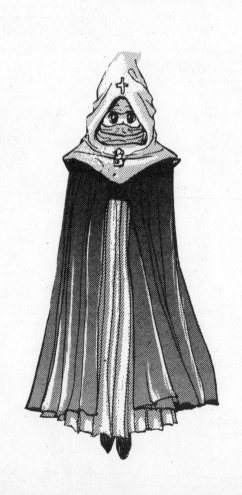

CHAPTER 18: ACTION!!

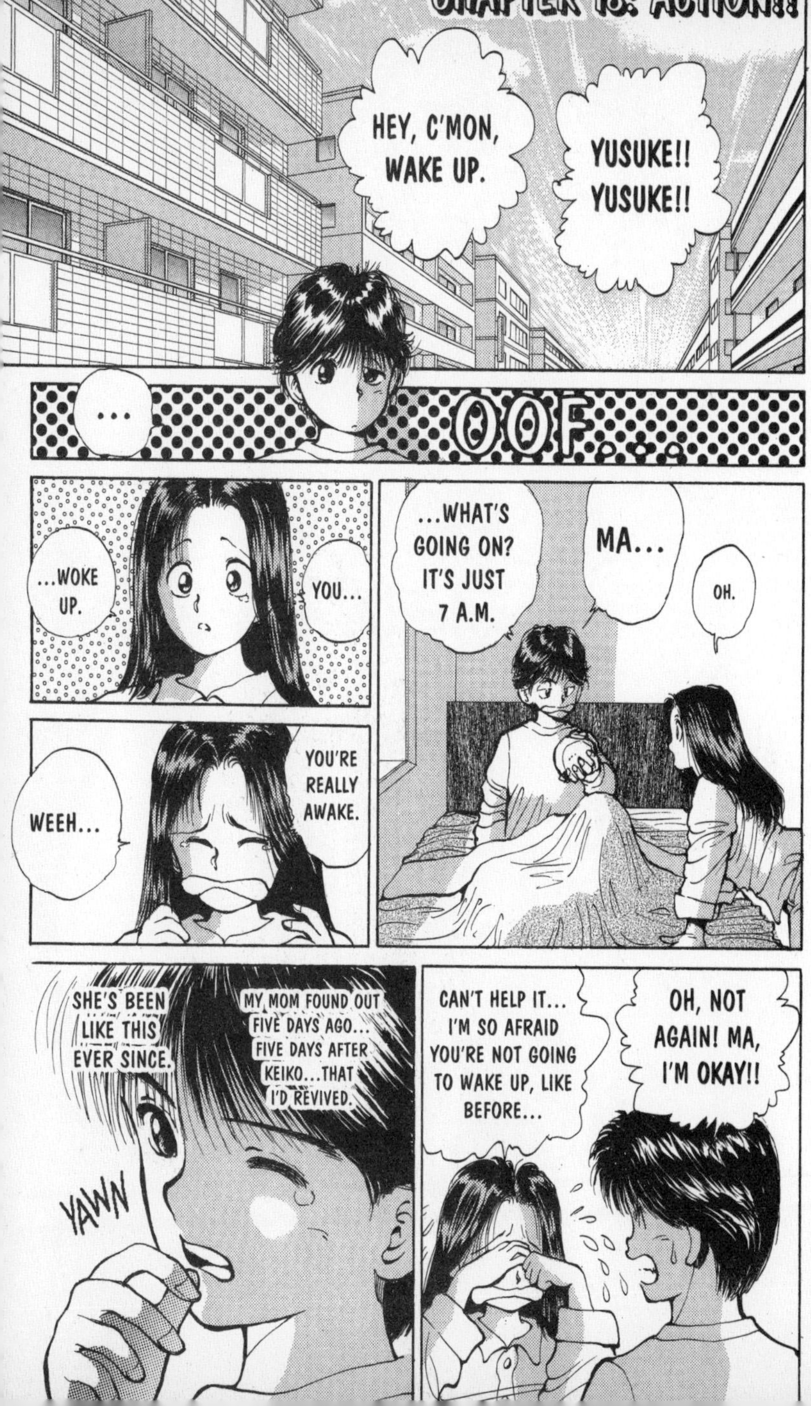
YUSUKE!! YUSUKE!!
HEY, C'MON, WAKE UP.
OOF...
...
MA...
OH.
...WHAT'S GOING ON? IT'S JUST 7 A.M.
YOU...
...WOKE UP.
YOU'RE REALLY AWAKE.
WEEH...
OH, NOT AGAIN! MA, I'M OKAY!!
CAN'T HELP IT... I'M SO AFRAID YOU'RE NOT GOING TO WAKE UP, LIKE BEFORE...
MY MOM FOUND OUT FIVE DAYS AGO... FIVE DAYS AFTER KEIKO...THAT I'D REVIVED.
SHE'S BEEN LIKE THIS EVER SINCE.
YAWN

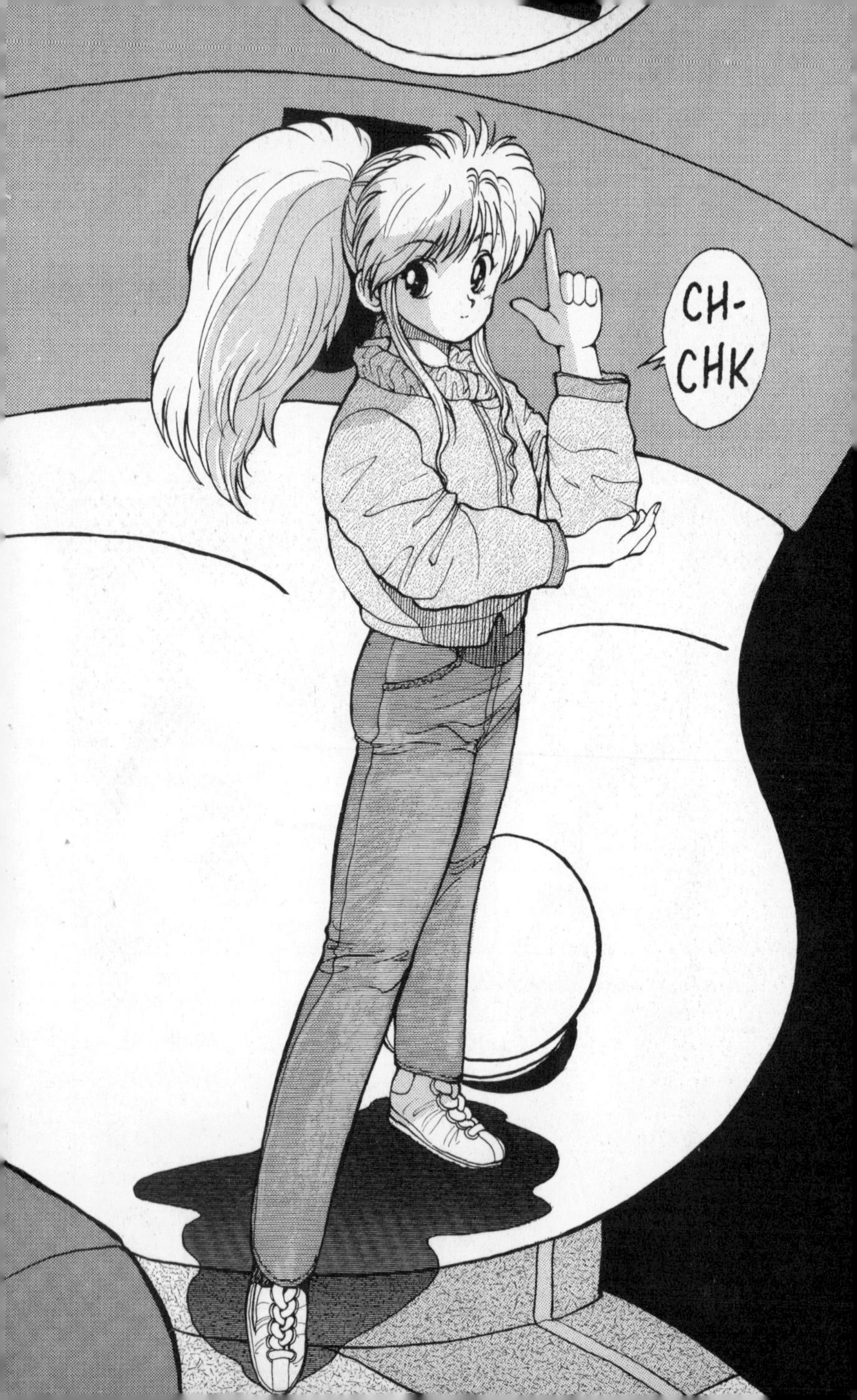
CH-
CHK

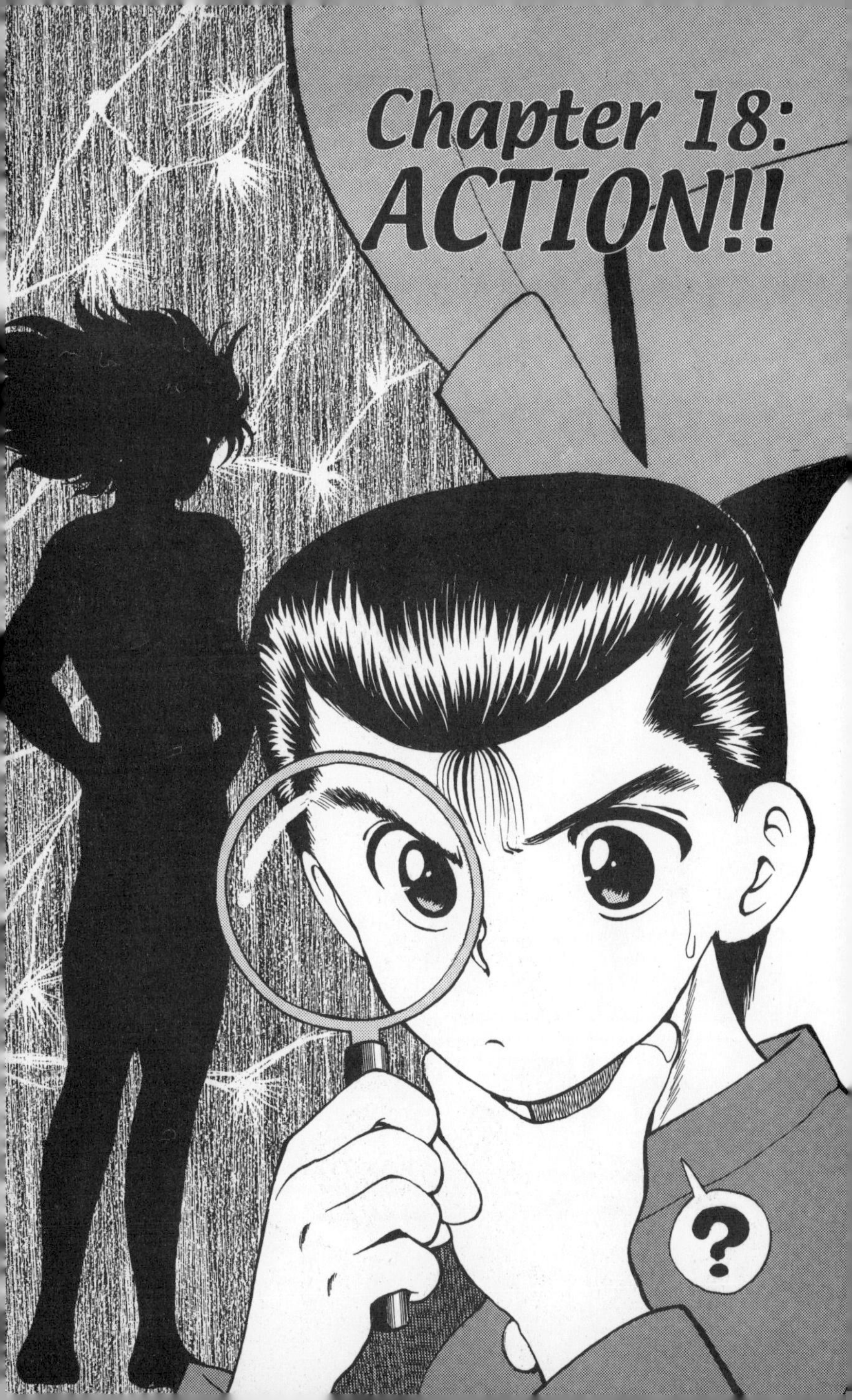
Chapter 18:
ACTION!!
?

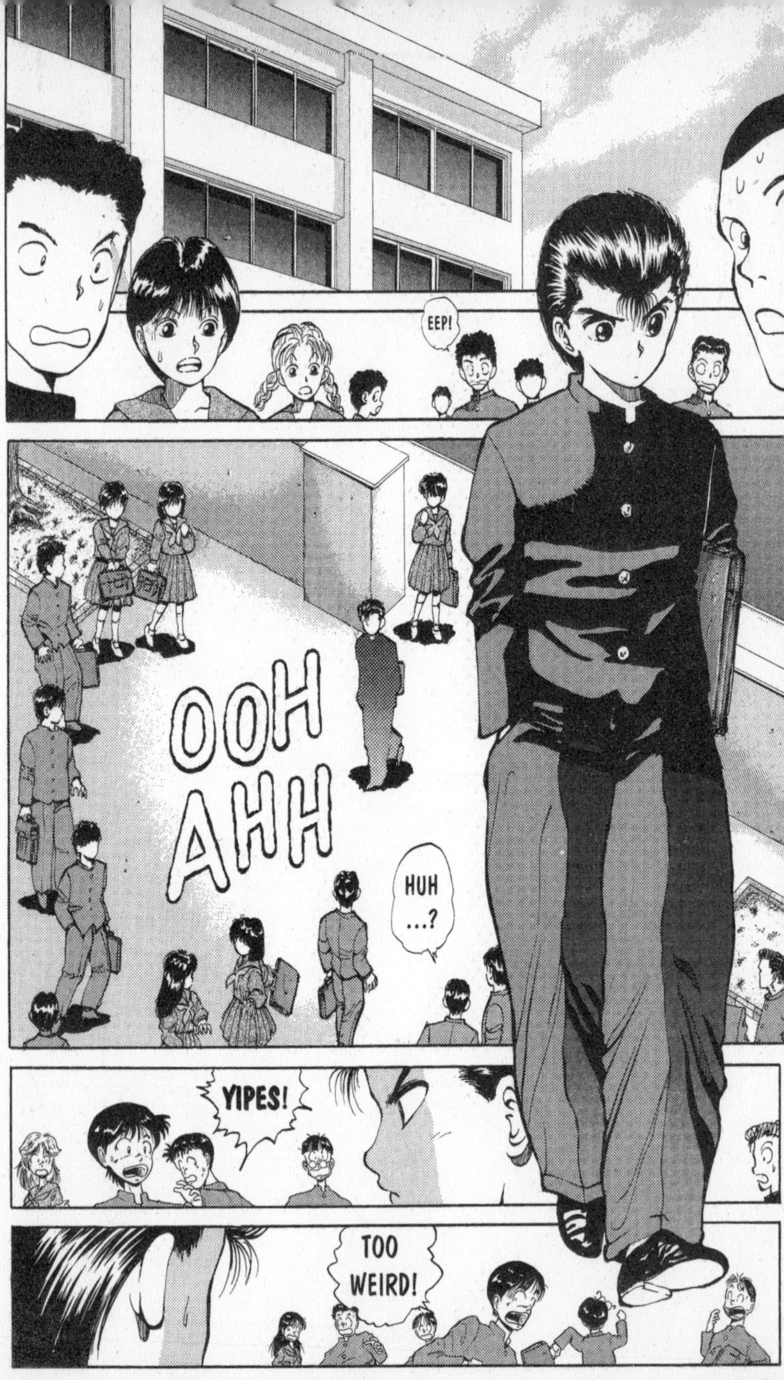
EEP!
OOH AHH
HUH ...?
YIPES!
TOO WEIRD!

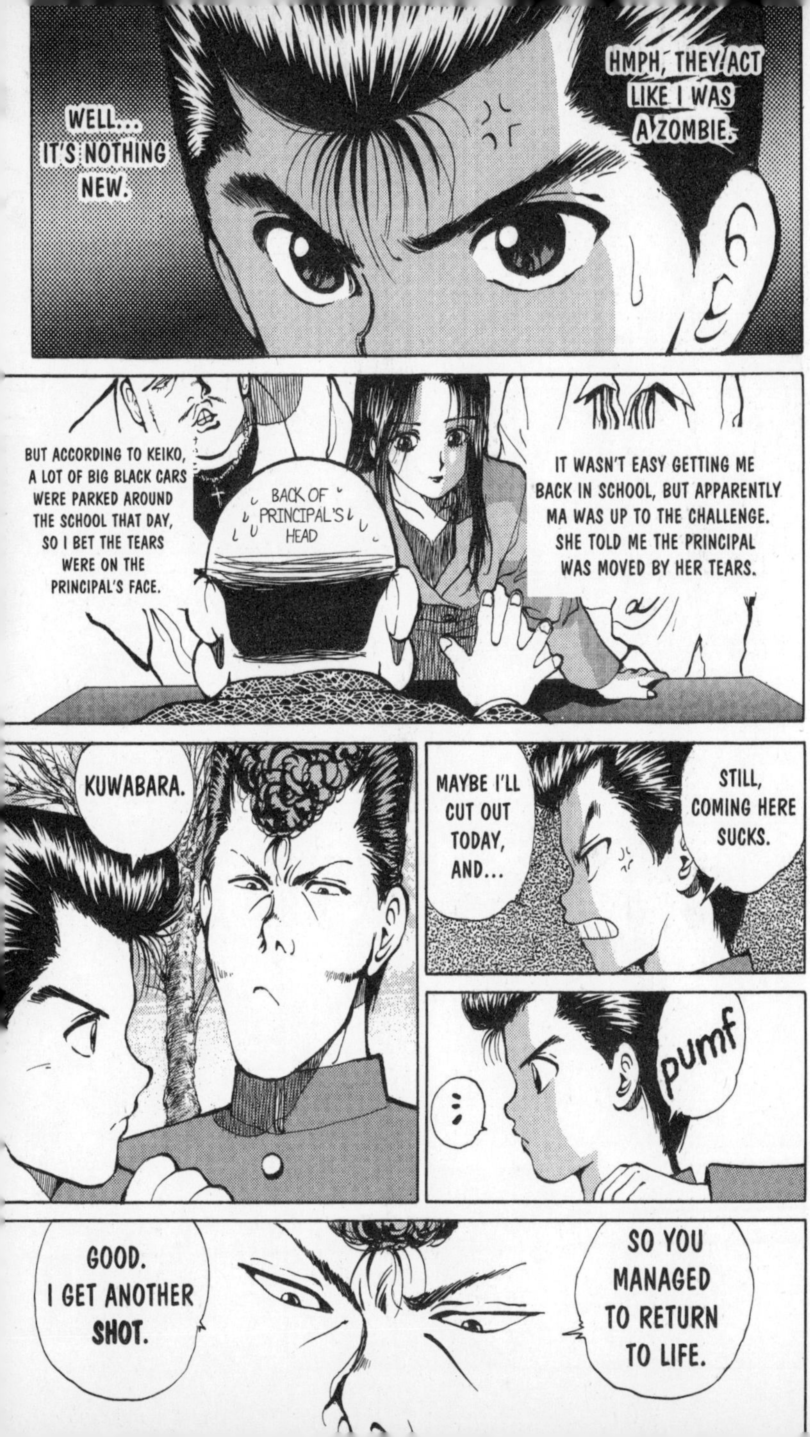
HMPH, THEY ACT LIKE I WAS A ZOMBIE.
WELL... IT'S NOTHING NEW.
IT WASN'T EASY GETTING ME BACK IN SCHOOL, BUT APPARENTLY MA WAS UP TO THE CHALLENGE. SHE TOLD ME THE PRINCIPAL WAS MOVED BY HER TEARS.
BUT ACCORDING TO KEIKO, A LOT OF BIG BLACK CARS WERE PARKED AROUND THE SCHOOL THAT DAY, SO I BET THE TEARS WERE ON THE PRINCIPAL'S FACE.
BACK OF PRINCIPAL'S HEAD
STILL, COMING HERE SUCKS.
MAYBE I'LL CUT OUT TODAY, AND...
pumf
...
KUWABARA.
SO YOU MANAGED TO RETURN TO LIFE.
GOOD. I GET ANOTHER SHOT.

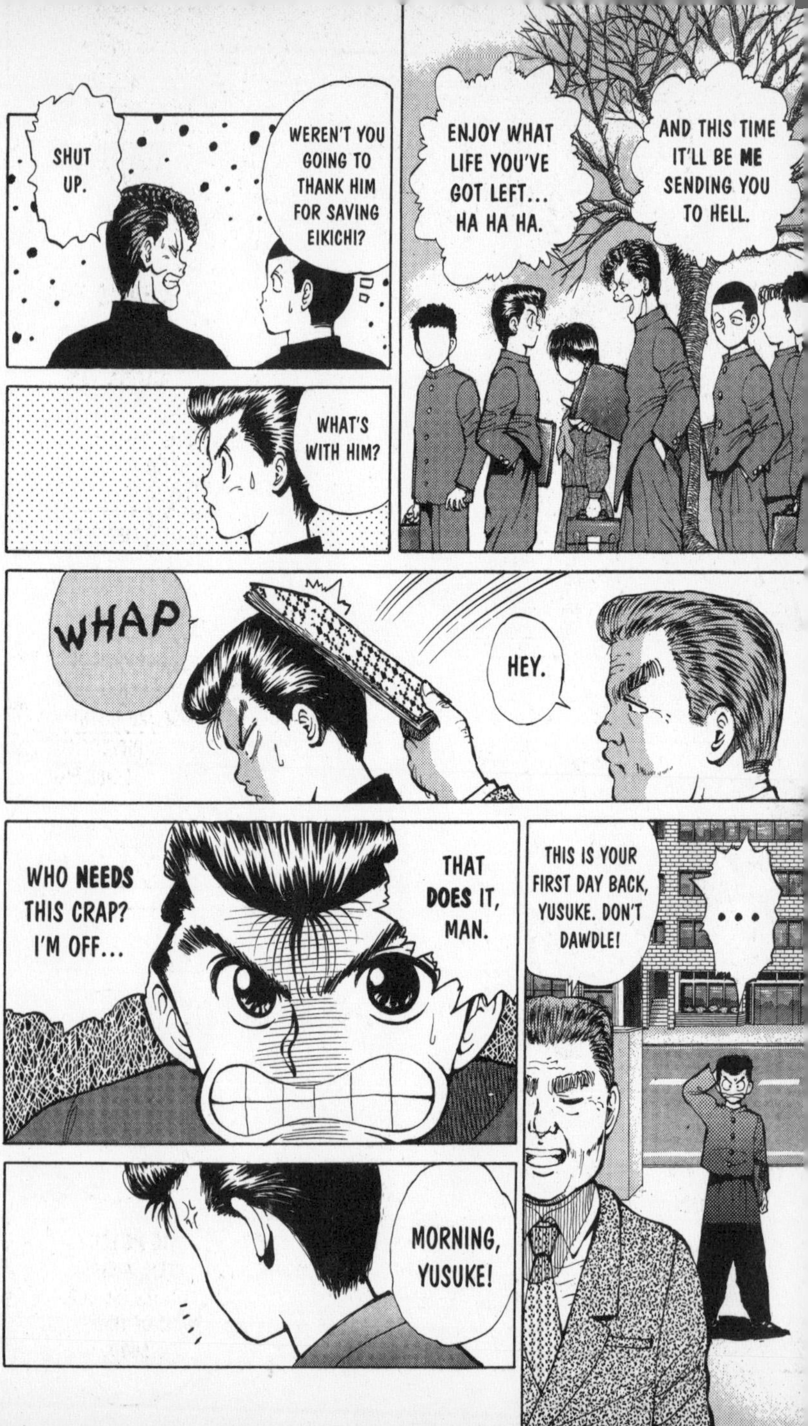
AND THIS TIME IT'LL BE **ME** SENDING YOU TO HELL.
ENJOY WHAT LIFE YOU'VE GOT LEFT... HA HA HA.
WEREN'T YOU GOING TO THANK HIM FOR SAVING EIKICHI?
SHUT UP.
WHAT'S WITH HIM?
HEY.
WHAP
...
THIS IS YOUR FIRST DAY BACK, YUSUKE. DON'T DAWDLE!
THAT **DOES** IT, MAN.
WHO **NEEDS** THIS CRAP? I'M OFF...
MORNING, YUSUKE!

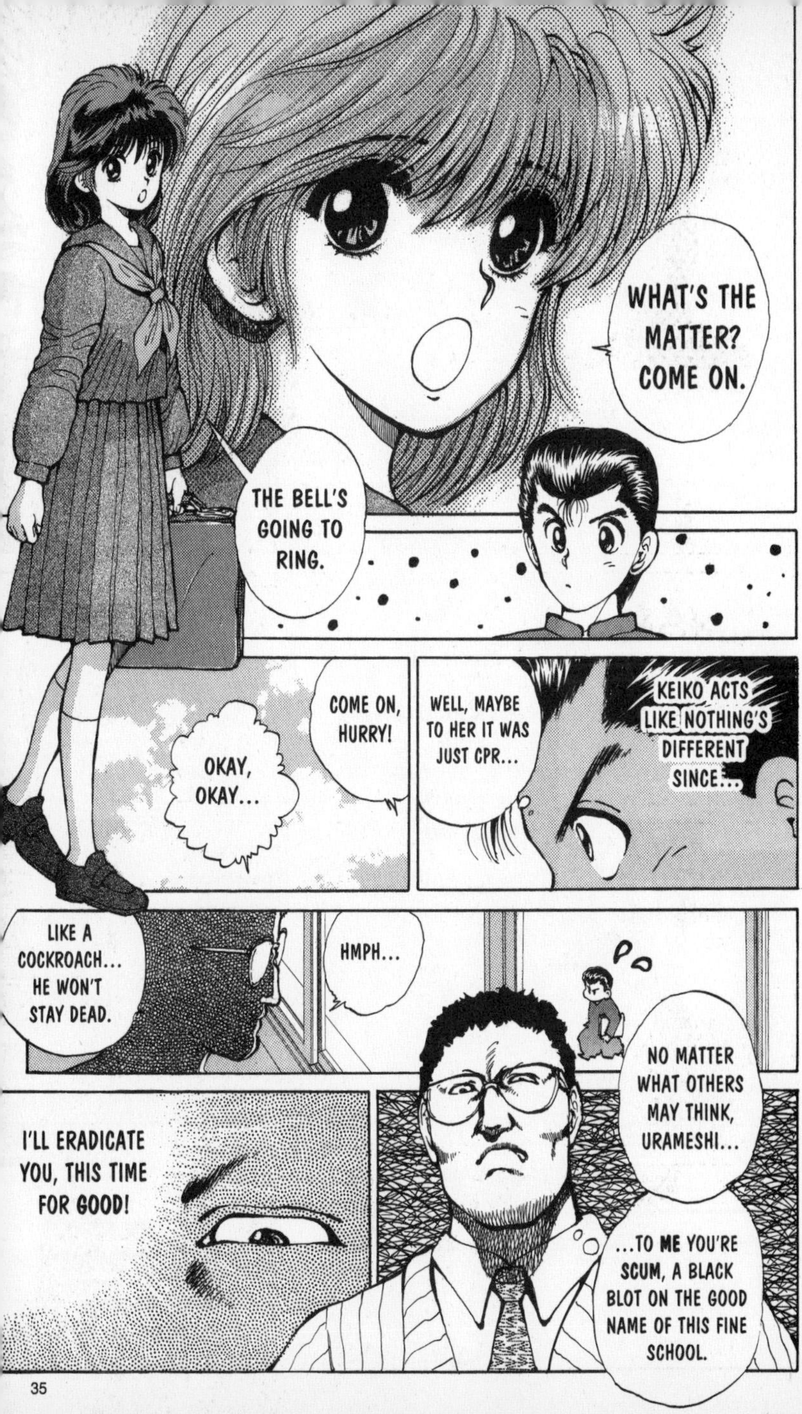
WHAT'S THE MATTER? COME ON.
THE BELL'S GOING TO RING.
KEIKO ACTS LIKE NOTHING'S DIFFERENT SINCE...
WELL, MAYBE TO HER IT WAS JUST CPR...
COME ON, HURRY!
OKAY, OKAY...
HMPH...
LIKE A COCKROACH... HE WON'T STAY DEAD.
NO MATTER WHAT OTHERS MAY THINK, URAMESHI...
...TO ME YOU'RE SCUM, A BLACK BLOT ON THE GOOD NAME OF THIS FINE SCHOOL.
I'LL ERADICATE YOU, THIS TIME FOR GOOD!

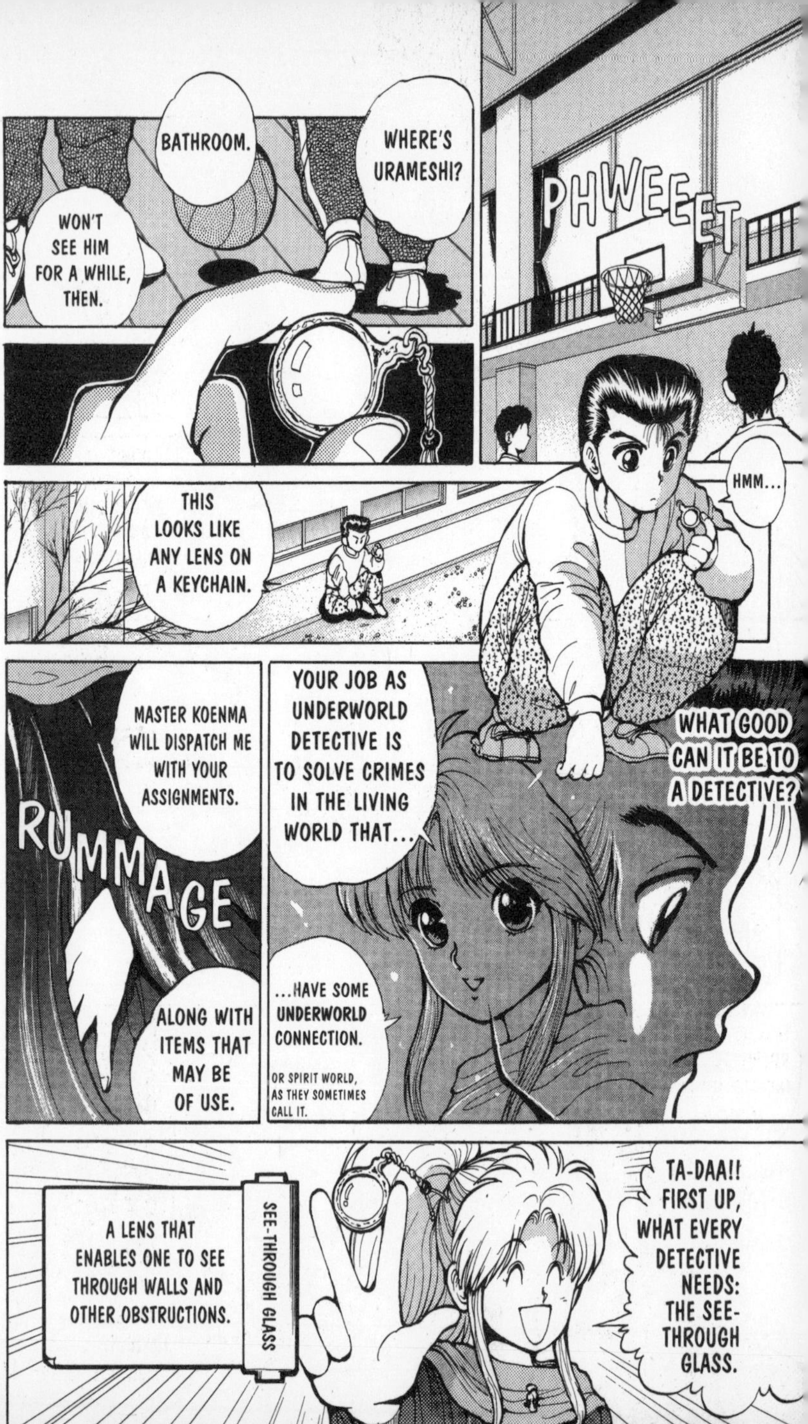
PHWEEEET
HMM...
WHERE'S URAMESHI?
BATHROOM.
WON'T SEE HIM FOR A WHILE, THEN.
THIS LOOKS LIKE ANY LENS ON A KEYCHAIN.
WHAT GOOD CAN IT BE TO A DETECTIVE?
YOUR JOB AS UNDERWORLD DETECTIVE IS TO SOLVE CRIMES IN THE LIVING WORLD THAT...
...HAVE SOME UNDERWORLD CONNECTION.
OR SPIRIT WORLD, AS THEY SOMETIMES CALL IT.
MASTER KOENMA WILL DISPATCH ME WITH YOUR ASSIGNMENTS.
RUMMAGE
ALONG WITH ITEMS THAT MAY BE OF USE.
TA-DAA!! FIRST UP, WHAT EVERY DETECTIVE NEEDS: THE SEE-THROUGH GLASS.
SEE-THROUGH GLASS
A LENS THAT ENABLES ONE TO SEE THROUGH WALLS AND OTHER OBSTRUCTIONS.

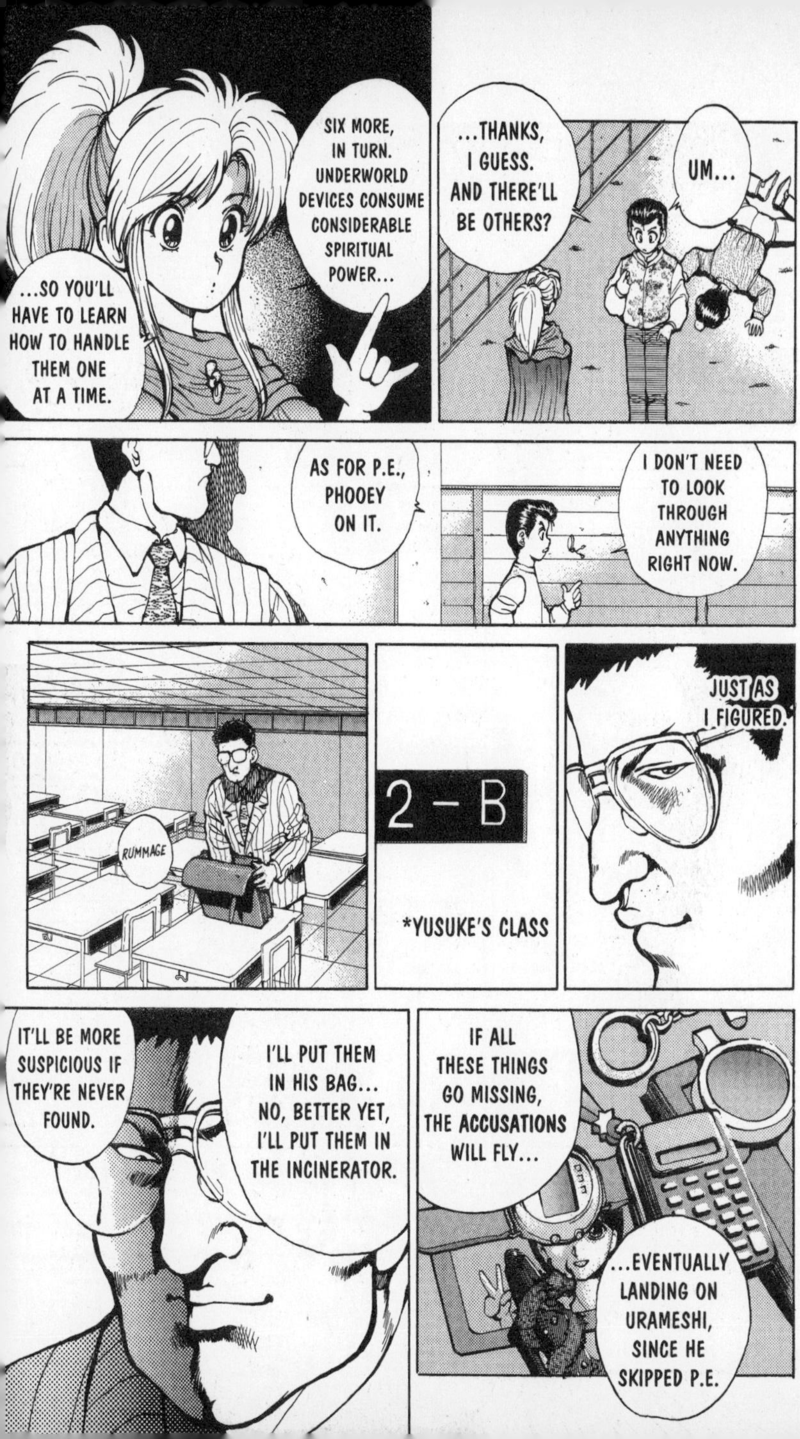
UM...
...THANKS, I GUESS. AND THERE'LL BE OTHERS?
SIX MORE, IN TURN. UNDERWORLD DEVICES CONSUME CONSIDERABLE SPIRITUAL POWER...
...SO YOU'LL HAVE TO LEARN HOW TO HANDLE THEM ONE AT A TIME.
I DON'T NEED TO LOOK THROUGH ANYTHING RIGHT NOW.
AS FOR P.E., PHOOEY ON IT.
JUST AS I FIGURED.
2 – B
*YUSUKE'S CLASS
RUMMAGE
IF ALL THESE THINGS GO MISSING, THE ACCUSATIONS WILL FLY...
...EVENTUALLY LANDING ON URAMESHI, SINCE HE SKIPPED P.E.
I'LL PUT THEM IN HIS BAG... NO, BETTER YET, I'LL PUT THEM IN THE INCINERATOR.
IT'LL BE MORE SUSPICIOUS IF THEY'RE NEVER FOUND.

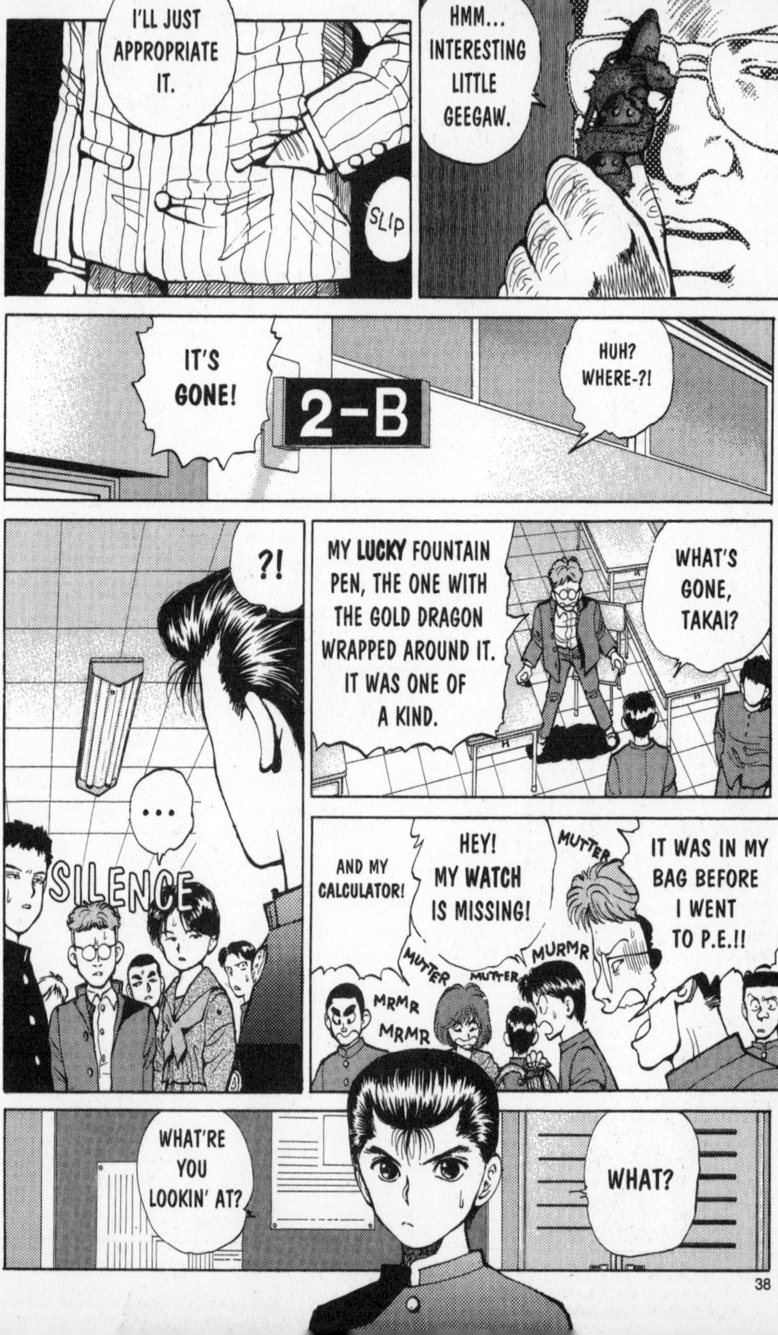
HMM... INTERESTING LITTLE GEEGAW.
I'LL JUST APPROPRIATE IT.
SLIP
HUH? WHERE-?!
2-B
IT'S GONE!
WHAT'S GONE, TAKAI?
MY LUCKY FOUNTAIN PEN, THE ONE WITH THE GOLD DRAGON WRAPPED AROUND IT. IT WAS ONE OF A KIND.
IT WAS IN MY BAG BEFORE I WENT TO P.E.!!
MUTTER
HEY! MY WATCH IS MISSING!
AND MY CALCULATOR!
MURMR
MUTTER
MUTTER
MRMR
MRMR
?!
...
SILENCE
WHAT?
WHAT'RE YOU LOOKIN' AT?

READ THIS WAY

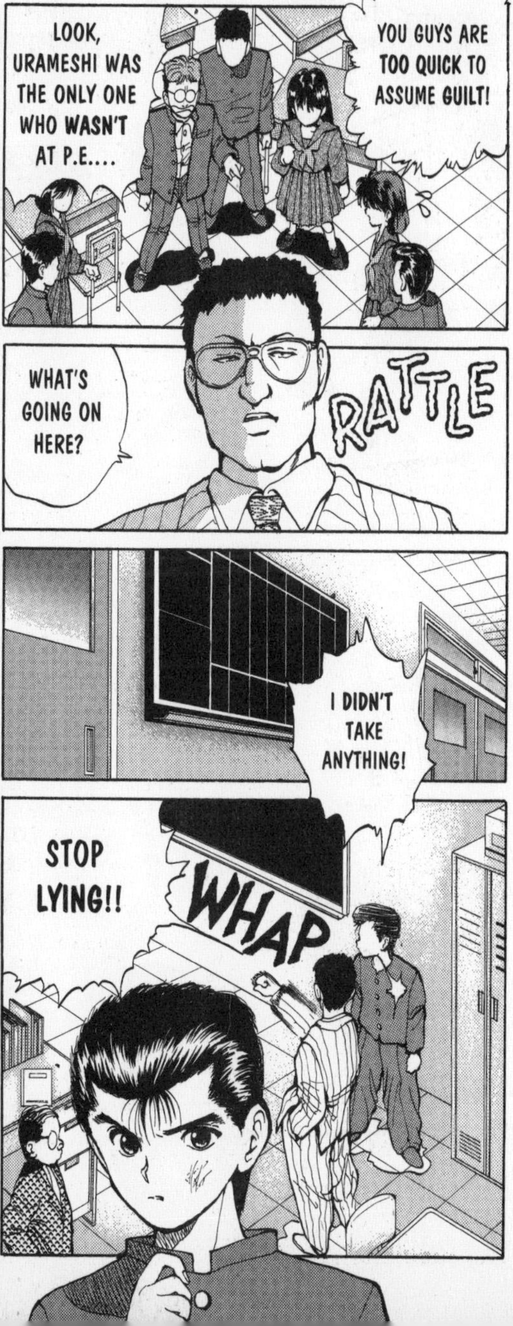
YOU GUYS ARE TOO QUICK TO ASSUME GUILT!
LOOK, URAMESHI WAS THE ONLY ONE WHO WASN'T AT P.E....
RATTLE
WHAT'S GOING ON HERE?
I DIDN'T TAKE ANYTHING!
WHAP
STOP LYING!!

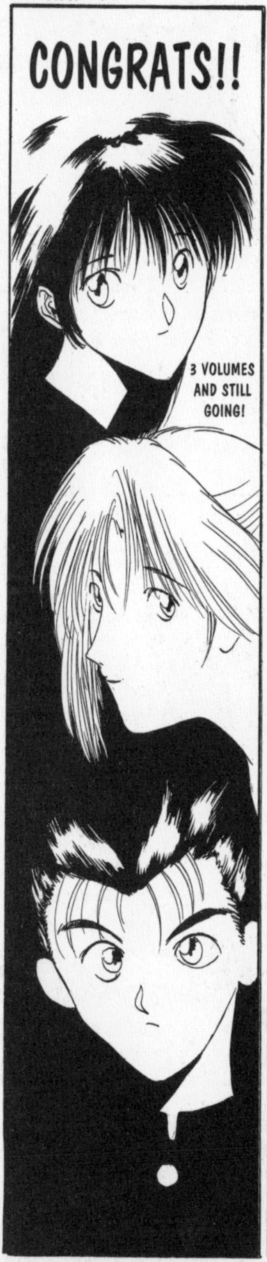
CONGRATS!!
3 VOLUMES AND STILL GOING!

* THIS IS A BONUS DRAWING BY ANOTHER ARTIST, CONGRATULATING TOGASHI ON REACHING THE THIRD VOLUME OF YUYU HAKUSHO.

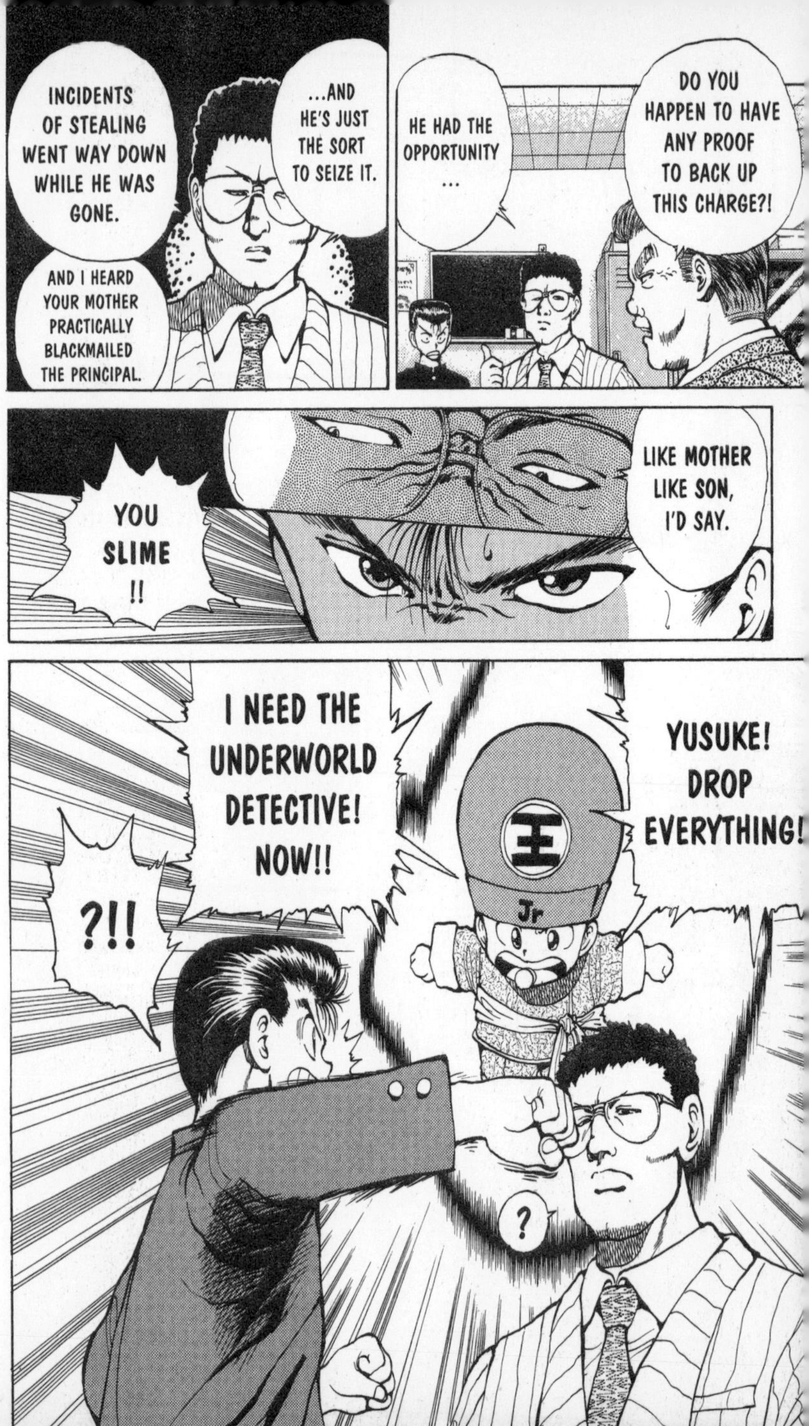
DO YOU HAPPEN TO HAVE ANY PROOF TO BACK UP THIS CHARGE?!
HE HAD THE OPPORTUNITY...
...AND HE'S JUST THE SORT TO SEIZE IT.
INCIDENTS OF STEALING WENT WAY DOWN WHILE HE WAS GONE.
AND I HEARD YOUR MOTHER PRACTICALLY BLACKMAILED THE PRINCIPAL.
LIKE MOTHER LIKE SON, I'D SAY.
YOU SLIME!!
YUSUKE! DROP EVERYTHING!
I NEED THE UNDERWORLD DETECTIVE! NOW!!
?!!
?

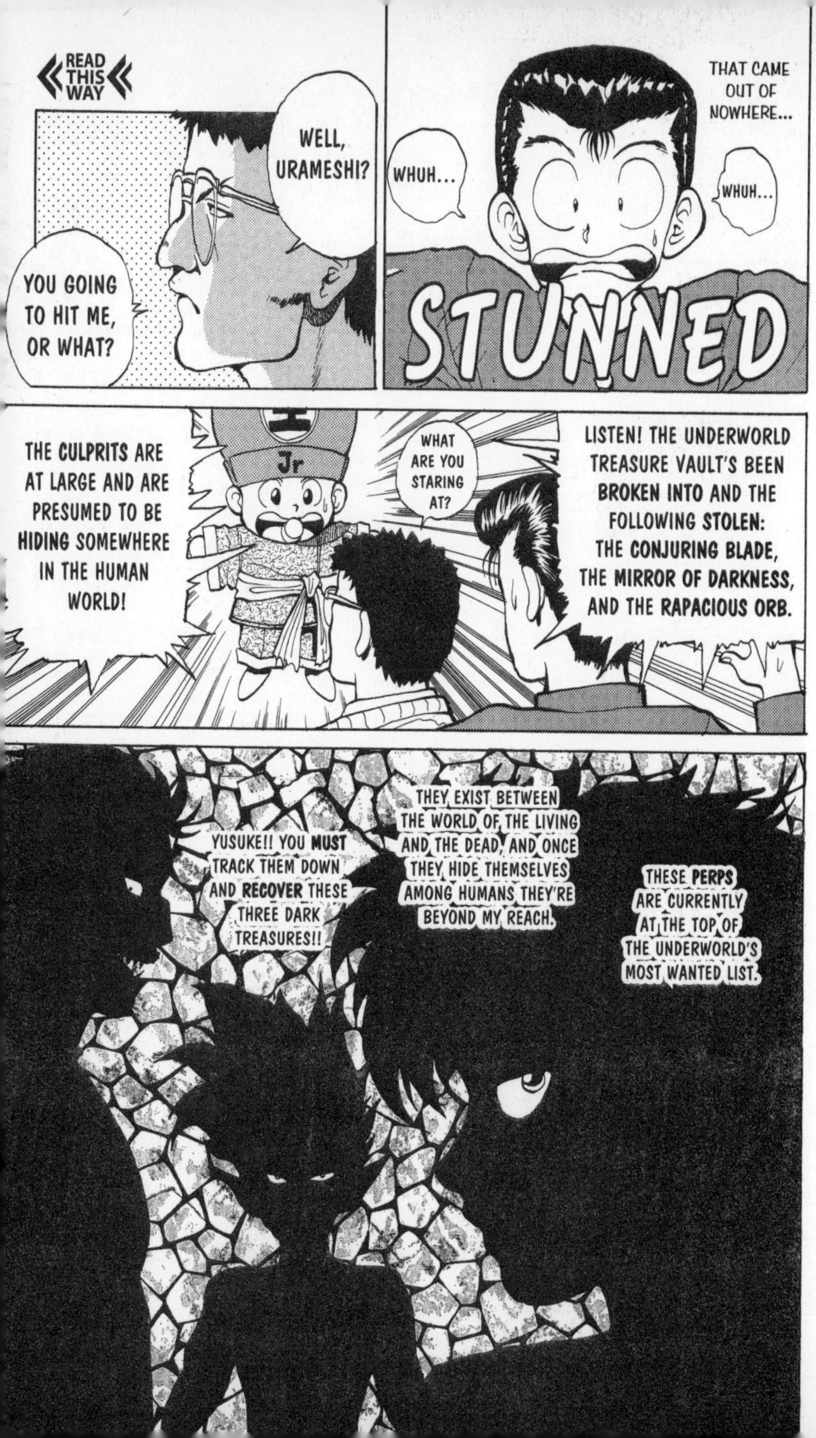
READ THIS WAY
THAT CAME OUT OF NOWHERE...
WHUH...
WHUH...
STUNNED
WELL, URAMESHI?
YOU GOING TO HIT ME, OR WHAT?
LISTEN! THE UNDERWORLD TREASURE VAULT'S BEEN BROKEN INTO AND THE FOLLOWING STOLEN: THE CONJURING BLADE, THE MIRROR OF DARKNESS, AND THE RAPACIOUS ORB.
WHAT ARE YOU STARING AT?
THE CULPRITS ARE AT LARGE AND ARE PRESUMED TO BE HIDING SOMEWHERE IN THE HUMAN WORLD!
THESE PERPS ARE CURRENTLY AT THE TOP OF THE UNDERWORLD'S MOST WANTED LIST.
THEY EXIST BETWEEN THE WORLD OF THE LIVING AND THE DEAD, AND ONCE THEY HIDE THEMSELVES AMONG HUMANS THEY'RE BEYOND MY REACH.
YUSUKE!! YOU MUST TRACK THEM DOWN AND RECOVER THESE THREE DARK TREASURES!!

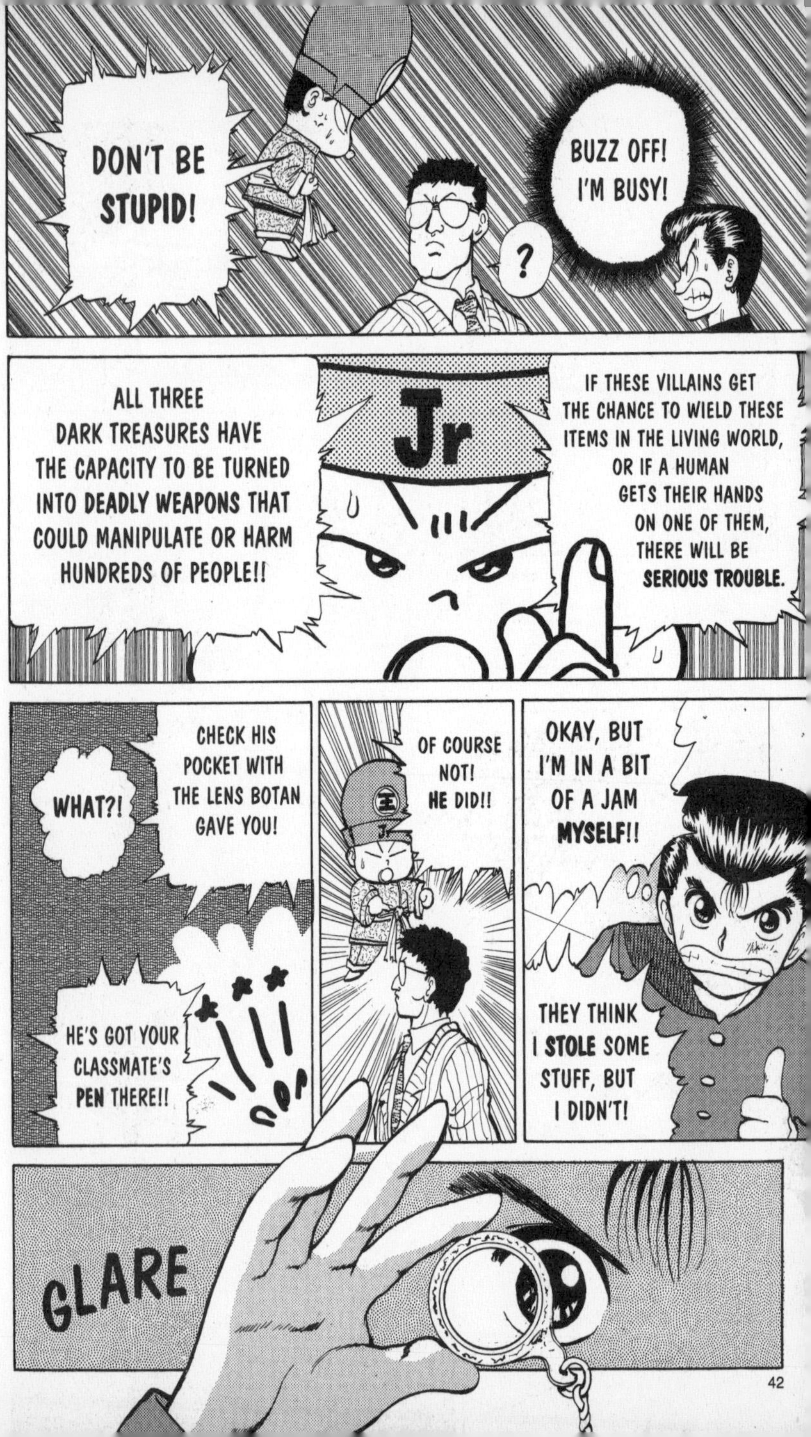
BUZZ OFF! I'M BUSY!
?
DON'T BE STUPID!
IF THESE VILLAINS GET THE CHANCE TO WIELD THESE ITEMS IN THE LIVING WORLD, OR IF A HUMAN GETS THEIR HANDS ON ONE OF THEM, THERE WILL BE SERIOUS TROUBLE.
ALL THREE DARK TREASURES HAVE THE CAPACITY TO BE TURNED INTO DEADLY WEAPONS THAT COULD MANIPULATE OR HARM HUNDREDS OF PEOPLE!!
Jr
OKAY, BUT I'M IN A BIT OF A JAM MYSELF!!
THEY THINK I STOLE SOME STUFF, BUT I DIDN'T!
OF COURSE NOT! HE DID!!
CHECK HIS POCKET WITH THE LENS BOTAN GAVE YOU!
WHAT?!
HE'S GOT YOUR CLASSMATE'S PEN THERE!!
GLARE

READ THIS WAY

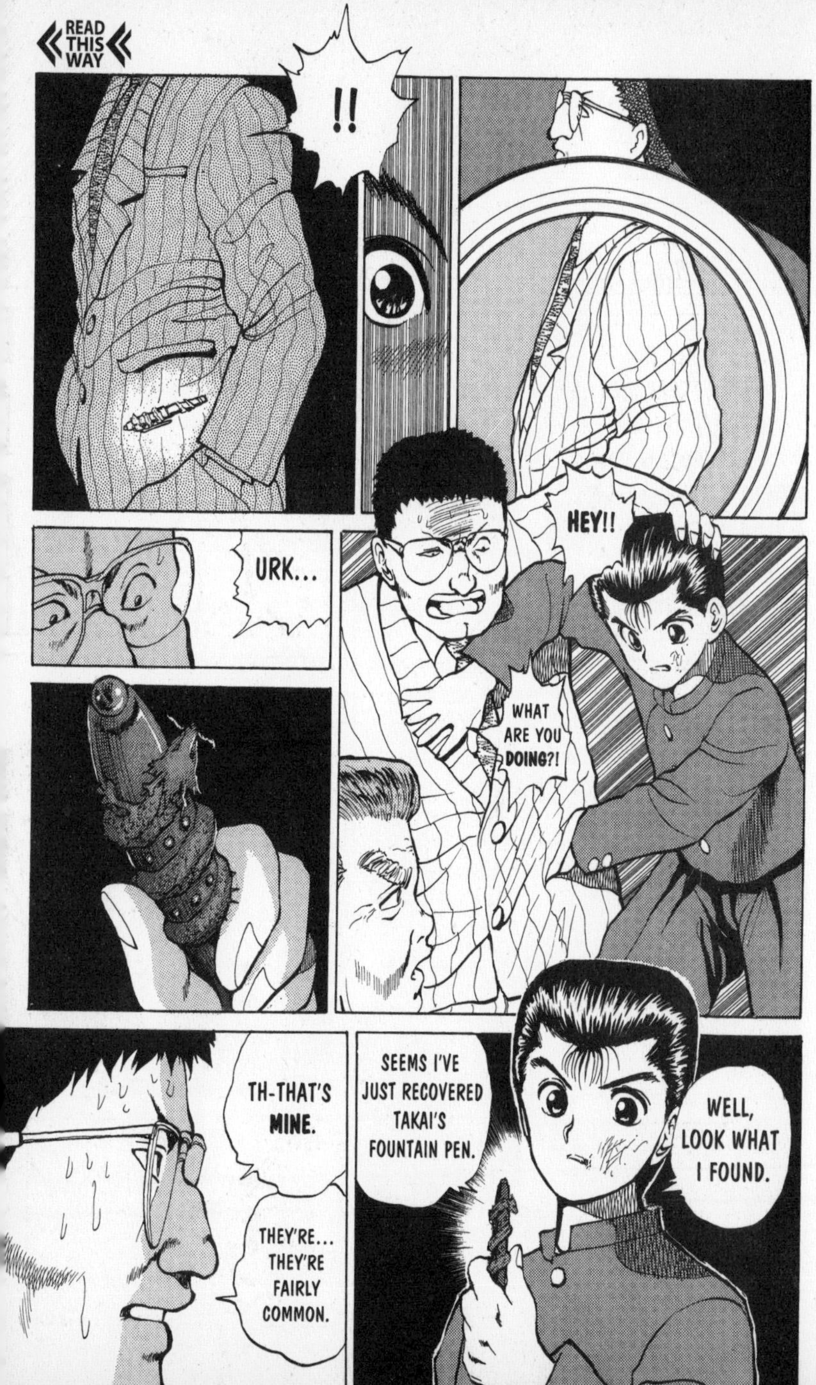
!!
HEY!!
WHAT ARE YOU DOING?!
URK...
WELL, LOOK WHAT I FOUND.
SEEMS I'VE JUST RECOVERED TAKAI'S FOUNTAIN PEN.
TH-THAT'S MINE.
THEY'RE... THEY'RE FAIRLY COMMON.

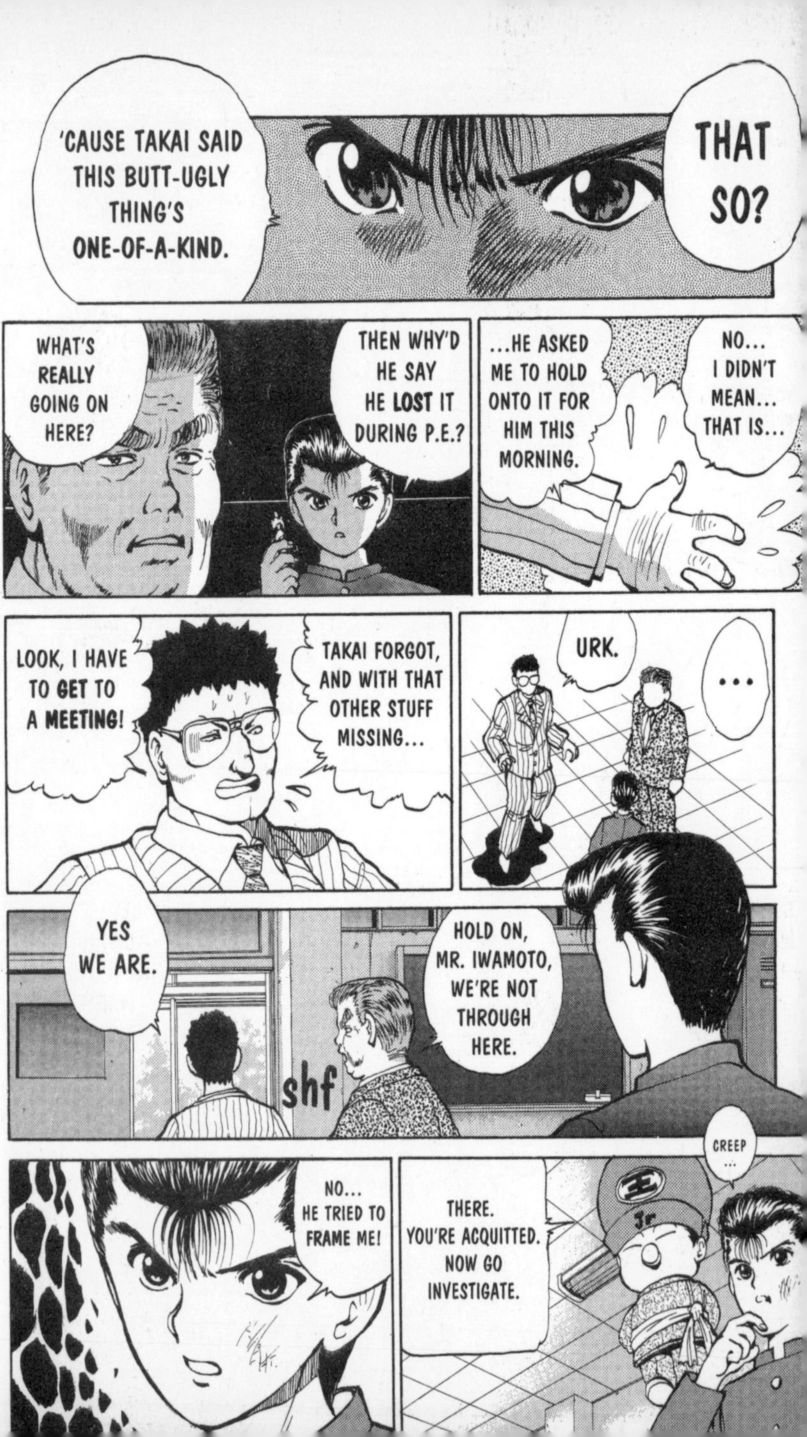
THAT SO?
'CAUSE TAKAI SAID THIS BUTT-UGLY THING'S ONE-OF-A-KIND.
NO... I DIDN'T MEAN... THAT IS...
...HE ASKED ME TO HOLD ONTO IT FOR HIM THIS MORNING.
THEN WHY'D HE SAY HE LOST IT DURING P.E.?
WHAT'S REALLY GOING ON HERE?
...
URK.
TAKAI FORGOT, AND WITH THAT OTHER STUFF MISSING...
LOOK, I HAVE TO GET TO A MEETING!
HOLD ON, MR. IWAMOTO, WE'RE NOT THROUGH HERE.
shf
YES WE ARE.
CREEP ...
THERE. YOU'RE ACQUITTED. NOW GO INVESTIGATE.
NO... HE TRIED TO FRAME ME!

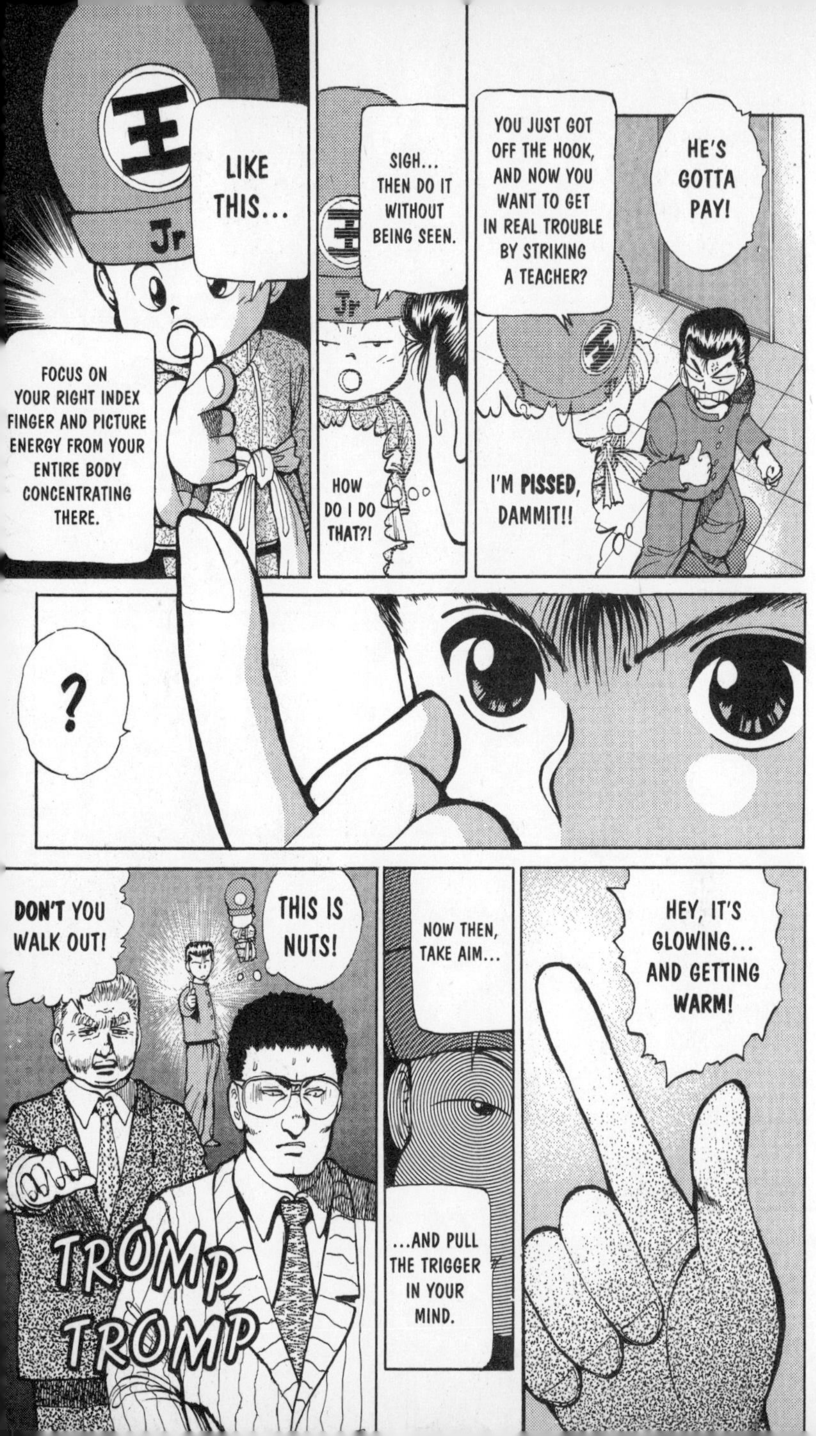
HE'S GOTTA PAY!
YOU JUST GOT OFF THE HOOK, AND NOW YOU WANT TO GET IN REAL TROUBLE BY STRIKING A TEACHER?
I'M **PISSED**, DAMMIT!!
SIGH... THEN DO IT WITHOUT BEING SEEN.
HOW DO I DO THAT?!
LIKE THIS...
FOCUS ON YOUR RIGHT INDEX FINGER AND PICTURE ENERGY FROM YOUR ENTIRE BODY CONCENTRATING THERE.
?
HEY, IT'S GLOWING... AND GETTING WARM!
NOW THEN, TAKE AIM...
...AND PULL THE TRIGGER IN YOUR MIND.
THIS IS NUTS!
DON'T YOU WALK OUT!
TROMP TROMP

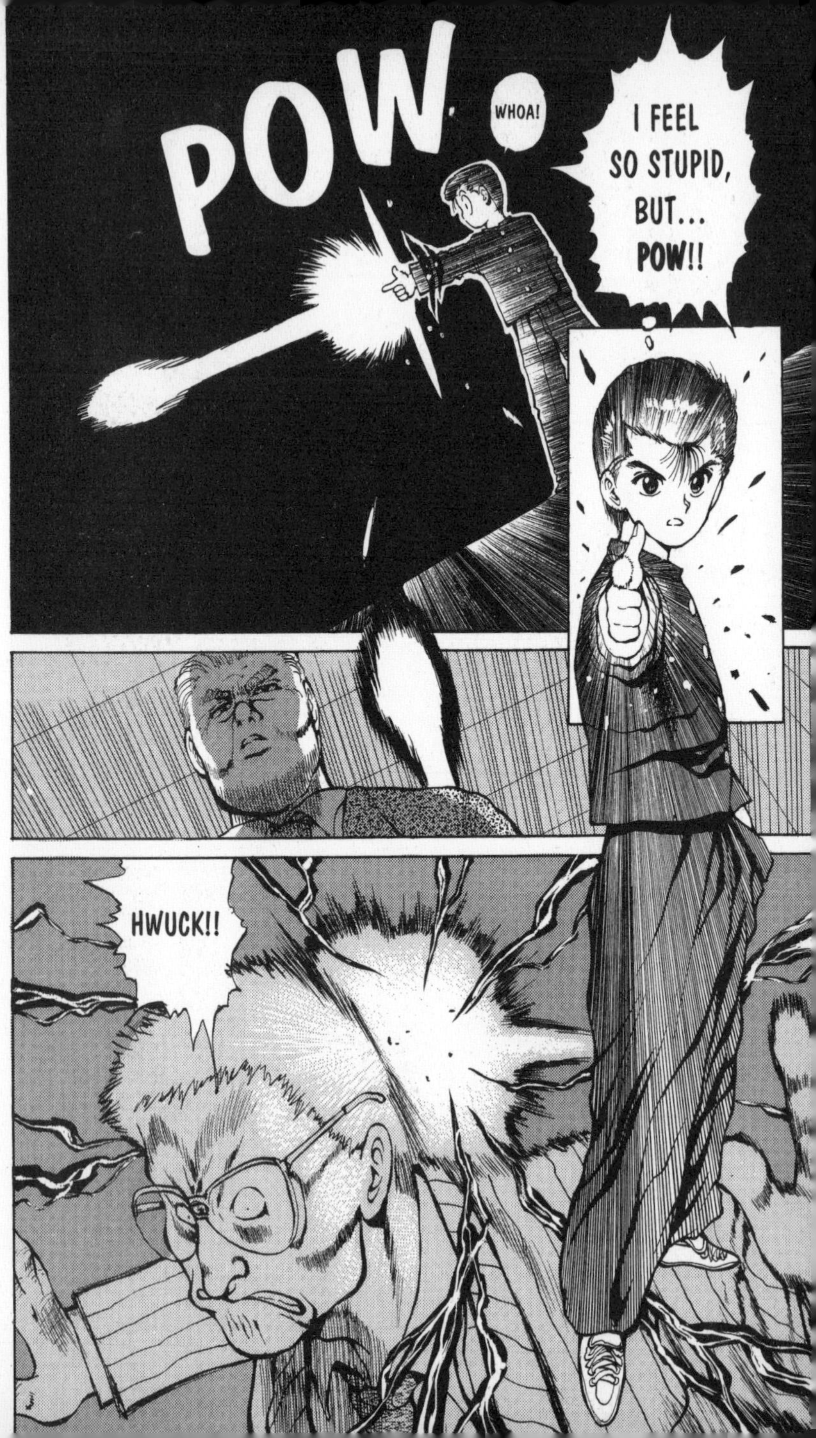
I FEEL SO STUPID, BUT... POW!!
WHOA!
POW
HWUCK!!

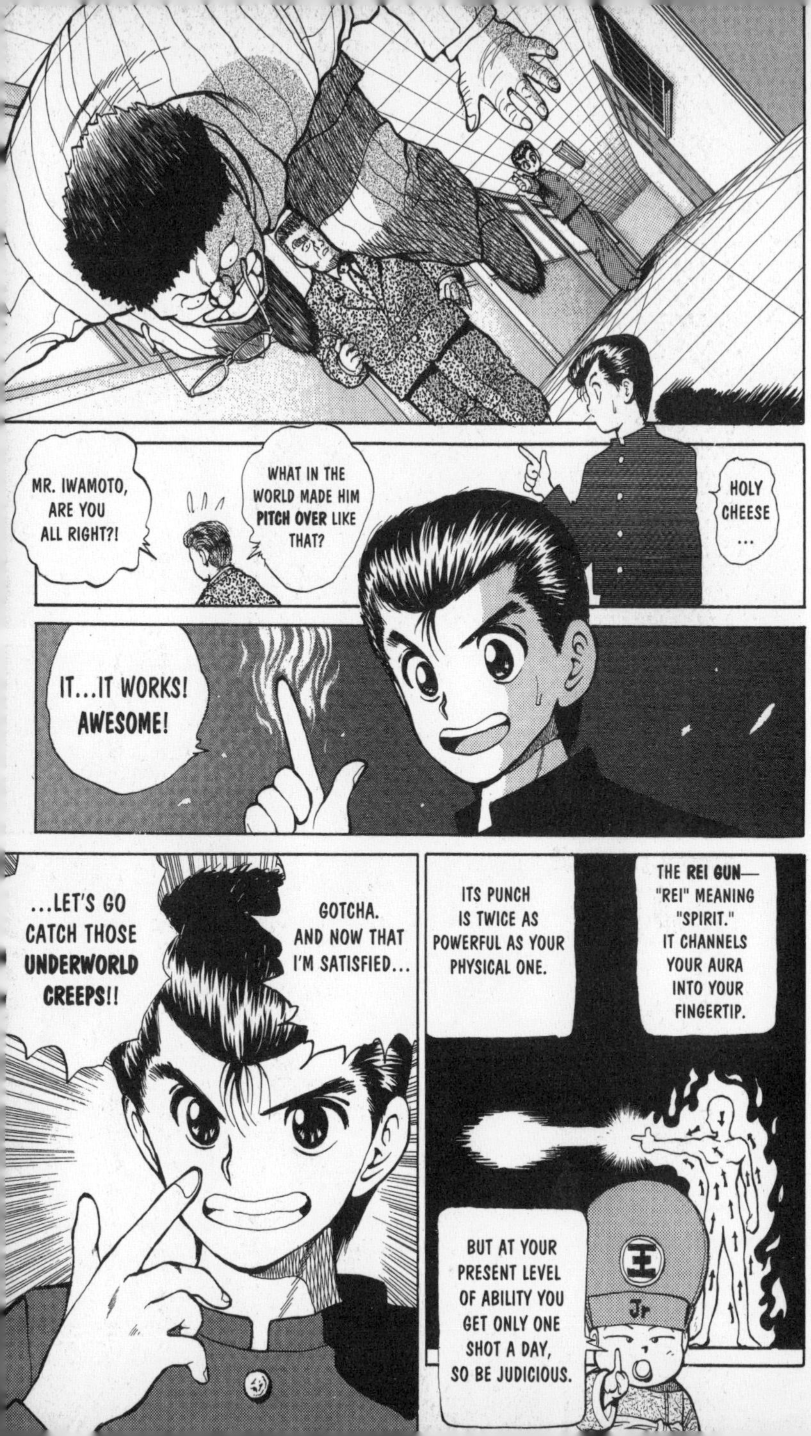
HOLY CHEESE ...
WHAT IN THE WORLD MADE HIM **PITCH OVER** LIKE THAT?
MR. IWAMOTO, ARE YOU ALL RIGHT?!
IT...IT WORKS! **AWESOME!**
THE **REI GUN**— "REI" MEANING "SPIRIT." IT CHANNELS YOUR AURA INTO YOUR FINGERTIP.
ITS PUNCH IS TWICE AS POWERFUL AS YOUR PHYSICAL ONE.
BUT AT YOUR PRESENT LEVEL OF ABILITY YOU GET ONLY ONE SHOT A DAY, SO BE JUDICIOUS.
GOTCHA. AND NOW THAT I'M SATISFIED...
...LET'S GO CATCH THOSE **UNDERWORLD CREEPS!!**

CHAPTER 19: THE DEADLY TRIO

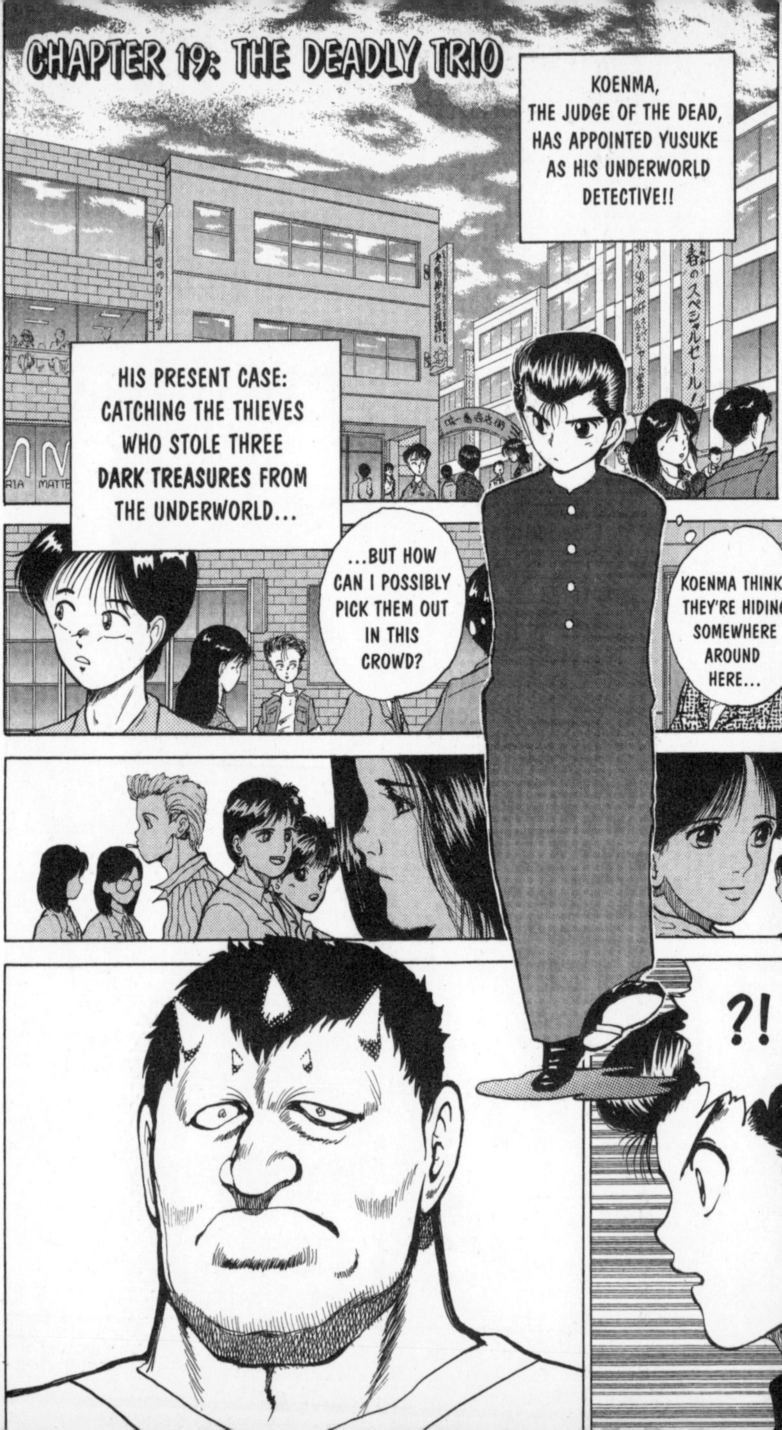
KOENMA, THE JUDGE OF THE DEAD, HAS APPOINTED YUSUKE AS HIS UNDERWORLD DETECTIVE!!
HIS PRESENT CASE: CATCHING THE THIEVES WHO STOLE THREE DARK TREASURES FROM THE UNDERWORLD...
KOENMA THINKS THEY'RE HIDING SOMEWHERE AROUND HERE...
...BUT HOW CAN I POSSIBLY PICK THEM OUT IN THIS CROWD?
?!

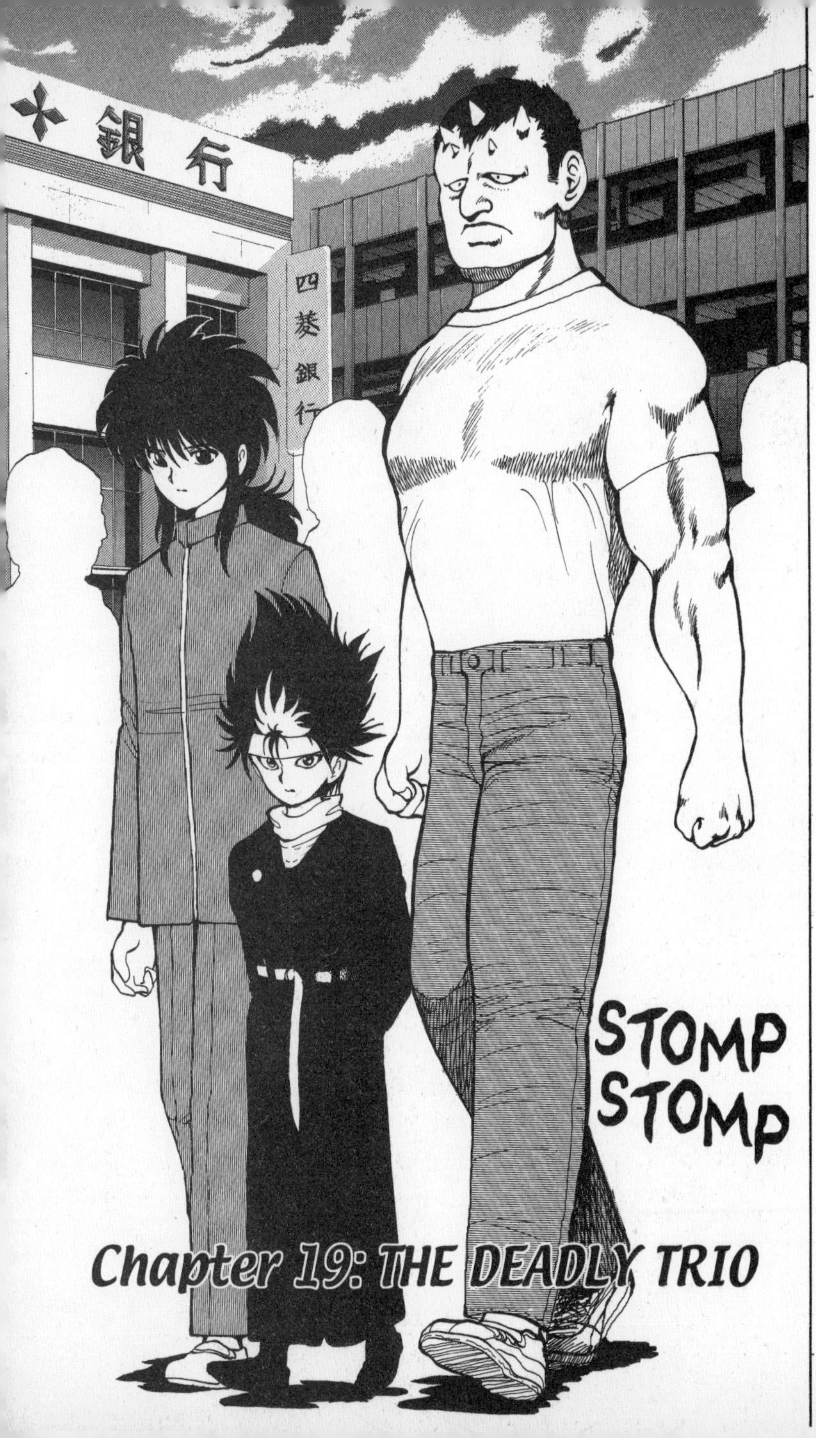
銀行
四菱銀行
STOMP
STOMP

Chapter 19: THE DEADLY TRIO

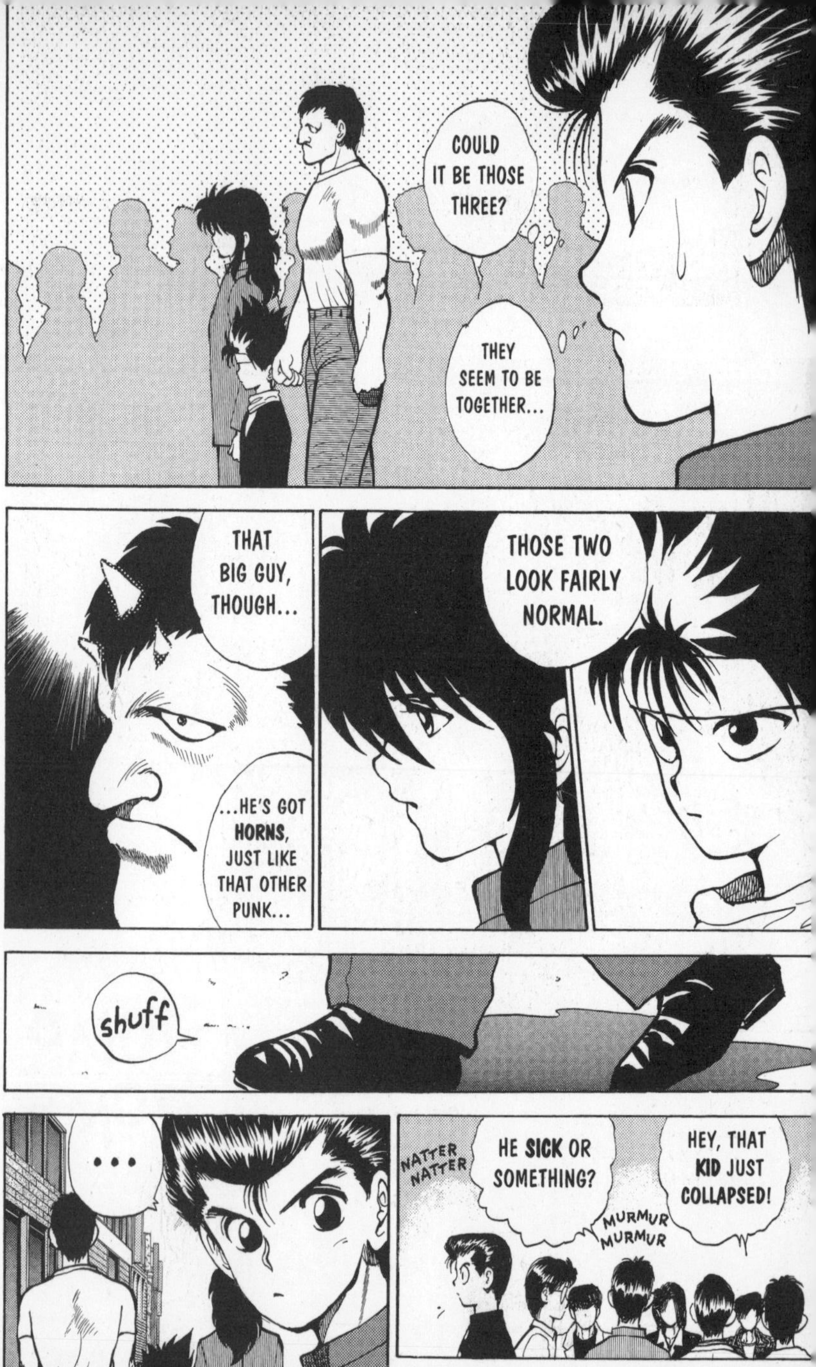
COULD IT BE THOSE THREE?
THEY SEEM TO BE TOGETHER...
THOSE TWO LOOK FAIRLY NORMAL.
THAT BIG GUY, THOUGH...
...HE'S GOT **HORNS**, JUST LIKE THAT OTHER PUNK...
shuff
HEY, THAT **KID** JUST COLLAPSED!
MURMUR MURMUR
HE **SICK** OR SOMETHING?
NATTER NATTER
...

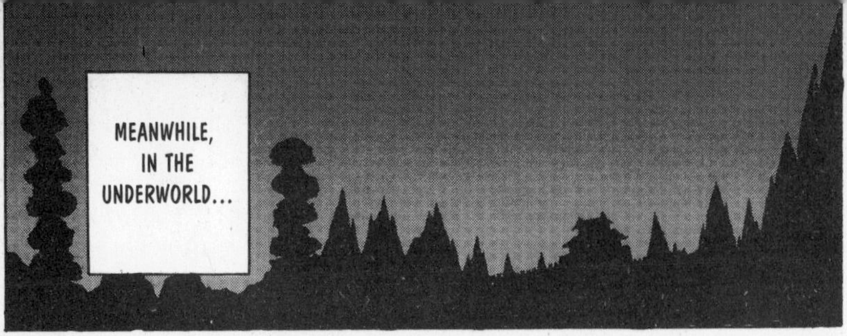
MEANWHILE, IN THE UNDERWORLD...

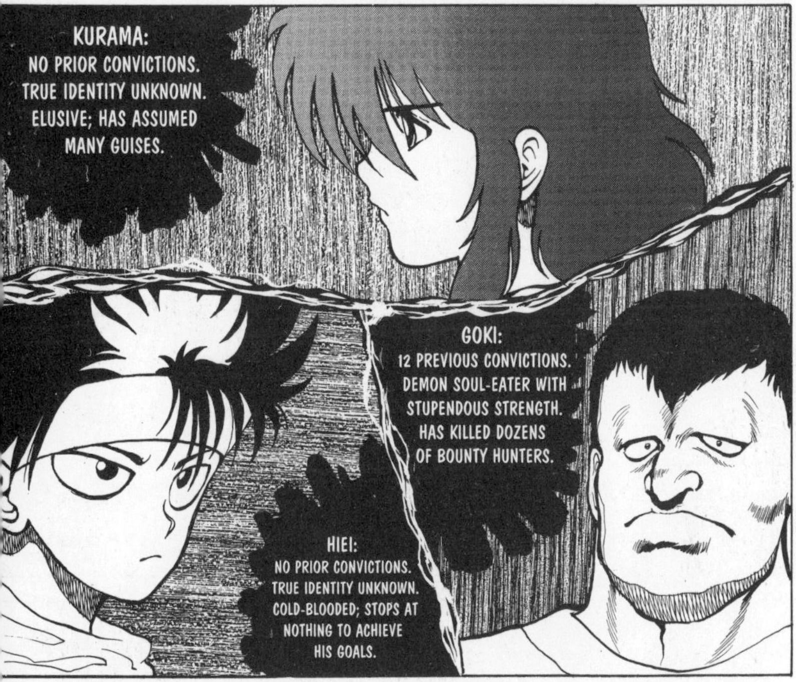
KURAMA:
NO PRIOR CONVICTIONS. TRUE IDENTITY UNKNOWN. ELUSIVE; HAS ASSUMED MANY GUISES.
GOKI:
12 PREVIOUS CONVICTIONS. DEMON SOUL-EATER WITH STUPENDOUS STRENGTH. HAS KILLED DOZENS OF BOUNTY HUNTERS.
HIEI:
NO PRIOR CONVICTIONS. TRUE IDENTITY UNKNOWN. COLD-BLOODED; STOPS AT NOTHING TO ACHIEVE HIS GOALS.

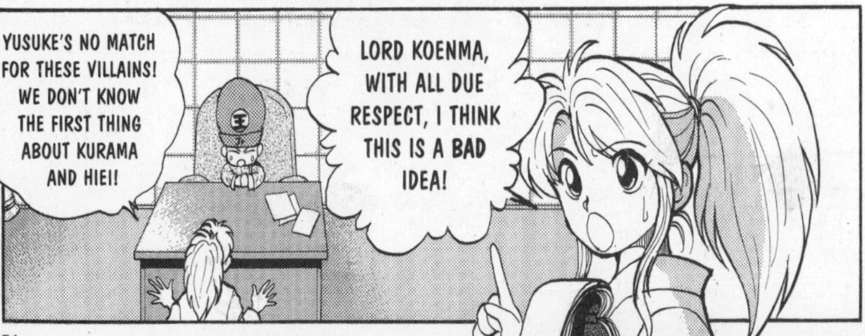
LORD KOENMA, WITH ALL DUE RESPECT, I THINK THIS IS A BAD IDEA!
YUSUKE'S NO MATCH FOR THESE VILLAINS! WE DON'T KNOW THE FIRST THING ABOUT KURAMA AND HIEI!

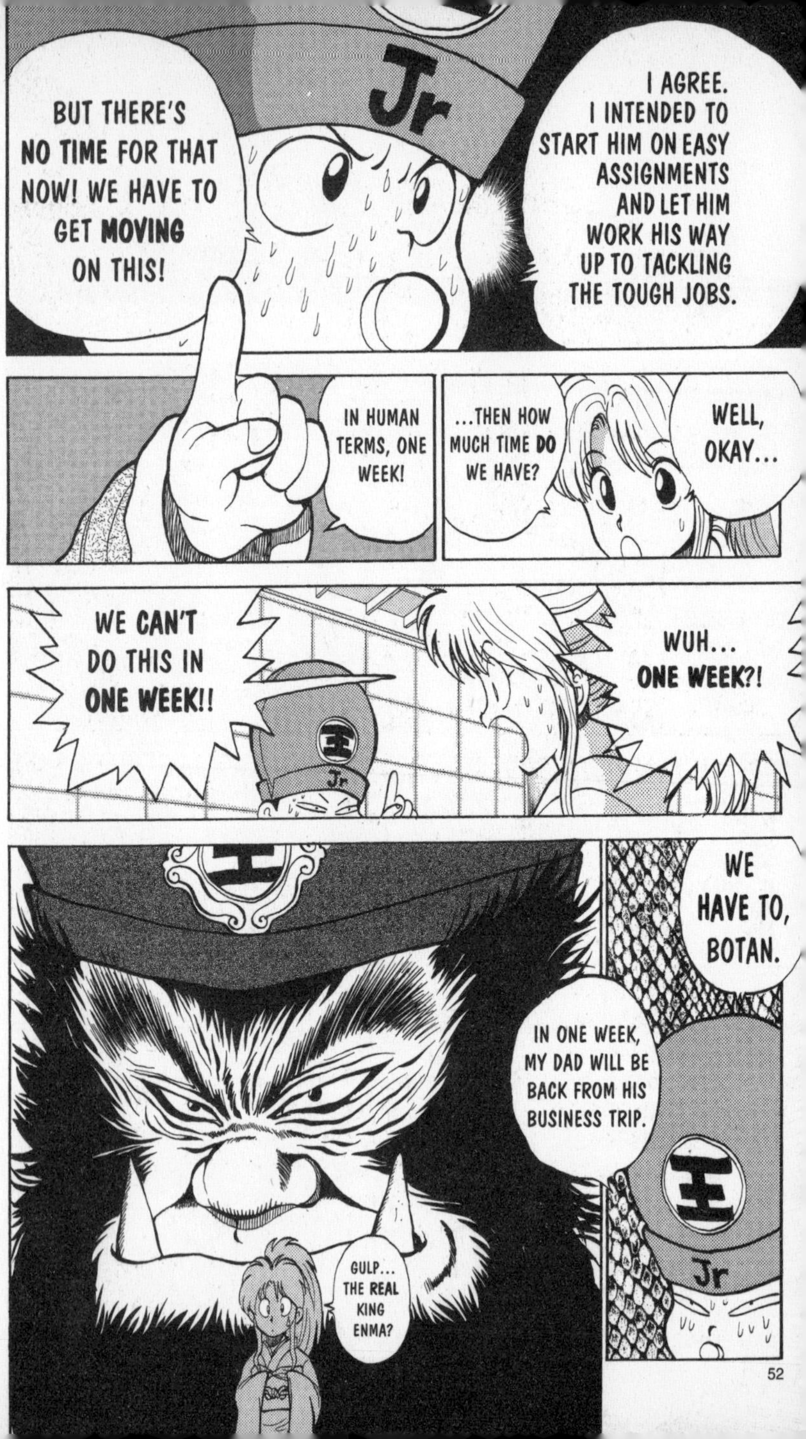
I AGREE. I INTENDED TO START HIM ON EASY ASSIGNMENTS AND LET HIM WORK HIS WAY UP TO TACKLING THE TOUGH JOBS.
BUT THERE'S NO TIME FOR THAT NOW! WE HAVE TO GET **MOVING** ON THIS!
WELL, OKAY...
...THEN HOW MUCH TIME **DO** WE HAVE?
IN HUMAN TERMS, ONE WEEK!
WUH... **ONE WEEK?!**
WE **CAN'T** DO THIS IN **ONE WEEK!!**
WE HAVE TO, BOTAN.
IN ONE WEEK, MY DAD WILL BE BACK FROM HIS BUSINESS TRIP.
GULP... THE **REAL** KING ENMA?

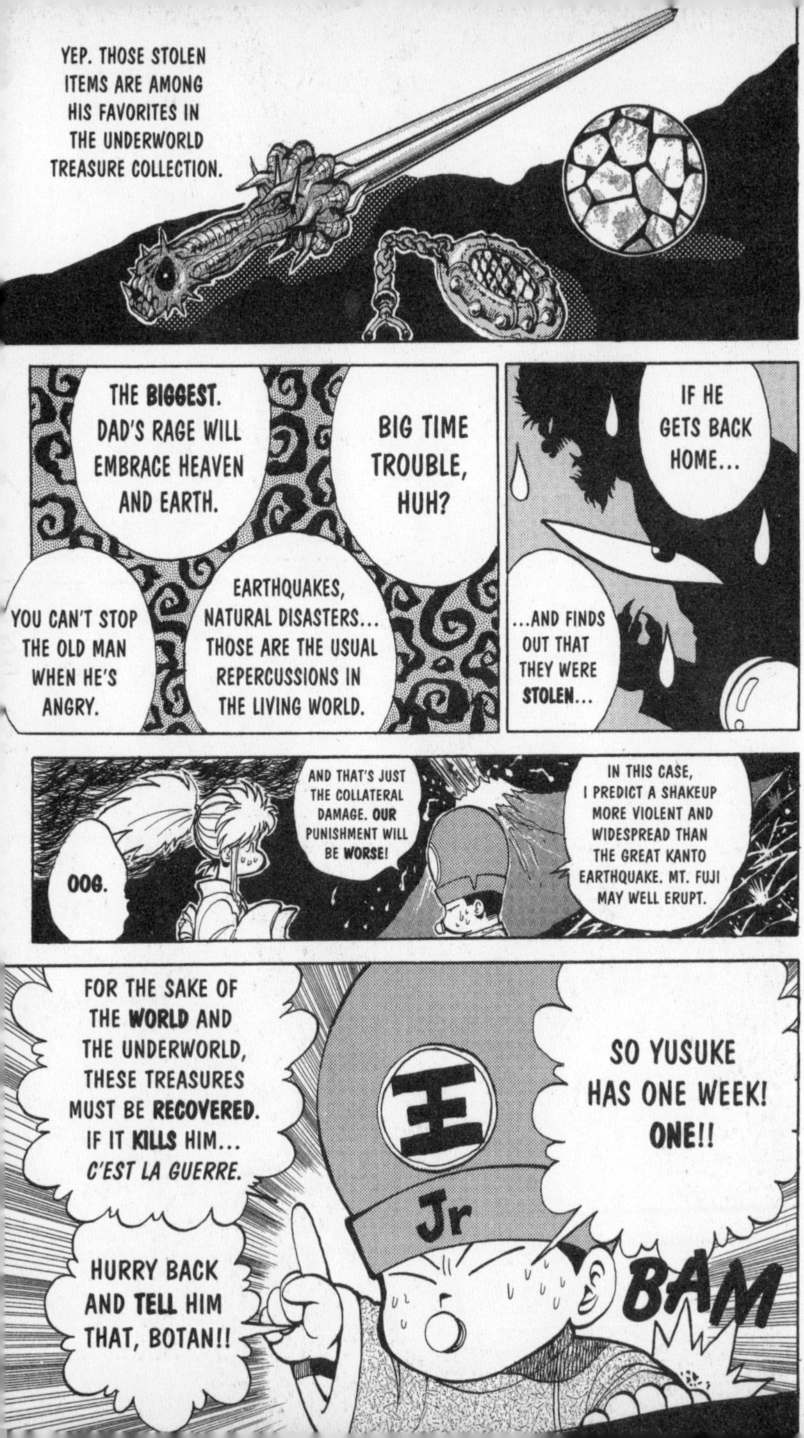
YEP. THOSE STOLEN ITEMS ARE AMONG HIS FAVORITES IN THE UNDERWORLD TREASURE COLLECTION.
IF HE GETS BACK HOME...
...AND FINDS OUT THAT THEY WERE **STOLEN**...
BIG TIME TROUBLE, HUH?
THE **BIGGEST**. DAD'S RAGE WILL EMBRACE HEAVEN AND EARTH.
EARTHQUAKES, NATURAL DISASTERS... THOSE ARE THE USUAL REPERCUSSIONS IN THE LIVING WORLD.
YOU CAN'T STOP THE OLD MAN WHEN HE'S ANGRY.
IN THIS CASE, I PREDICT A SHAKEUP MORE VIOLENT AND WIDESPREAD THAN THE GREAT KANTO EARTHQUAKE. MT. FUJI MAY WELL ERUPT.
AND THAT'S JUST THE COLLATERAL DAMAGE. **OUR** PUNISHMENT WILL BE **WORSE**!
OOG.
SO YUSUKE HAS ONE WEEK! **ONE**!!
BAM
FOR THE SAKE OF THE **WORLD** AND THE UNDERWORLD, THESE TREASURES MUST BE **RECOVERED**. IF IT **KILLS** HIM... *C'EST LA GUERRE.*
HURRY BACK AND **TELL** HIM THAT, BOTAN!!

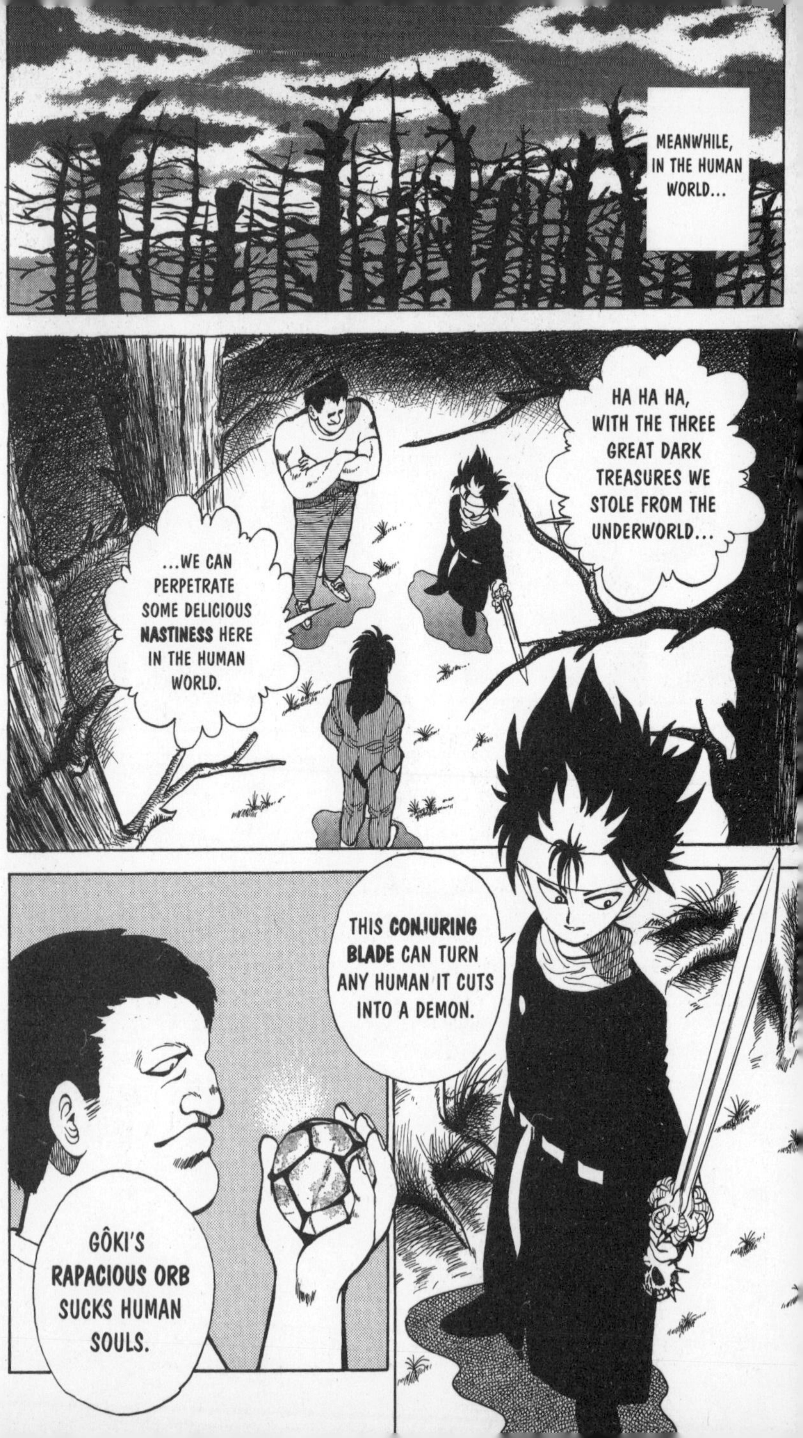
MEANWHILE, IN THE HUMAN WORLD...
HA HA HA, WITH THE THREE GREAT DARK TREASURES WE STOLE FROM THE UNDERWORLD...
...WE CAN PERPETRATE SOME DELICIOUS **NASTINESS** HERE IN THE HUMAN WORLD.
THIS **CONJURING BLADE** CAN TURN ANY HUMAN IT CUTS INTO A DEMON.
GÔKI'S **RAPACIOUS ORB** SUCKS HUMAN SOULS.

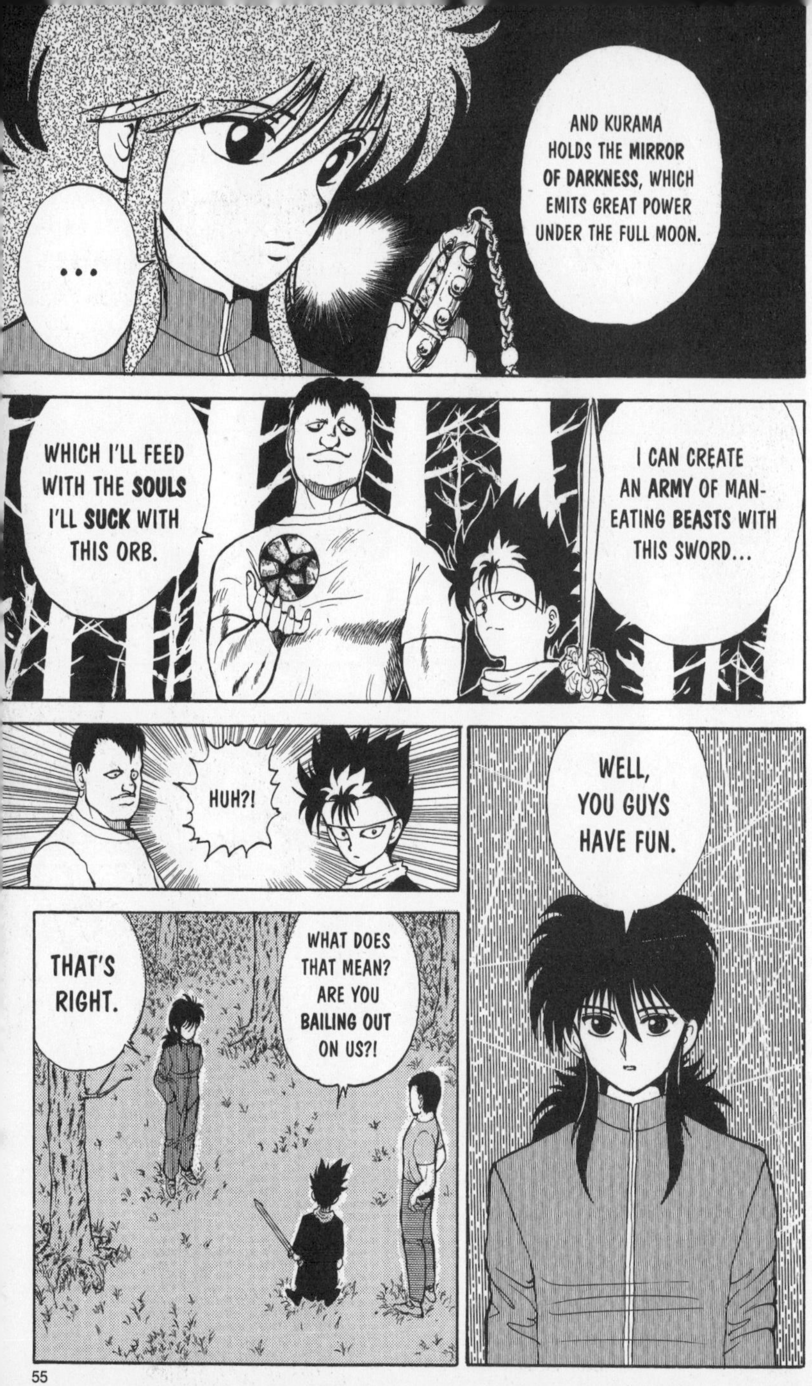
AND KURAMA HOLDS THE MIRROR OF DARKNESS, WHICH EMITS GREAT POWER UNDER THE FULL MOON.
...
I CAN CREATE AN ARMY OF MAN-EATING BEASTS WITH THIS SWORD...
WHICH I'LL FEED WITH THE SOULS I'LL SUCK WITH THIS ORB.
WELL, YOU GUYS HAVE FUN.
HUH?!
WHAT DOES THAT MEAN? ARE YOU BAILING OUT ON US?!
THAT'S RIGHT.

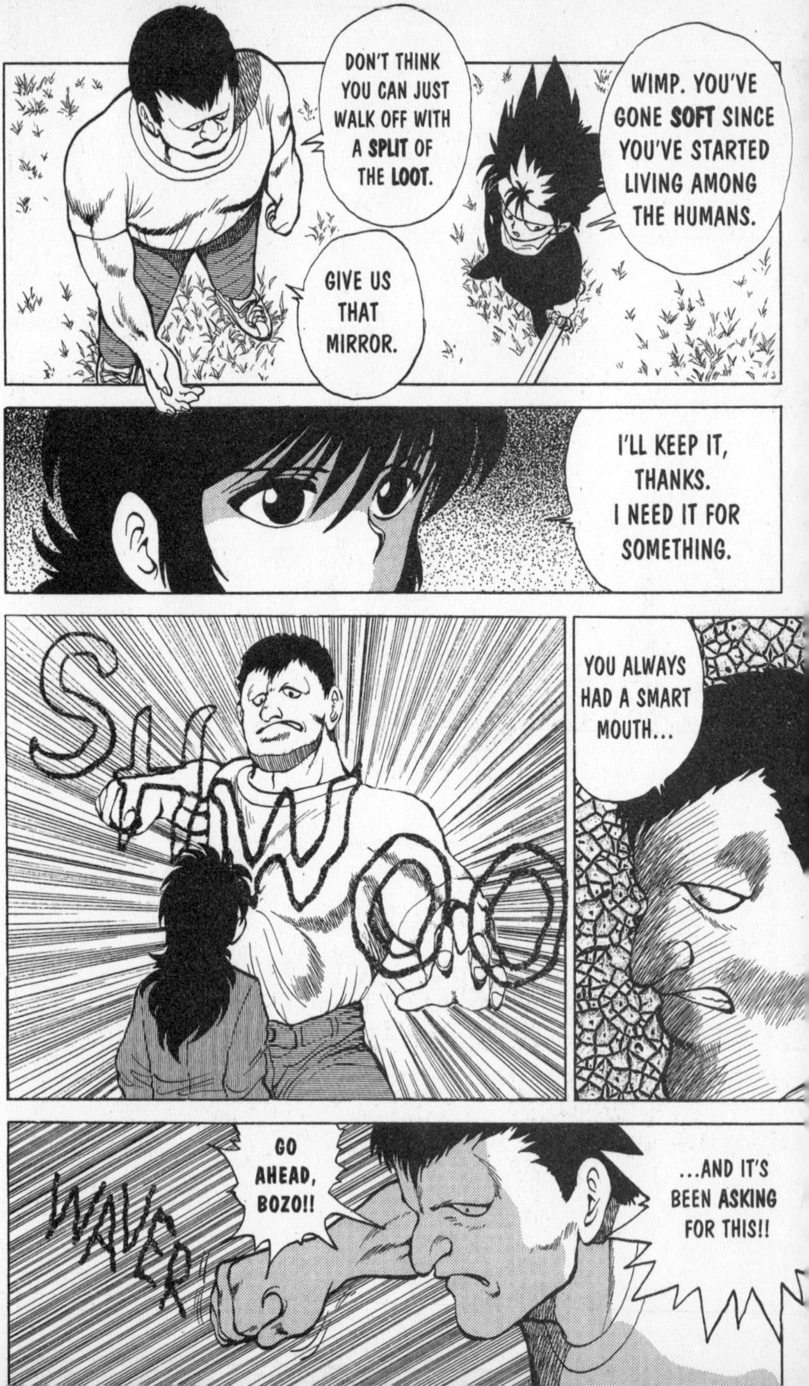
WIMP. YOU'VE GONE SOFT SINCE YOU'VE STARTED LIVING AMONG THE HUMANS.
DON'T THINK YOU CAN JUST WALK OFF WITH A SPLIT OF THE LOOT.
GIVE US THAT MIRROR.
I'LL KEEP IT, THANKS. I NEED IT FOR SOMETHING.
YOU ALWAYS HAD A SMART MOUTH...
...AND IT'S BEEN ASKING FOR THIS!!
GO AHEAD, BOZO!!
WAVER

READ THIS WAY

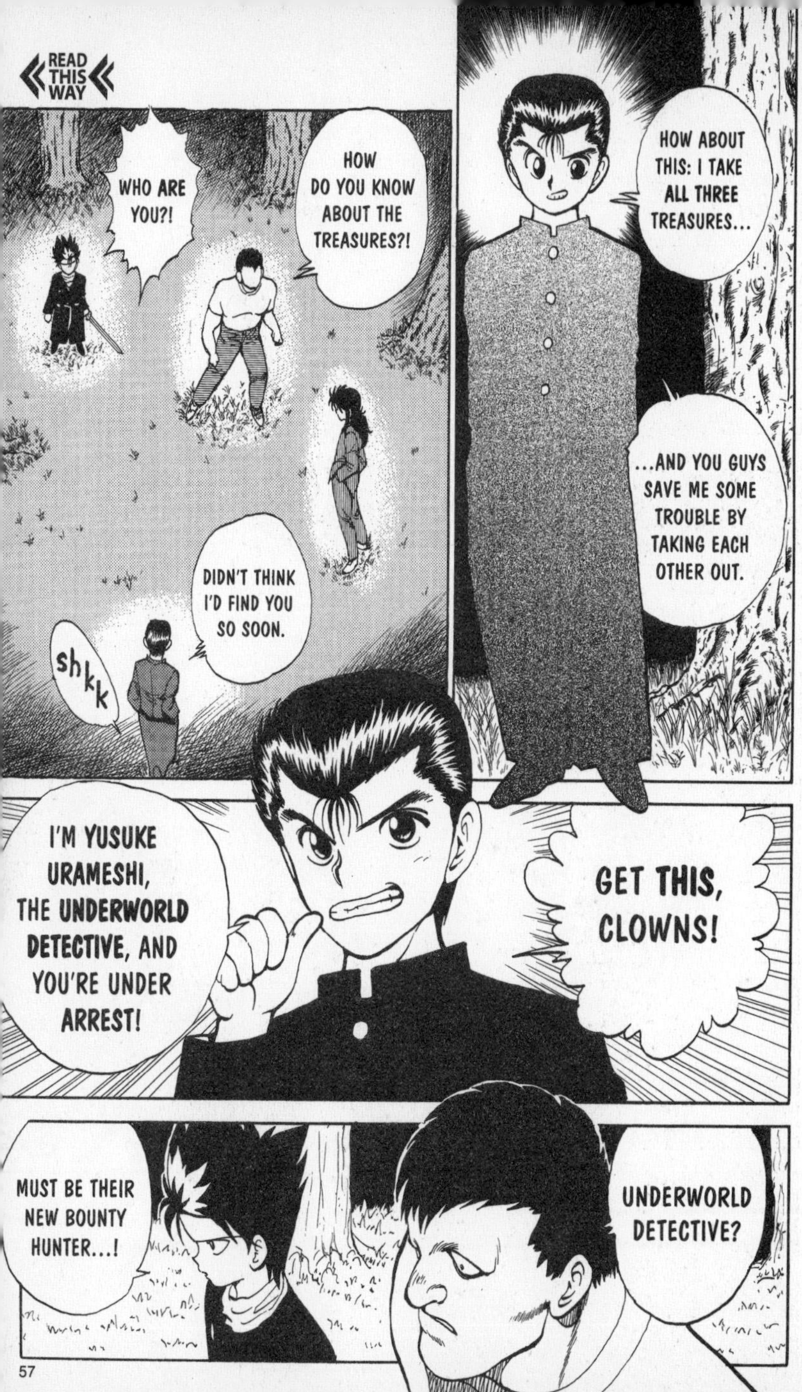

HOW ABOUT THIS: I TAKE ALL THREE TREASURES...
...AND YOU GUYS SAVE ME SOME TROUBLE BY TAKING EACH OTHER OUT.
HOW DO YOU KNOW ABOUT THE TREASURES?!
WHO ARE YOU?!
DIDN'T THINK I'D FIND YOU SO SOON.
shkk
GET THIS, CLOWNS!
I'M YUSUKE URAMESHI, THE UNDERWORLD DETECTIVE, AND YOU'RE UNDER ARREST!
UNDERWORLD DETECTIVE?
MUST BE THEIR NEW BOUNTY HUNTER...!

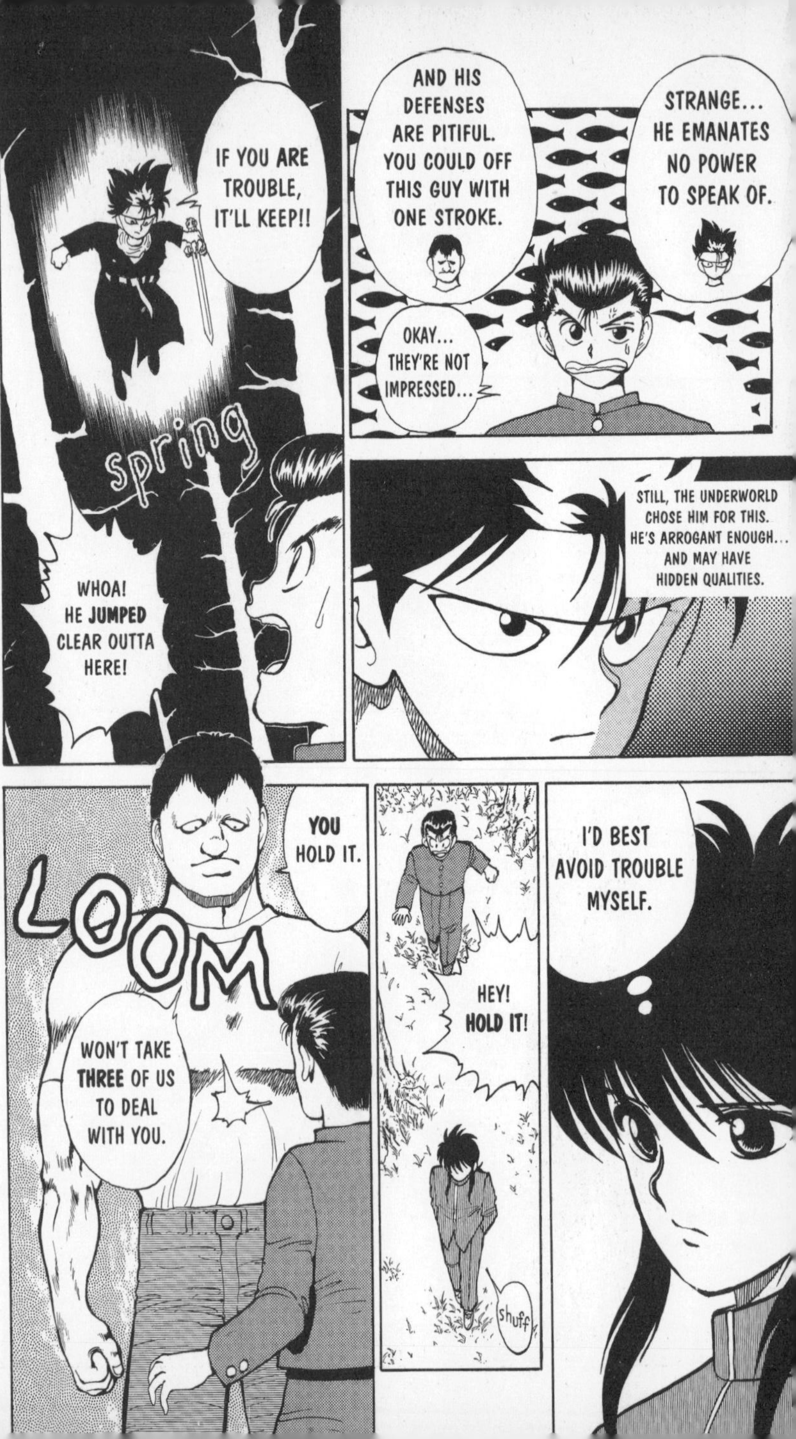
STRANGE... HE EMANATES NO POWER TO SPEAK OF.
AND HIS DEFENSES ARE PITIFUL. YOU COULD OFF THIS GUY WITH ONE STROKE.
OKAY... THEY'RE NOT IMPRESSED...
STILL, THE UNDERWORLD CHOSE HIM FOR THIS. HE'S ARROGANT ENOUGH... AND MAY HAVE HIDDEN QUALITIES.
IF YOU ARE TROUBLE, IT'LL KEEP!!
spring
WHOA! HE JUMPED CLEAR OUTTA HERE!
I'D BEST AVOID TROUBLE MYSELF.
HEY! HOLD IT!
shuff
YOU HOLD IT.
LOOM
WON'T TAKE THREE OF US TO DEAL WITH YOU.

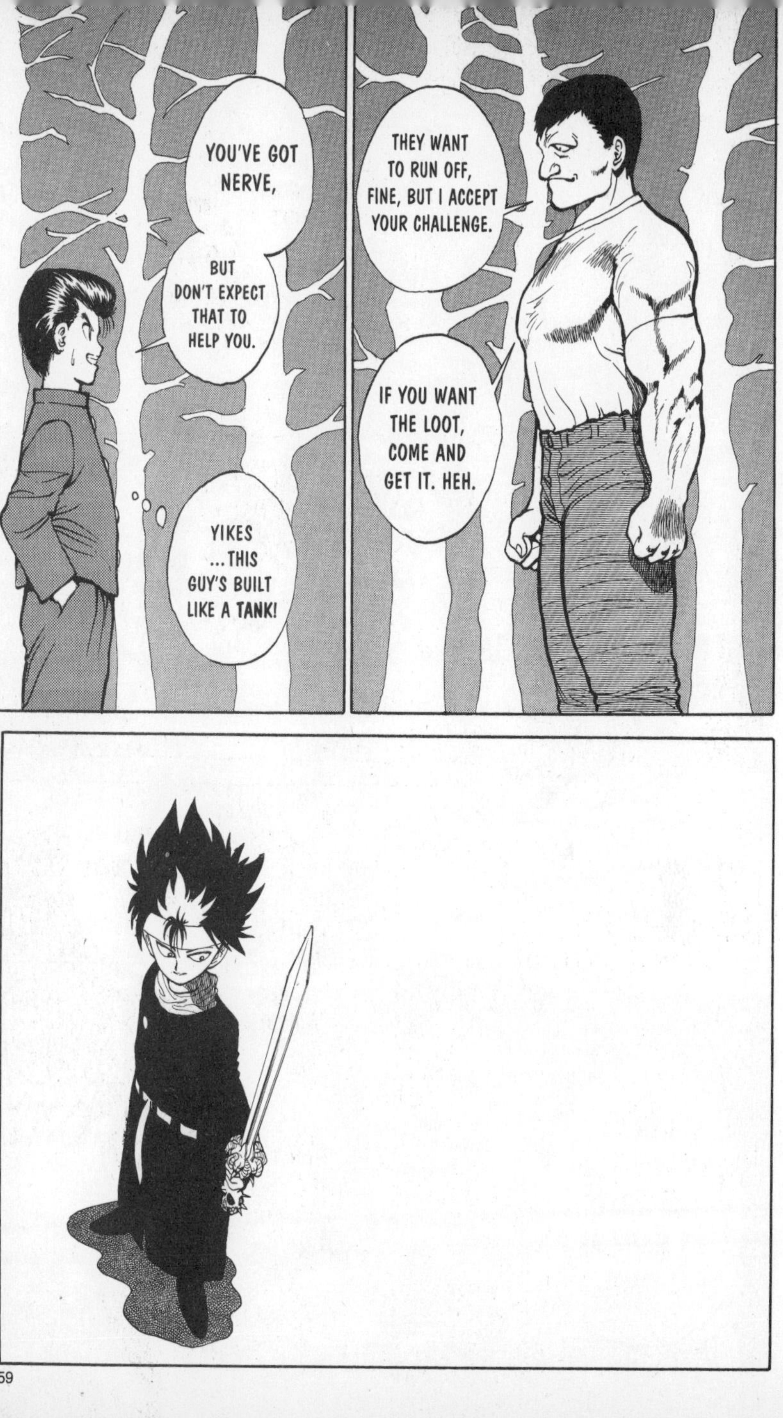
THEY WANT TO RUN OFF, FINE, BUT I ACCEPT YOUR CHALLENGE.
IF YOU WANT THE LOOT, COME AND GET IT. HEH.
YOU'VE GOT NERVE,
BUT DON'T EXPECT THAT TO HELP YOU.
YIKES ...THIS GUY'S BUILT LIKE A TANK!

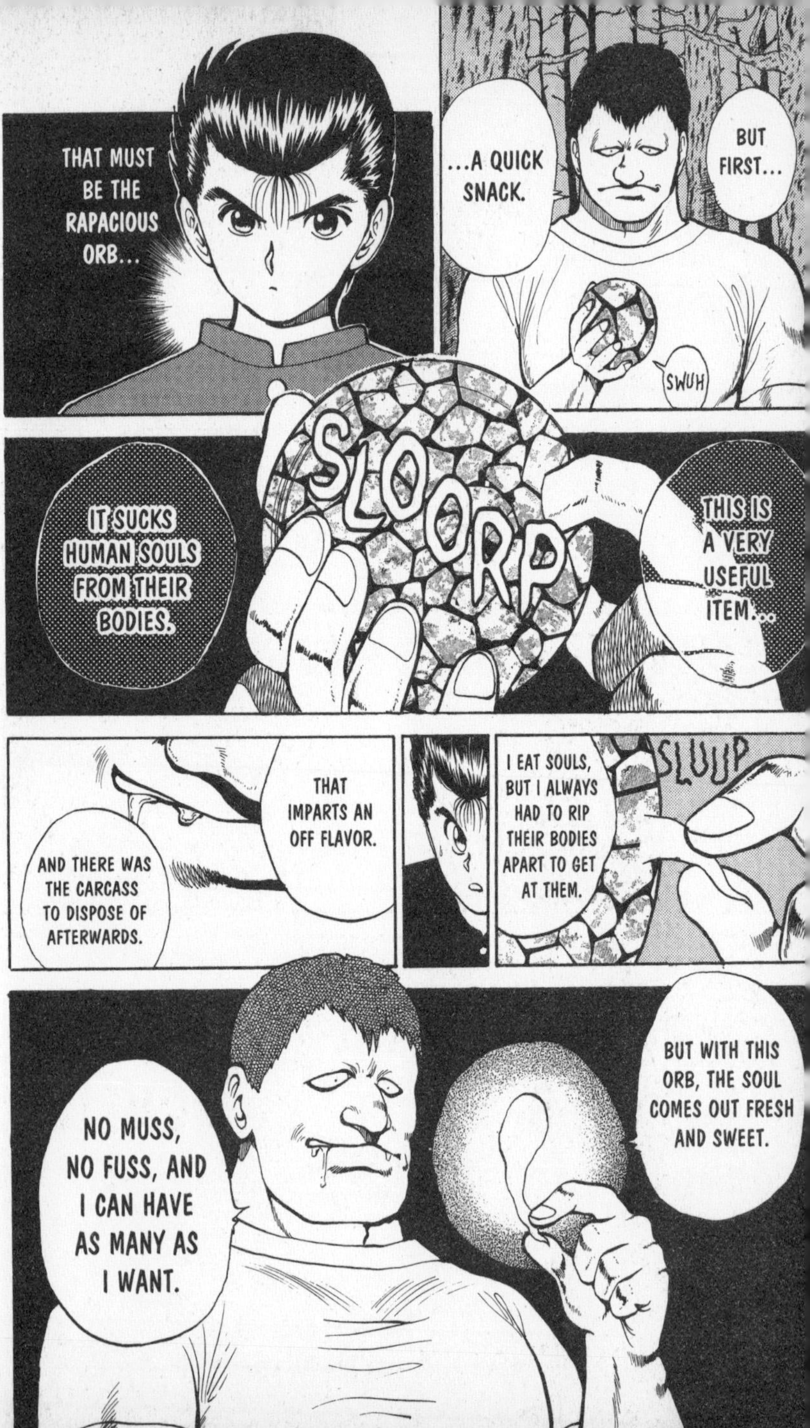
BUT FIRST...
...A QUICK SNACK.
SWUH
THAT MUST BE THE RAPACIOUS ORB...
THIS IS A VERY USEFUL ITEM...
SLOORP
IT SUCKS HUMAN SOULS FROM THEIR BODIES.
SLUUP
I EAT SOULS, BUT I ALWAYS HAD TO RIP THEIR BODIES APART TO GET AT THEM.
THAT IMPARTS AN OFF FLAVOR.
AND THERE WAS THE CARCASS TO DISPOSE OF AFTERWARDS.
BUT WITH THIS ORB, THE SOUL COMES OUT FRESH AND SWEET.
NO MUSS, NO FUSS, AND I CAN HAVE AS MANY AS I WANT.

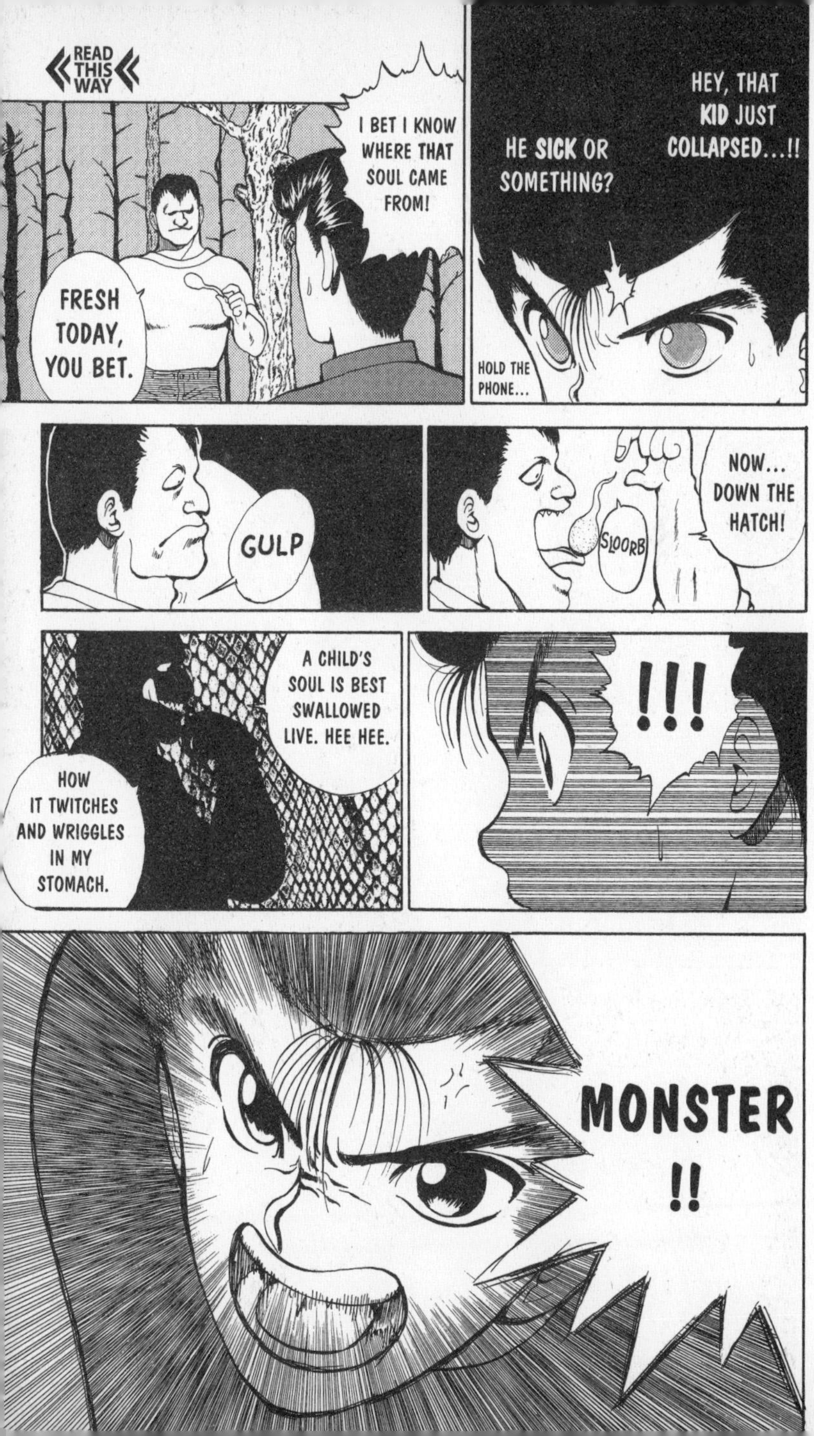
READ THIS WAY
HEY, THAT KID JUST COLLAPSED...!!
HE SICK OR SOMETHING?
HOLD THE PHONE...
I BET I KNOW WHERE THAT SOUL CAME FROM!
FRESH TODAY, YOU BET.
NOW... DOWN THE HATCH!
SLOORB
GULP
!!!
A CHILD'S SOUL IS BEST SWALLOWED LIVE. HEE HEE.
HOW IT TWITCHES AND WRIGGLES IN MY STOMACH.
MONSTER !!

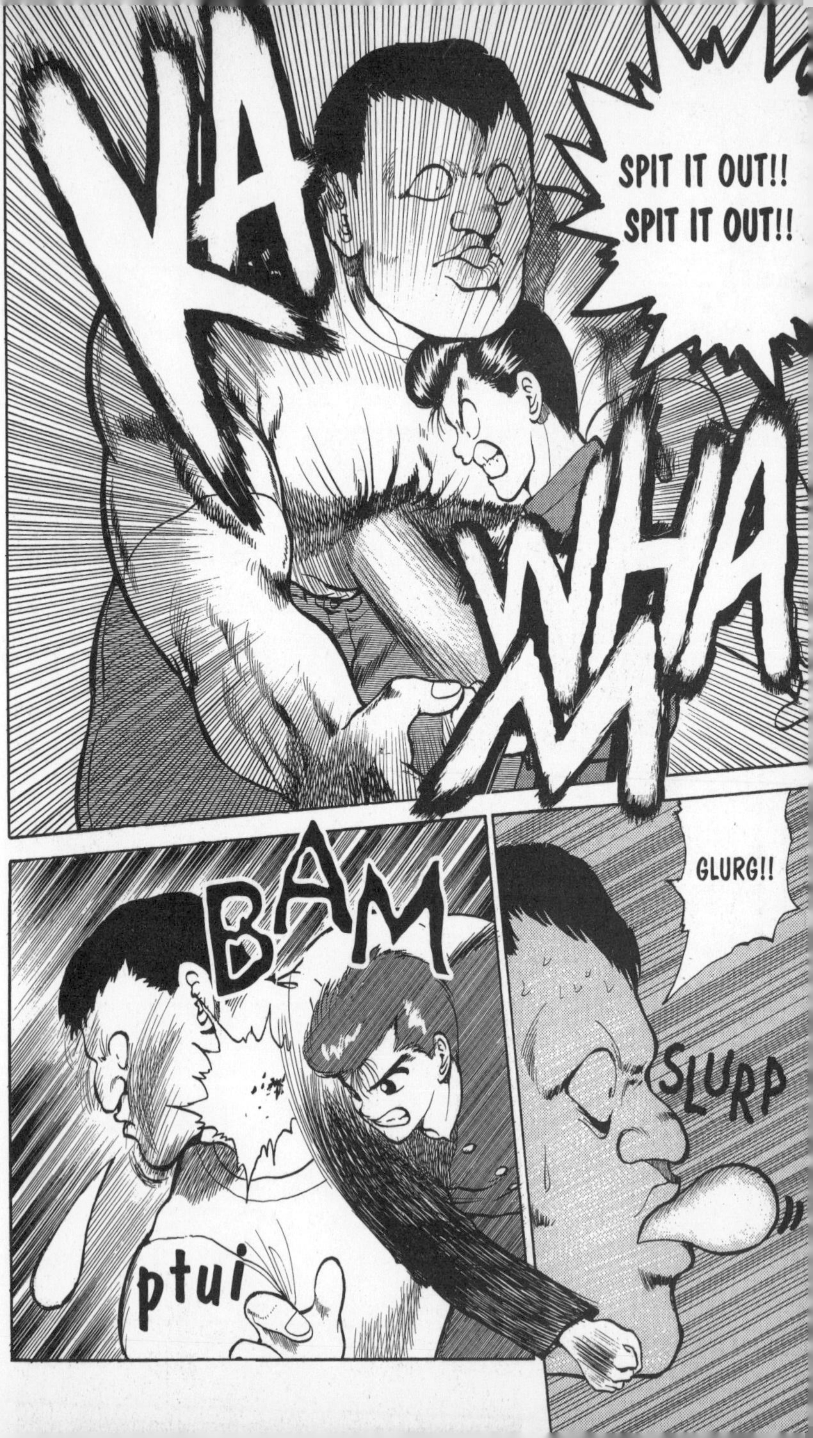
SPIT IT OUT!!
SPIT IT OUT!!
WHAM
GLURG!!
SLURP
BAM
ptui

READ THIS WAY

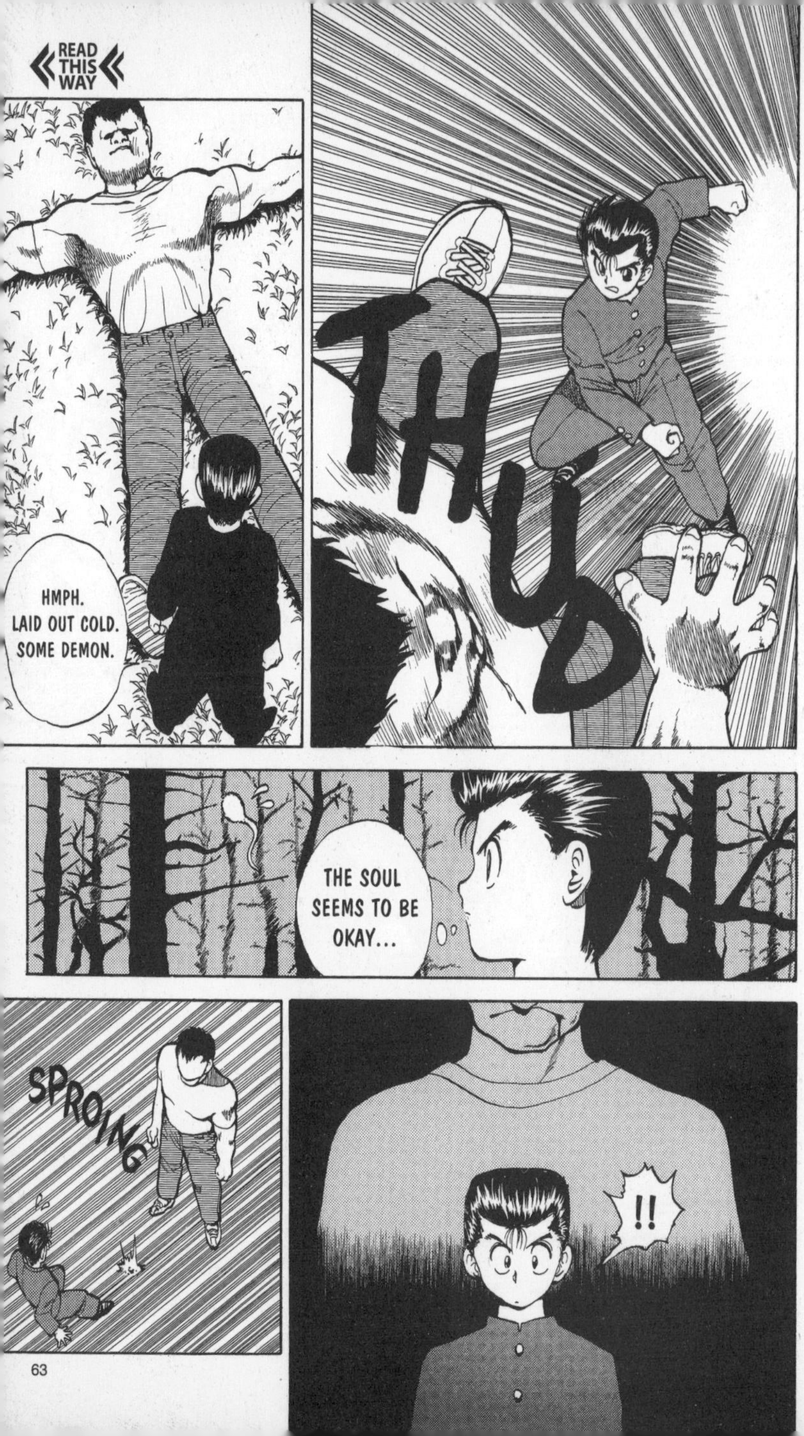
THUD
HMPH. LAID OUT COLD. SOME DEMON.
THE SOUL SEEMS TO BE OKAY...
!!
SPROING

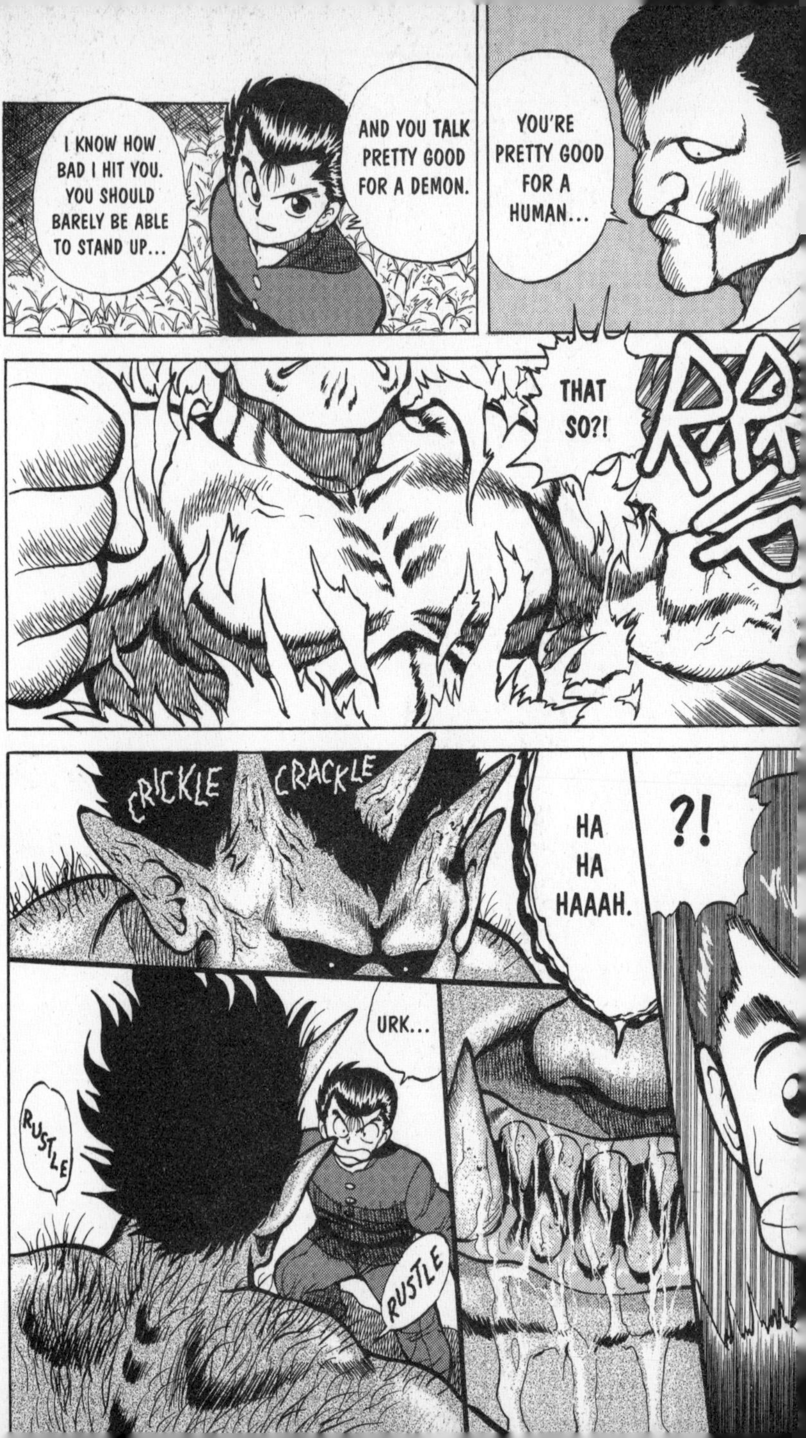
YOU'RE PRETTY GOOD FOR A HUMAN...
AND YOU TALK PRETTY GOOD FOR A DEMON.
I KNOW HOW BAD I HIT YOU. YOU SHOULD BARELY BE ABLE TO STAND UP...
RRRIP
THAT SO?!
?!
HA HA HAAAH.
CRACKLE
CRICKLE
URK...
RUSTLE
RUSTLE

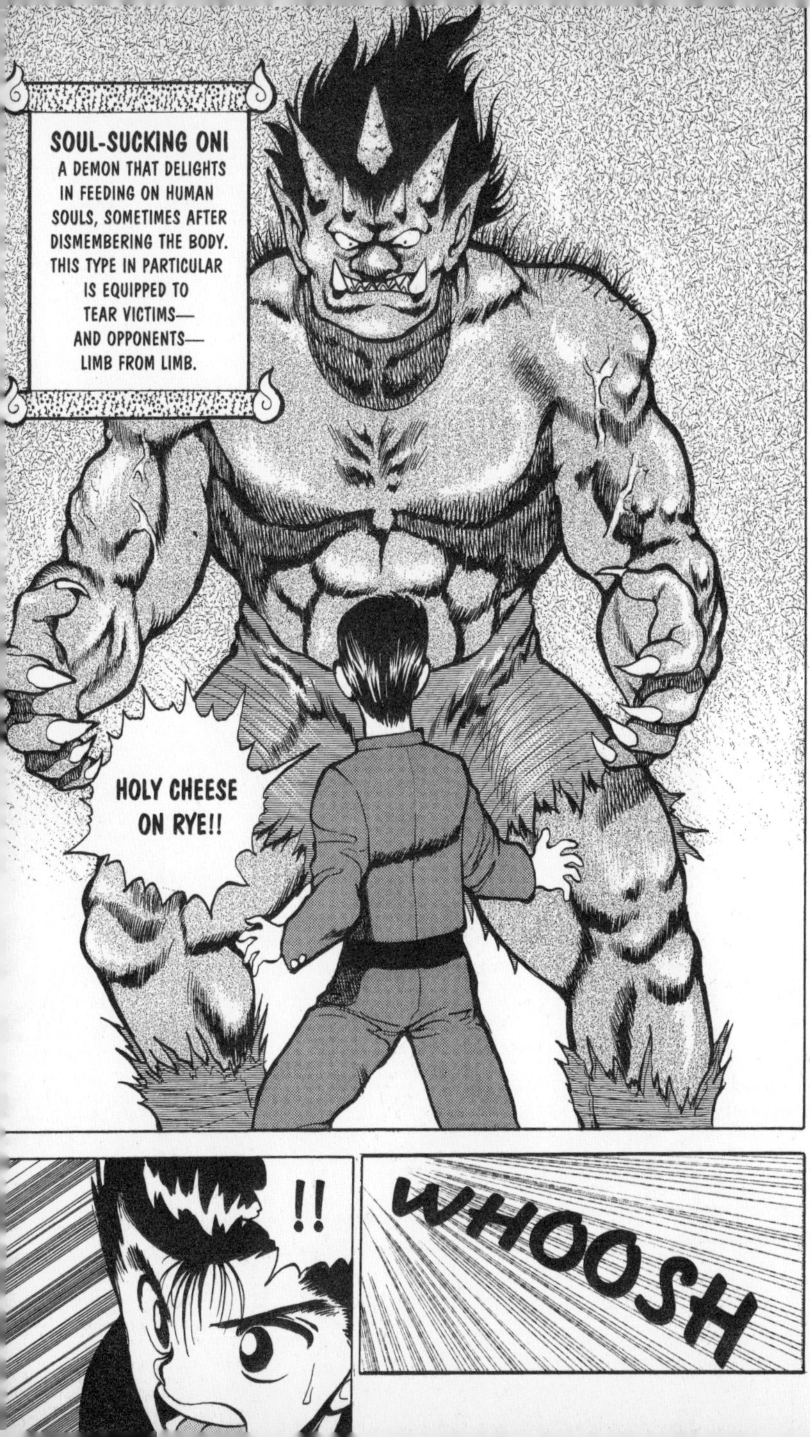
SOUL-SUCKING ONI
A DEMON THAT DELIGHTS IN FEEDING ON HUMAN SOULS, SOMETIMES AFTER DISMEMBERING THE BODY. THIS TYPE IN PARTICULAR IS EQUIPPED TO TEAR VICTIMS— AND OPPONENTS— LIMB FROM LIMB.
HOLY CHEESE ON RYE!!
WHOOSH
!!

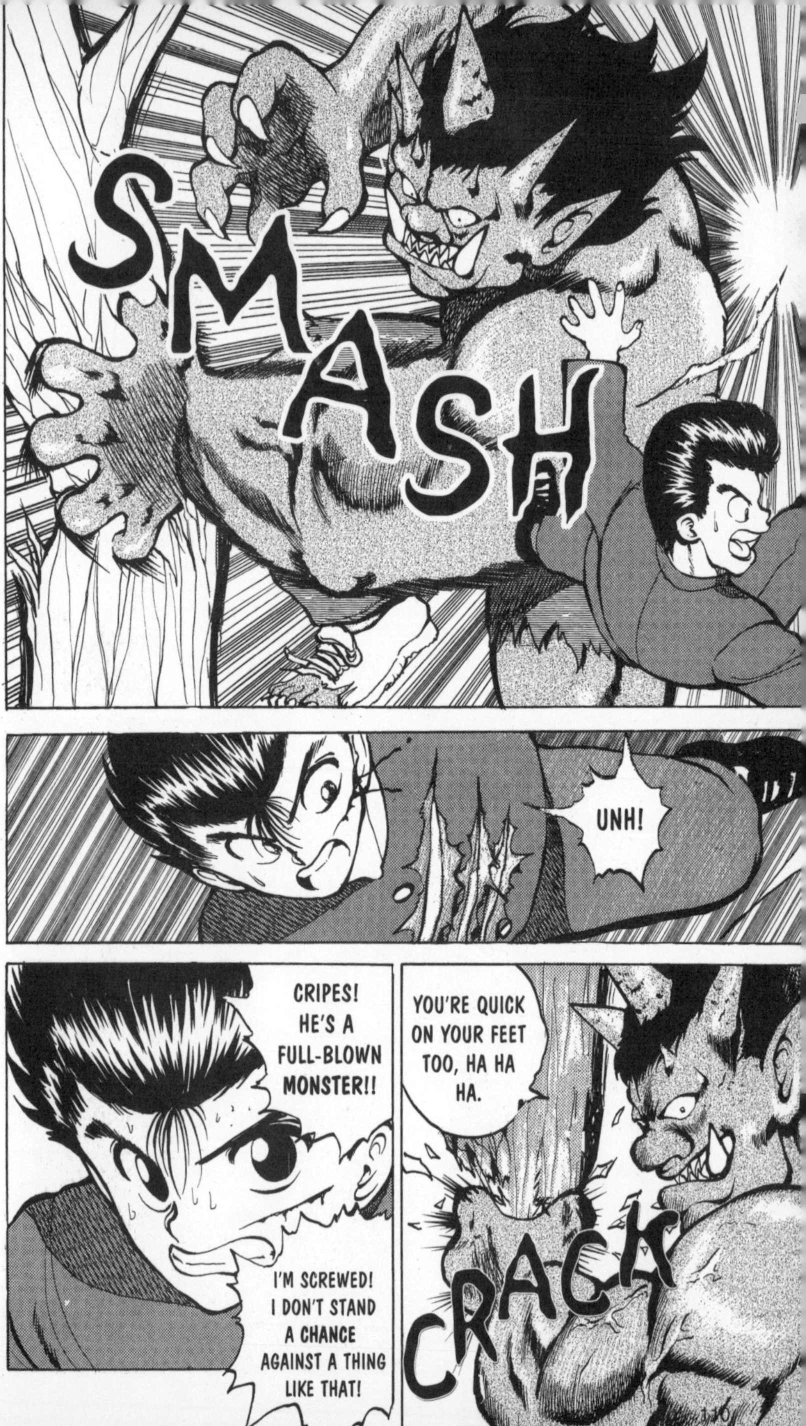
SMASH
UNH!
YOU'RE QUICK ON YOUR FEET TOO, HA HA HA.
CRACK
CRIPES! HE'S A FULL-BLOWN MONSTER!!
I'M SCREWED! I DON'T STAND A CHANCE AGAINST A THING LIKE THAT!

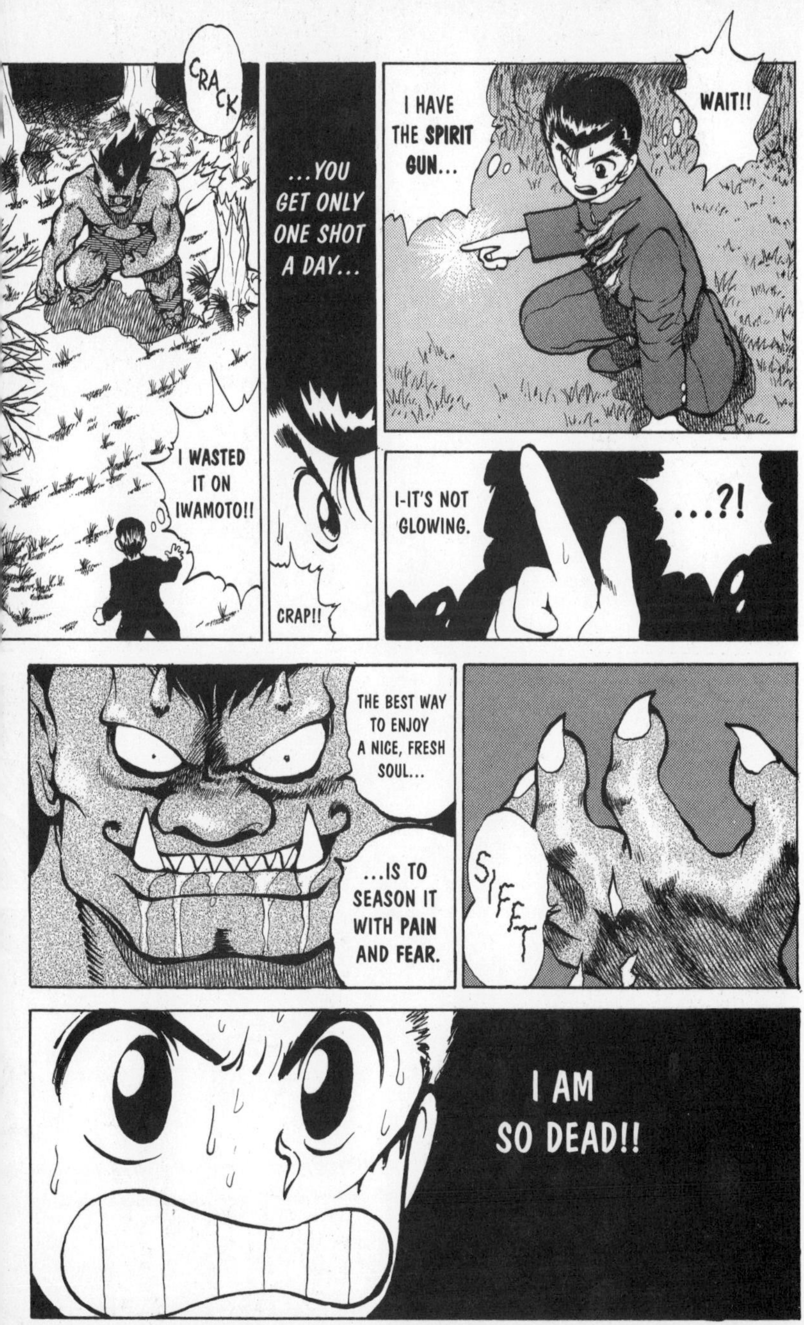
WAIT!!
I HAVE THE SPIRIT GUN...
...?!
I-IT'S NOT GLOWING.
...YOU GET ONLY ONE SHOT A DAY...
CRAP!!
CRACK
I WASTED IT ON IWAMOTO!!
SIFFT
THE BEST WAY TO ENJOY A NICE, FRESH SOUL...
...IS TO SEASON IT WITH PAIN AND FEAR.
I AM SO DEAD!!

CHAPTER 20: THE MUNCHER OF SOULS!!

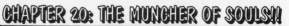

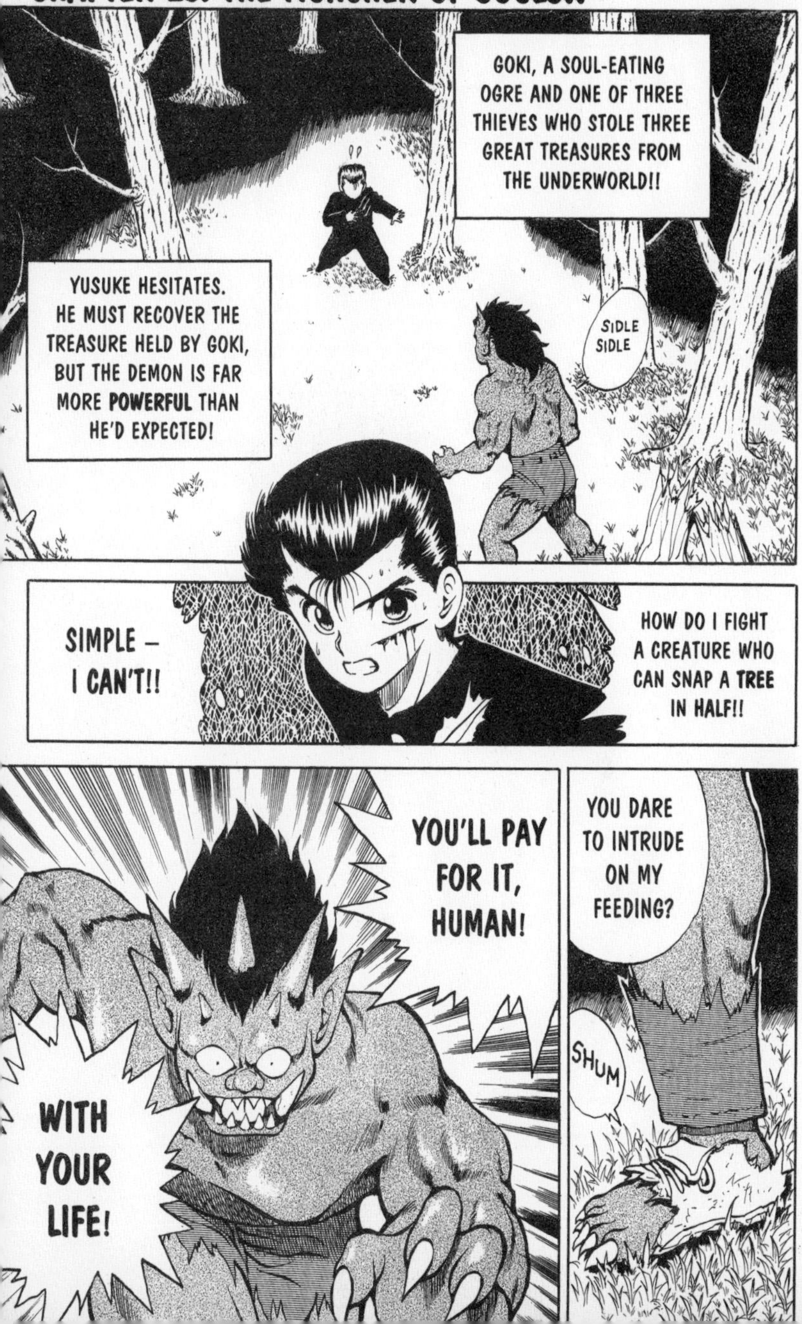
GOKI, A SOUL-EATING OGRE AND ONE OF THREE THIEVES WHO STOLE THREE GREAT TREASURES FROM THE UNDERWORLD!!
SIDLE SIDLE
YUSUKE HESITATES. HE MUST RECOVER THE TREASURE HELD BY GOKI, BUT THE DEMON IS FAR MORE **POWERFUL** THAN HE'D EXPECTED!
HOW DO I FIGHT A CREATURE WHO CAN SNAP A **TREE** IN **HALF**!!
SIMPLE – I **CAN'T**!!
YOU DARE TO INTRUDE ON MY FEEDING?
SHUM
YOU'LL PAY FOR IT, HUMAN!
WITH YOUR LIFE!

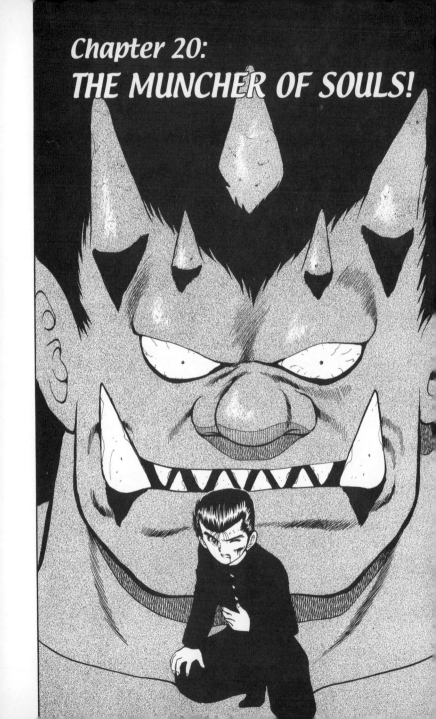

Chapter 20:
THE MUNCHER OF SOULS!

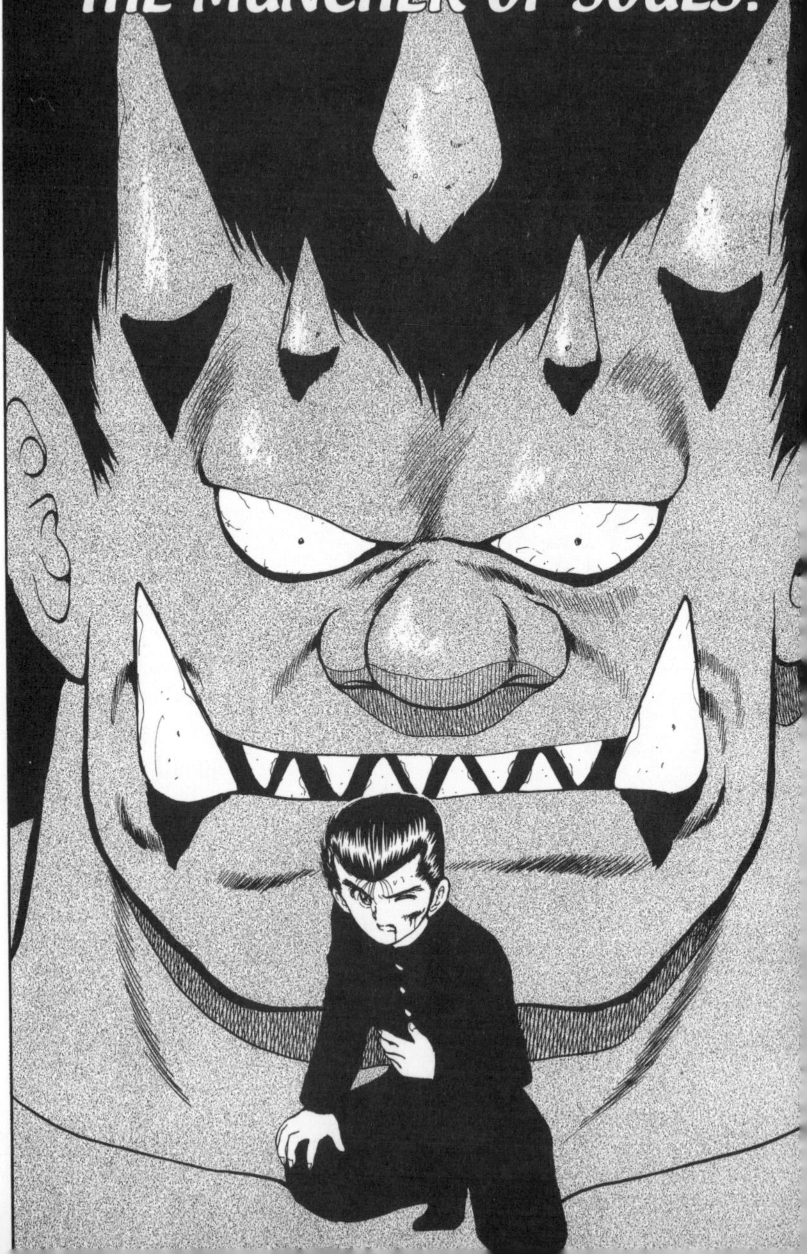

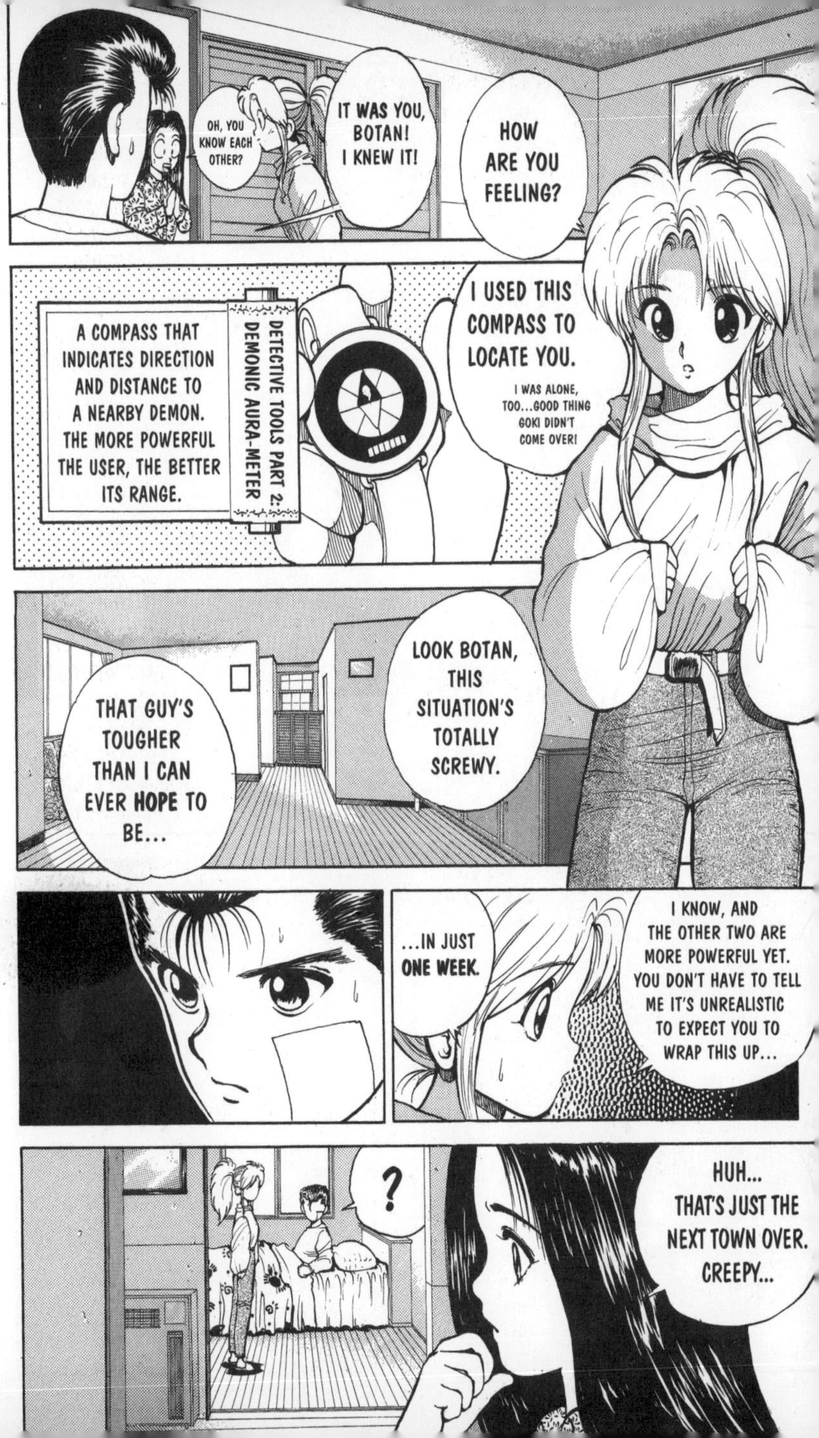
HOW ARE YOU FEELING?
IT WAS YOU, BOTAN! I KNEW IT!
OH, YOU KNOW EACH OTHER?
I USED THIS COMPASS TO LOCATE YOU.
I WAS ALONE, TOO...GOOD THING GOKI DIDN'T COME OVER!
DETECTIVE TOOLS PART 2: DEMONIC AURA-METER
A COMPASS THAT INDICATES DIRECTION AND DISTANCE TO A NEARBY DEMON. THE MORE POWERFUL THE USER, THE BETTER ITS RANGE.
LOOK BOTAN, THIS SITUATION'S TOTALLY SCREWY.
THAT GUY'S TOUGHER THAN I CAN EVER HOPE TO BE...
I KNOW, AND THE OTHER TWO ARE MORE POWERFUL YET. YOU DON'T HAVE TO TELL ME IT'S UNREALISTIC TO EXPECT YOU TO WRAP THIS UP...
...IN JUST ONE WEEK.
HUH... THAT'S JUST THE NEXT TOWN OVER. CREEPY...
?

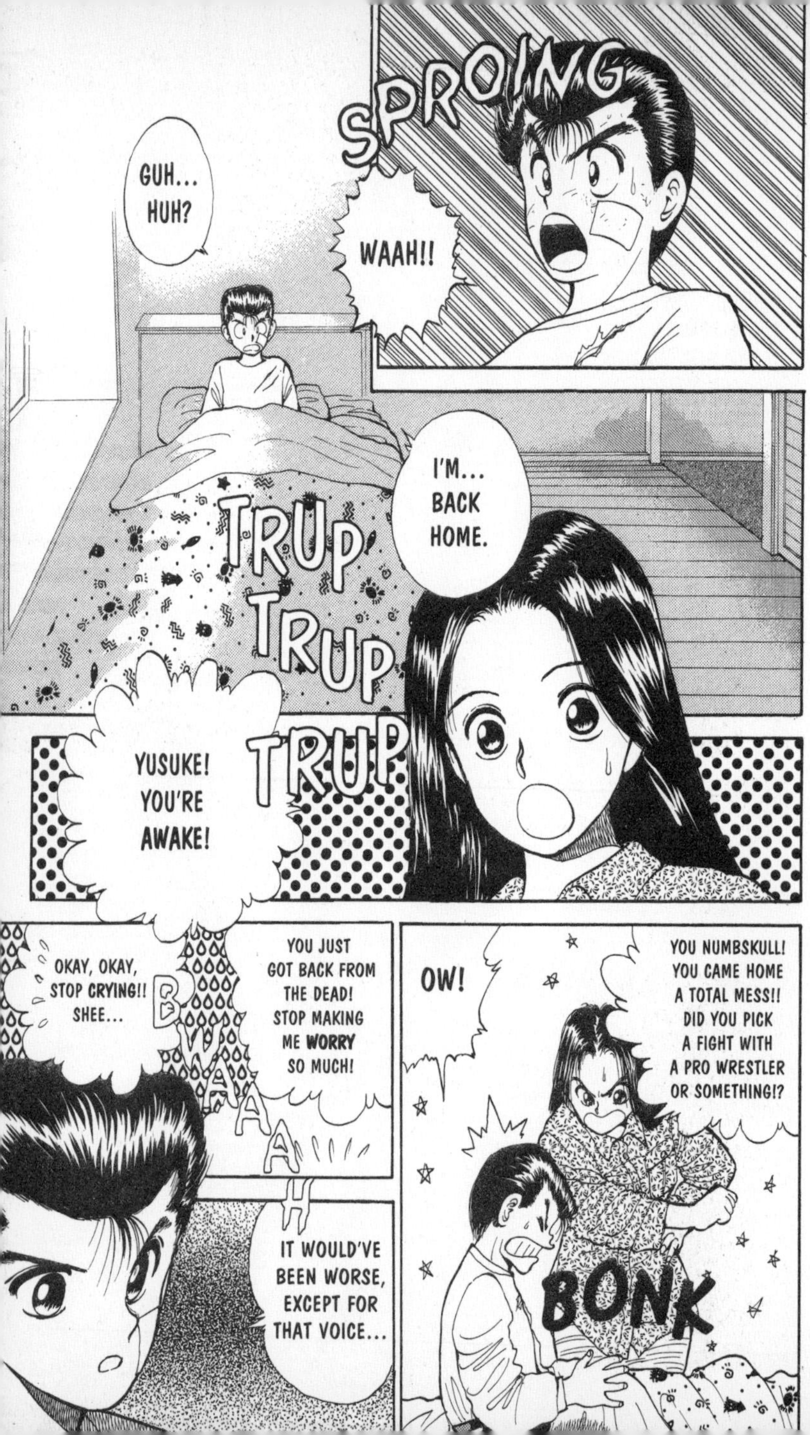
SPROING
WAAH!!
GUH... HUH?
I'M... BACK HOME.
TRUP TRUP TRUP
YUSUKE! YOU'RE AWAKE!
YOU NUMBSKULL!! YOU CAME HOME A TOTAL MESS!! DID YOU PICK A FIGHT WITH A PRO WRESTLER OR SOMETHING!?
OW!
BONK
YOU JUST GOT BACK FROM THE DEAD! STOP MAKING ME WORRY SO MUCH!
OKAY, OKAY, STOP CRYING!! SHEE...
BWAAAAH
IT WOULD'VE BEEN WORSE, EXCEPT FOR THAT VOICE...

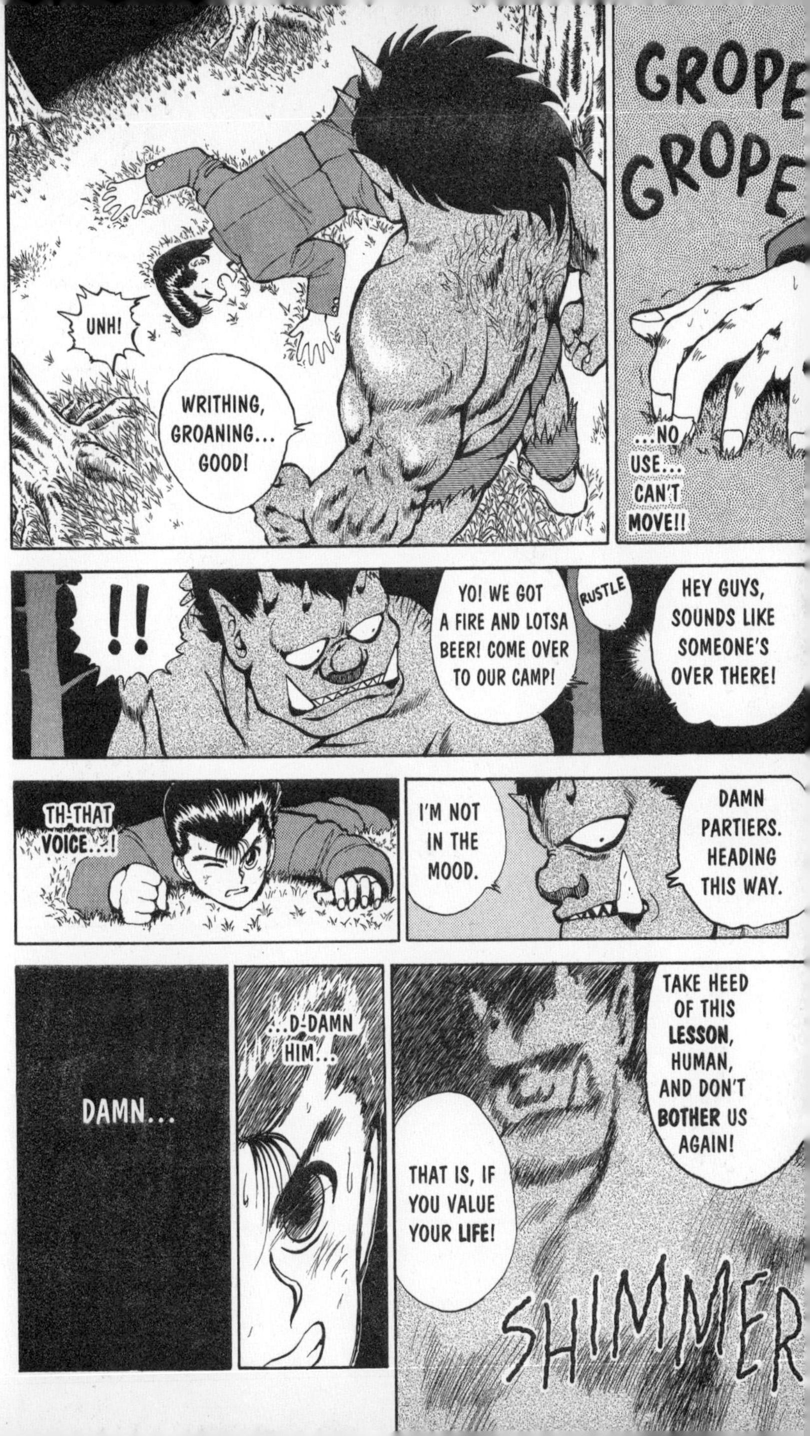
GROPE GROPE
...NO USE... CAN'T MOVE!!
UNH!
WRITHING, GROANING... GOOD!
HEY GUYS, SOUNDS LIKE SOMEONE'S OVER THERE!
RUSTLE
YO! WE GOT A FIRE AND LOTSA BEER! COME OVER TO OUR CAMP!
!!
DAMN PARTIERS. HEADING THIS WAY.
I'M NOT IN THE MOOD.
TH-THAT VOICE...!
TAKE HEED OF THIS LESSON, HUMAN, AND DON'T BOTHER US AGAIN!
THAT IS, IF YOU VALUE YOUR LIFE!
SHIMMER
...D-DAMN HIM...
DAMN...

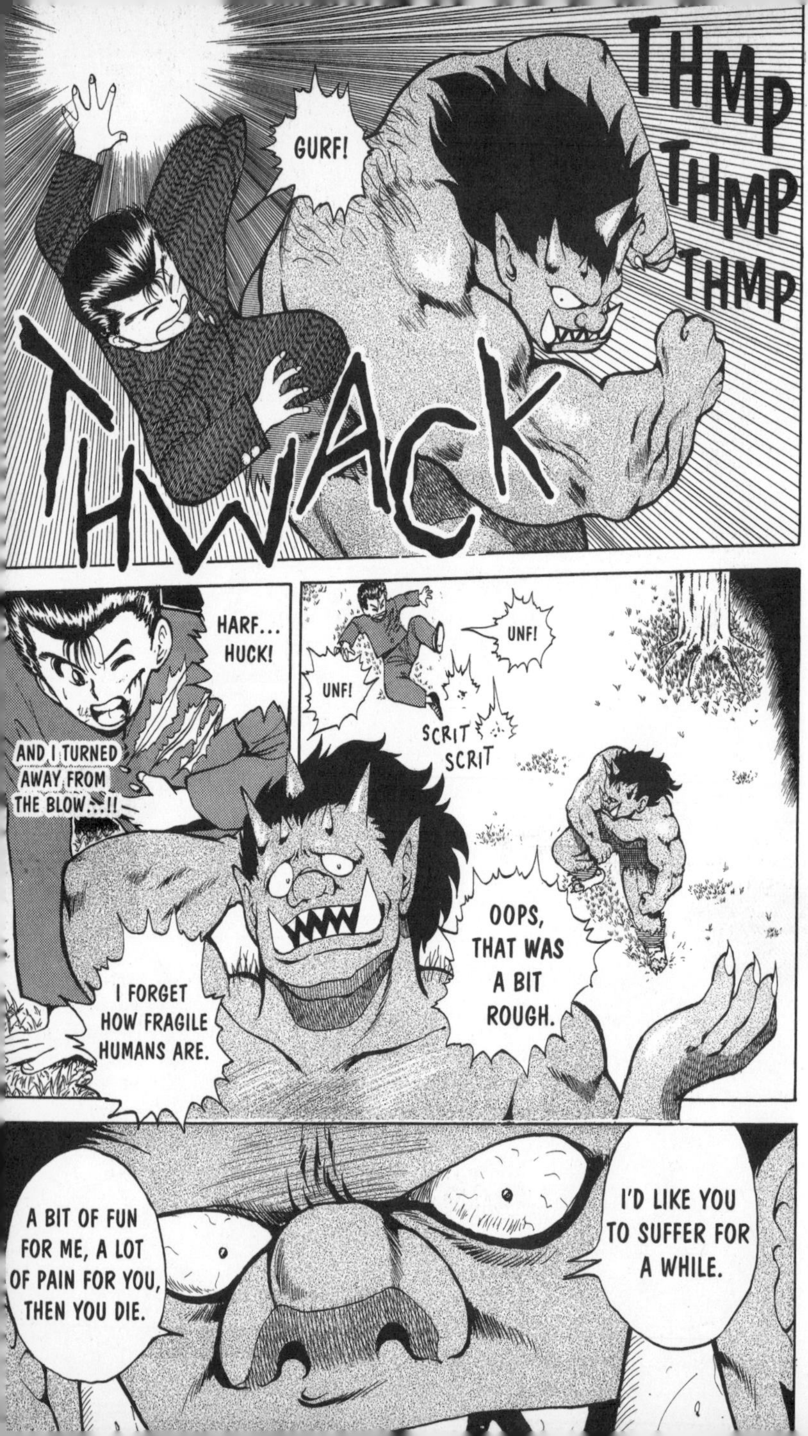
THMP THMP THMP
GURF!
THWACK
UNF!
UNF!
SCRIT SCRIT
HARF... HUCK!
AND I TURNED AWAY FROM THE BLOW...!!
OOPS, THAT WAS A BIT ROUGH.
I FORGET HOW FRAGILE HUMANS ARE.
I'D LIKE YOU TO SUFFER FOR A WHILE.
A BIT OF FUN FOR ME, A LOT OF PAIN FOR YOU, THEN YOU DIE.

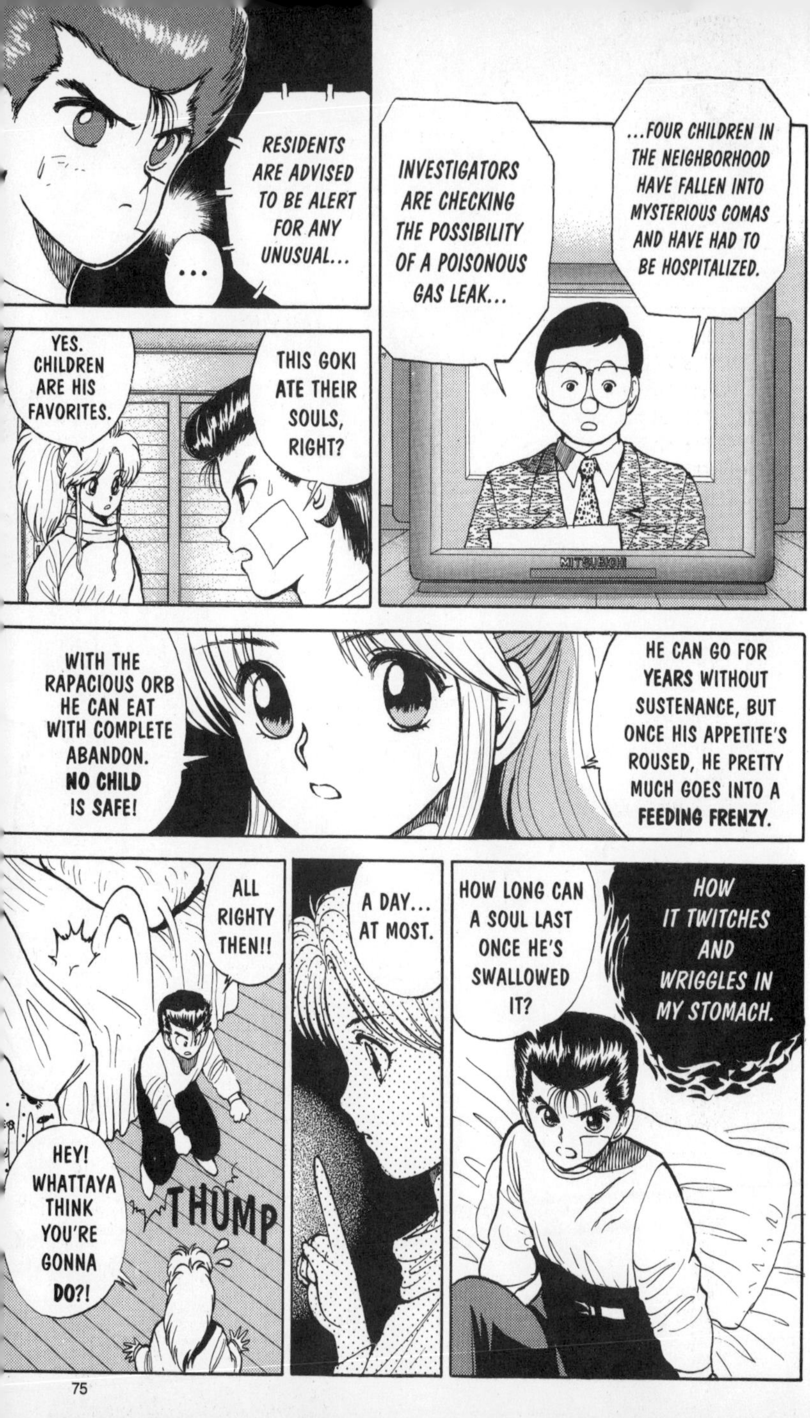
...FOUR CHILDREN IN THE NEIGHBORHOOD HAVE FALLEN INTO MYSTERIOUS COMAS AND HAVE HAD TO BE HOSPITALIZED.
INVESTIGATORS ARE CHECKING THE POSSIBILITY OF A POISONOUS GAS LEAK...
RESIDENTS ARE ADVISED TO BE ALERT FOR ANY UNUSUAL...
...
THIS GOKI ATE THEIR SOULS, RIGHT?
YES. CHILDREN ARE HIS FAVORITES.
HE CAN GO FOR YEARS WITHOUT SUSTENANCE, BUT ONCE HIS APPETITE'S ROUSED, HE PRETTY MUCH GOES INTO A FEEDING FRENZY.
WITH THE RAPACIOUS ORB HE CAN EAT WITH COMPLETE ABANDON. NO CHILD IS SAFE!
HOW IT TWITCHES AND WRIGGLES IN MY STOMACH.
HOW LONG CAN A SOUL LAST ONCE HE'S SWALLOWED IT?
A DAY... AT MOST.
ALL RIGHTY THEN!!
THUMP
HEY! WHATTAYA THINK YOU'RE GONNA DO?!

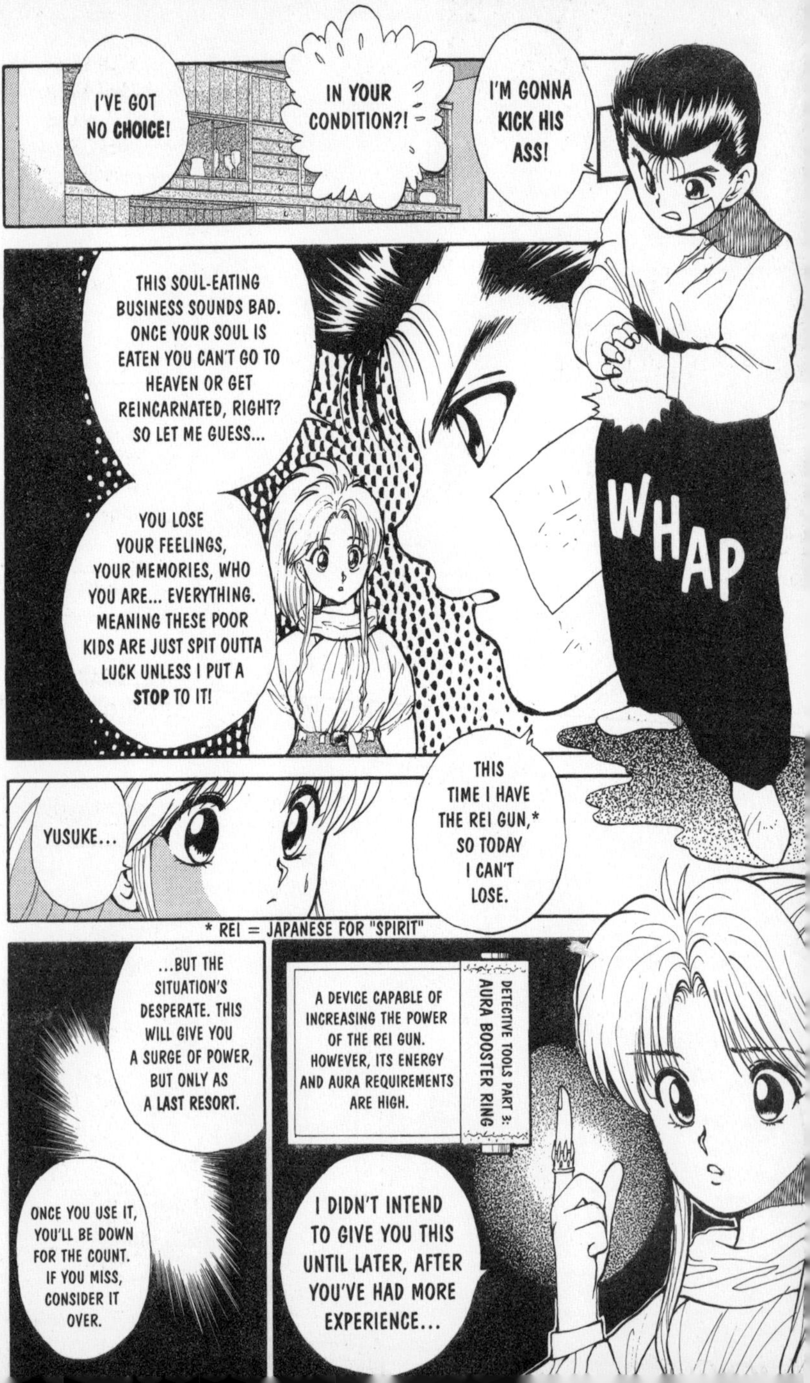
I'M GONNA KICK HIS ASS!
IN YOUR CONDITION?!
I'VE GOT NO CHOICE!
WHAP
THIS SOUL-EATING BUSINESS SOUNDS BAD. ONCE YOUR SOUL IS EATEN YOU CAN'T GO TO HEAVEN OR GET REINCARNATED, RIGHT? SO LET ME GUESS...
YOU LOSE YOUR FEELINGS, YOUR MEMORIES, WHO YOU ARE... EVERYTHING. MEANING THESE POOR KIDS ARE JUST SPIT OUTTA LUCK UNLESS I PUT A STOP TO IT!
THIS TIME I HAVE THE REI GUN,* SO TODAY I CAN'T LOSE.
YUSUKE...
* REI = JAPANESE FOR "SPIRIT"
DETECTIVE TOOLS PART 3: AURA BOOSTER RING
A DEVICE CAPABLE OF INCREASING THE POWER OF THE REI GUN. HOWEVER, ITS ENERGY AND AURA REQUIREMENTS ARE HIGH.
I DIDN'T INTEND TO GIVE YOU THIS UNTIL LATER, AFTER YOU'VE HAD MORE EXPERIENCE...
...BUT THE SITUATION'S DESPERATE. THIS WILL GIVE YOU A SURGE OF POWER, BUT ONLY AS A LAST RESORT.
ONCE YOU USE IT, YOU'LL BE DOWN FOR THE COUNT. IF YOU MISS, CONSIDER IT OVER.

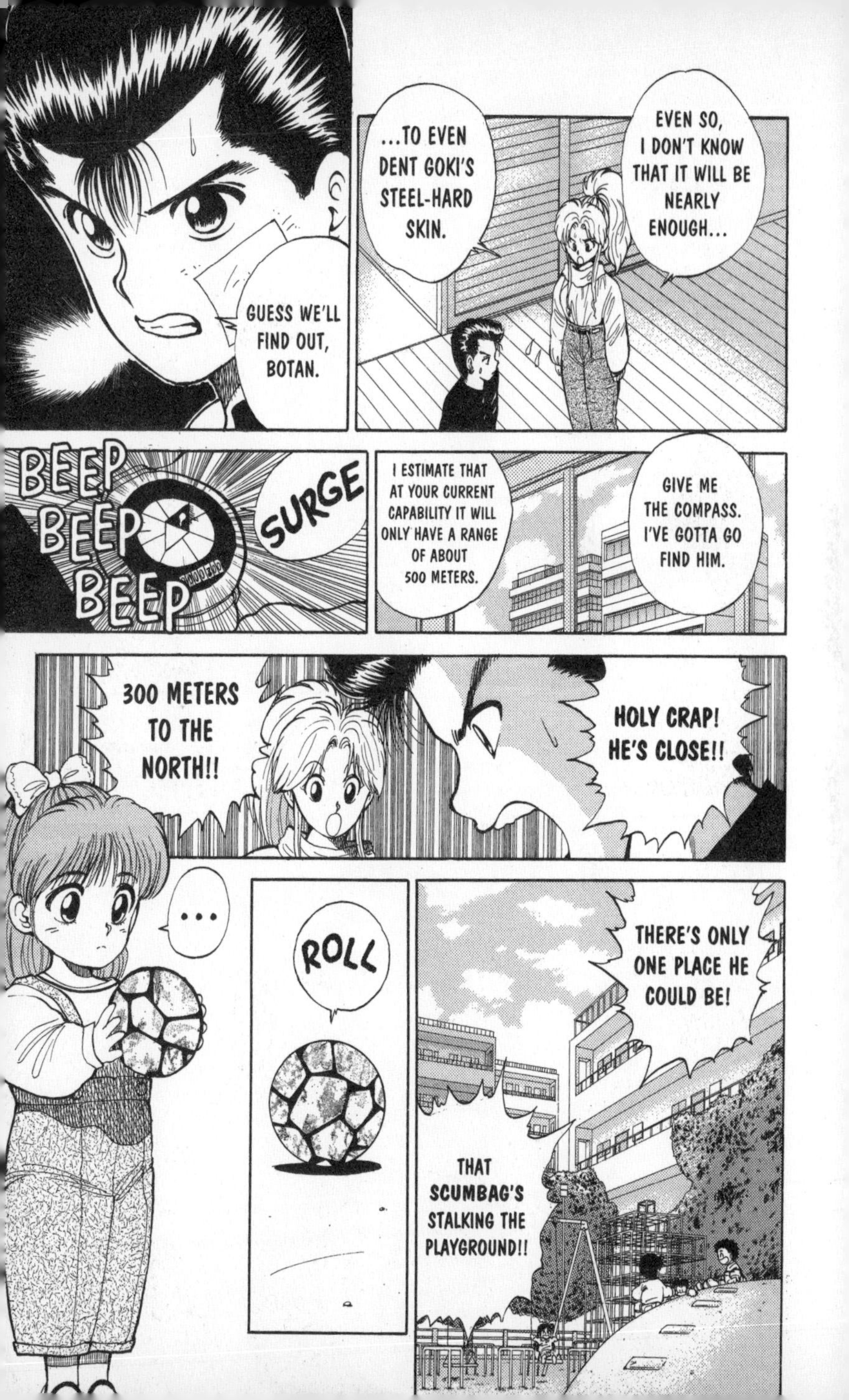
EVEN SO, I DON'T KNOW THAT IT WILL BE NEARLY ENOUGH...
...TO EVEN DENT GOKI'S STEEL-HARD SKIN.
GUESS WE'LL FIND OUT, BOTAN.
GIVE ME THE COMPASS. I'VE GOTTA GO FIND HIM.
I ESTIMATE THAT AT YOUR CURRENT CAPABILITY IT WILL ONLY HAVE A RANGE OF ABOUT 500 METERS.
SURGE
BEEP BEEP BEEP
HOLY CRAP! HE'S CLOSE!!
300 METERS TO THE NORTH!!
THERE'S ONLY ONE PLACE HE COULD BE!
THAT SCUMBAG'S STALKING THE PLAYGROUND!!
ROLL
...

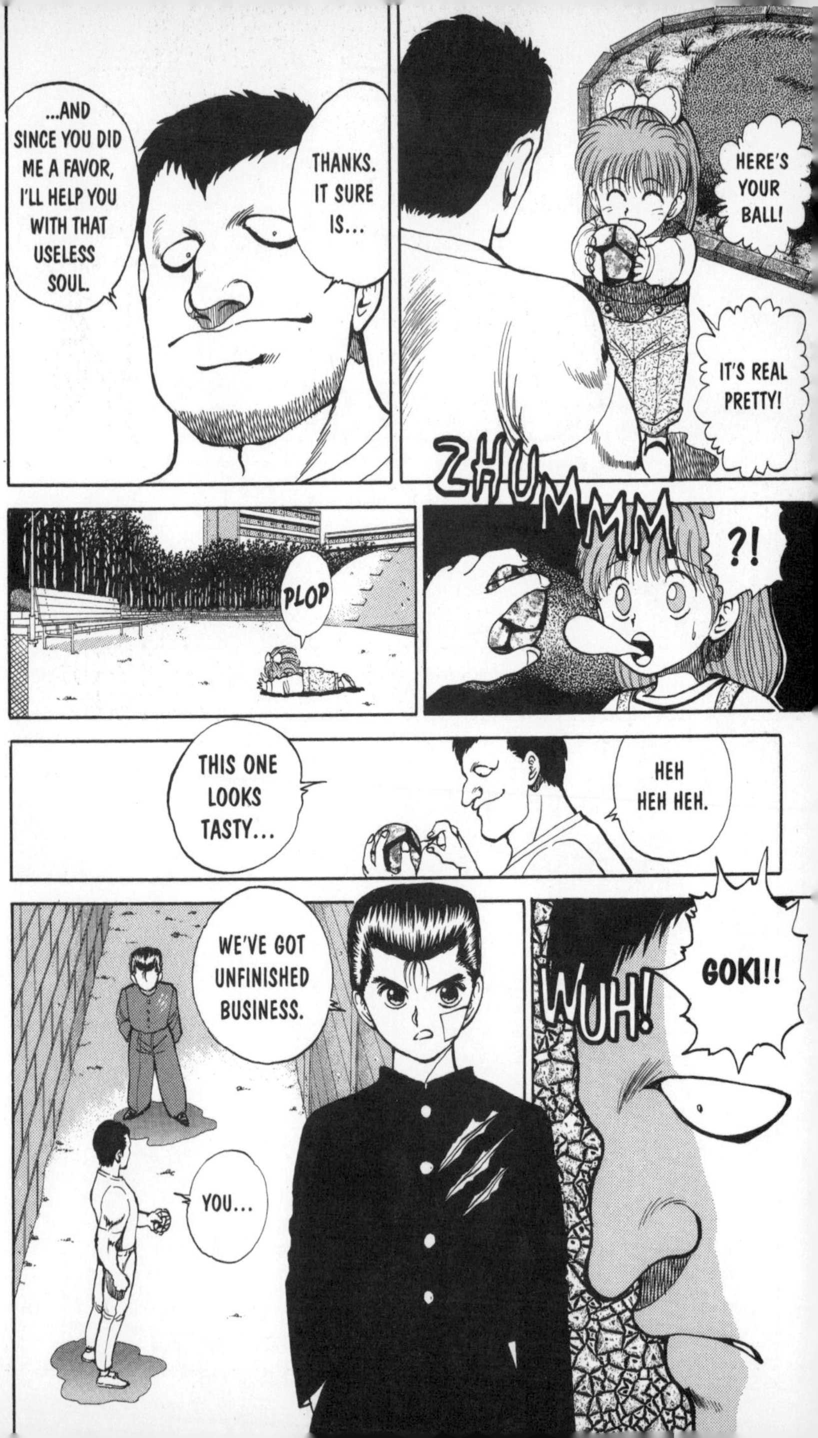
HERE'S YOUR BALL!
IT'S REAL PRETTY!
THANKS. IT SURE IS...
...AND SINCE YOU DID ME A FAVOR, I'LL HELP YOU WITH THAT USELESS SOUL.
ZHUMMMM
?!
PLOP
HEH HEH HEH.
THIS ONE LOOKS TASTY...
GOKI!!
WUH!
WE'VE GOT UNFINISHED BUSINESS.
YOU...

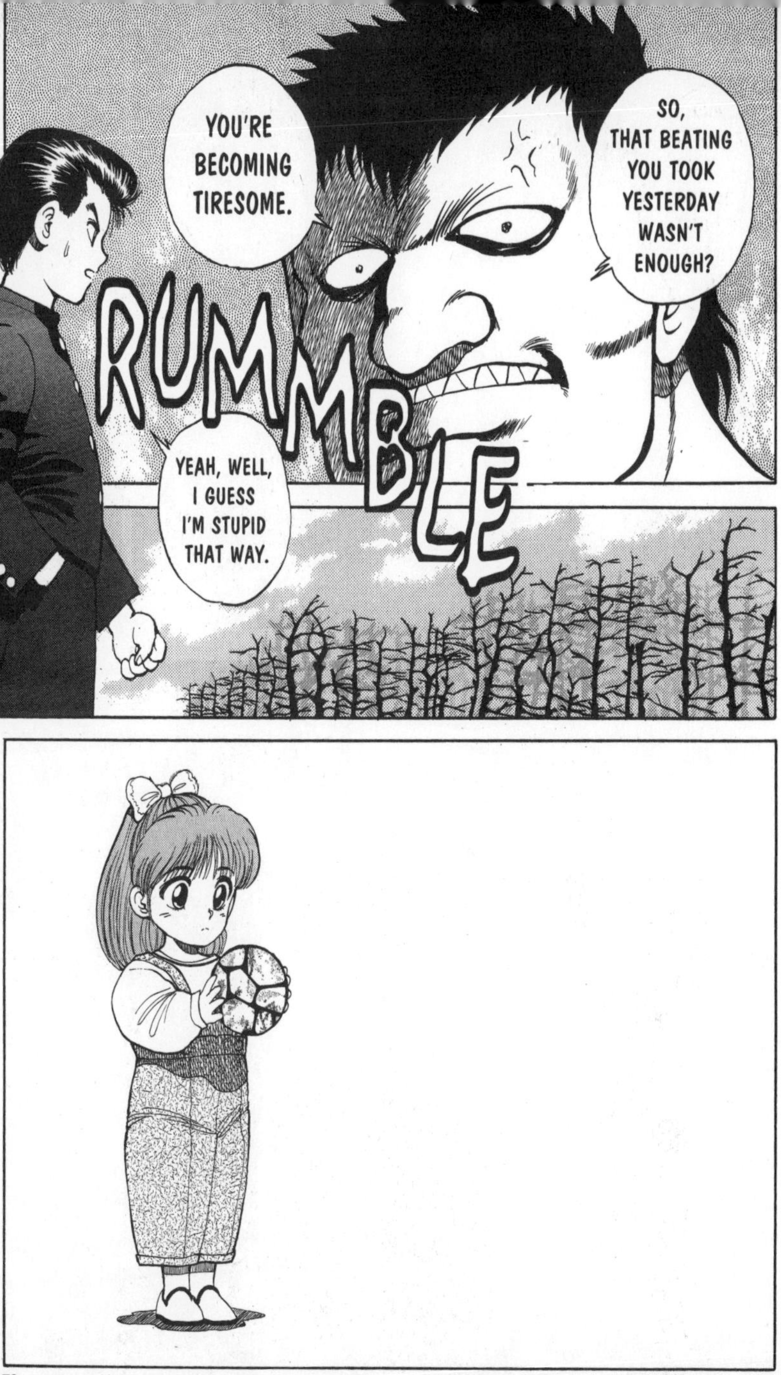
SO, THAT BEATING YOU TOOK YESTERDAY WASN'T ENOUGH?
YOU'RE BECOMING TIRESOME.
RUMMBLE
YEAH, WELL, I GUESS I'M STUPID THAT WAY.

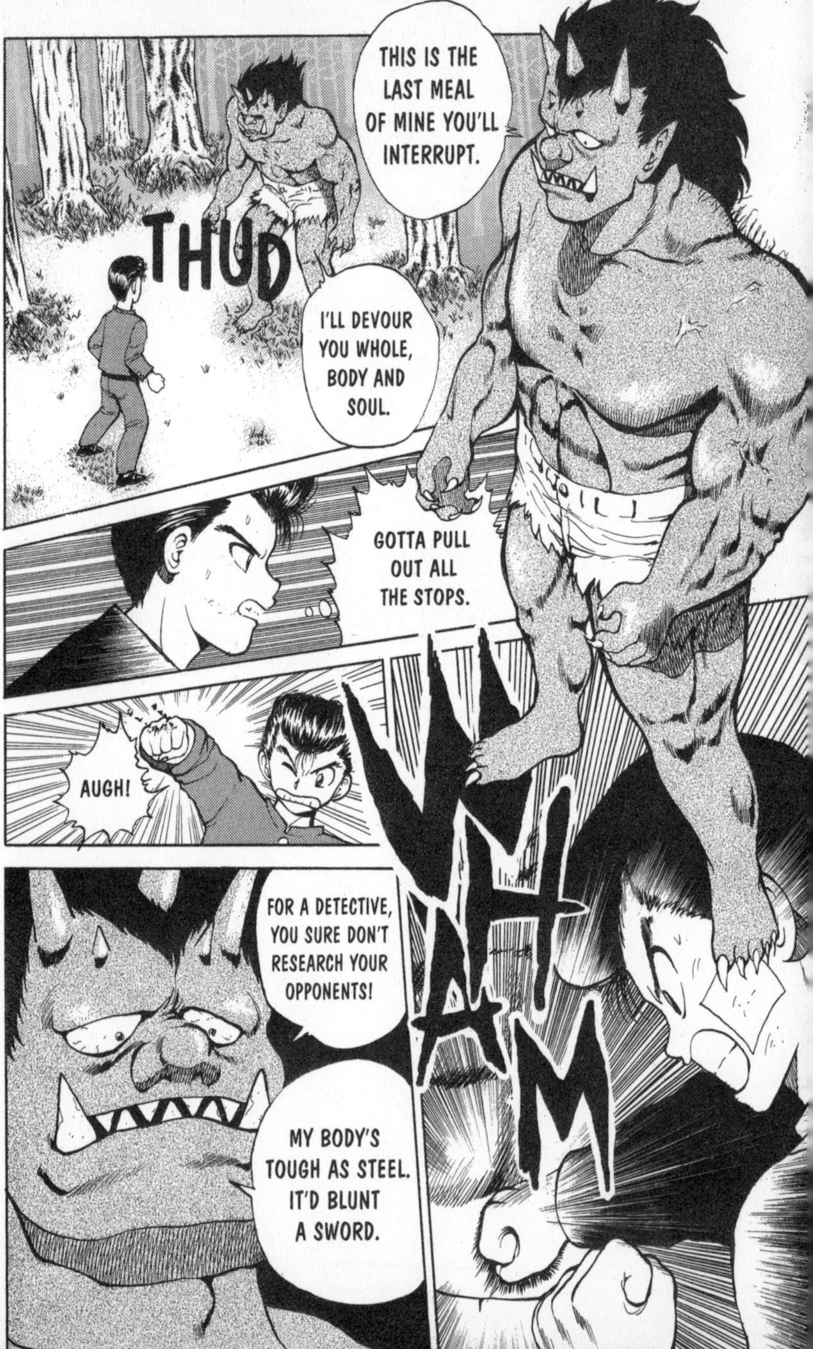
THIS IS THE LAST MEAL OF MINE YOU'LL INTERRUPT.
THUD
I'LL DEVOUR YOU WHOLE, BODY AND SOUL.
GOTTA PULL OUT ALL THE STOPS.
AUGH!
WHAM
FOR A DETECTIVE, YOU SURE DON'T RESEARCH YOUR OPPONENTS!
MY BODY'S TOUGH AS STEEL. IT'D BLUNT A SWORD.

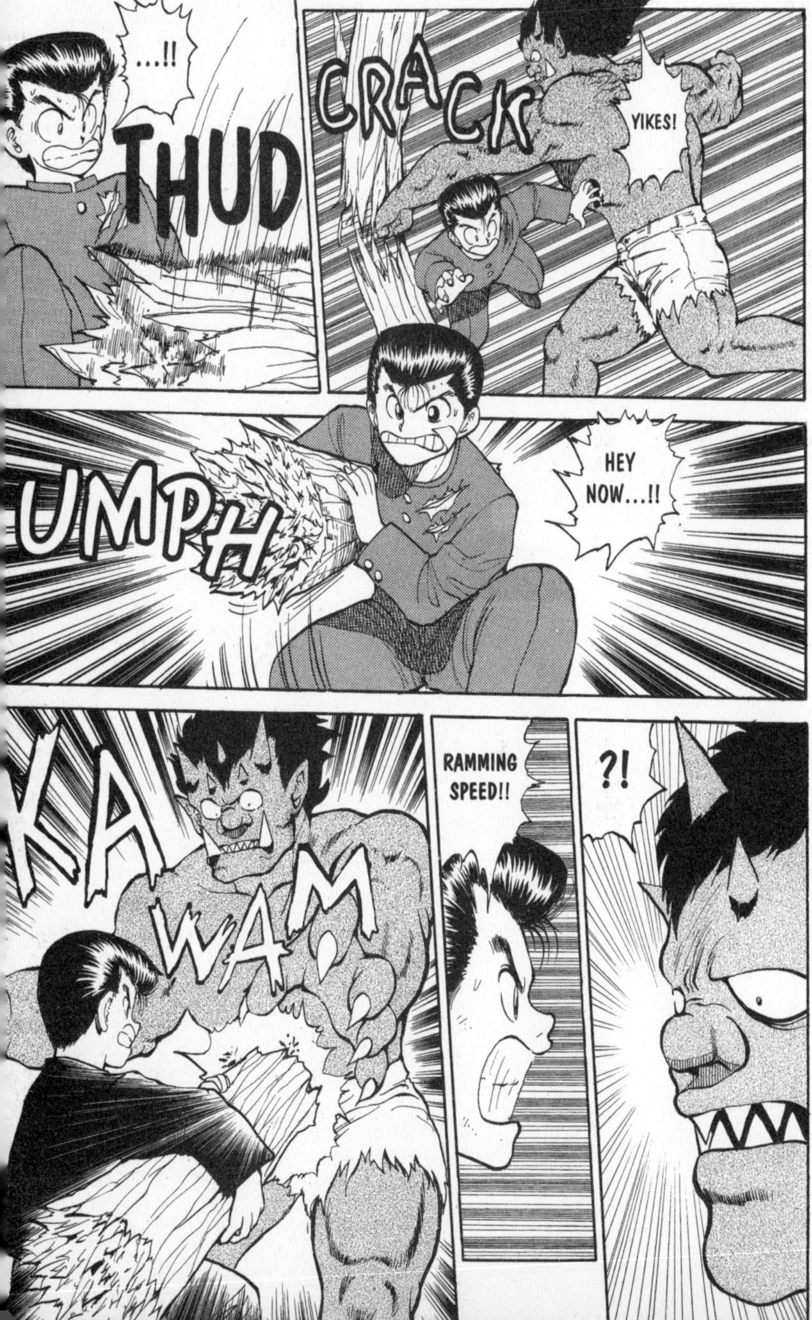
CRACK
YIKES!
...!!
THUD
HEY NOW...!!
UMPH
?!
RAMMING SPEED!!
KA WAM

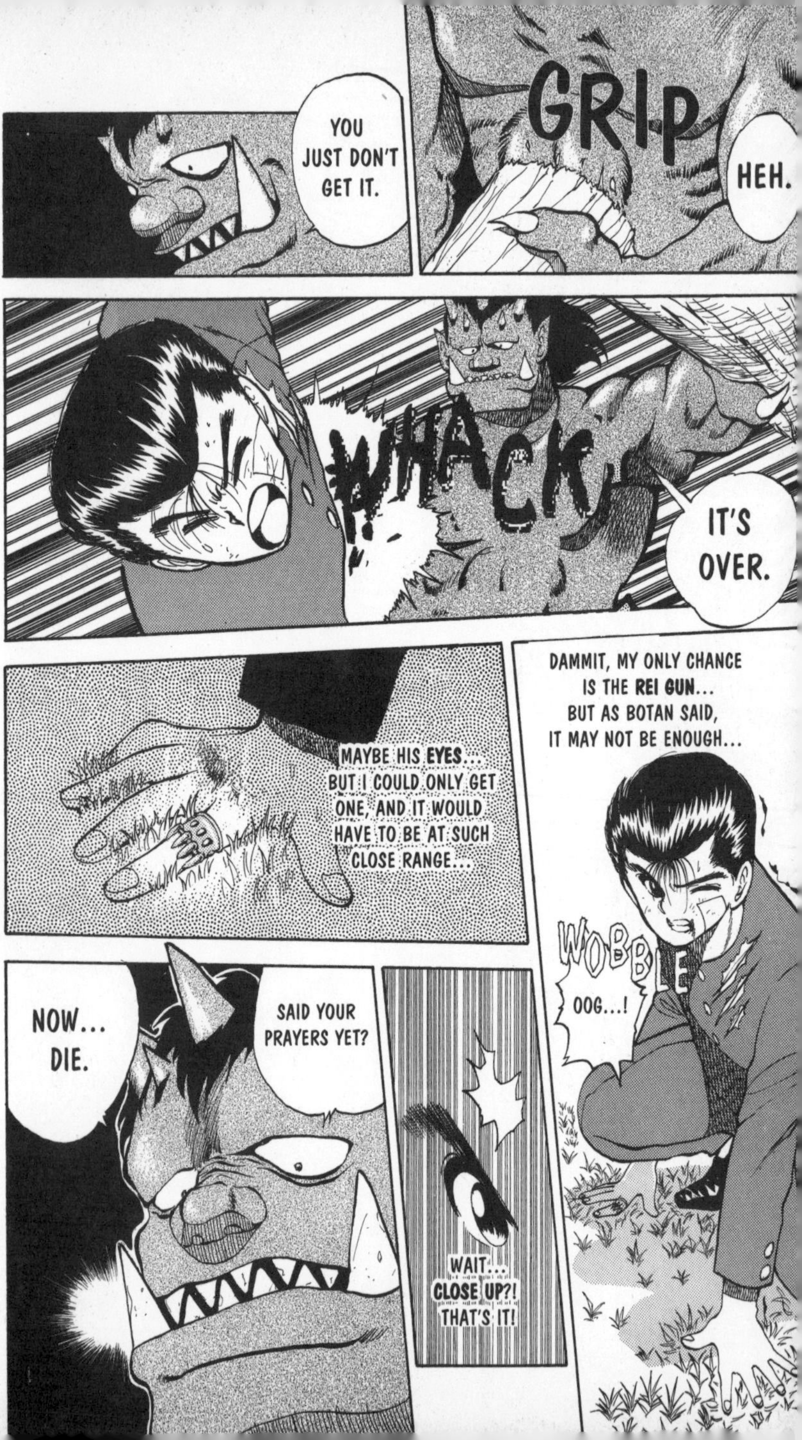
GRIP
HEH.
YOU JUST DON'T GET IT.
WHACK
IT'S OVER.
DAMMIT, MY ONLY CHANCE IS THE REI GUN... BUT AS BOTAN SAID, IT MAY NOT BE ENOUGH...
WOBBLE
OOG...!
MAYBE HIS EYES... BUT I COULD ONLY GET ONE, AND IT WOULD HAVE TO BE AT SUCH CLOSE RANGE...
WAIT... CLOSE UP?! THAT'S IT!
SAID YOUR PRAYERS YET?
NOW... DIE.

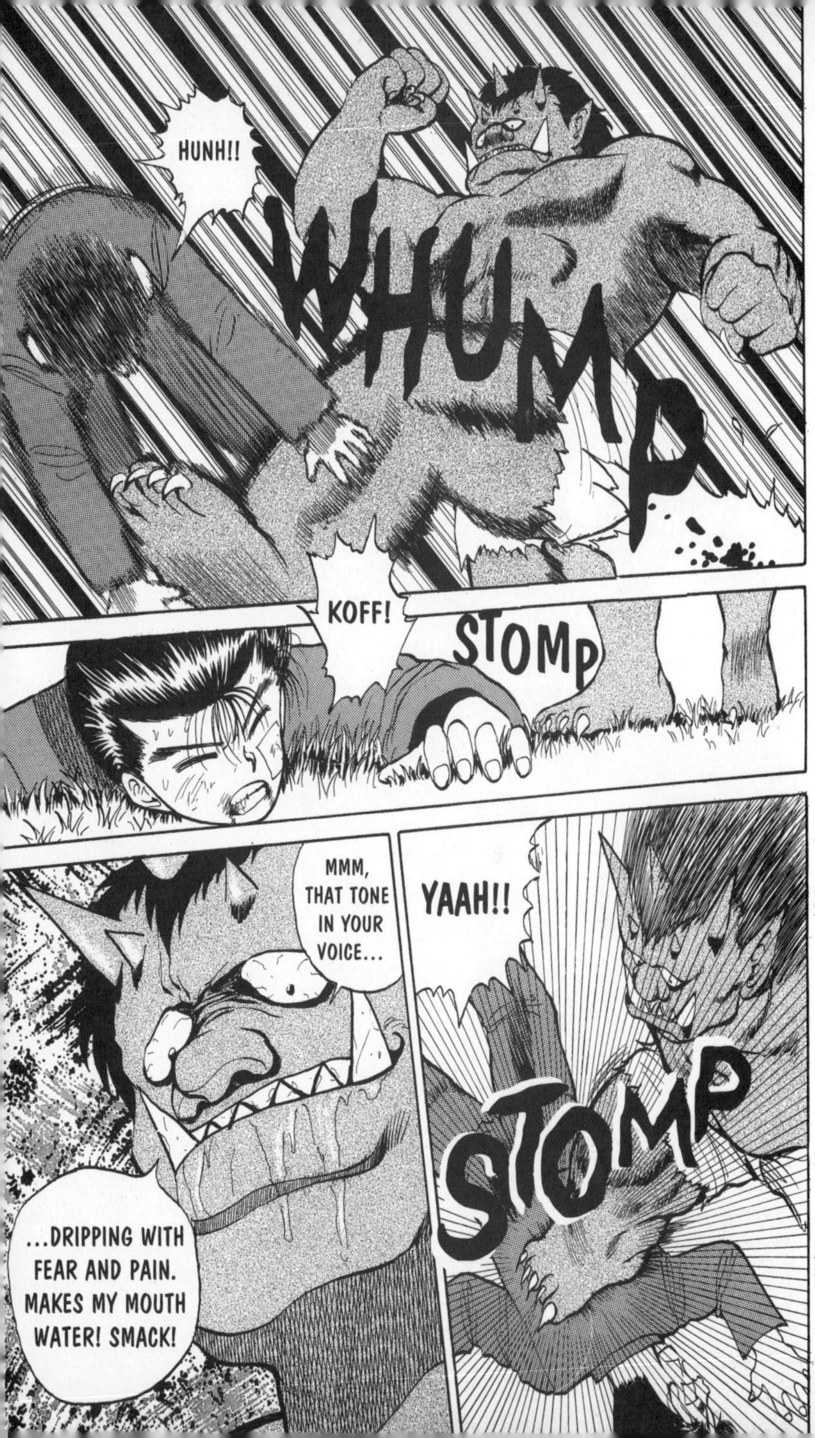
HUNH!!
WHUMP
KOFF!
STOMP
YAAH!!
STOMP
MMM, THAT TONE IN YOUR VOICE...
...DRIPPING WITH FEAR AND PAIN. MAKES MY MOUTH WATER! SMACK!

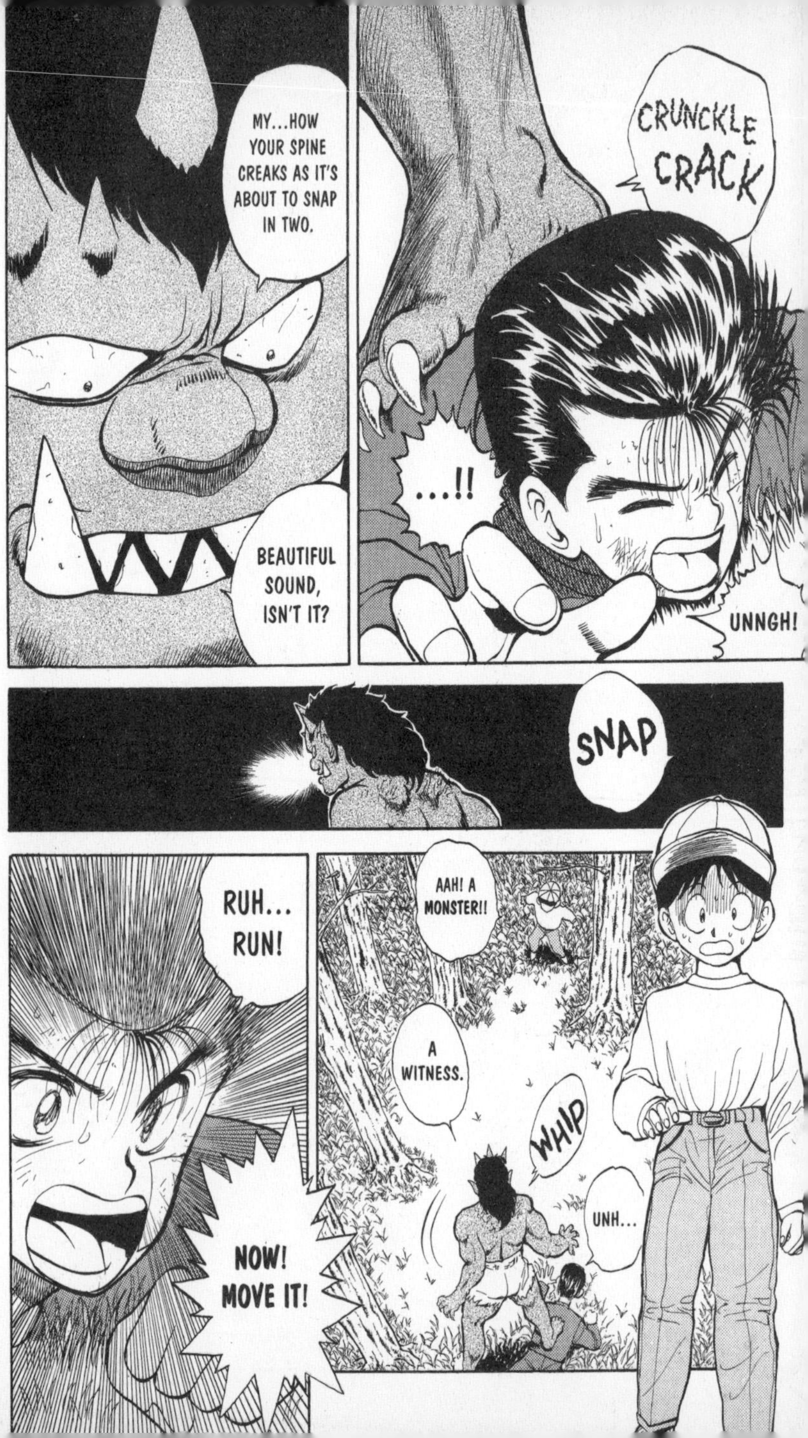
CRUNCKLE CRACK
...!!
UNNGH!
MY...HOW YOUR SPINE CREAKS AS IT'S ABOUT TO SNAP IN TWO.
BEAUTIFUL SOUND, ISN'T IT?
SNAP
AAH! A MONSTER!!
A WITNESS.
WHIP
UNH...
RUH... RUN!
NOW! MOVE IT!

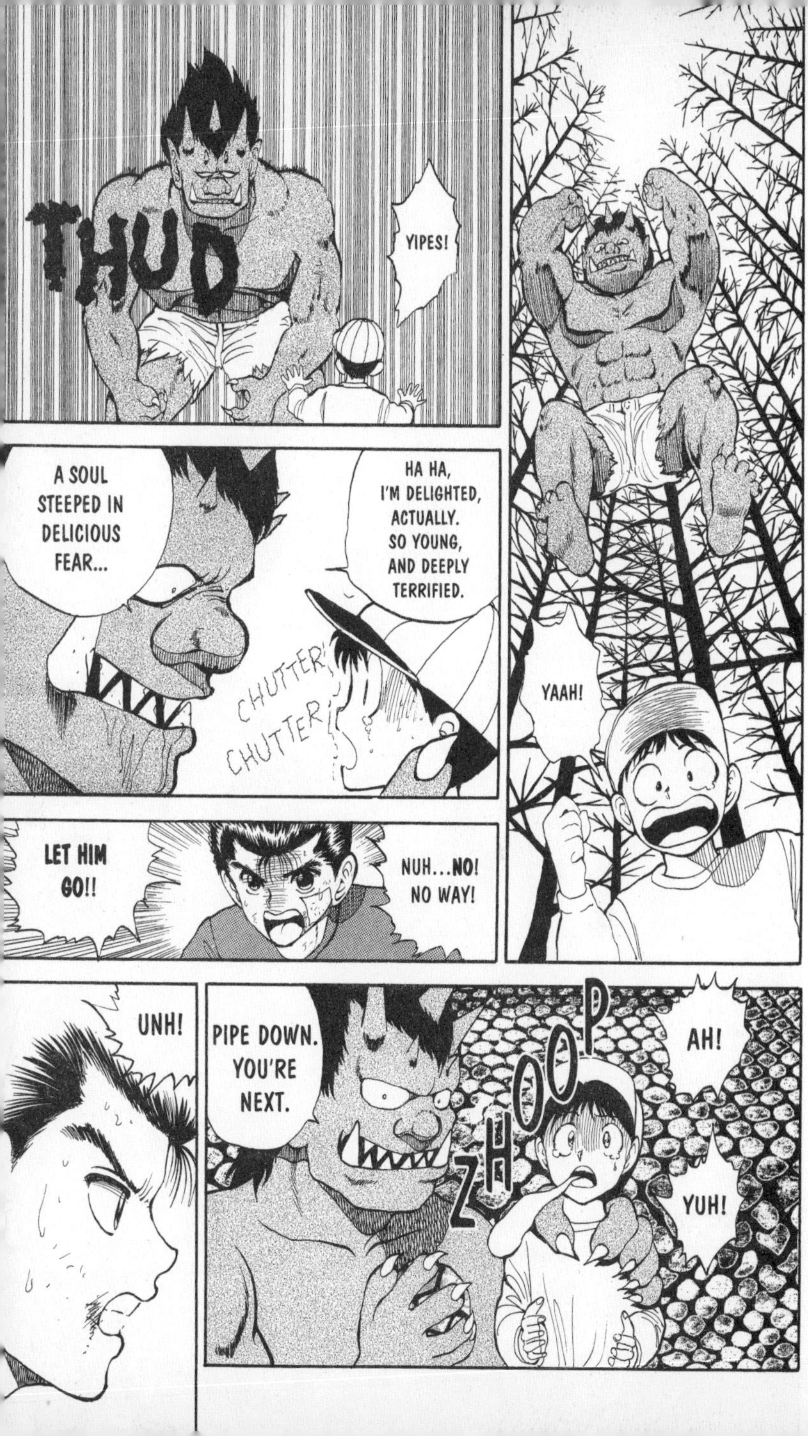
YAAH!
THUD
YIPES!
HA HA, I'M DELIGHTED, ACTUALLY. SO YOUNG, AND DEEPLY TERRIFIED.
A SOUL STEEPED IN DELICIOUS FEAR...
CHUTTER CHUTTER
NUH...NO! NO WAY!
LET HIM GO!!
AH!
ZHOOOP
YUH!
PIPE DOWN. YOU'RE NEXT.
UNH!

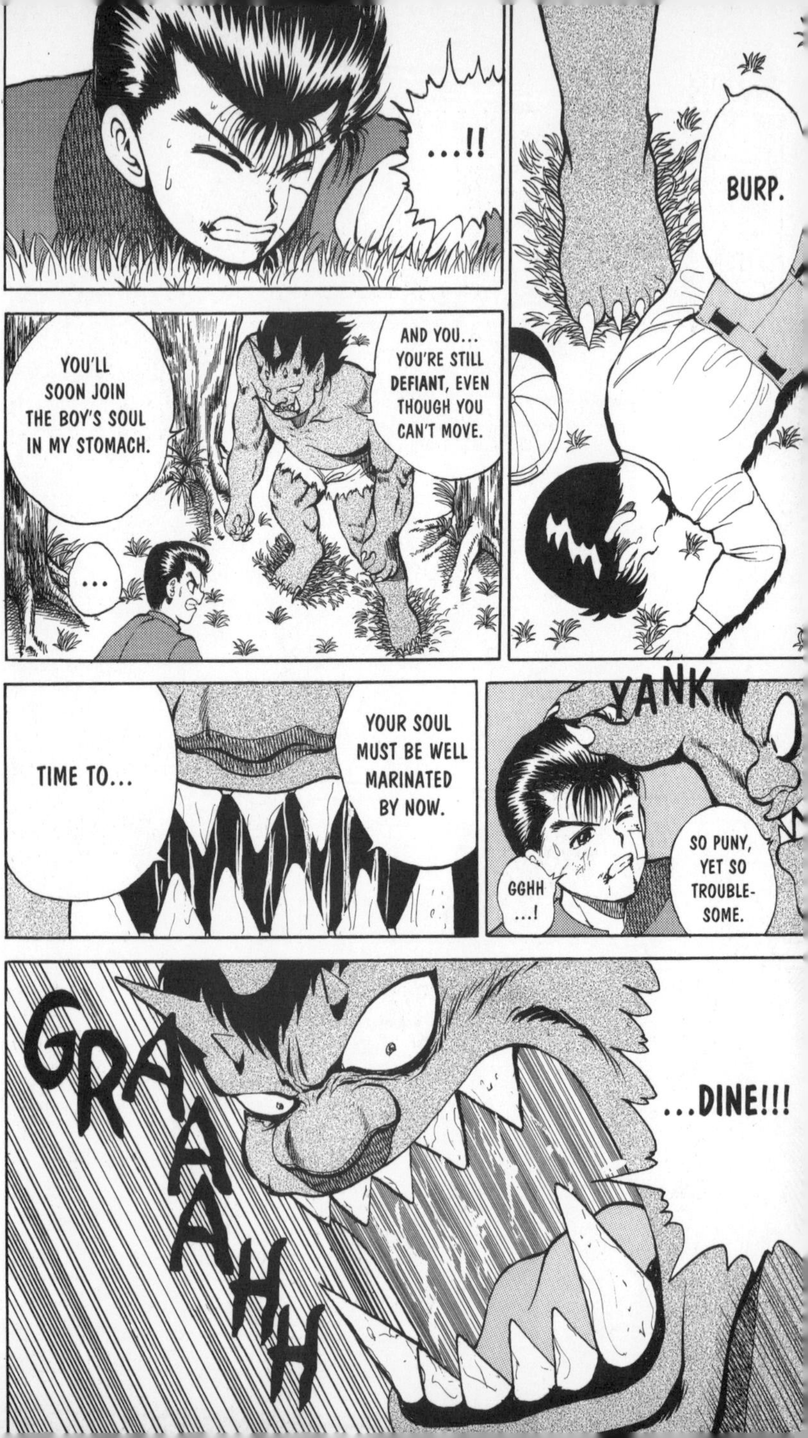
BURP.
...!!
AND YOU... YOU'RE STILL DEFIANT, EVEN THOUGH YOU CAN'T MOVE.
YOU'LL SOON JOIN THE BOY'S SOUL IN MY STOMACH.
...
YANK
SO PUNY, YET SO TROUBLE-SOME.
GGHH ...!
YOUR SOUL MUST BE WELL MARINATED BY NOW.
TIME TO...
...DINE!!!
GRAAAHHH

READ THIS WAY

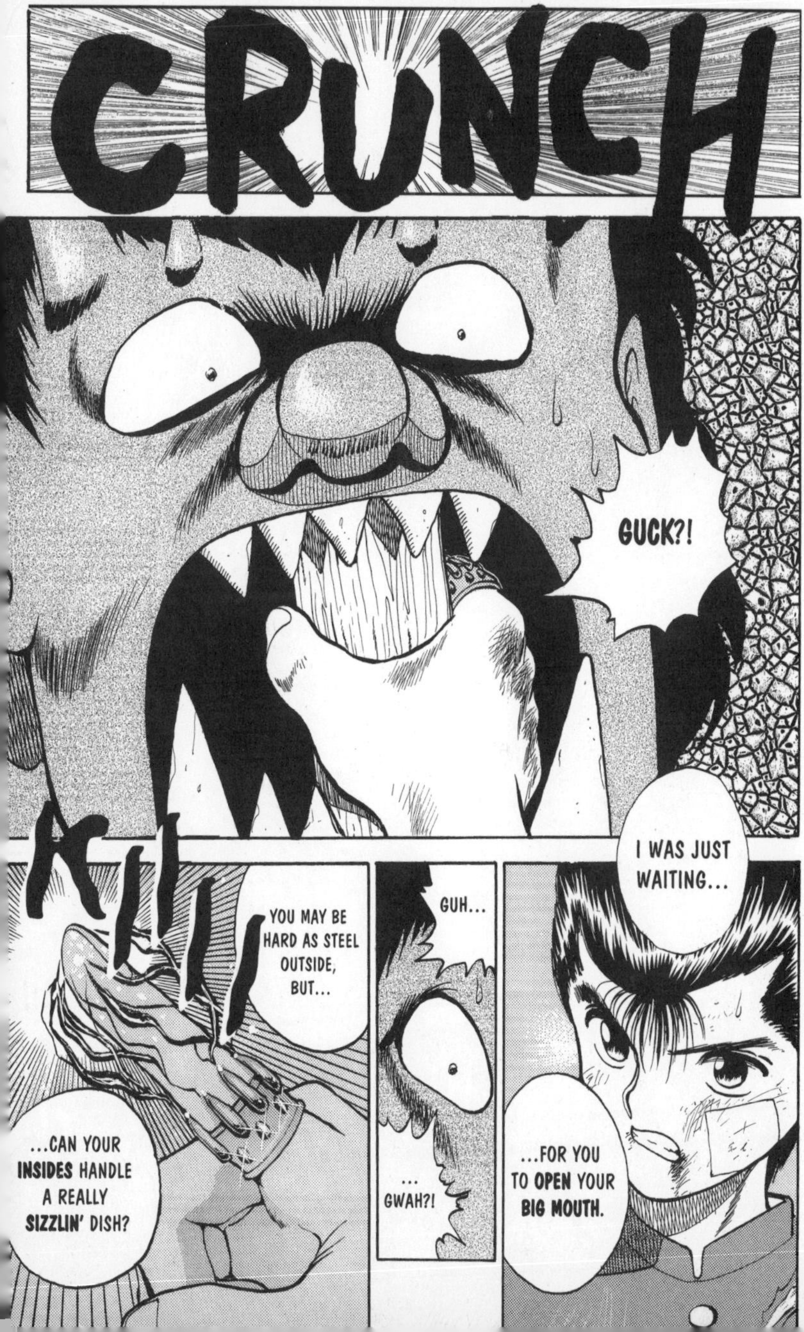
CRUNCH
GUCK?!
I WAS JUST WAITING...
...FOR YOU TO OPEN YOUR BIG MOUTH.
GUH...
...GWAH?!
YOU MAY BE HARD AS STEEL OUTSIDE, BUT...
...CAN YOUR INSIDES HANDLE A REALLY SIZZLIN' DISH?

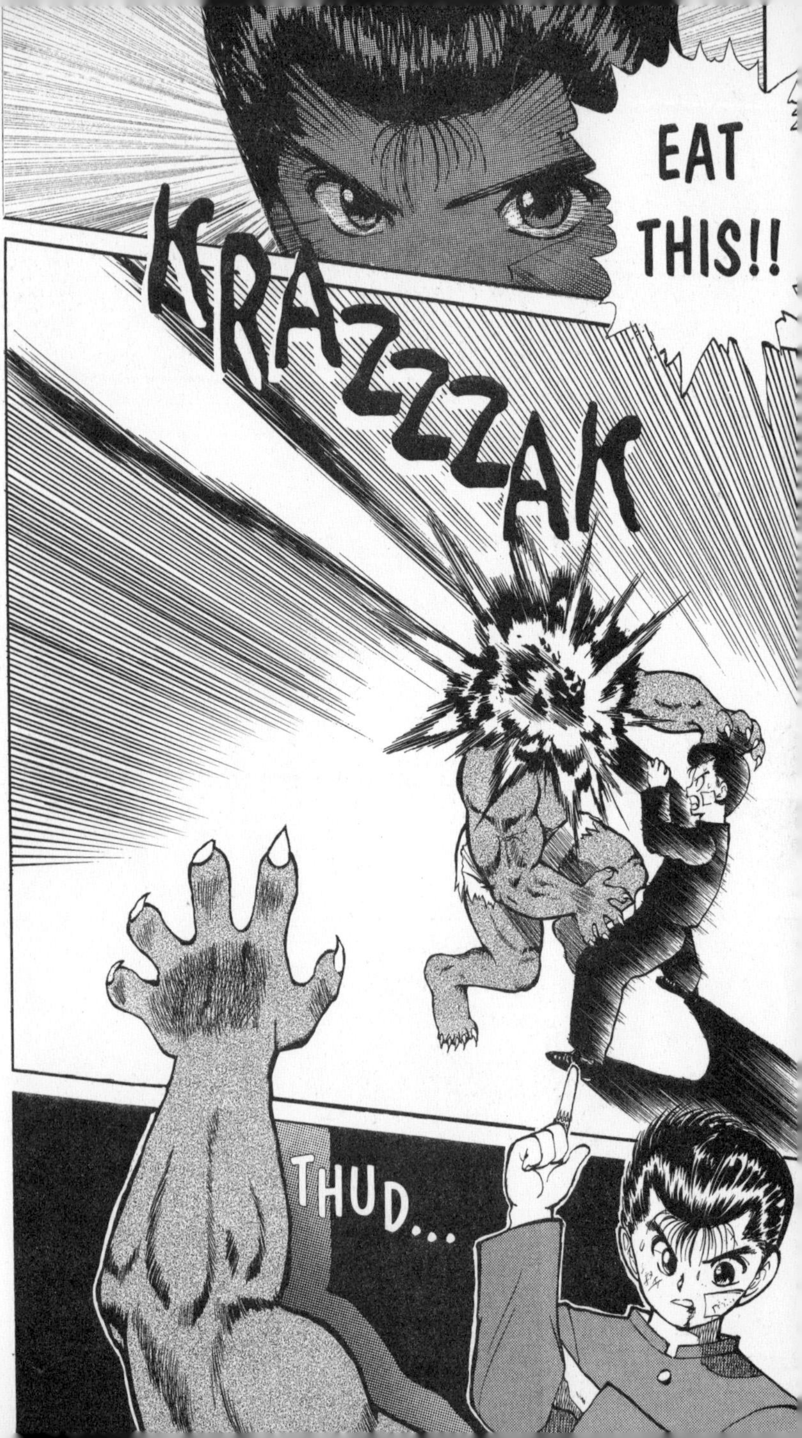
EAT THIS!!
KRAZZZAK
THUD...

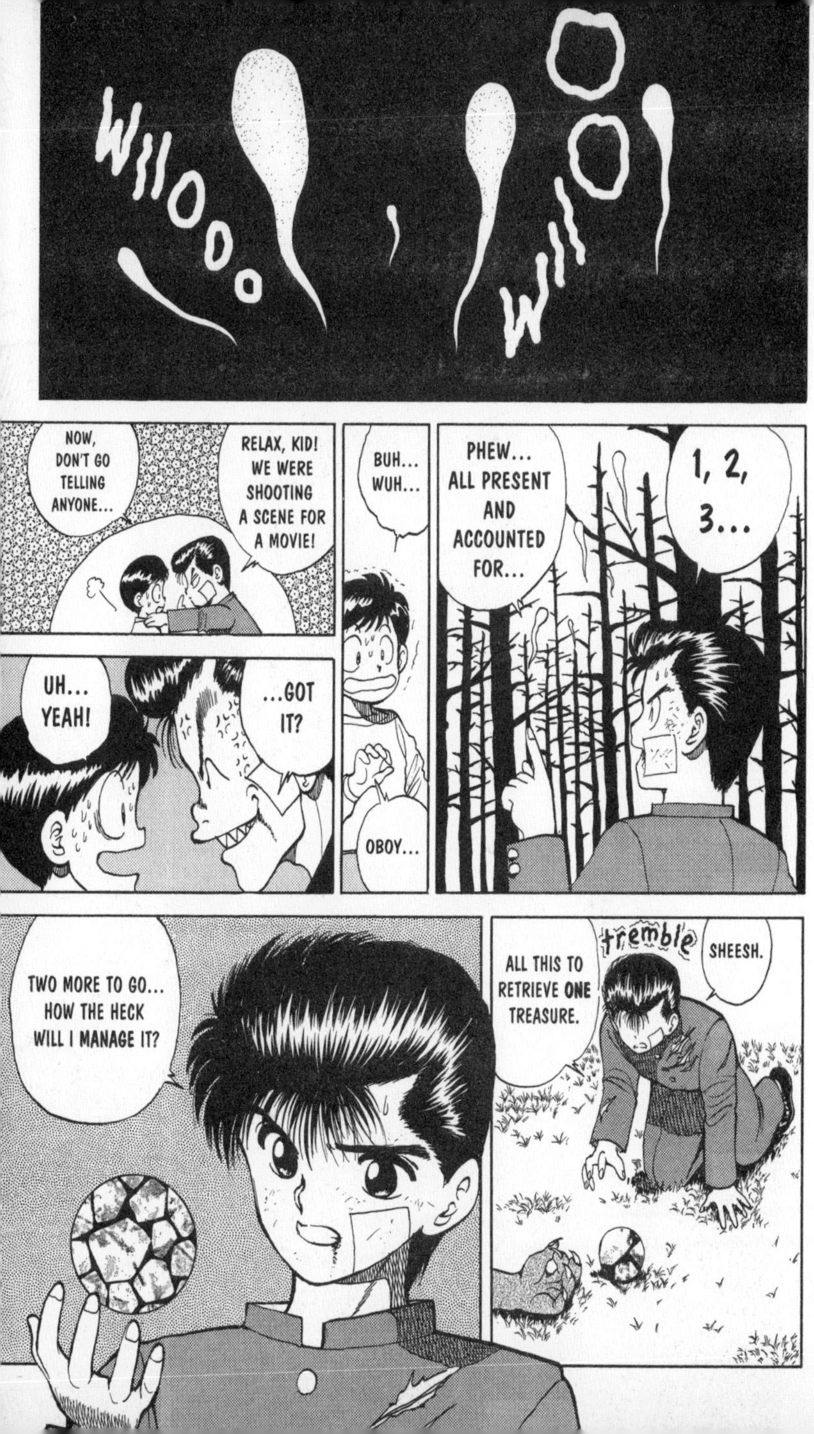
WHOOO
WHOOO
1, 2, 3...
PHEW... ALL PRESENT AND ACCOUNTED FOR...
BUH... WUH...
OBOY...
RELAX, KID! WE WERE SHOOTING A SCENE FOR A MOVIE!
NOW, DON'T GO TELLING ANYONE...
...GOT IT?
UH... YEAH!
SHEESH.
tremble
ALL THIS TO RETRIEVE **ONE** TREASURE.
TWO MORE TO GO... HOW THE HECK WILL I MANAGE IT?

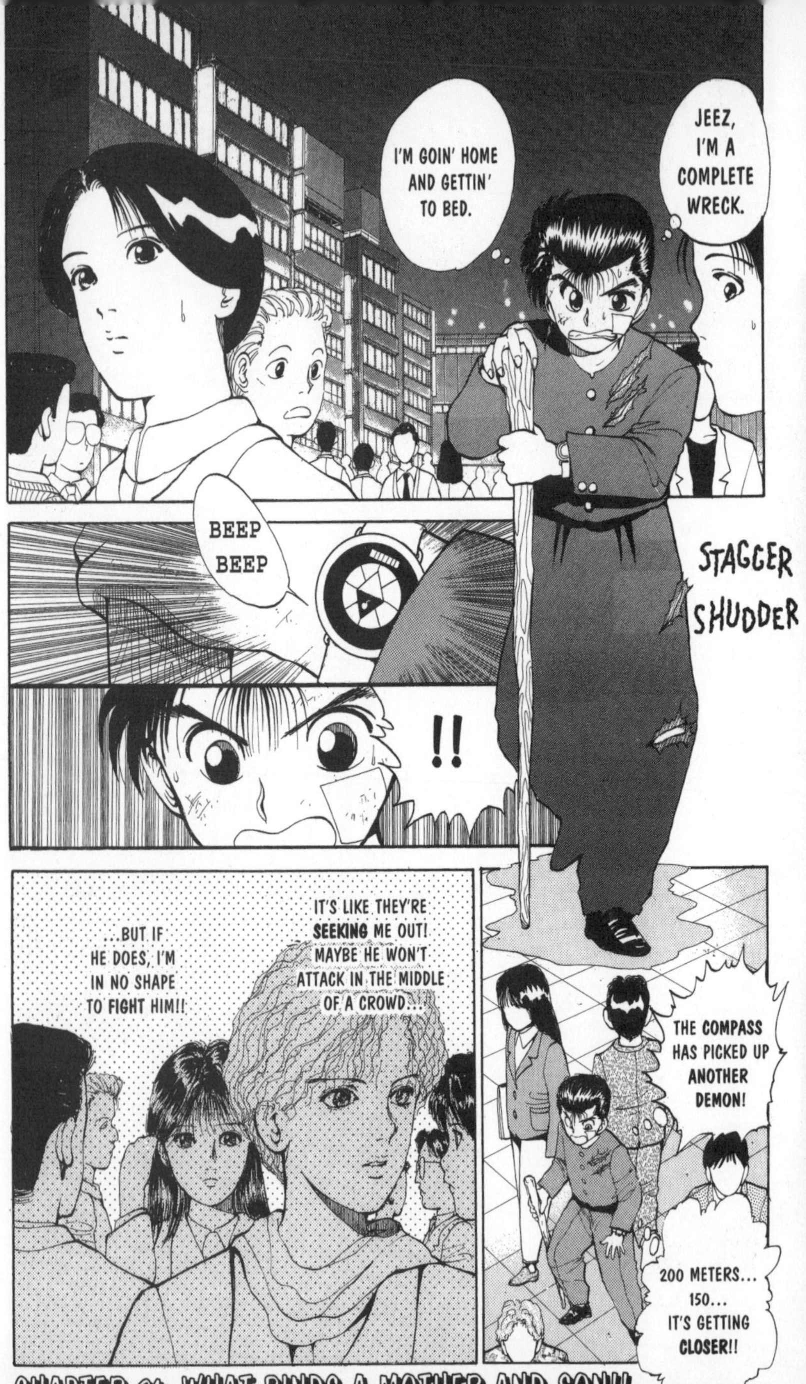
JEEZ, I'M A COMPLETE WRECK.
I'M GOIN' HOME AND GETTIN' TO BED.
STAGGER
SHUDDER
BEEP BEEP
!!
THE COMPASS HAS PICKED UP ANOTHER DEMON!
200 METERS... 150... IT'S GETTING CLOSER!!
IT'S LIKE THEY'RE SEEKING ME OUT! MAYBE HE WON'T ATTACK IN THE MIDDLE OF A CROWD...
...BUT IF HE DOES, I'M IN NO SHAPE TO FIGHT HIM!!

CHAPTER 21: WHAT BINDS A MOTHER AND SON!!

Chapter 21:
WHAT BINDS A MOTHER AND SON!!

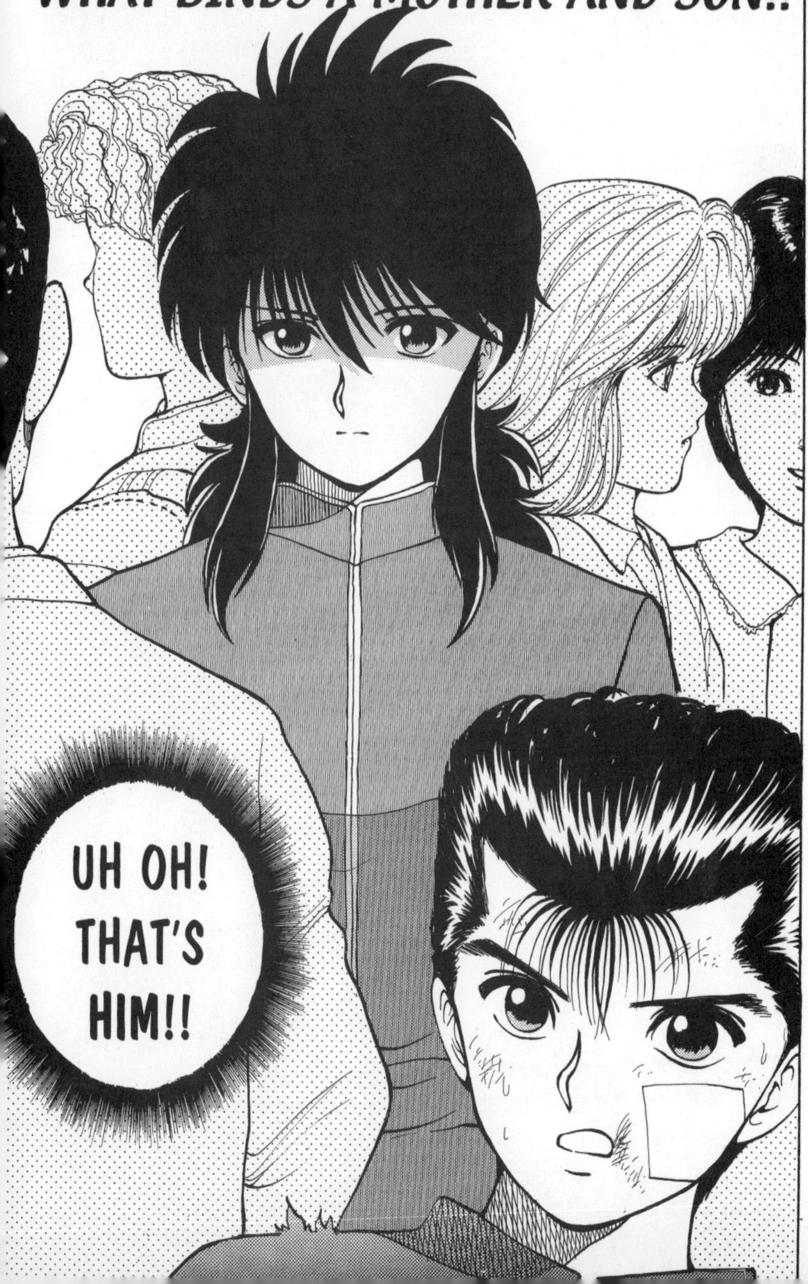
UH OH! THAT'S HIM!!

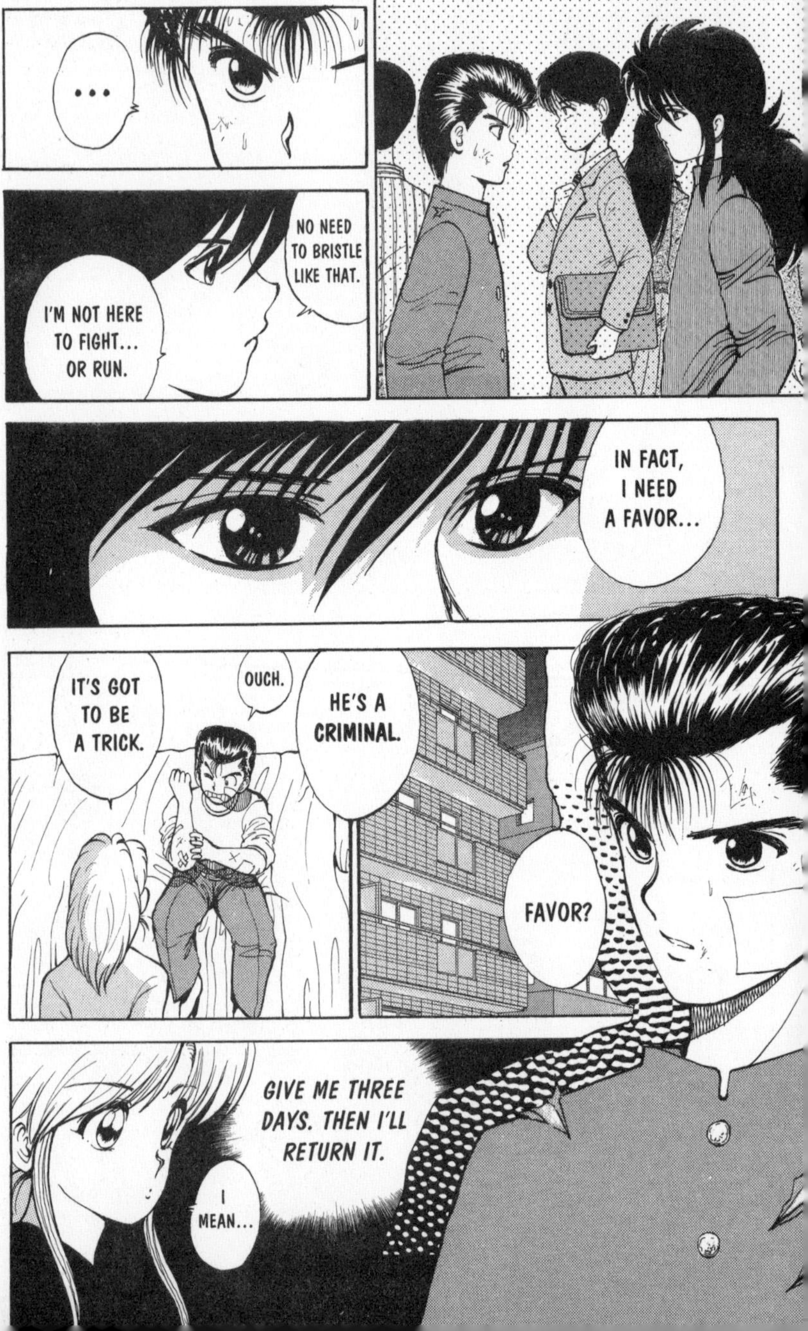
...
NO NEED TO BRISTLE LIKE THAT.
I'M NOT HERE TO FIGHT... OR RUN.
IN FACT, I NEED A FAVOR...
FAVOR?
HE'S A CRIMINAL.
OUCH.
IT'S GOT TO BE A TRICK.
GIVE ME THREE DAYS. THEN I'LL RETURN IT.
I MEAN...

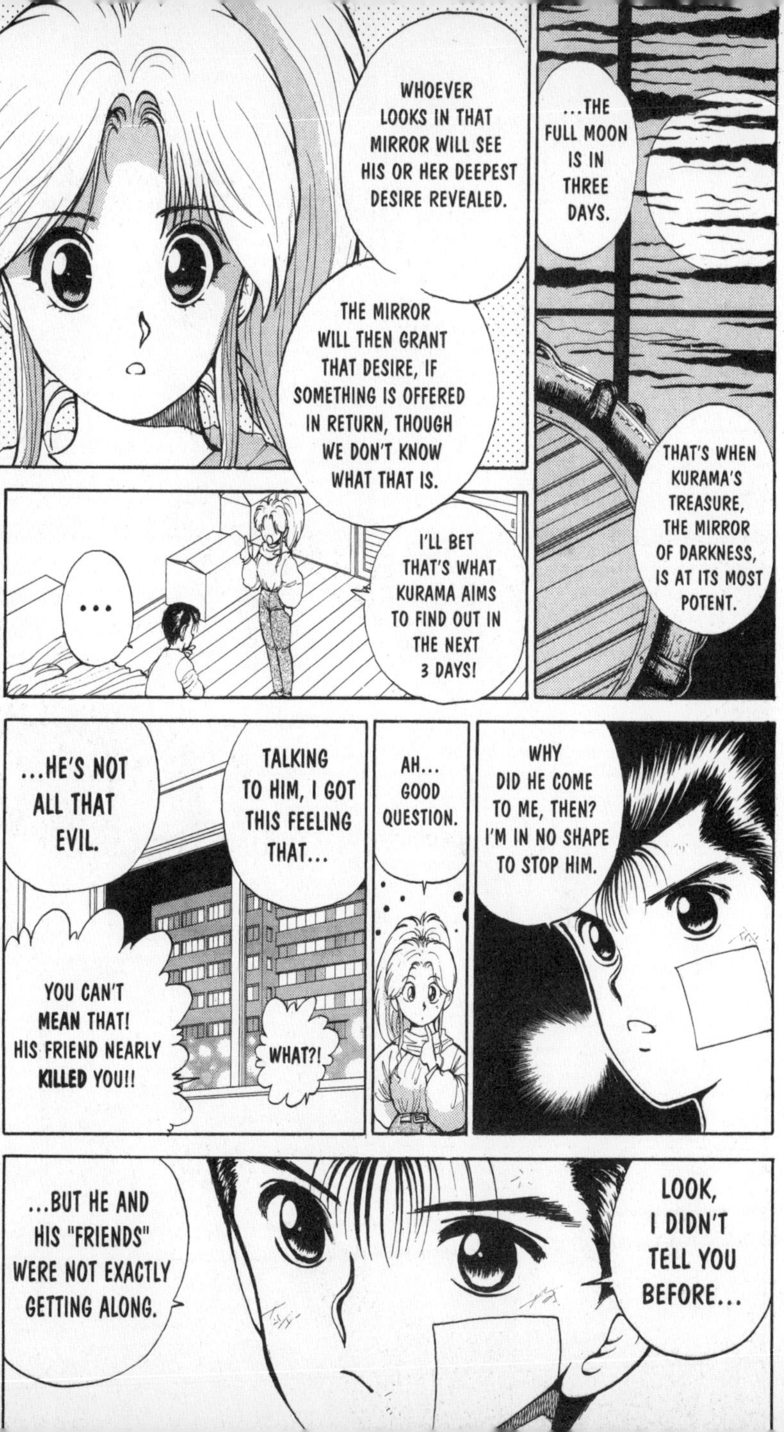
...THE FULL MOON IS IN THREE DAYS.
THAT'S WHEN KURAMA'S TREASURE, THE MIRROR OF DARKNESS, IS AT ITS MOST POTENT.
WHOEVER LOOKS IN THAT MIRROR WILL SEE HIS OR HER DEEPEST DESIRE REVEALED.
THE MIRROR WILL THEN GRANT THAT DESIRE, IF SOMETHING IS OFFERED IN RETURN, THOUGH WE DON'T KNOW WHAT THAT IS.
I'LL BET THAT'S WHAT KURAMA AIMS TO FIND OUT IN THE NEXT 3 DAYS!
...
WHY DID HE COME TO ME, THEN? I'M IN NO SHAPE TO STOP HIM.
AH... GOOD QUESTION.
TALKING TO HIM, I GOT THIS FEELING THAT...
...HE'S NOT ALL THAT EVIL.
WHAT?!
YOU CAN'T MEAN THAT! HIS FRIEND NEARLY **KILLED** YOU!!
LOOK, I DIDN'T TELL YOU BEFORE...
...BUT HE AND HIS "FRIENDS" WERE NOT EXACTLY GETTING ALONG.

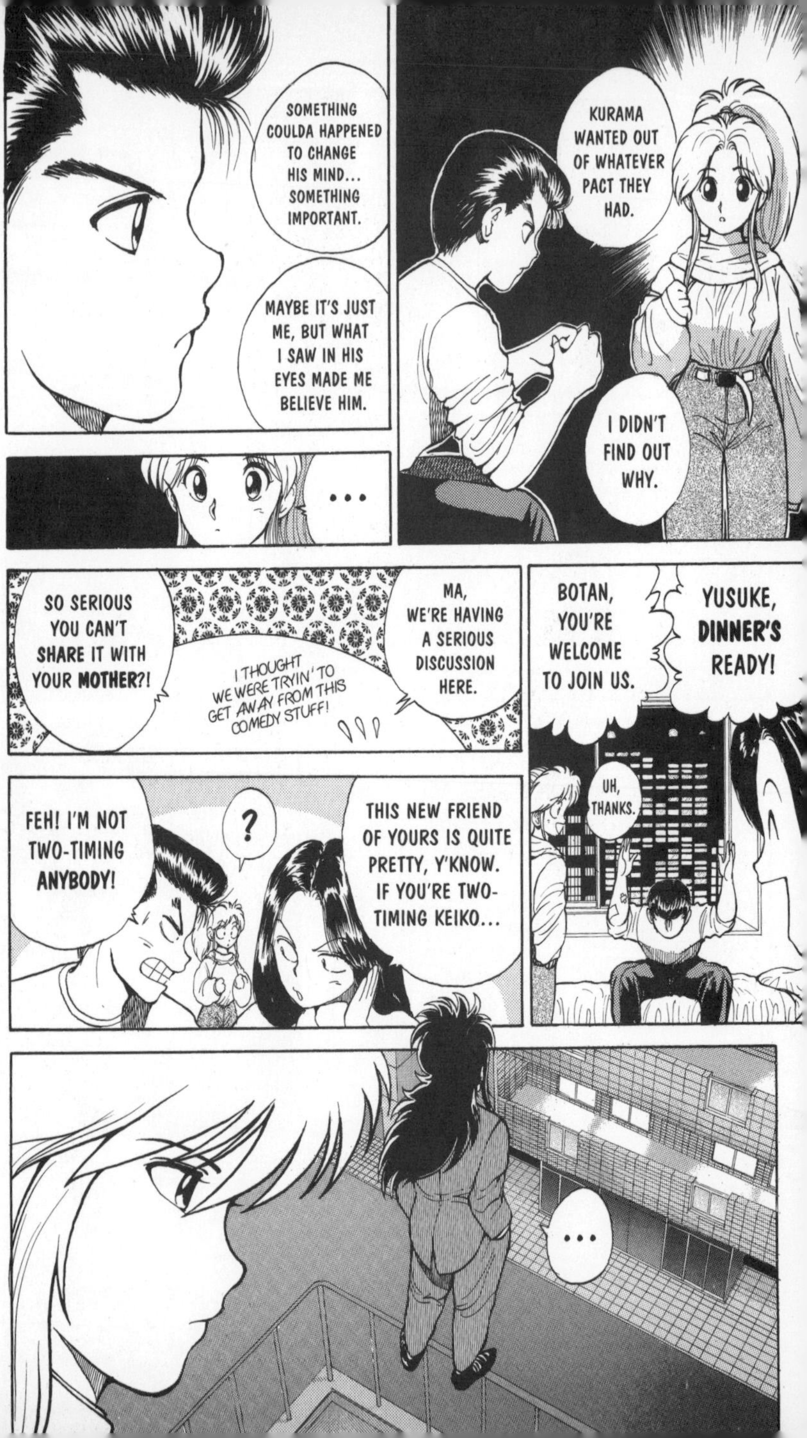
KURAMA WANTED OUT OF WHATEVER PACT THEY HAD.
I DIDN'T FIND OUT WHY.
SOMETHING COULDA HAPPENED TO CHANGE HIS MIND... SOMETHING IMPORTANT.
MAYBE IT'S JUST ME, BUT WHAT I SAW IN HIS EYES MADE ME BELIEVE HIM.
...
YUSUKE, **DINNER'S** READY!
BOTAN, YOU'RE WELCOME TO JOIN US.
UH, THANKS.
MA, WE'RE HAVING A SERIOUS DISCUSSION HERE.
I THOUGHT WE WERE TRYIN' TO GET AWAY FROM THIS COMEDY STUFF!
SO SERIOUS YOU CAN'T **SHARE** IT WITH YOUR **MOTHER**?!
THIS NEW FRIEND OF YOURS IS QUITE PRETTY, Y'KNOW. IF YOU'RE TWO-TIMING KEIKO...
?
FEH! I'M NOT TWO-TIMING **ANYBODY**!
...

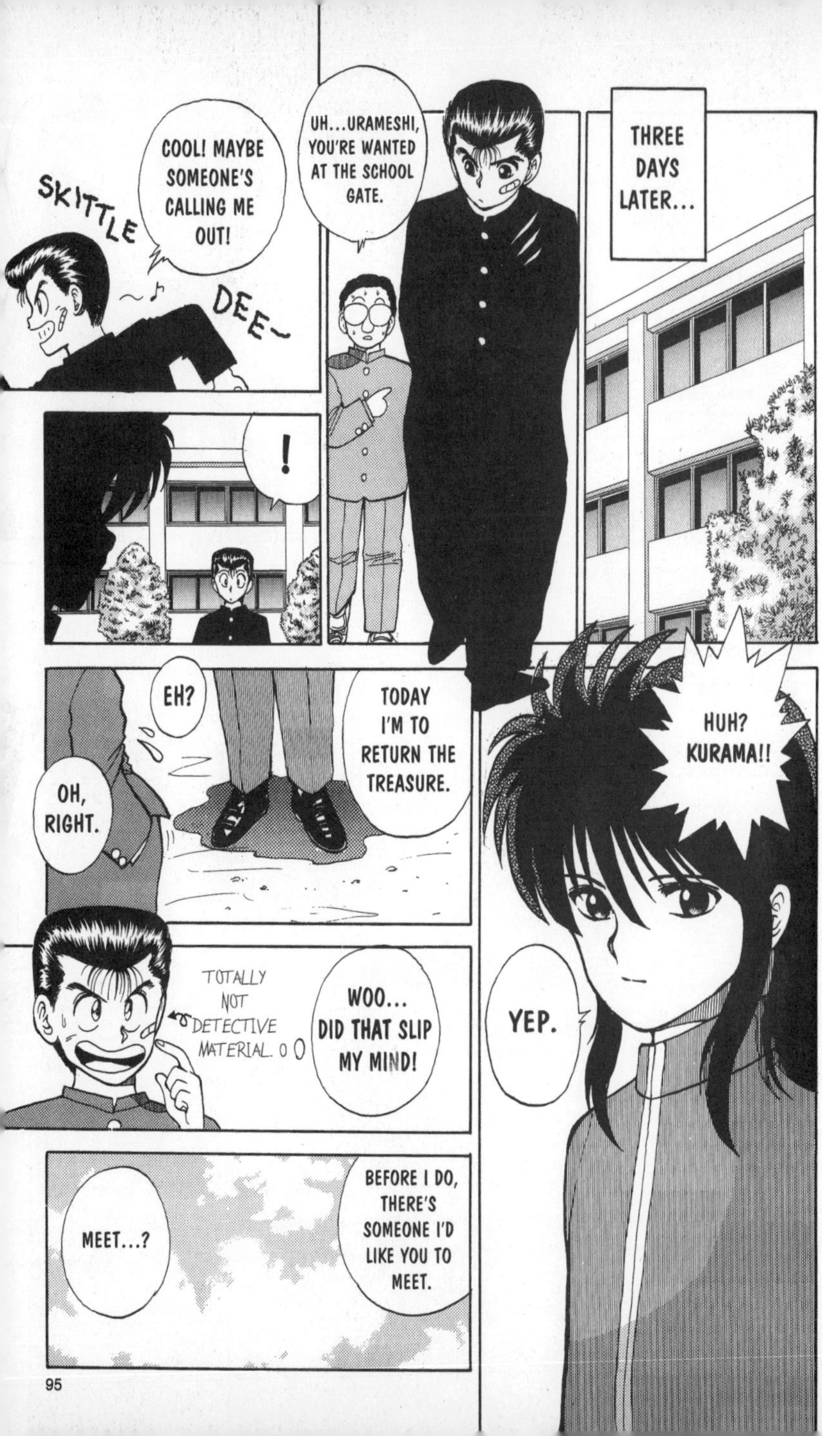
THREE DAYS LATER...
UH...URAMESHI, YOU'RE WANTED AT THE SCHOOL GATE.
COOL! MAYBE SOMEONE'S CALLING ME OUT!
SKITTLE
DEE~
!
HUH? KURAMA!!
YEP.
TODAY I'M TO RETURN THE TREASURE.
EH?
OH, RIGHT.
WOO... DID THAT SLIP MY MIND!
TOTALLY NOT DETECTIVE MATERIAL.
BEFORE I DO, THERE'S SOMEONE I'D LIKE YOU TO MEET.
MEET...?

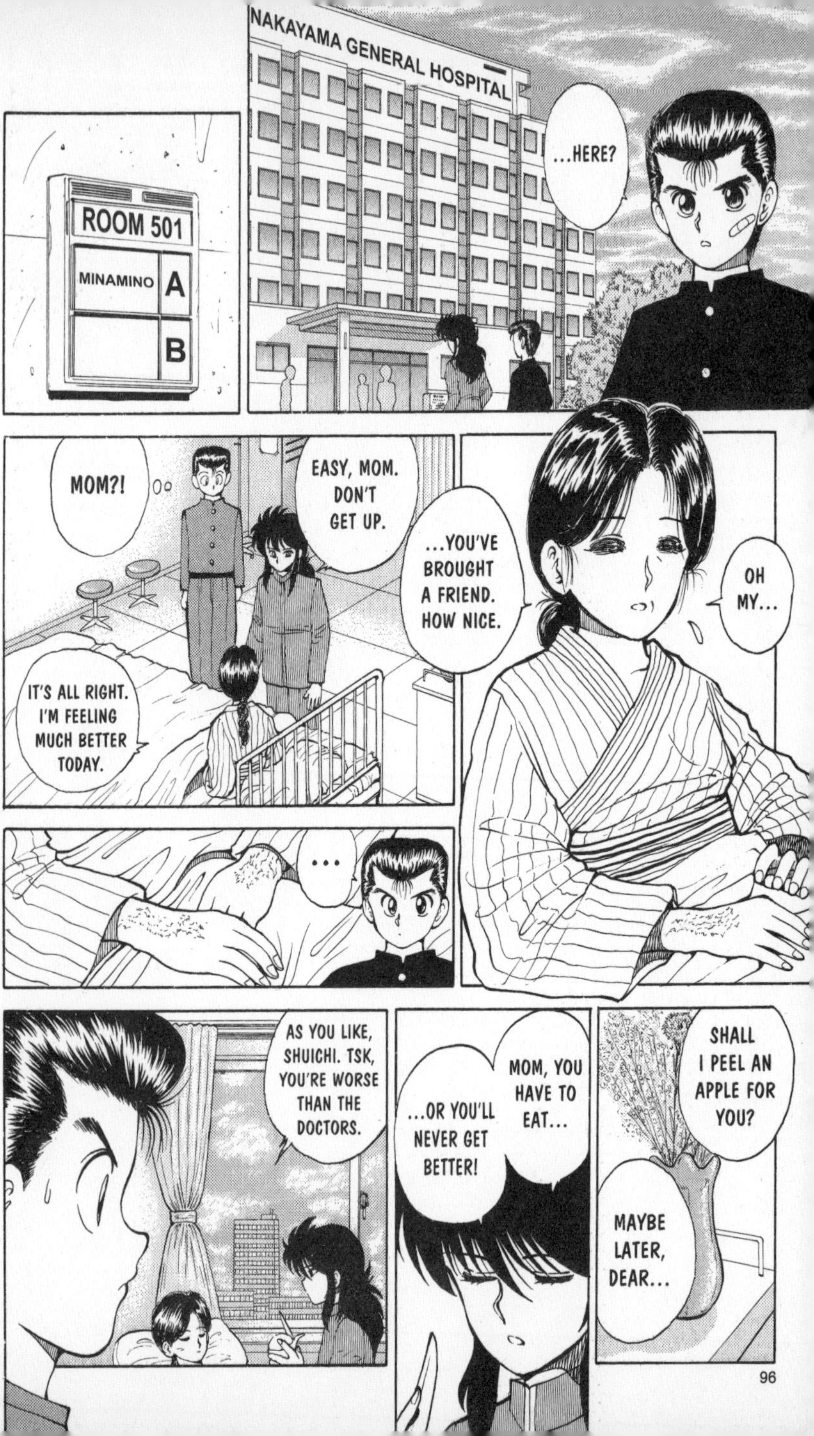
NAKAYAMA GENERAL HOSPITAL
...HERE?
ROOM 501
MINAMINO
A
B
OH MY...
...YOU'VE BROUGHT A FRIEND. HOW NICE.
EASY, MOM. DON'T GET UP.
MOM?!
IT'S ALL RIGHT. I'M FEELING MUCH BETTER TODAY.
...
SHALL I PEEL AN APPLE FOR YOU?
MAYBE LATER, DEAR...
MOM, YOU HAVE TO EAT...
...OR YOU'LL NEVER GET BETTER!
AS YOU LIKE, SHUICHI. TSK, YOU'RE WORSE THAN THE DOCTORS.

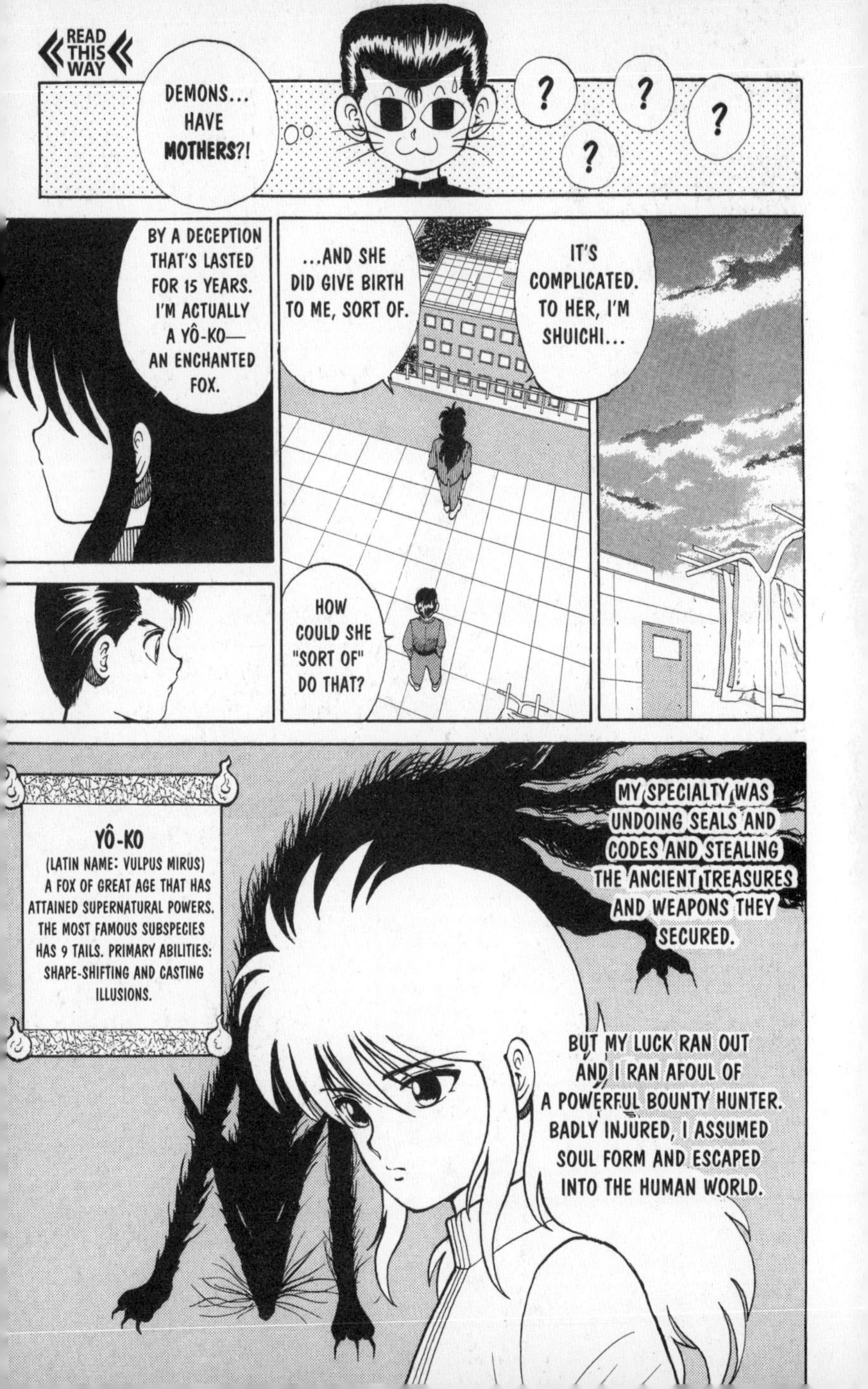
READ THIS WAY
DEMONS... HAVE MOTHERS?!
? ? ? ?
IT'S COMPLICATED. TO HER, I'M SHUICHI...
...AND SHE DID GIVE BIRTH TO ME, SORT OF.
HOW COULD SHE "SORT OF" DO THAT?
BY A DECEPTION THAT'S LASTED FOR 15 YEARS. I'M ACTUALLY A YÔ-KO— AN ENCHANTED FOX.
MY SPECIALTY WAS UNDOING SEALS AND CODES AND STEALING THE ANCIENT TREASURES AND WEAPONS THEY SECURED.
YÔ-KO
(LATIN NAME: VULPUS MIRUS) A FOX OF GREAT AGE THAT HAS ATTAINED SUPERNATURAL POWERS. THE MOST FAMOUS SUBSPECIES HAS 9 TAILS. PRIMARY ABILITIES: SHAPE-SHIFTING AND CASTING ILLUSIONS.
BUT MY LUCK RAN OUT AND I RAN AFOUL OF A POWERFUL BOUNTY HUNTER. BADLY INJURED, I ASSUMED SOUL FORM AND ESCAPED INTO THE HUMAN WORLD.

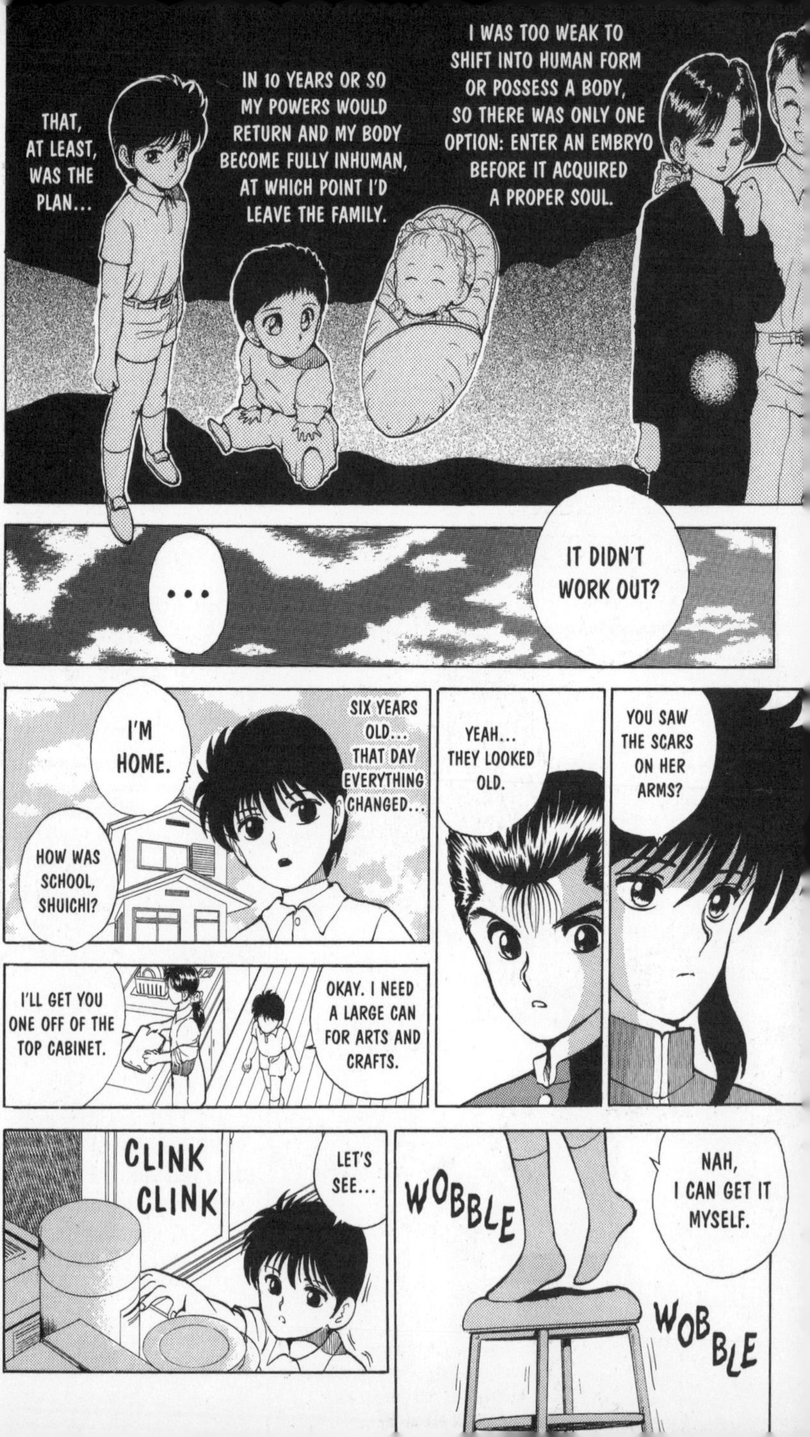
I WAS TOO WEAK TO SHIFT INTO HUMAN FORM OR POSSESS A BODY, SO THERE WAS ONLY ONE OPTION: ENTER AN EMBRYO BEFORE IT ACQUIRED A PROPER SOUL.
IN 10 YEARS OR SO MY POWERS WOULD RETURN AND MY BODY BECOME FULLY INHUMAN, AT WHICH POINT I'D LEAVE THE FAMILY.
THAT, AT LEAST, WAS THE PLAN...
IT DIDN'T WORK OUT?
...
YOU SAW THE SCARS ON HER ARMS?
YEAH... THEY LOOKED OLD.
SIX YEARS OLD... THAT DAY EVERYTHING CHANGED...
I'M HOME.
HOW WAS SCHOOL, SHUICHI?
OKAY. I NEED A LARGE CAN FOR ARTS AND CRAFTS.
I'LL GET YOU ONE OFF OF THE TOP CABINET.
NAH, I CAN GET IT MYSELF.
WOBBLE
WOBBLE
LET'S SEE...
CLINK
CLINK

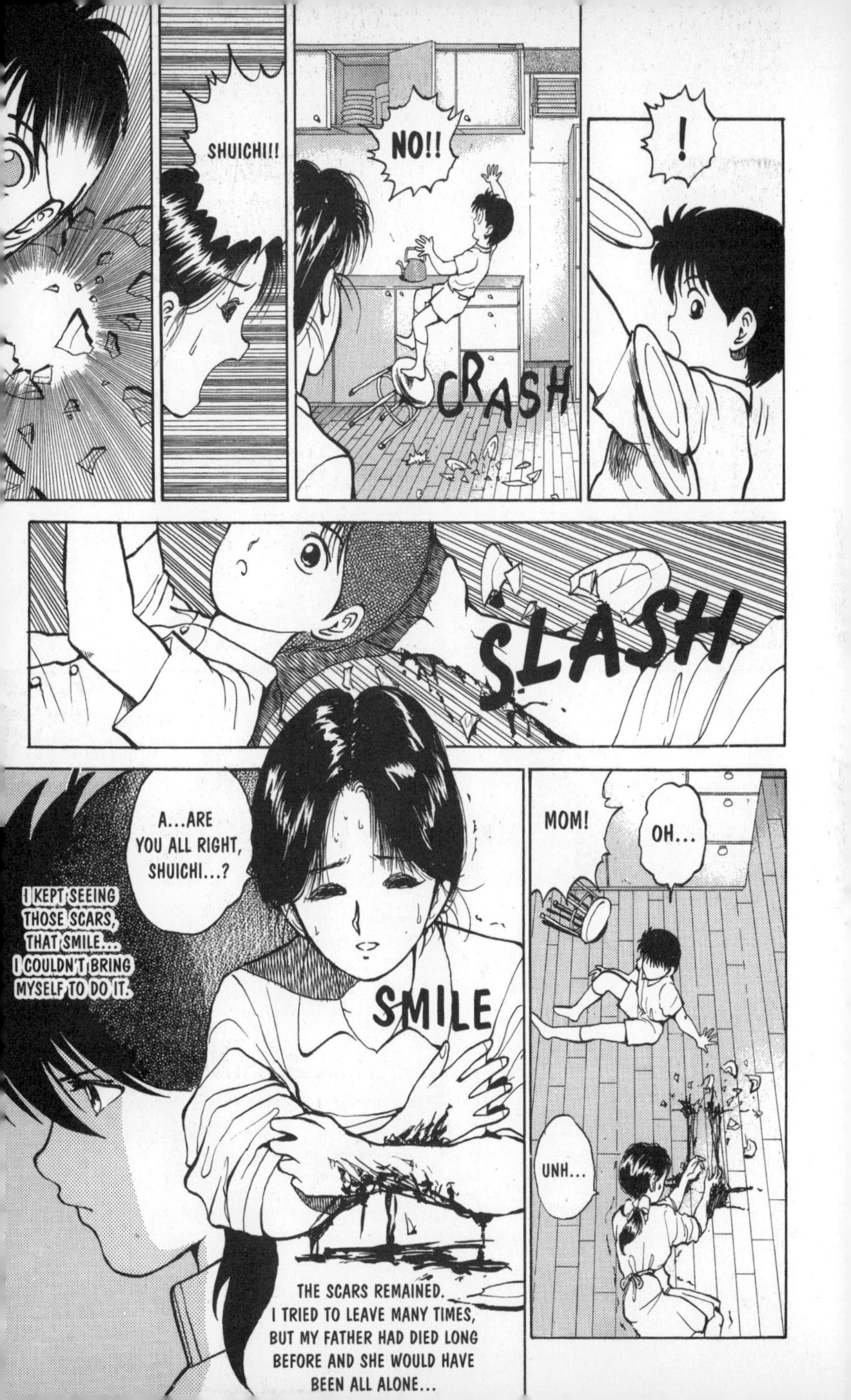
!
NO!!
CRASH
SHUICHI!!
SLASH
OH...
MOM!
UNH...
A...ARE YOU ALL RIGHT, SHUICHI...?
SMILE
I KEPT SEEING THOSE SCARS, THAT SMILE... I COULDN'T BRING MYSELF TO DO IT.
THE SCARS REMAINED. I TRIED TO LEAVE MANY TIMES, BUT MY FATHER HAD DIED LONG BEFORE AND SHE WOULD HAVE BEEN ALL ALONE...

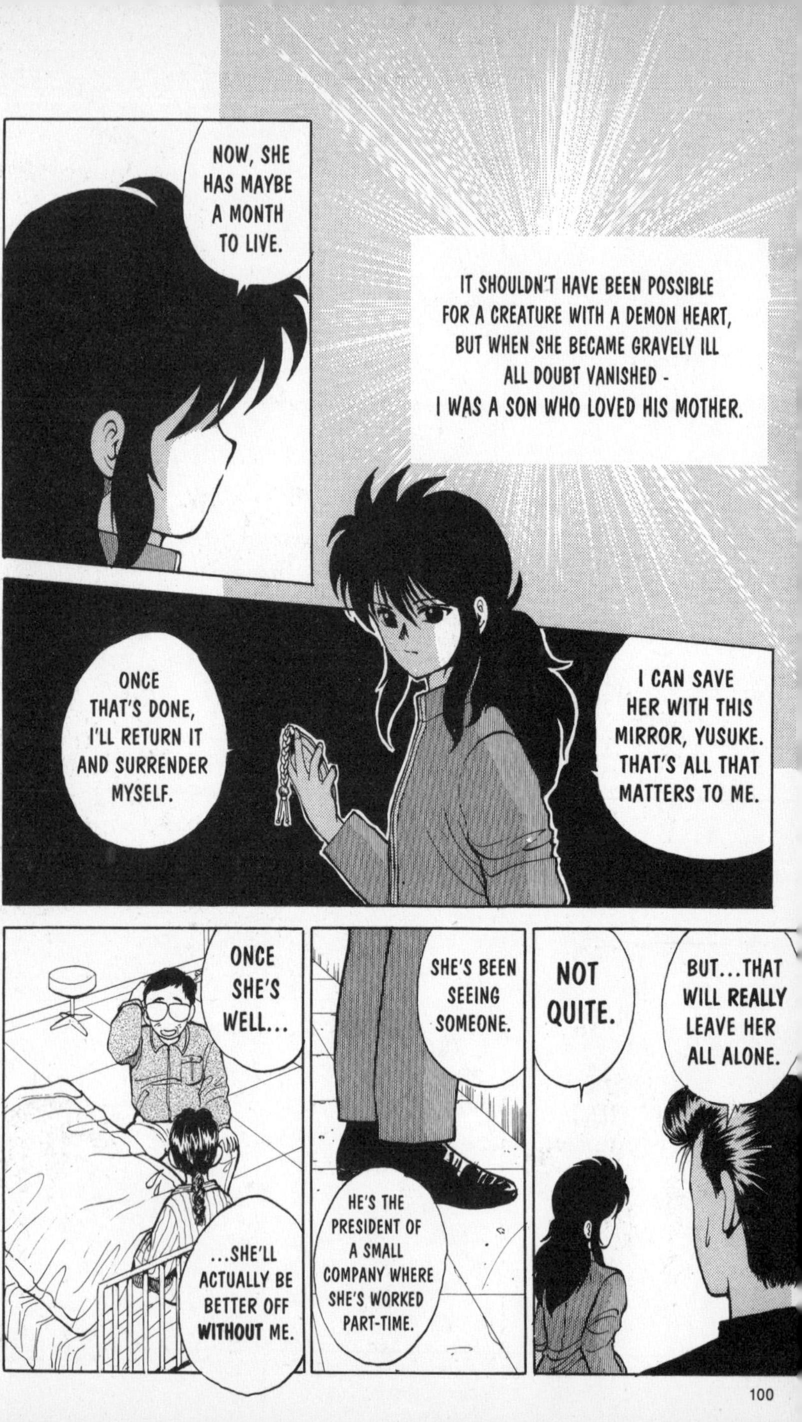
IT SHOULDN'T HAVE BEEN POSSIBLE FOR A CREATURE WITH A DEMON HEART, BUT WHEN SHE BECAME GRAVELY ILL ALL DOUBT VANISHED - I WAS A SON WHO LOVED HIS MOTHER.
NOW, SHE HAS MAYBE A MONTH TO LIVE.
I CAN SAVE HER WITH THIS MIRROR, YUSUKE. THAT'S ALL THAT MATTERS TO ME.
ONCE THAT'S DONE, I'LL RETURN IT AND SURRENDER MYSELF.
BUT...THAT WILL **REALLY** LEAVE HER ALL ALONE.
NOT QUITE.
SHE'S BEEN SEEING SOMEONE.
HE'S THE PRESIDENT OF A SMALL COMPANY WHERE SHE'S WORKED PART-TIME.
ONCE SHE'S WELL...
...SHE'LL ACTUALLY BE BETTER OFF **WITHOUT** ME.

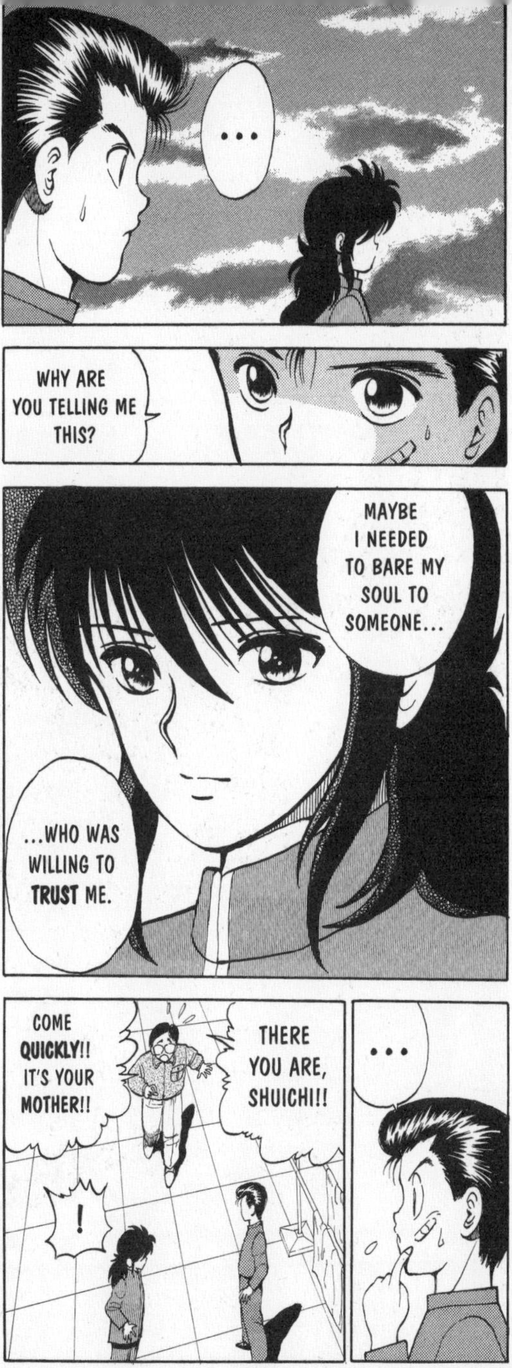
...
WHY ARE YOU TELLING ME THIS?
MAYBE I NEEDED TO BARE MY SOUL TO SOMEONE...
...WHO WAS WILLING TO **TRUST** ME.
...
THERE YOU ARE, SHUICHI!!
COME **QUICKLY!!** IT'S YOUR MOTHER!!
!
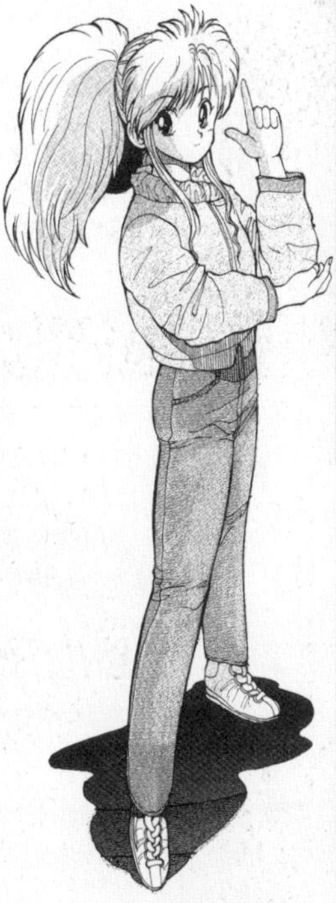

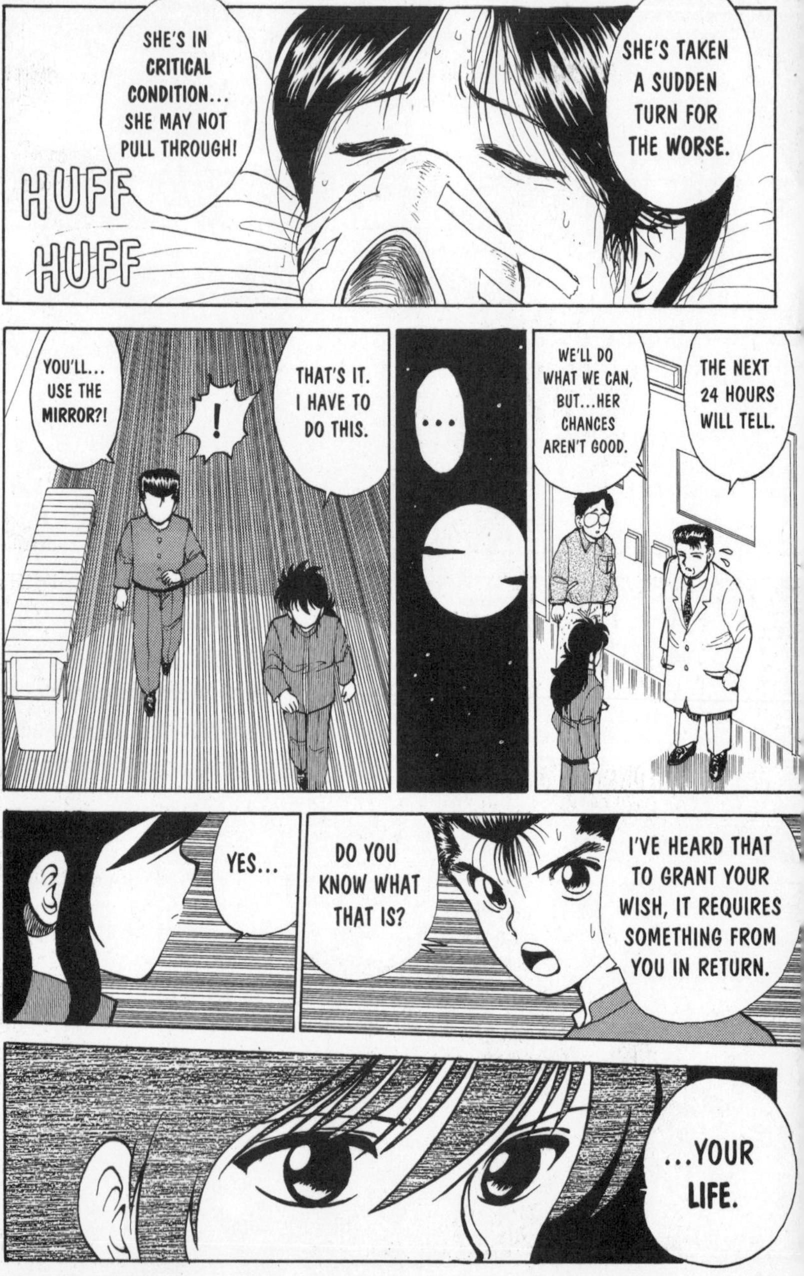
SHE'S TAKEN A SUDDEN TURN FOR THE WORSE.
SHE'S IN CRITICAL CONDITION... SHE MAY NOT PULL THROUGH!
HUFF
HUFF
THE NEXT 24 HOURS WILL TELL.
WE'LL DO WHAT WE CAN, BUT...HER CHANCES AREN'T GOOD.
...
THAT'S IT. I HAVE TO DO THIS.
!
YOU'LL... USE THE MIRROR?!
I'VE HEARD THAT TO GRANT YOUR WISH, IT REQUIRES SOMETHING FROM YOU IN RETURN.
DO YOU KNOW WHAT THAT IS?
YES...
...YOUR LIFE.

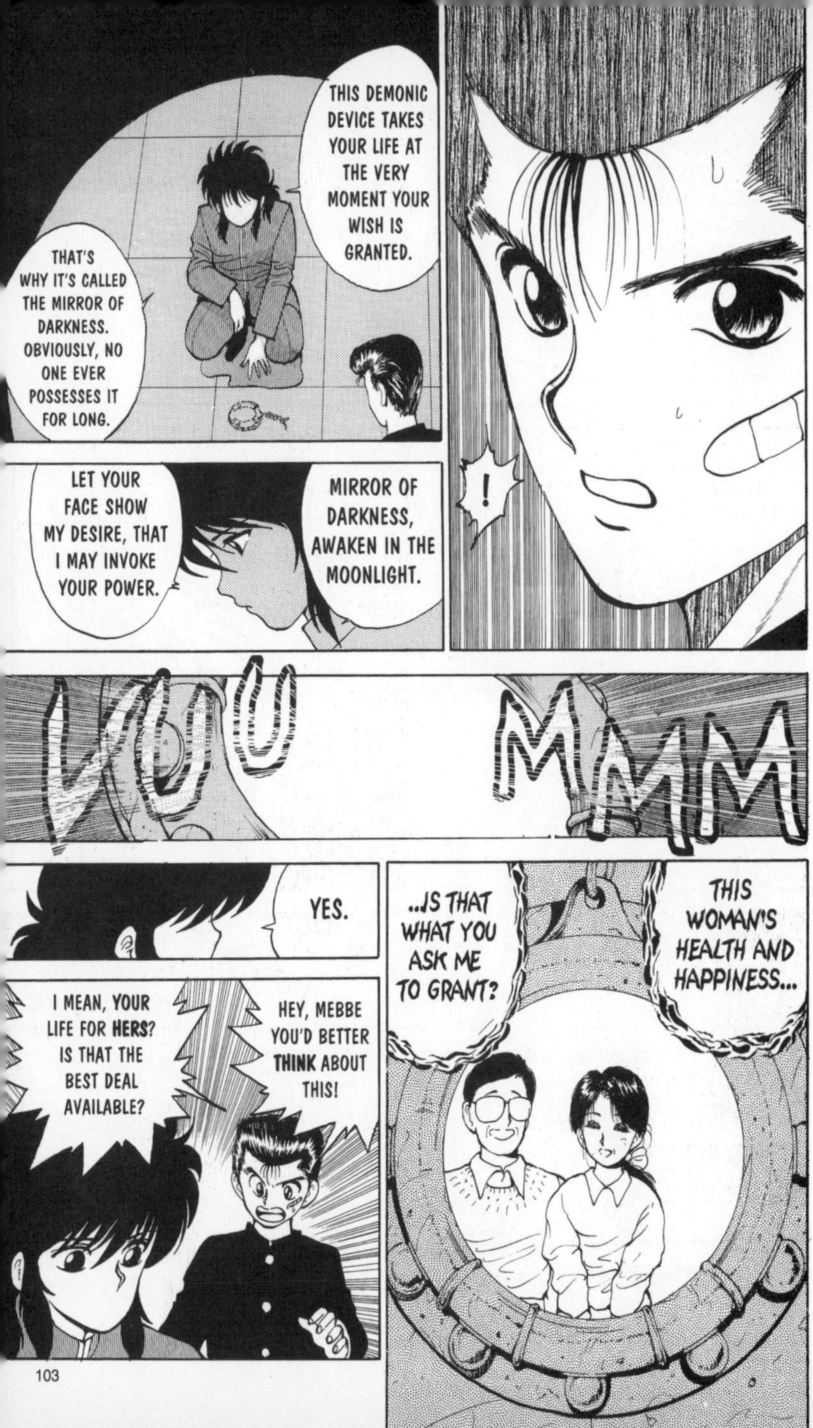
!
THIS DEMONIC DEVICE TAKES YOUR LIFE AT THE VERY MOMENT YOUR WISH IS GRANTED.
THAT'S WHY IT'S CALLED THE MIRROR OF DARKNESS. OBVIOUSLY, NO ONE EVER POSSESSES IT FOR LONG.
MIRROR OF DARKNESS, AWAKEN IN THE MOONLIGHT.
LET YOUR FACE SHOW MY DESIRE, THAT I MAY INVOKE YOUR POWER.
WUUU MMMM
THIS WOMAN'S HEALTH AND HAPPINESS...
...IS THAT WHAT YOU ASK ME TO GRANT?
YES.
HEY, MEBBE YOU'D BETTER **THINK** ABOUT THIS!
I MEAN, **YOUR** LIFE FOR **HERS**? IS THAT THE BEST DEAL AVAILABLE?

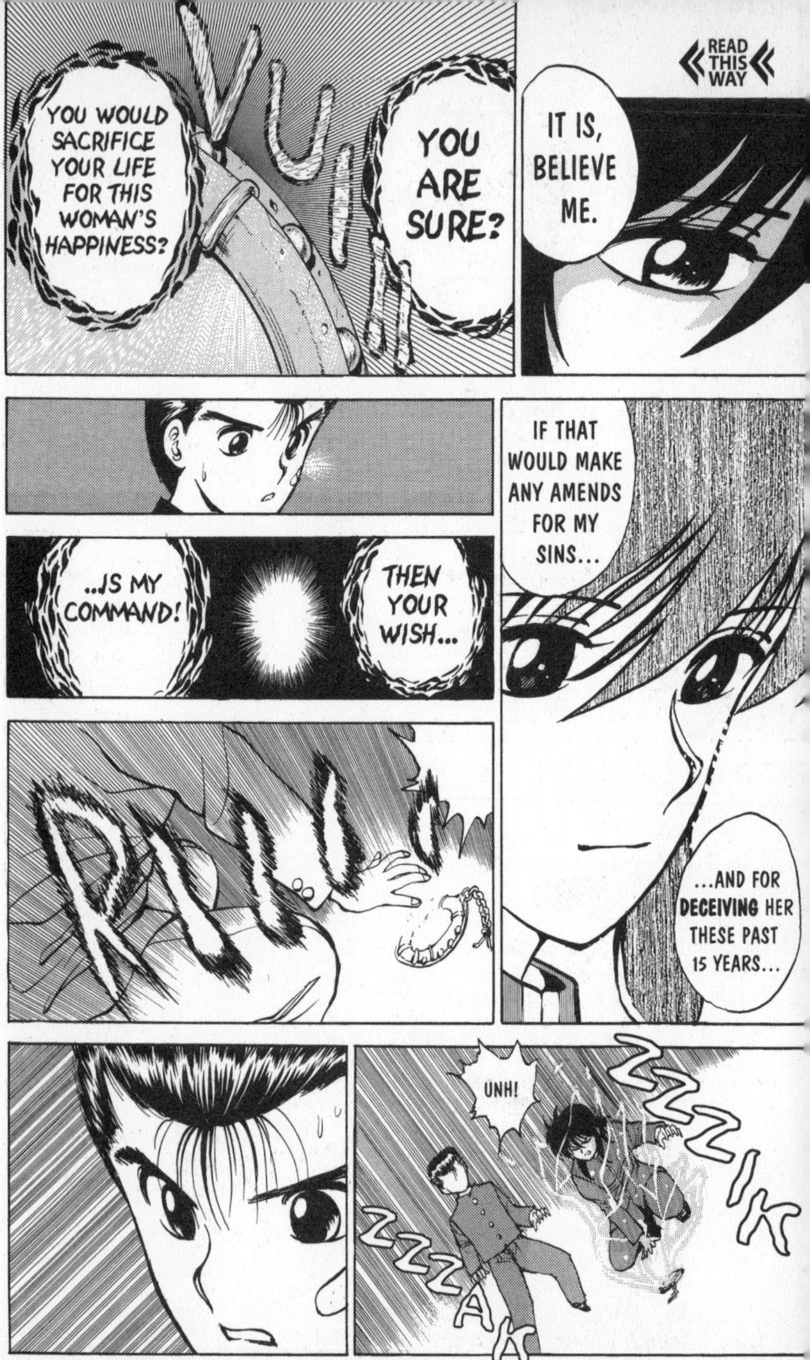
IT IS, BELIEVE ME.
YOU ARE SURE?
YOU WOULD SACRIFICE YOUR LIFE FOR THIS WOMAN'S HAPPINESS?
IF THAT WOULD MAKE ANY AMENDS FOR MY SINS...
...AND FOR **DECEIVING** HER THESE PAST 15 YEARS...
THEN YOUR WISH...
...IS MY COMMAND!
UNH!
ZZZZIK
ZZZZAK

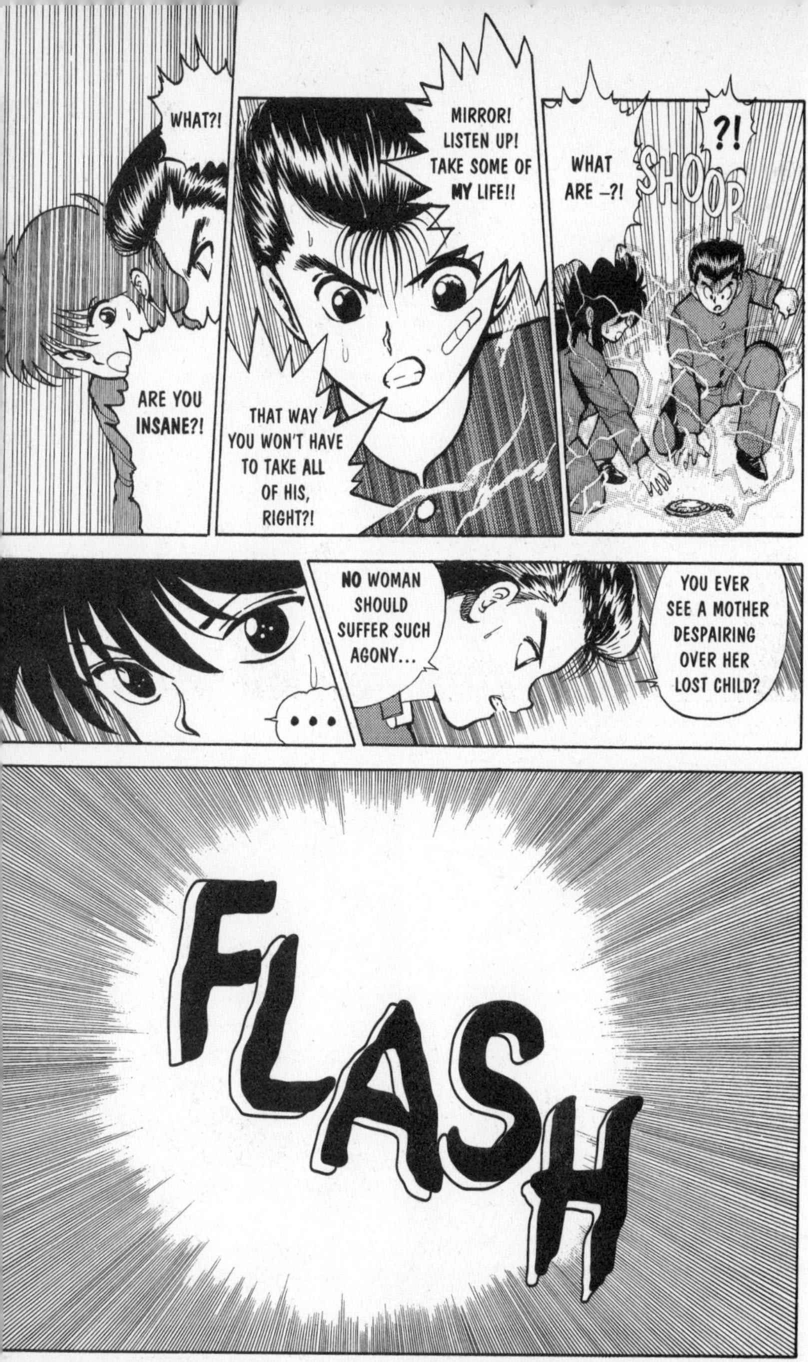
?!
SHOOP
WHAT ARE –?!
MIRROR! LISTEN UP! TAKE SOME OF MY LIFE!!
THAT WAY YOU WON'T HAVE TO TAKE ALL OF HIS, RIGHT?!
WHAT?!
ARE YOU INSANE?!
YOU EVER SEE A MOTHER DESPAIRING OVER HER LOST CHILD?
NO WOMAN SHOULD SUFFER SUCH AGONY...
...
FLASH

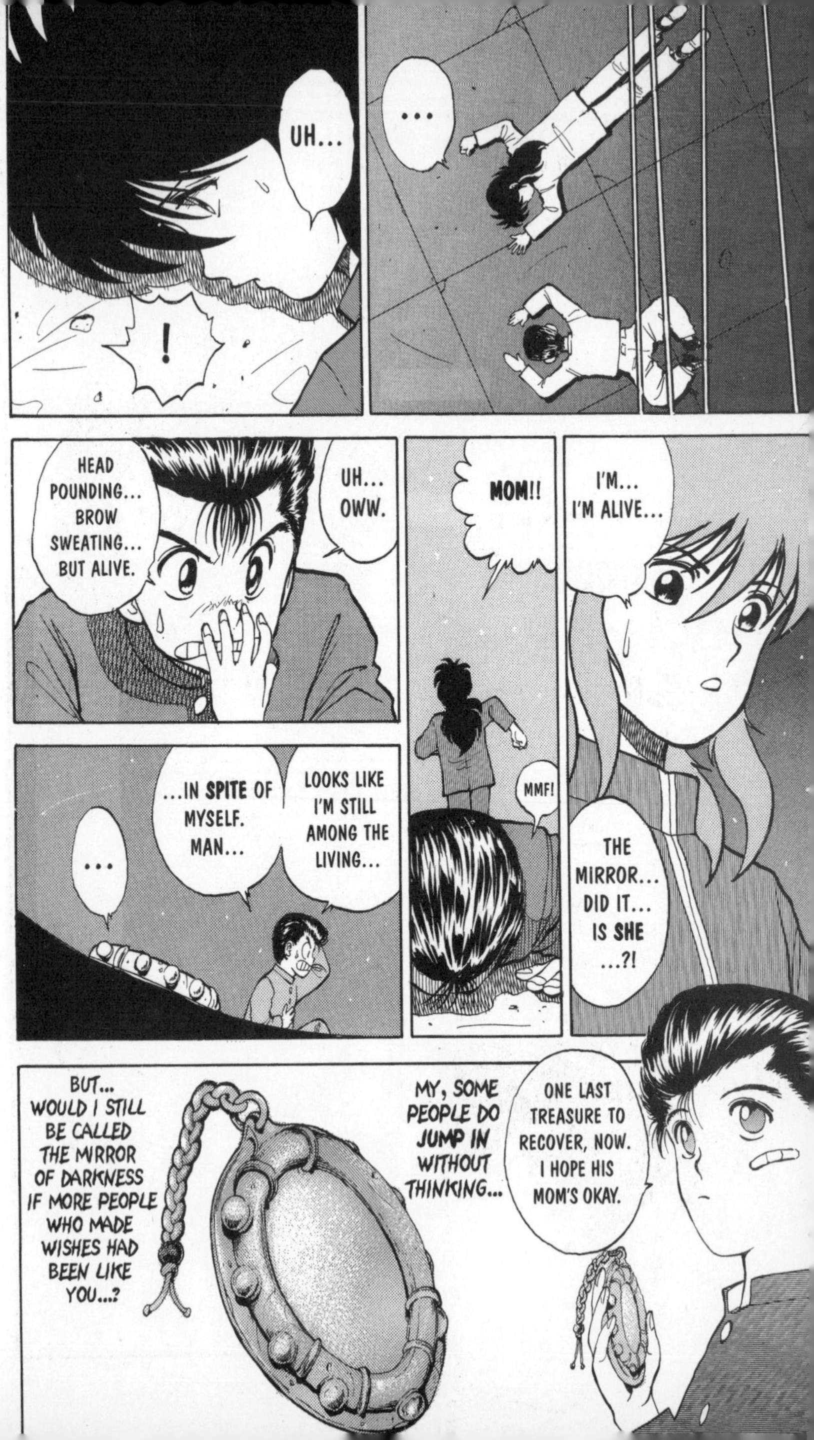
...
UH...
!
I'M... I'M ALIVE...
THE MIRROR... DID IT... IS SHE ...?!
MOM!!
MMF!
UH... OWW.
HEAD POUNDING... BROW SWEATING... BUT ALIVE.
LOOKS LIKE I'M STILL AMONG THE LIVING...
...IN SPITE OF MYSELF. MAN...
...
ONE LAST TREASURE TO RECOVER, NOW. I HOPE HIS MOM'S OKAY.
MY, SOME PEOPLE DO JUMP IN WITHOUT THINKING...
BUT... WOULD I STILL BE CALLED THE MIRROR OF DARKNESS IF MORE PEOPLE WHO MADE WISHES HAD BEEN LIKE YOU...?

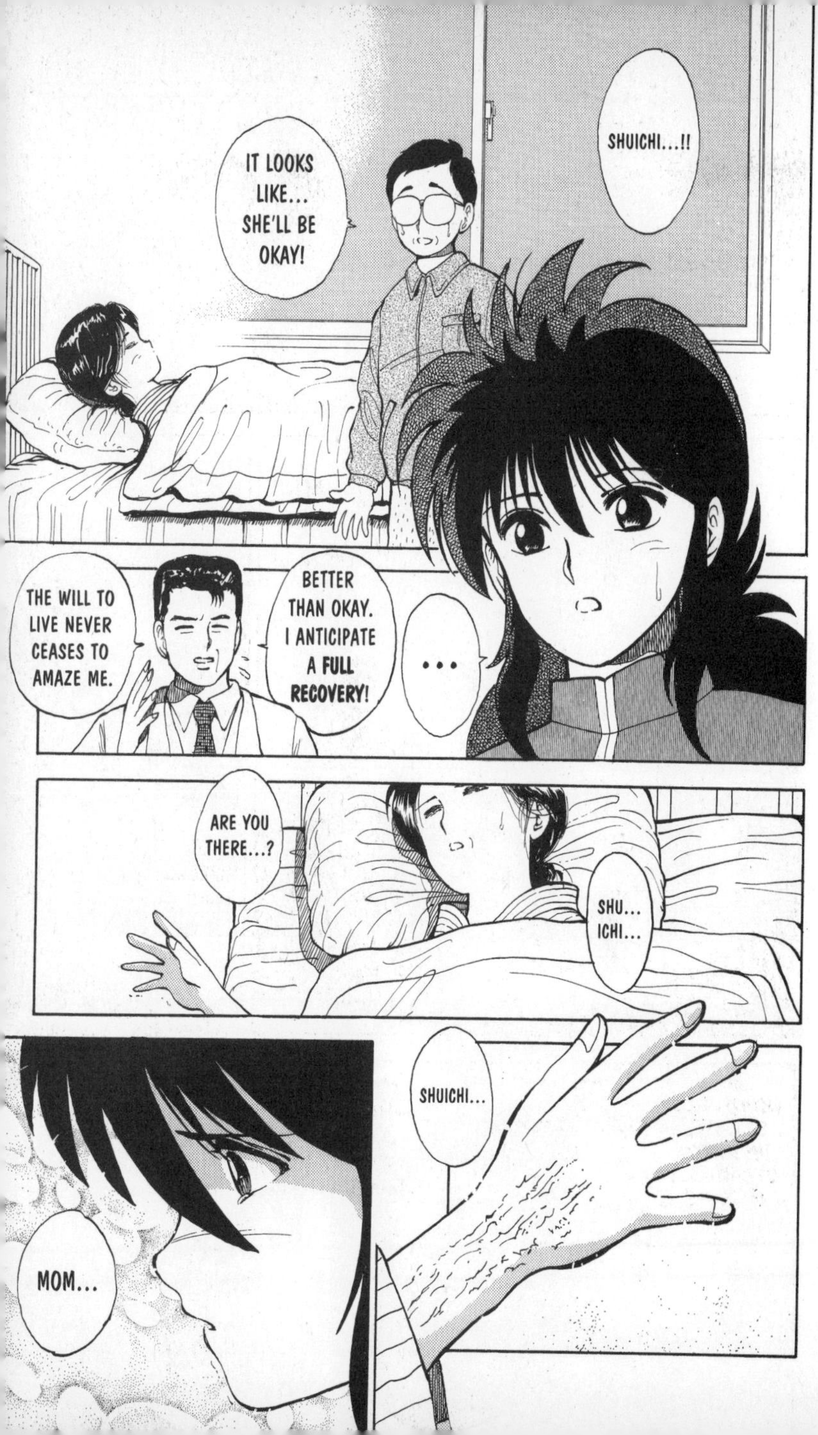
SHUICHI...!!
IT LOOKS LIKE... SHE'LL BE OKAY!
...
BETTER THAN OKAY. I ANTICIPATE A **FULL** RECOVERY!
THE WILL TO LIVE NEVER CEASES TO AMAZE ME.
SHU... ICHI...
ARE YOU THERE...?
SHUICHI...
MOM...

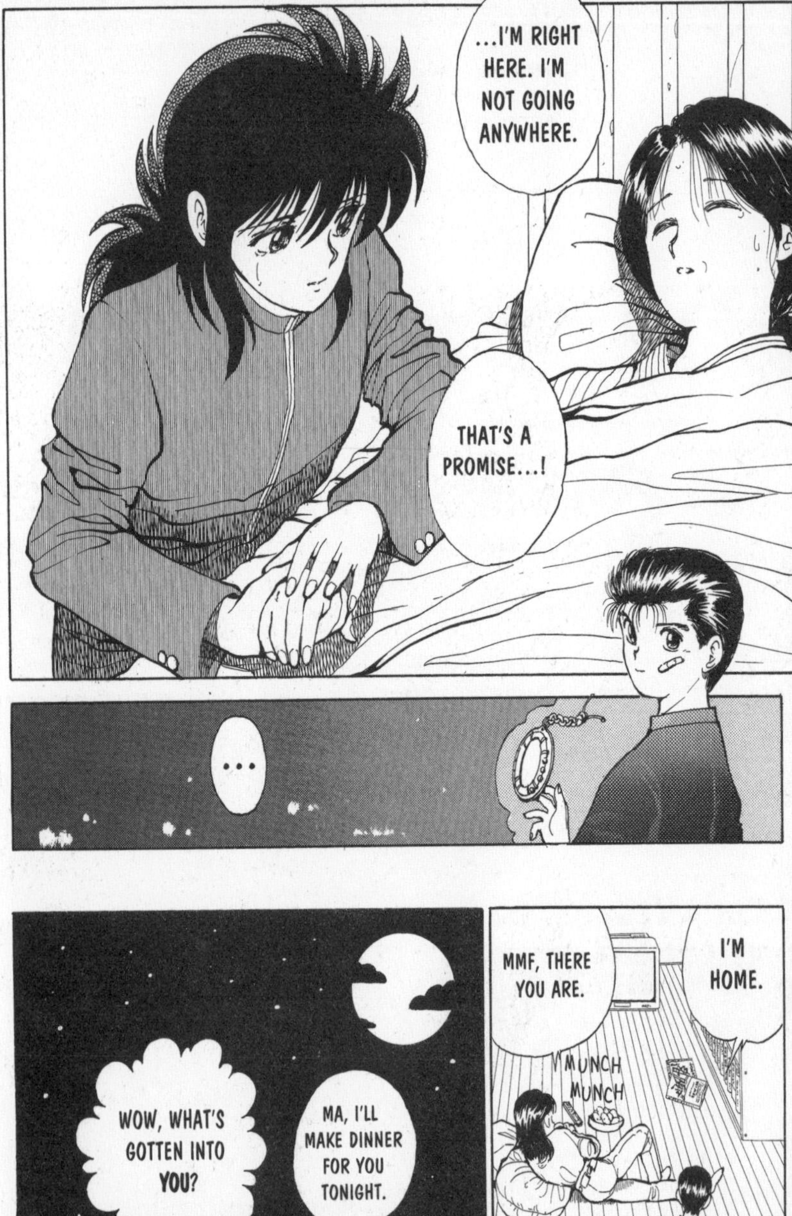
...I'M RIGHT HERE. I'M NOT GOING ANYWHERE.
THAT'S A PROMISE...!
...
I'M HOME.
MMF, THERE YOU ARE.
MUNCH MUNCH
MA, I'LL MAKE DINNER FOR YOU TONIGHT.
WOW, WHAT'S GOTTEN INTO YOU?

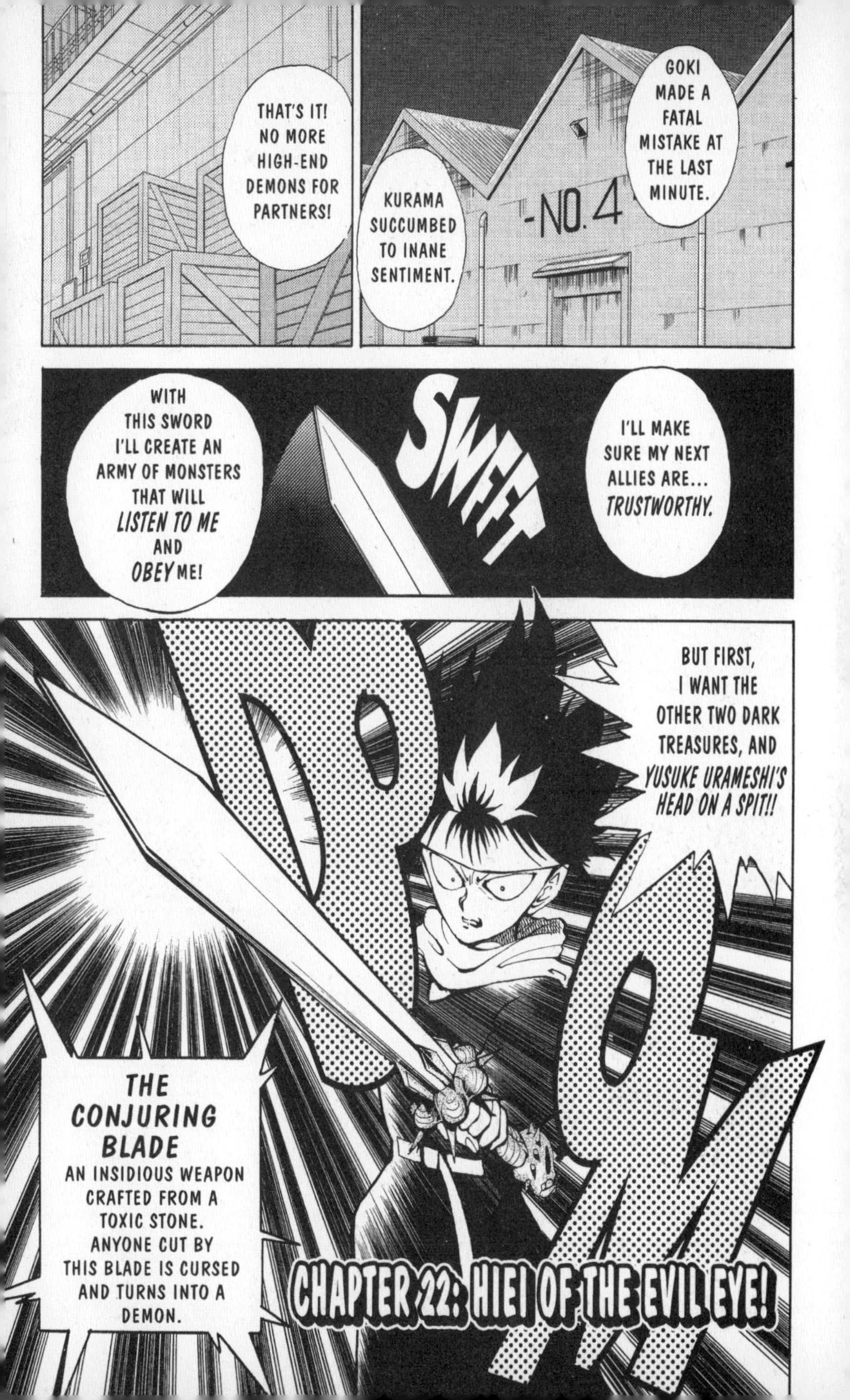

GOKI MADE A FATAL MISTAKE AT THE LAST MINUTE.
KURAMA SUCCUMBED TO INANE SENTIMENT.
THAT'S IT! NO MORE HIGH-END DEMONS FOR PARTNERS!
I'LL MAKE SURE MY NEXT ALLIES ARE... *TRUSTWORTHY.*
WITH THIS SWORD I'LL CREATE AN ARMY OF MONSTERS THAT WILL *LISTEN TO ME* AND *OBEY* ME!
BUT FIRST, I WANT THE OTHER TWO DARK TREASURES, AND *YUSUKE URAMESHI'S HEAD ON A SPIT!!*
THE CONJURING BLADE
AN INSIDIOUS WEAPON CRAFTED FROM A TOXIC STONE. ANYONE CUT BY THIS BLADE IS CURSED AND TURNS INTO A DEMON.
CHAPTER 22: HIEI OF THE EVIL EYE!

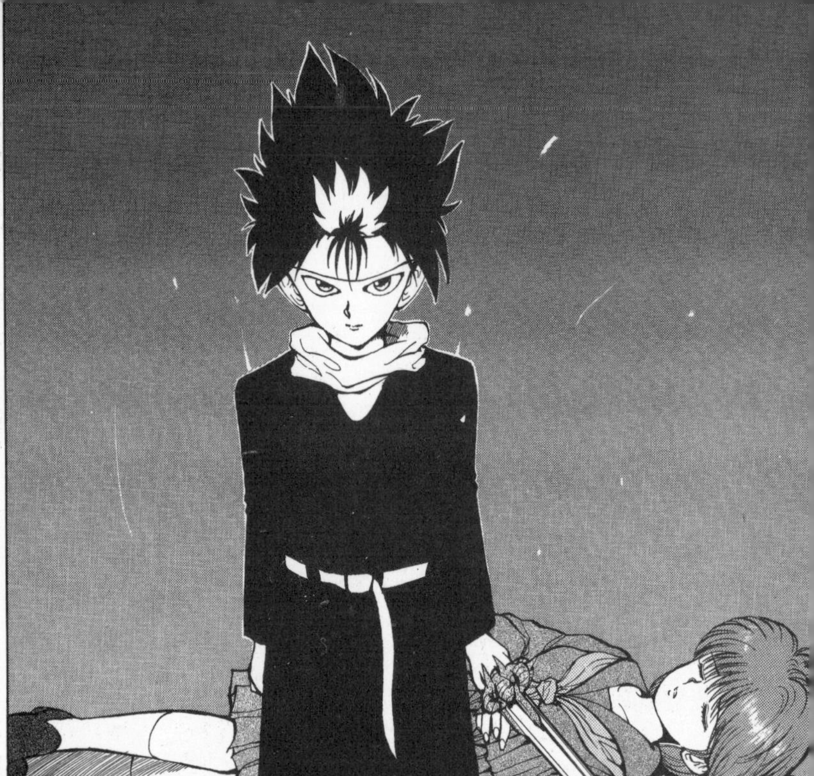

Chapter 22: HIEI OF THE EVIL EYE!!

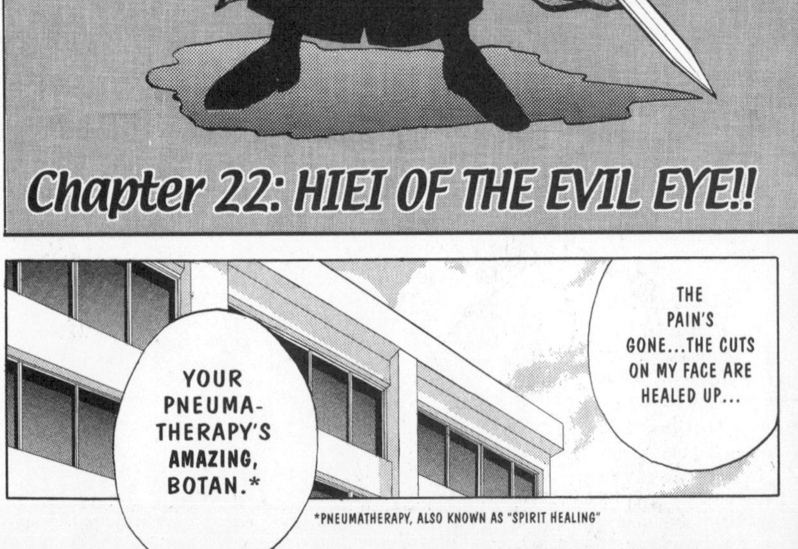
THE PAIN'S GONE...THE CUTS ON MY FACE ARE HEALED UP...
YOUR PNEUMA-THERAPY'S AMAZING, BOTAN.*

*PNEUMATHERAPY, ALSO KNOWN AS "SPIRIT HEALING"

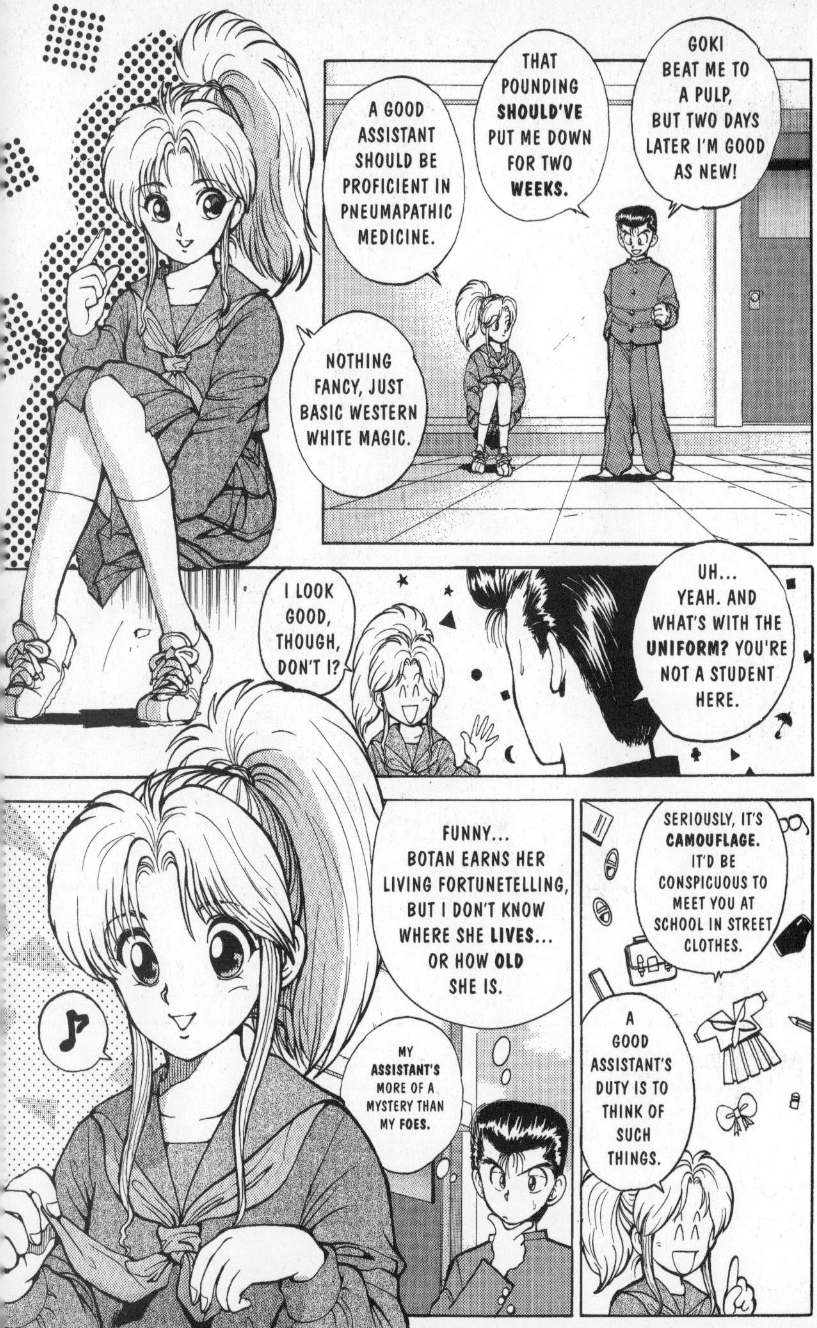
GOKI BEAT ME TO A PULP, BUT TWO DAYS LATER I'M GOOD AS NEW!
THAT POUNDING **SHOULD'VE** PUT ME DOWN FOR TWO **WEEKS.**
A GOOD ASSISTANT SHOULD BE PROFICIENT IN PNEUMAPATHIC MEDICINE.
NOTHING FANCY, JUST BASIC WESTERN WHITE MAGIC.
UH... YEAH. AND WHAT'S WITH THE **UNIFORM?** YOU'RE NOT A STUDENT HERE.
I LOOK GOOD, THOUGH, DON'T I?
SERIOUSLY, IT'S **CAMOUFLAGE.** IT'D BE CONSPICUOUS TO MEET YOU AT SCHOOL IN STREET CLOTHES.
A GOOD ASSISTANT'S DUTY IS TO THINK OF SUCH THINGS.
FUNNY... BOTAN EARNS HER LIVING FORTUNETELLING, BUT I DON'T KNOW WHERE SHE **LIVES**... OR HOW **OLD** SHE IS.
MY **ASSISTANT'S** MORE OF A MYSTERY THAN MY **FOES.**
♪

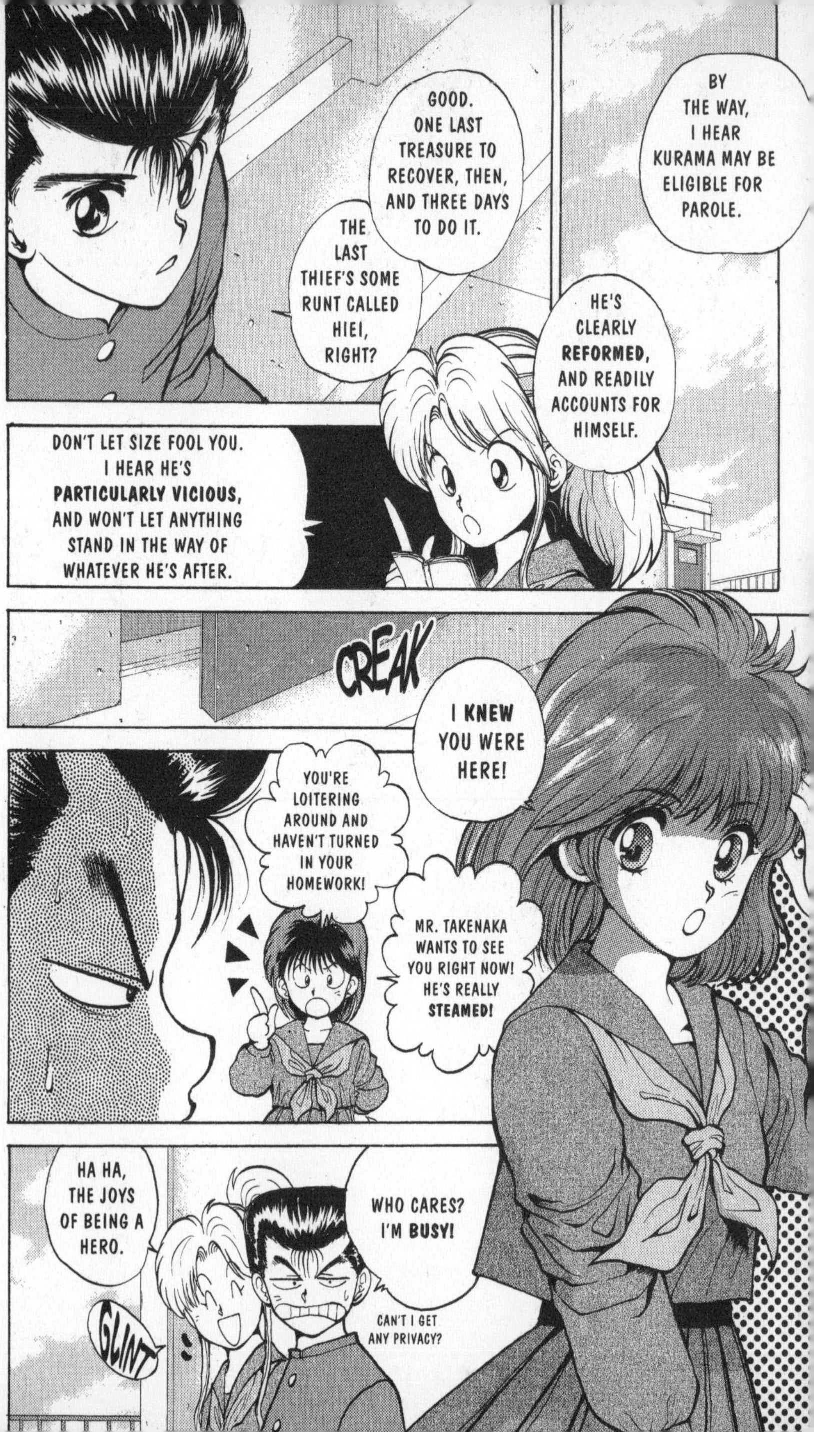
BY THE WAY, I HEAR KURAMA MAY BE ELIGIBLE FOR PAROLE.
HE'S CLEARLY **REFORMED**, AND READILY ACCOUNTS FOR HIMSELF.
GOOD. ONE LAST TREASURE TO RECOVER, THEN, AND THREE DAYS TO DO IT.
THE LAST THIEF'S SOME RUNT CALLED HIEI, RIGHT?
DON'T LET SIZE FOOL YOU. I HEAR HE'S **PARTICULARLY VICIOUS**, AND WON'T LET ANYTHING STAND IN THE WAY OF WHATEVER HE'S AFTER.
CREAK
I **KNEW** YOU WERE HERE!
YOU'RE LOITERING AROUND AND HAVEN'T TURNED IN YOUR HOMEWORK!
MR. TAKENAKA WANTS TO SEE YOU RIGHT NOW! HE'S REALLY **STEAMED!**
WHO CARES? I'M **BUSY!**
CAN'T I GET ANY PRIVACY?
HA HA, THE JOYS OF BEING A HERO.
GLINT

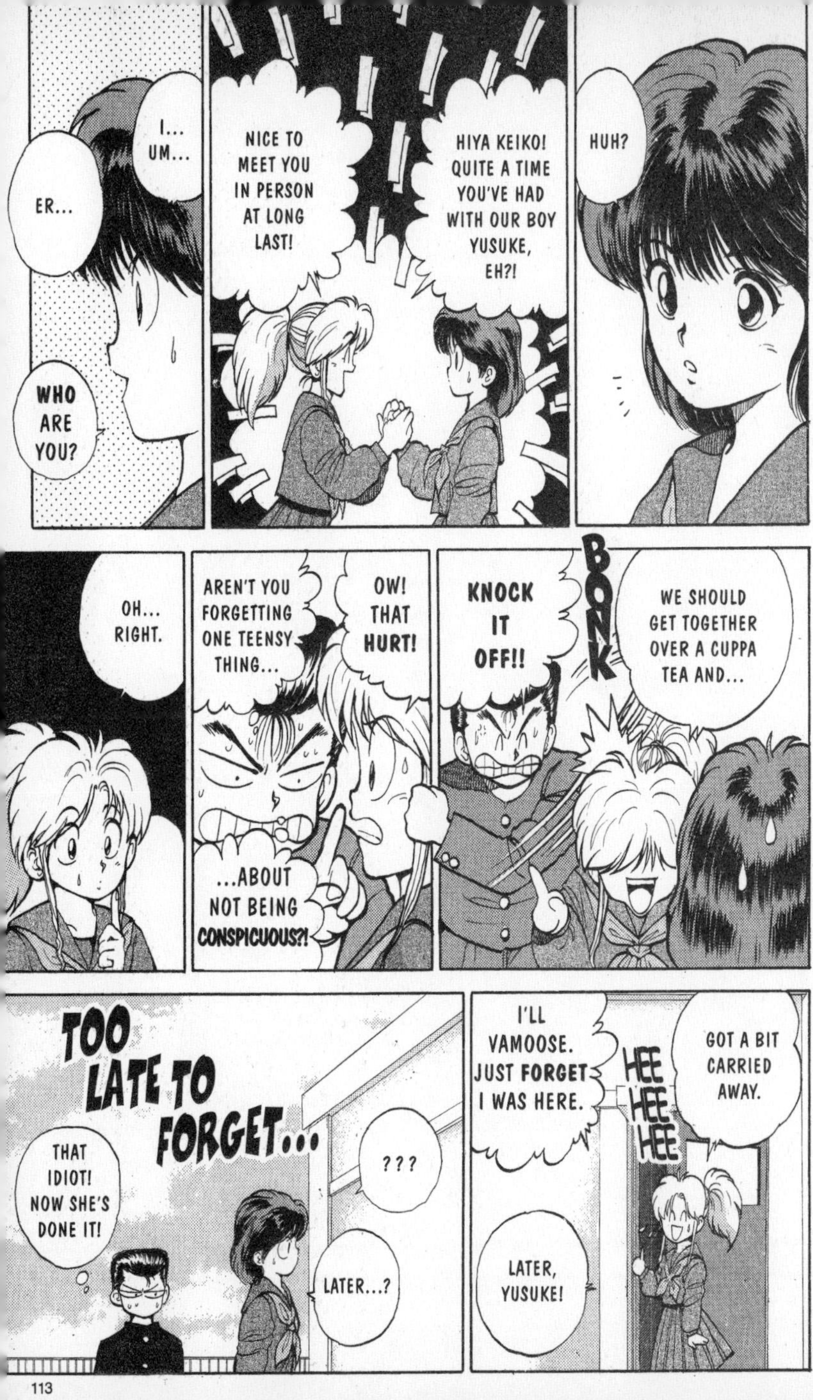
HUH?
HIYA KEIKO! QUITE A TIME YOU'VE HAD WITH OUR BOY YUSUKE, EH?!
NICE TO MEET YOU IN PERSON AT LONG LAST!
I... UM...
ER...
WHO ARE YOU?
WE SHOULD GET TOGETHER OVER A CUPPA TEA AND...
BONK
KNOCK IT OFF!!
OW! THAT HURT!
AREN'T YOU FORGETTING ONE TEENSY THING...
...ABOUT NOT BEING CONSPICUOUS?!
OH... RIGHT.
GOT A BIT CARRIED AWAY.
HEE HEE HEE
I'LL VAMOOSE. JUST FORGET I WAS HERE.
LATER, YUSUKE!
???
LATER...?
TOO LATE TO FORGET...
THAT IDIOT! NOW SHE'S DONE IT!

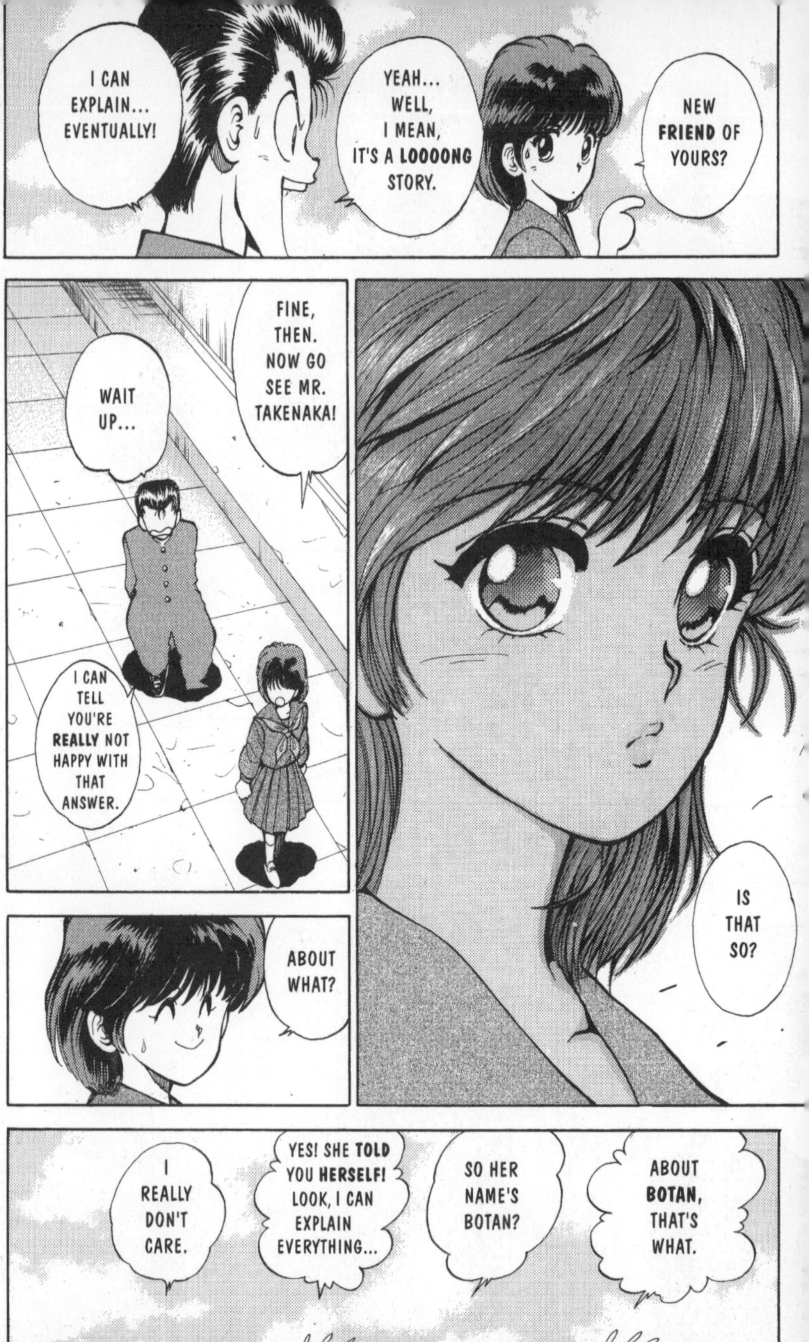
NEW **FRIEND** OF YOURS?
YEAH... WELL, I MEAN, IT'S A **LOOOONG** STORY.
I CAN EXPLAIN... EVENTUALLY!
IS THAT SO?
FINE, THEN. NOW GO SEE MR. TAKENAKA!
WAIT UP...
I CAN TELL YOU'RE **REALLY** NOT HAPPY WITH THAT ANSWER.
ABOUT WHAT?
ABOUT **BOTAN**, THAT'S WHAT.
SO HER NAME'S BOTAN?
YES! SHE **TOLD** YOU **HERSELF**! LOOK, I CAN EXPLAIN EVERYTHING...
I REALLY DON'T CARE.

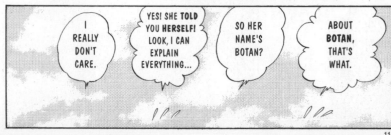

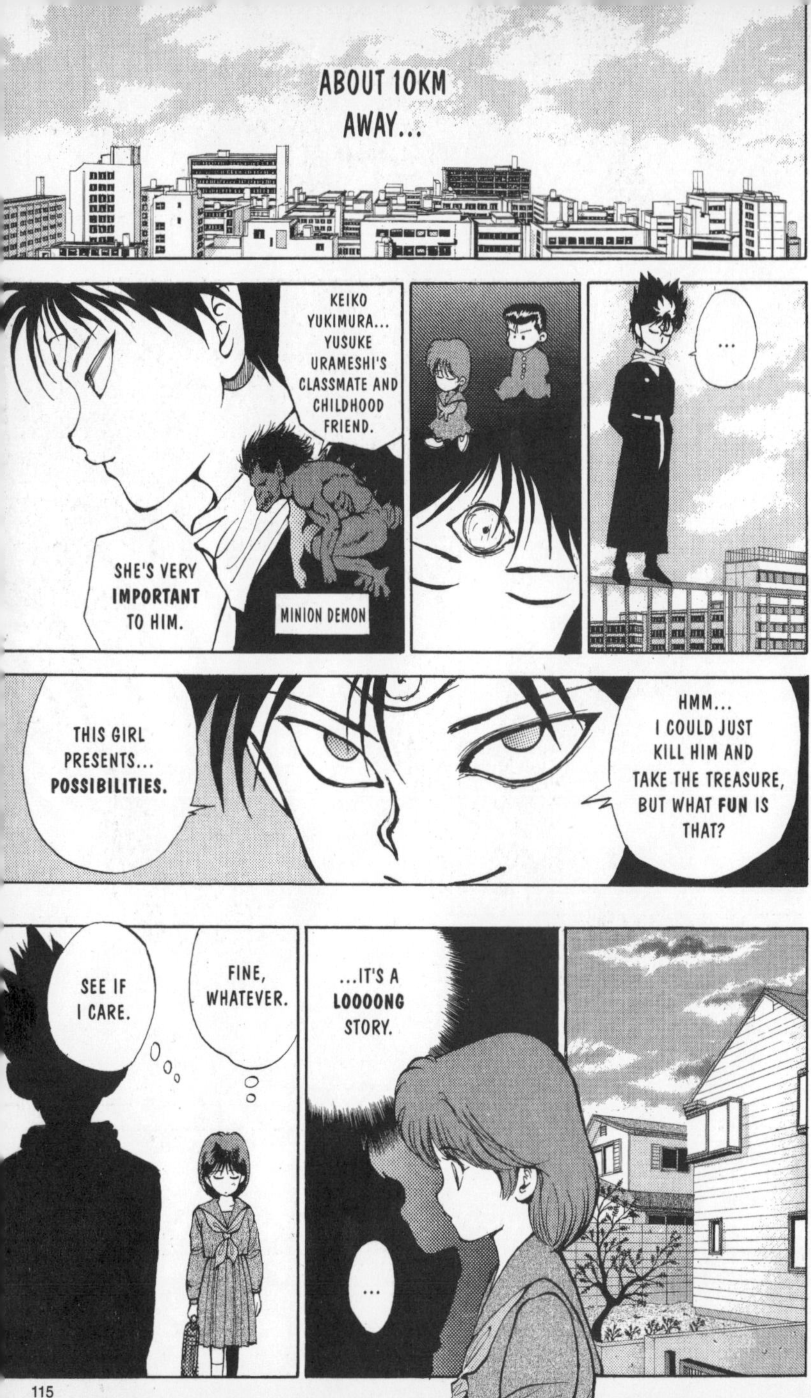
ABOUT 10KM AWAY...
...
KEIKO YUKIMURA... YUSUKE URAMESHI'S CLASSMATE AND CHILDHOOD FRIEND.
SHE'S VERY **IMPORTANT** TO HIM.
MINION DEMON
HMM... I COULD JUST KILL HIM AND TAKE THE TREASURE, BUT WHAT **FUN** IS THAT?
THIS GIRL PRESENTS... **POSSIBILITIES.**
...IT'S A **LOOOONG** STORY.
...
FINE, WHATEVER.
SEE IF I CARE.

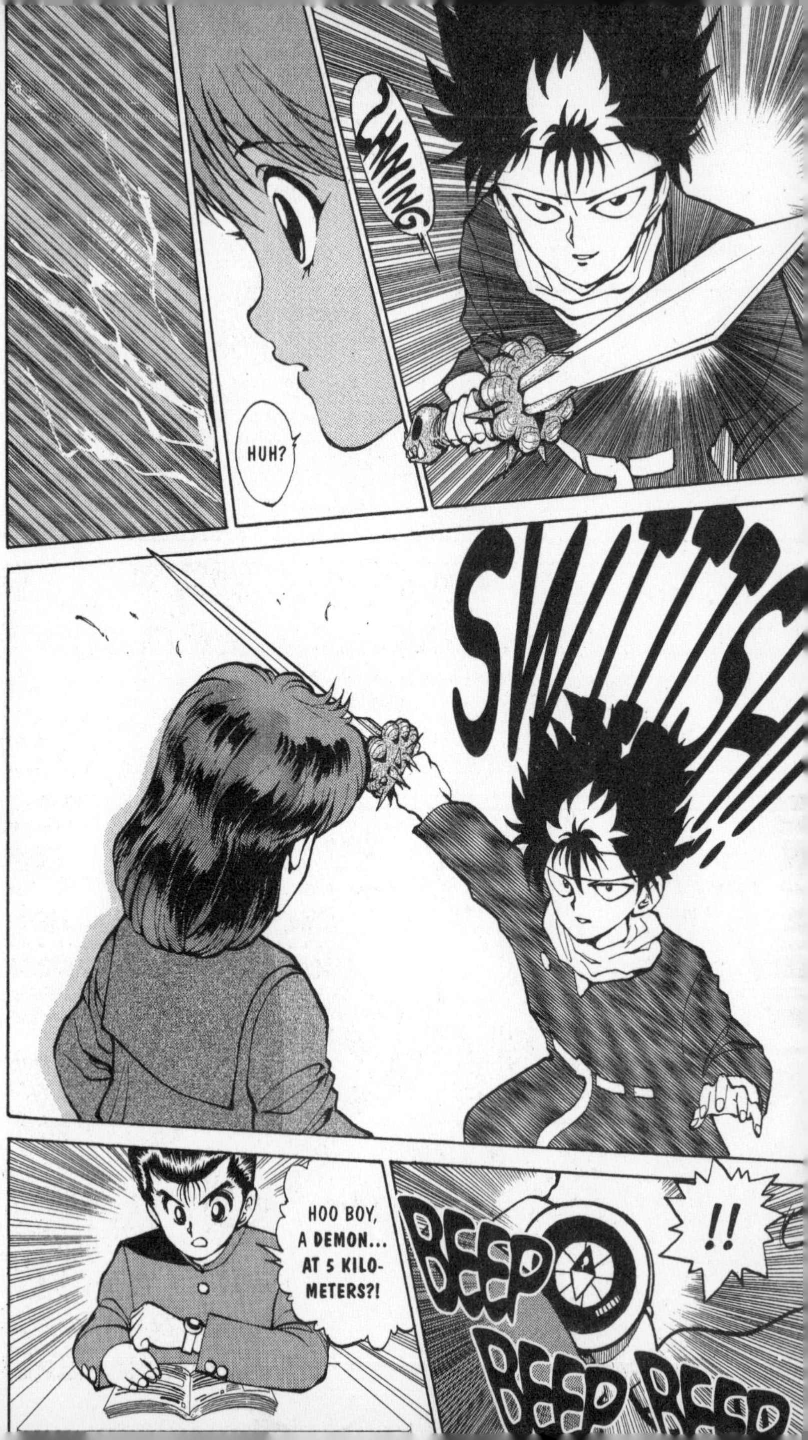
CHWING
HUH?
SWIISH!!
BEEP
BEEP BEEP
!!
HOO BOY, A DEMON... AT 5 KILO-METERS?!

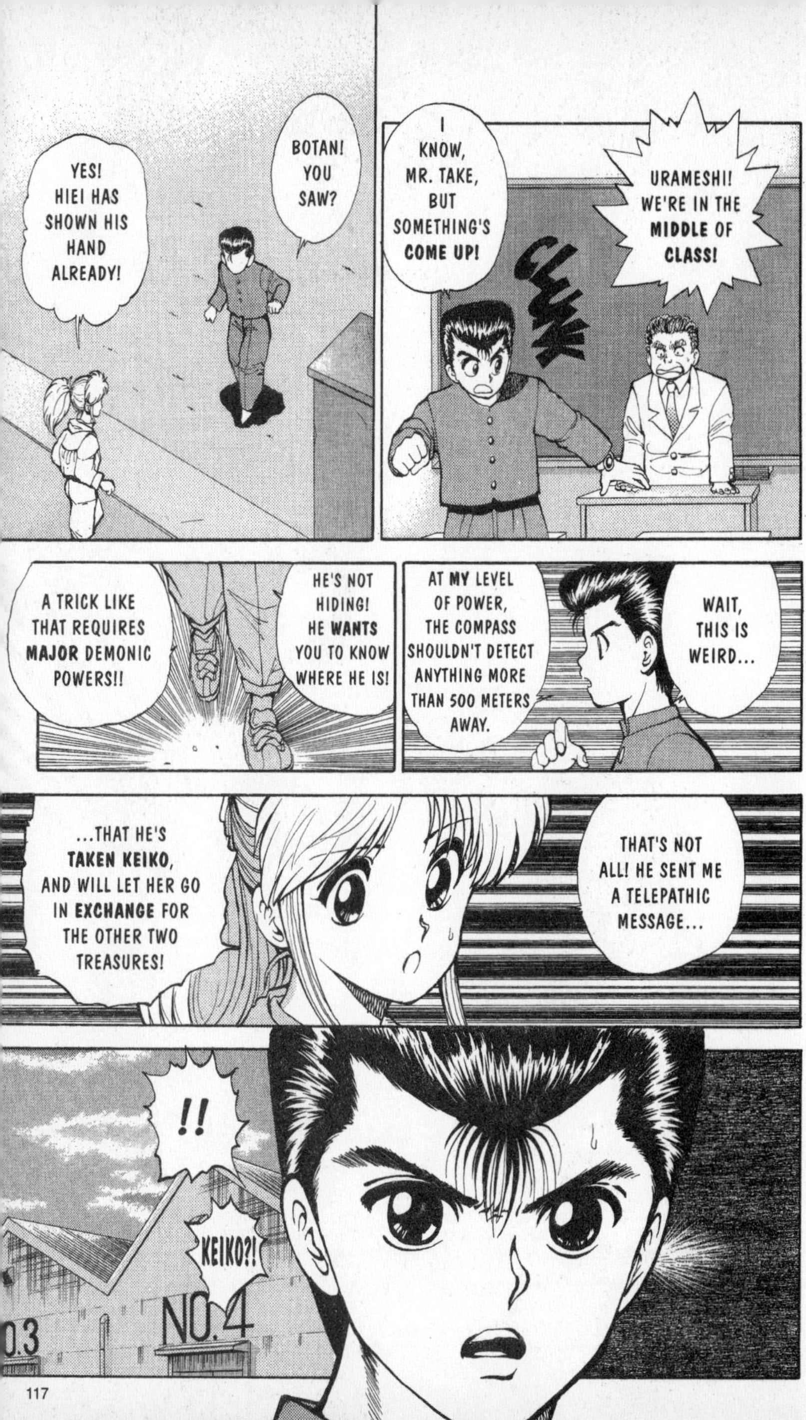
URAMESHI! WE'RE IN THE MIDDLE OF CLASS!
CLUNK
I KNOW, MR. TAKE, BUT SOMETHING'S COME UP!
BOTAN! YOU SAW?
YES! HIEI HAS SHOWN HIS HAND ALREADY!
WAIT, THIS IS WEIRD...
AT MY LEVEL OF POWER, THE COMPASS SHOULDN'T DETECT ANYTHING MORE THAN 500 METERS AWAY.
HE'S NOT HIDING! HE WANTS YOU TO KNOW WHERE HE IS!
A TRICK LIKE THAT REQUIRES MAJOR DEMONIC POWERS!!
THAT'S NOT ALL! HE SENT ME A TELEPATHIC MESSAGE...
...THAT HE'S TAKEN KEIKO, AND WILL LET HER GO IN EXCHANGE FOR THE OTHER TWO TREASURES!
!!
KEIKO?!
NO.4

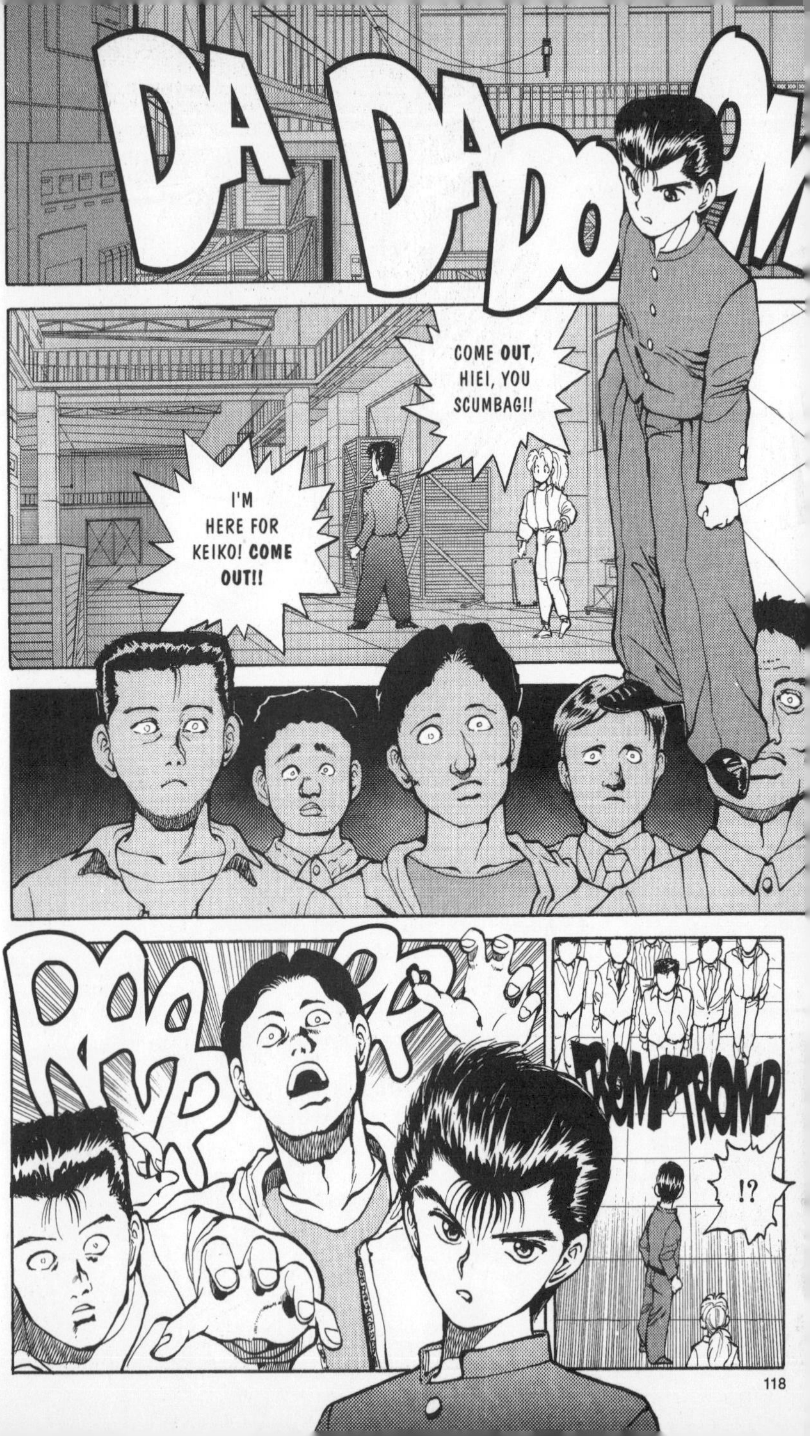
DA DADOOM
COME OUT, HIEI, YOU SCUMBAG!!
I'M HERE FOR KEIKO! COME OUT!!
TROMPTROMP
!?

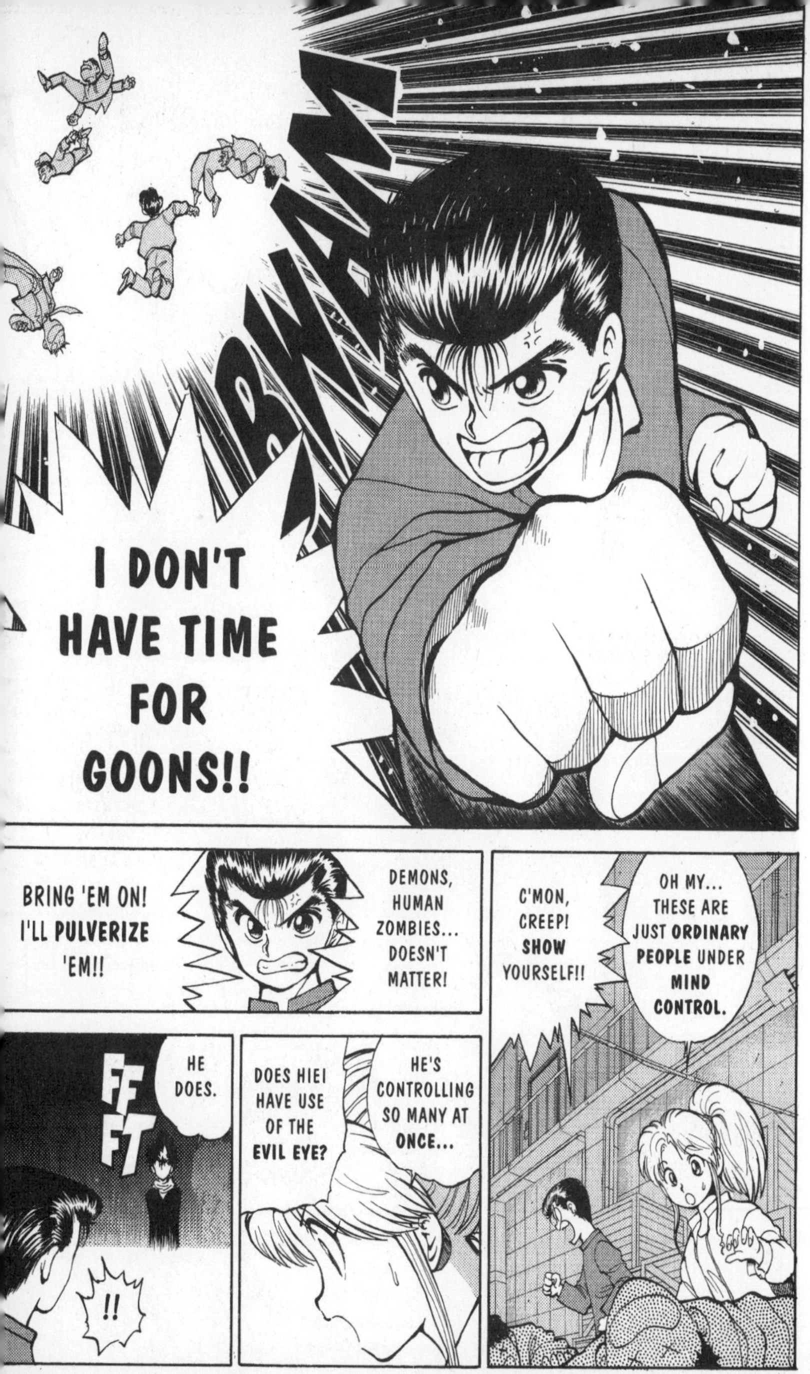
BWAM
I DON'T HAVE TIME FOR GOONS!!
OH MY... THESE ARE JUST ORDINARY PEOPLE UNDER MIND CONTROL.
C'MON, CREEP! SHOW YOURSELF!!
DEMONS, HUMAN ZOMBIES... DOESN'T MATTER!
BRING 'EM ON! I'LL PULVERIZE 'EM!!
HE'S CONTROLLING SO MANY AT ONCE...
DOES HIEI HAVE USE OF THE EVIL EYE?
HE DOES.
FFFT
!!

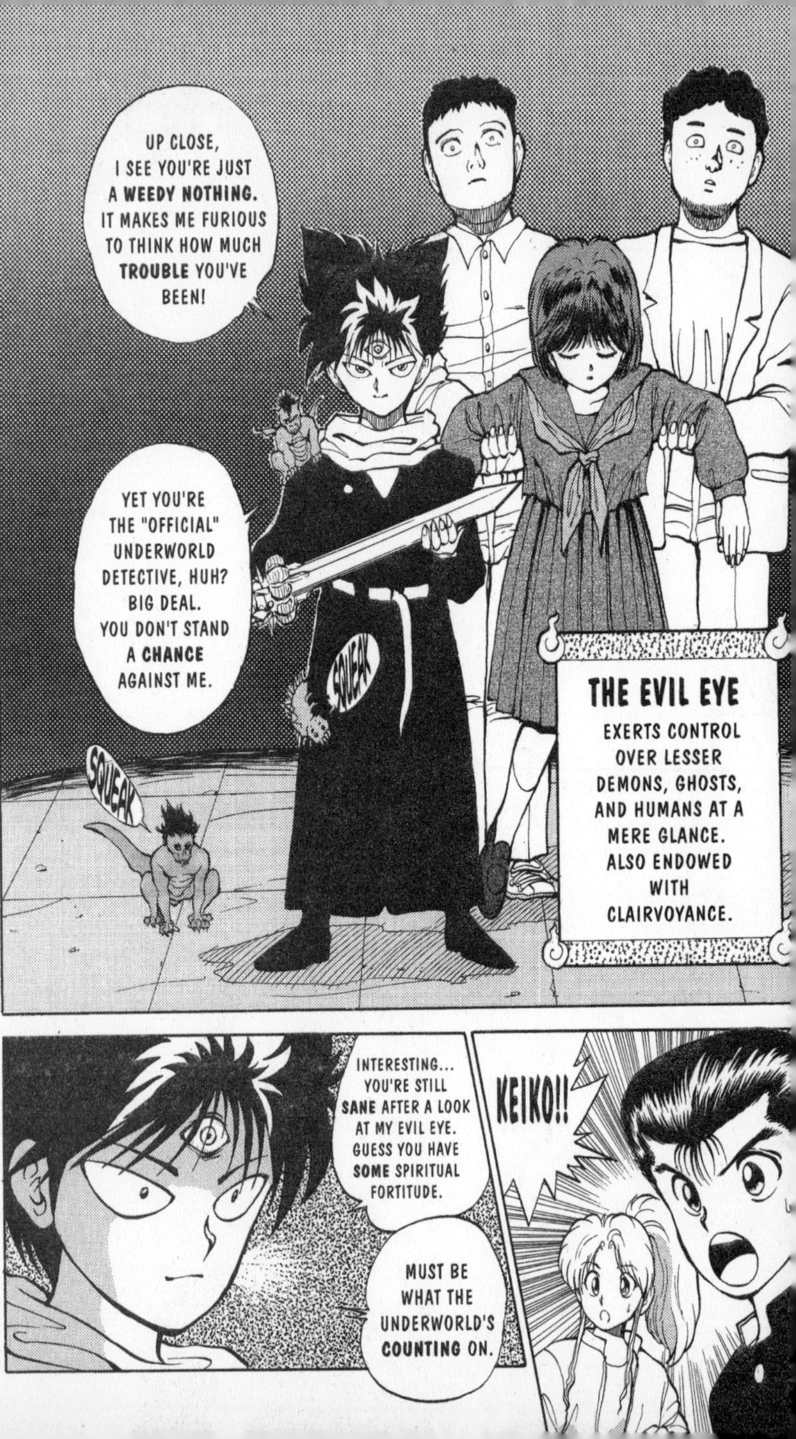
UP CLOSE, I SEE YOU'RE JUST A **WEEDY NOTHING.** IT MAKES ME FURIOUS TO THINK HOW MUCH **TROUBLE** YOU'VE BEEN!
YET YOU'RE THE "OFFICIAL" UNDERWORLD DETECTIVE, HUH? BIG DEAL. YOU DON'T STAND A **CHANCE** AGAINST ME.
SQUEAK
THE EVIL EYE
EXERTS CONTROL OVER LESSER DEMONS, GHOSTS, AND HUMANS AT A MERE GLANCE. ALSO ENDOWED WITH CLAIRVOYANCE.
SQUEAK
KEIKO!!
INTERESTING... YOU'RE STILL **SANE** AFTER A LOOK AT MY EVIL EYE. GUESS YOU HAVE **SOME** SPIRITUAL FORTITUDE.
MUST BE WHAT THE UNDERWORLD'S **COUNTING** ON.

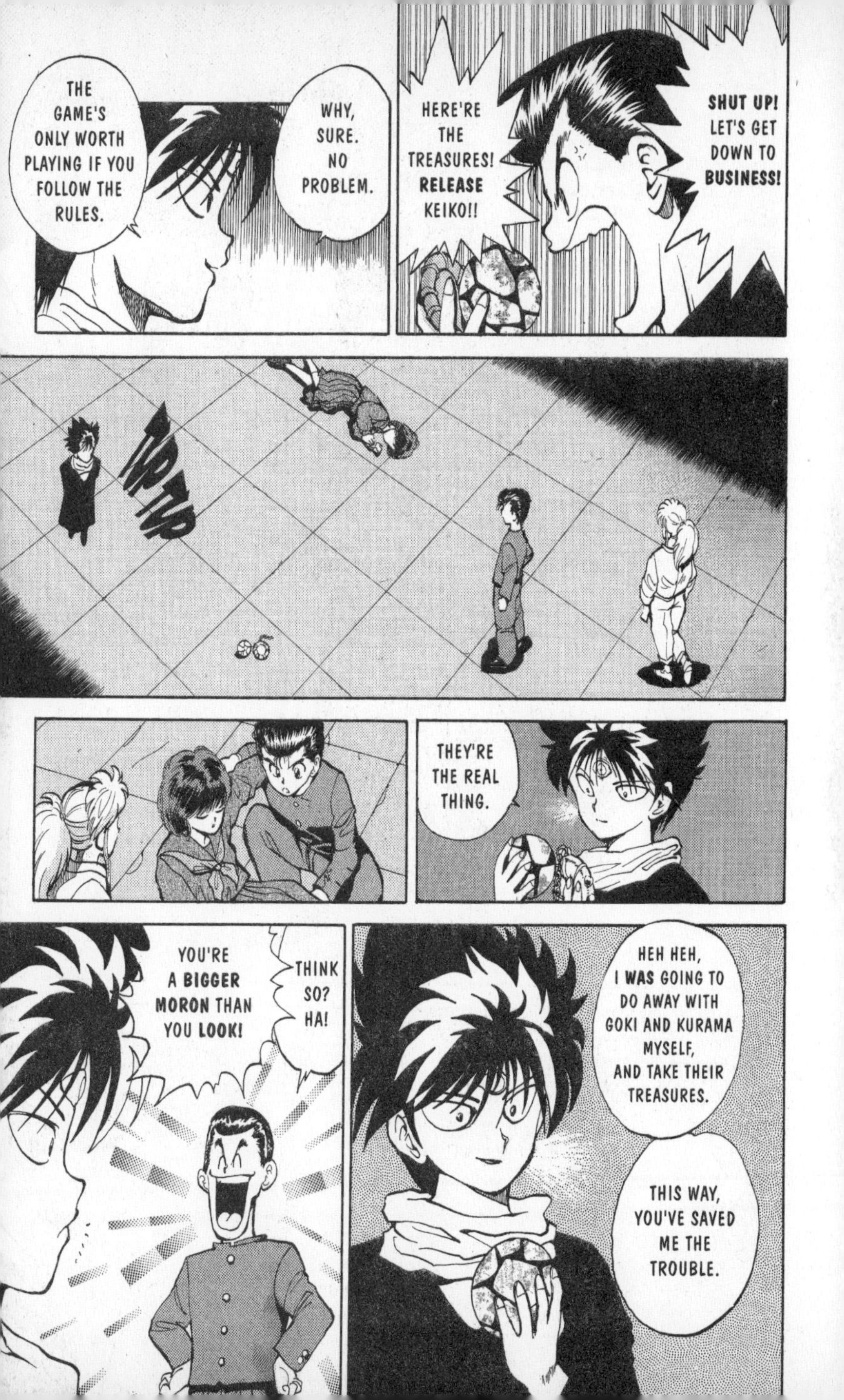
SHUT UP! LET'S GET DOWN TO BUSINESS!
HERE'RE THE TREASURES! RELEASE KEIKO!!
WHY, SURE. NO PROBLEM.
THE GAME'S ONLY WORTH PLAYING IF YOU FOLLOW THE RULES.
TUP TUP
THEY'RE THE REAL THING.
HEH HEH, I WAS GOING TO DO AWAY WITH GOKI AND KURAMA MYSELF, AND TAKE THEIR TREASURES.
THIS WAY, YOU'VE SAVED ME THE TROUBLE.
THINK SO? HA!
YOU'RE A BIGGER MORON THAN YOU LOOK!

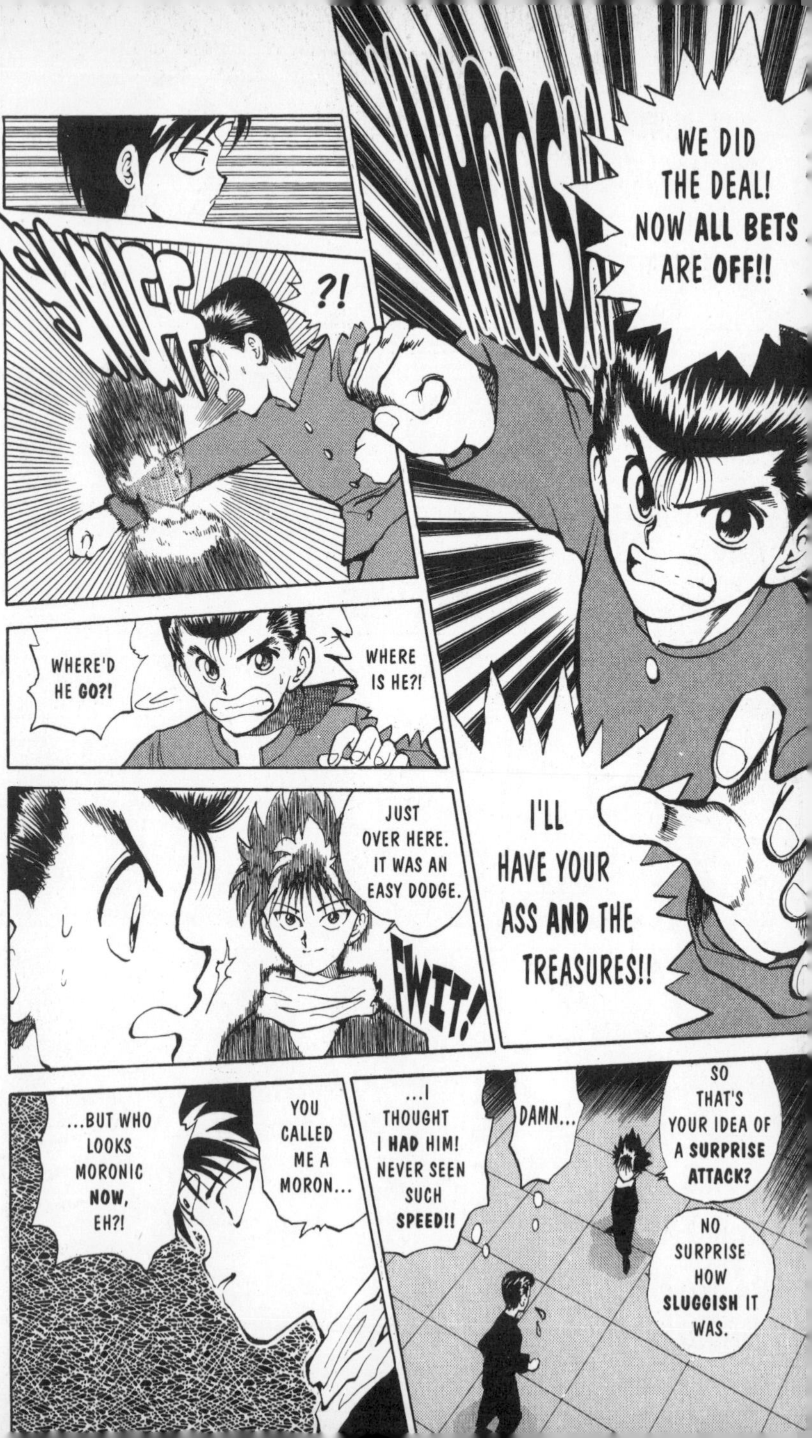

WE DID THE DEAL! NOW ALL BETS ARE OFF!!
I'LL HAVE YOUR ASS AND THE TREASURES!!
?!
WHERE IS HE?!
WHERE'D HE GO?!
JUST OVER HERE. IT WAS AN EASY DODGE.
FWIT!
SO THAT'S YOUR IDEA OF A SURPRISE ATTACK?
NO SURPRISE HOW SLUGGISH IT WAS.
DAMN...
...I THOUGHT I HAD HIM! NEVER SEEN SUCH SPEED!!
YOU CALLED ME A MORON...
...BUT WHO LOOKS MORONIC NOW, EH?!

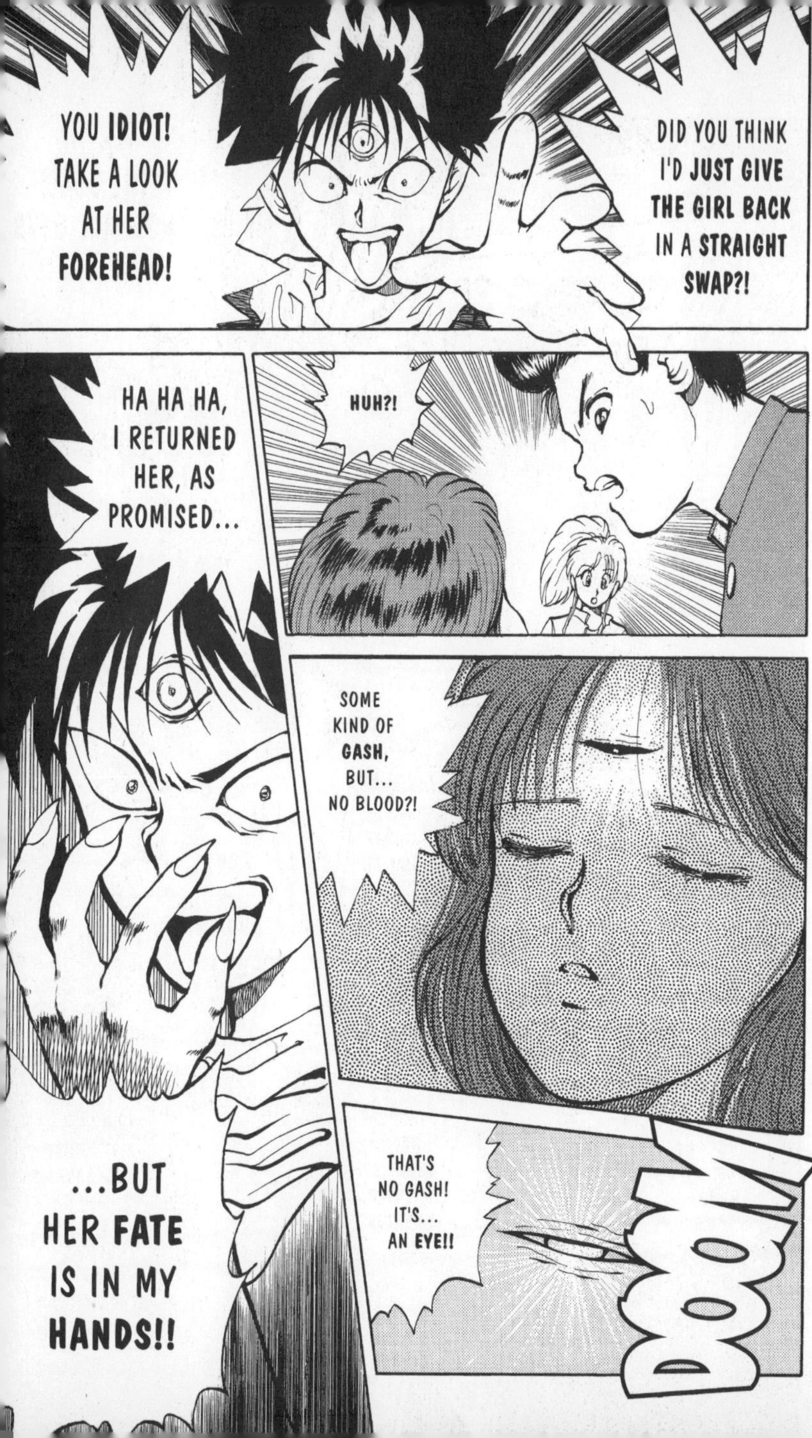
DID YOU THINK I'D JUST GIVE THE GIRL BACK IN A STRAIGHT SWAP?!
YOU IDIOT! TAKE A LOOK AT HER FOREHEAD!
HUH?!
SOME KIND OF GASH, BUT... NO BLOOD?!
THAT'S NO GASH! IT'S... AN EYE!!
DOOM
HA HA HA, I RETURNED HER, AS PROMISED...
...BUT HER FATE IS IN MY HANDS!!

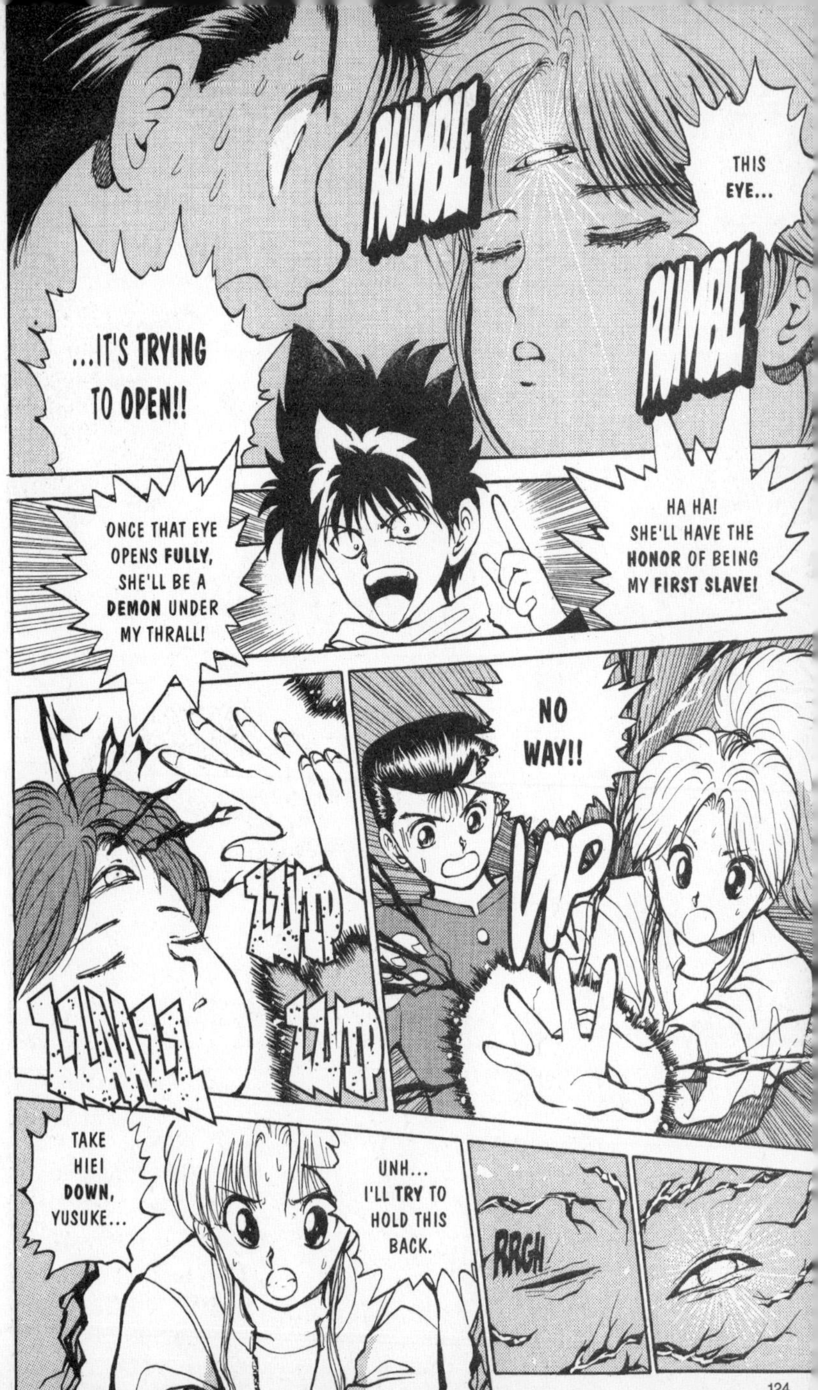
THIS EYE...
RUMBLE
RUMBLE
...IT'S TRYING TO OPEN!!
HA HA! SHE'LL HAVE THE HONOR OF BEING MY FIRST SLAVE!
ONCE THAT EYE OPENS FULLY, SHE'LL BE A DEMON UNDER MY THRALL!
NO WAY!!
RRGH
TAKE HIEI DOWN, YUSUKE...
UNH... I'LL TRY TO HOLD THIS BACK.

READ THIS WAY

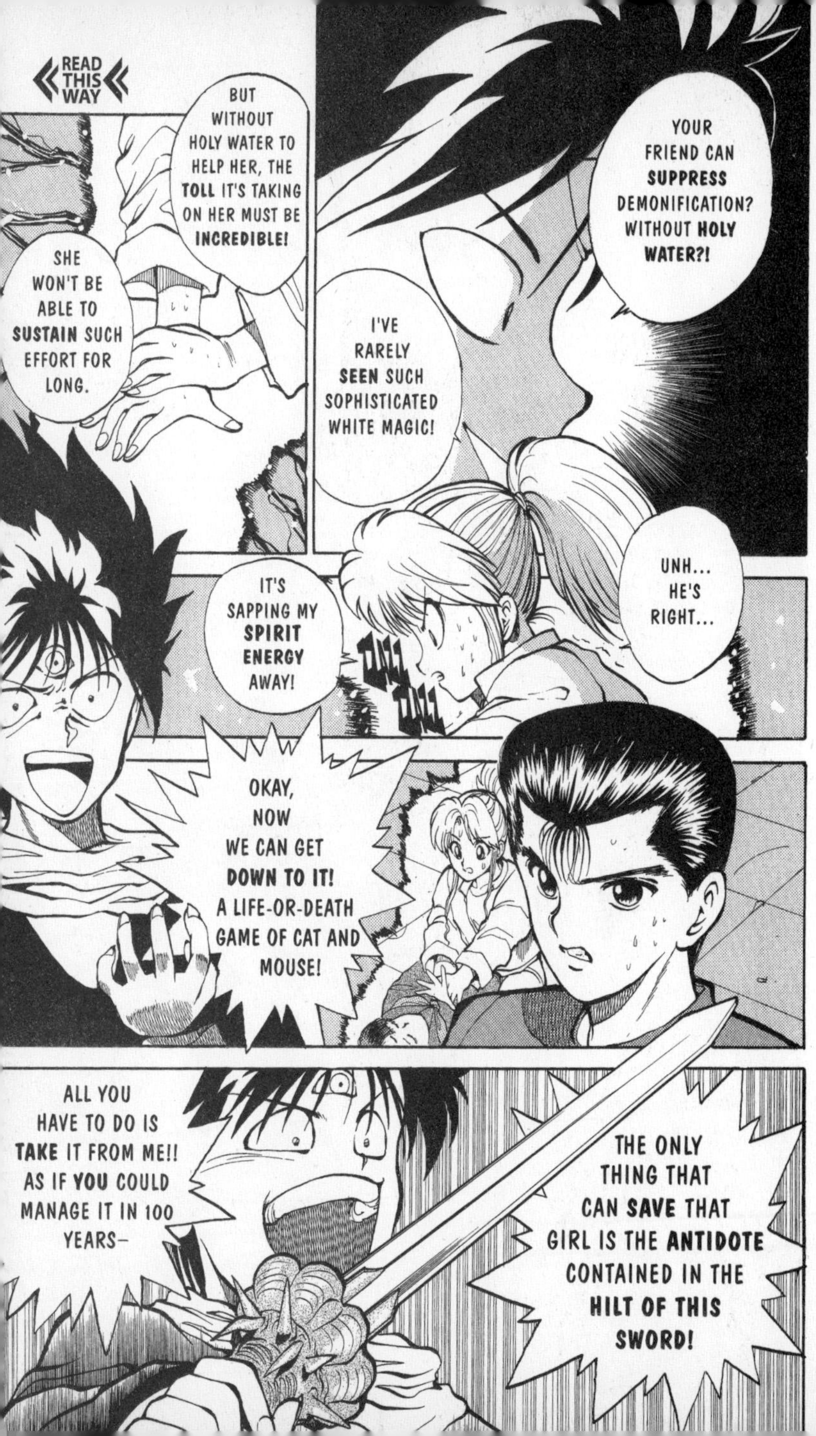
YOUR FRIEND CAN SUPPRESS DEMONIFICATION? WITHOUT HOLY WATER?!
I'VE RARELY SEEN SUCH SOPHISTICATED WHITE MAGIC!
BUT WITHOUT HOLY WATER TO HELP HER, THE TOLL IT'S TAKING ON HER MUST BE INCREDIBLE!
SHE WON'T BE ABLE TO SUSTAIN SUCH EFFORT FOR LONG.
UNH... HE'S RIGHT...
IT'S SAPPING MY SPIRIT ENERGY AWAY!
OKAY, NOW WE CAN GET DOWN TO IT! A LIFE-OR-DEATH GAME OF CAT AND MOUSE!
THE ONLY THING THAT CAN SAVE THAT GIRL IS THE ANTIDOTE CONTAINED IN THE HILT OF THIS SWORD!
ALL YOU HAVE TO DO IS TAKE IT FROM ME!! AS IF YOU COULD MANAGE IT IN 100 YEARS–

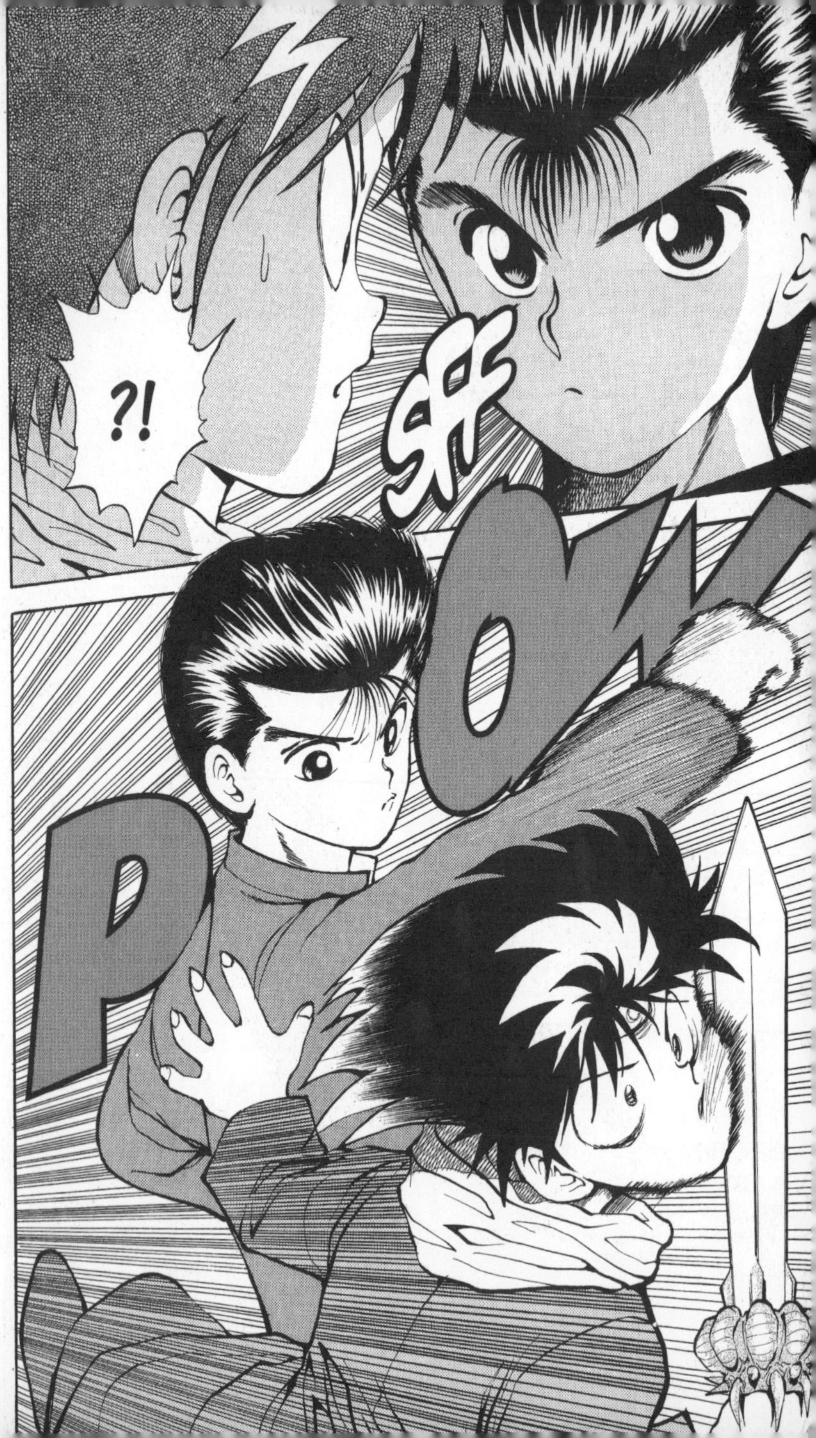
SFF
?!
POW

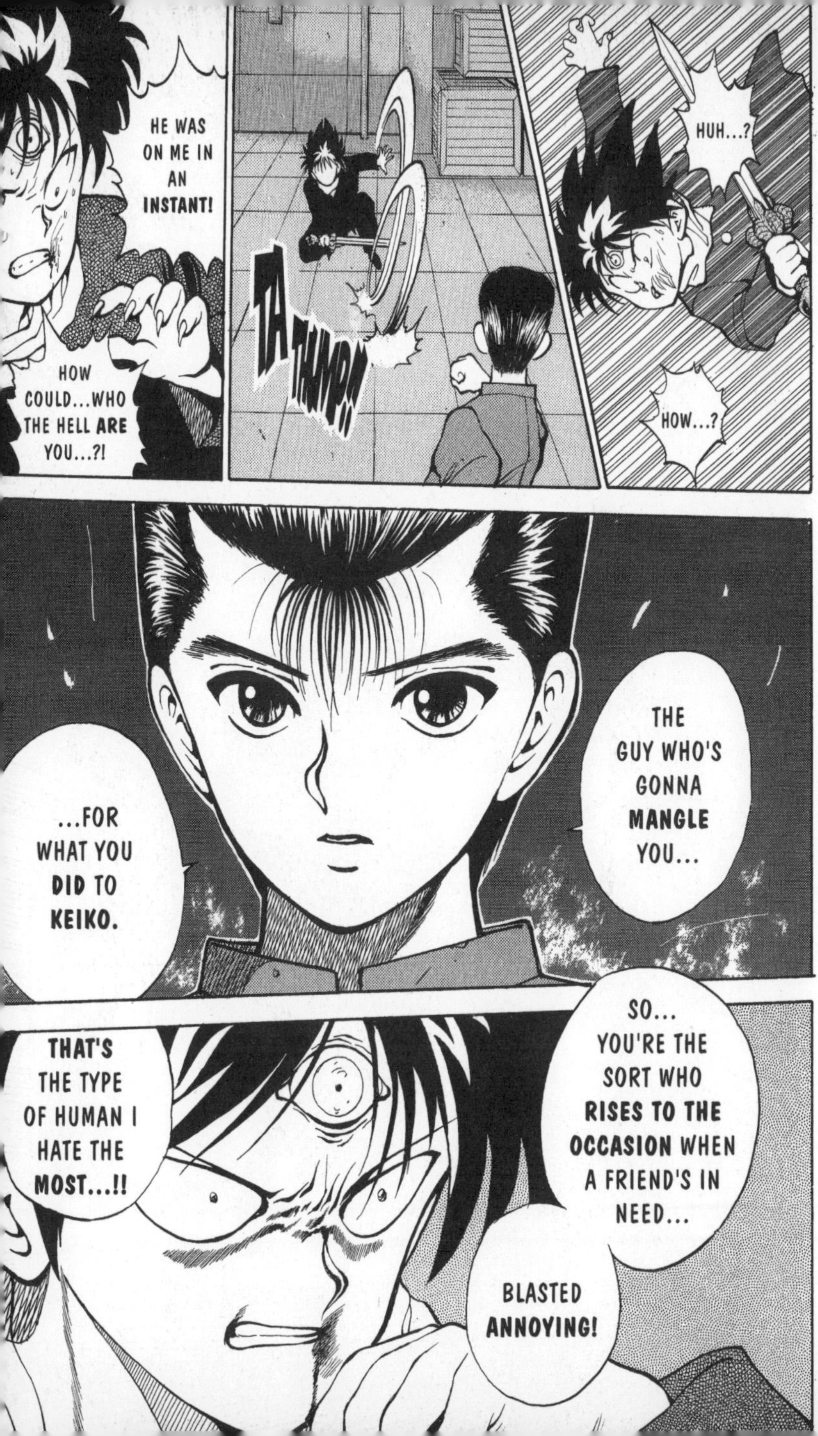
HUH...?
HOW...?
TA THUMP!!
HE WAS ON ME IN AN INSTANT!
HOW COULD...WHO THE HELL ARE YOU...?!
THE GUY WHO'S GONNA MANGLE YOU...
...FOR WHAT YOU DID TO KEIKO.
SO... YOU'RE THE SORT WHO RISES TO THE OCCASION WHEN A FRIEND'S IN NEED...
BLASTED ANNOYING!
THAT'S THE TYPE OF HUMAN I HATE THE MOST...!!

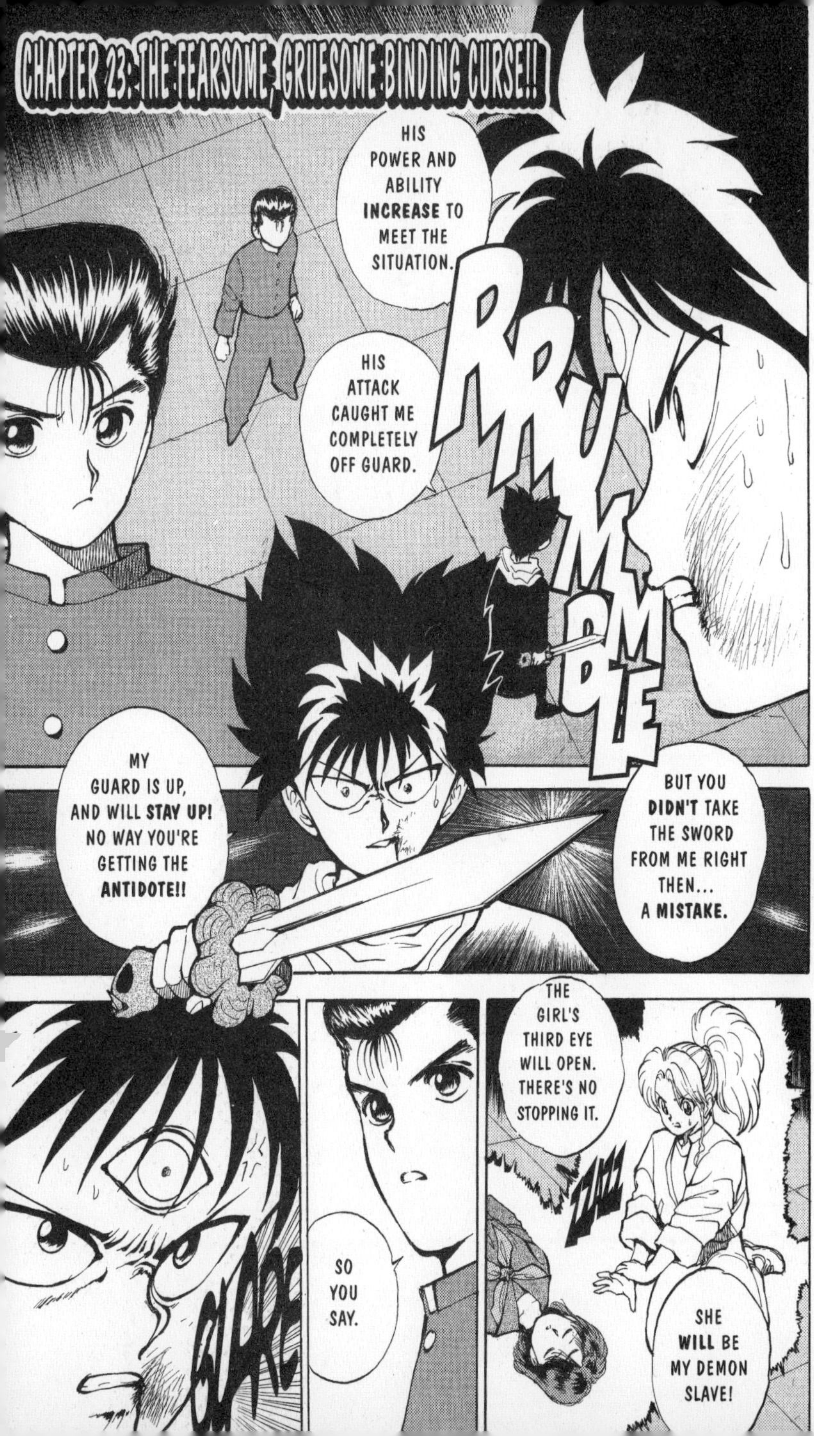
CHAPTER 23: THE FEARSOME, GRUESOME BINDING CURSE!!
HIS POWER AND ABILITY INCREASE TO MEET THE SITUATION.
HIS ATTACK CAUGHT ME COMPLETELY OFF GUARD.
BUT YOU DIDN'T TAKE THE SWORD FROM ME RIGHT THEN... A MISTAKE.
MY GUARD IS UP, AND WILL STAY UP! NO WAY YOU'RE GETTING THE ANTIDOTE!!
THE GIRL'S THIRD EYE WILL OPEN. THERE'S NO STOPPING IT.
SHE WILL BE MY DEMON SLAVE!
SO YOU SAY.
GLARE

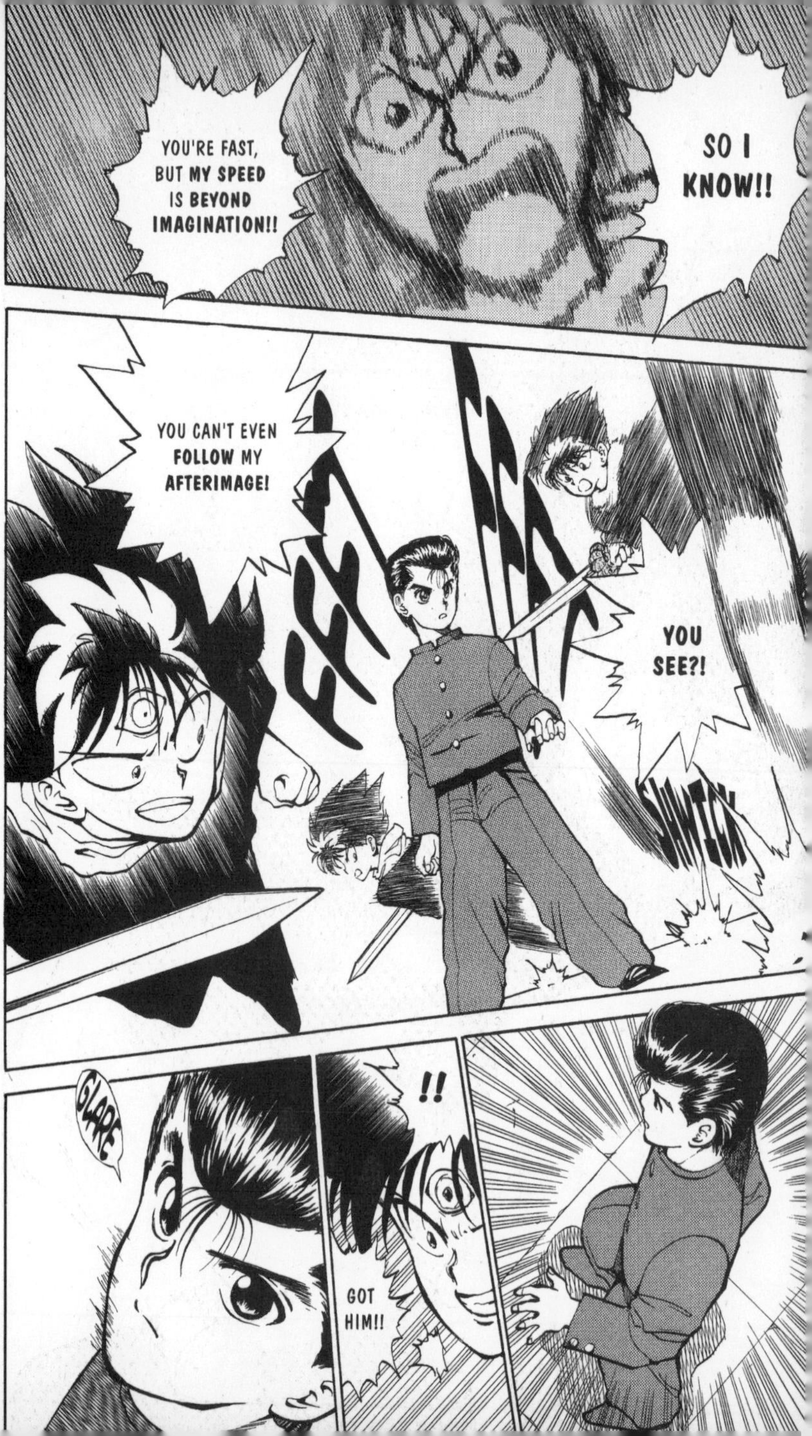
SO I KNOW!!
YOU'RE FAST, BUT MY SPEED IS BEYOND IMAGINATION!!
YOU SEE?!
YOU CAN'T EVEN FOLLOW MY AFTERIMAGE!
!!
GOT HIM!!
GLARE

Chapter23: THE FEARSOME, GRUESOME BINDING CURSE!!

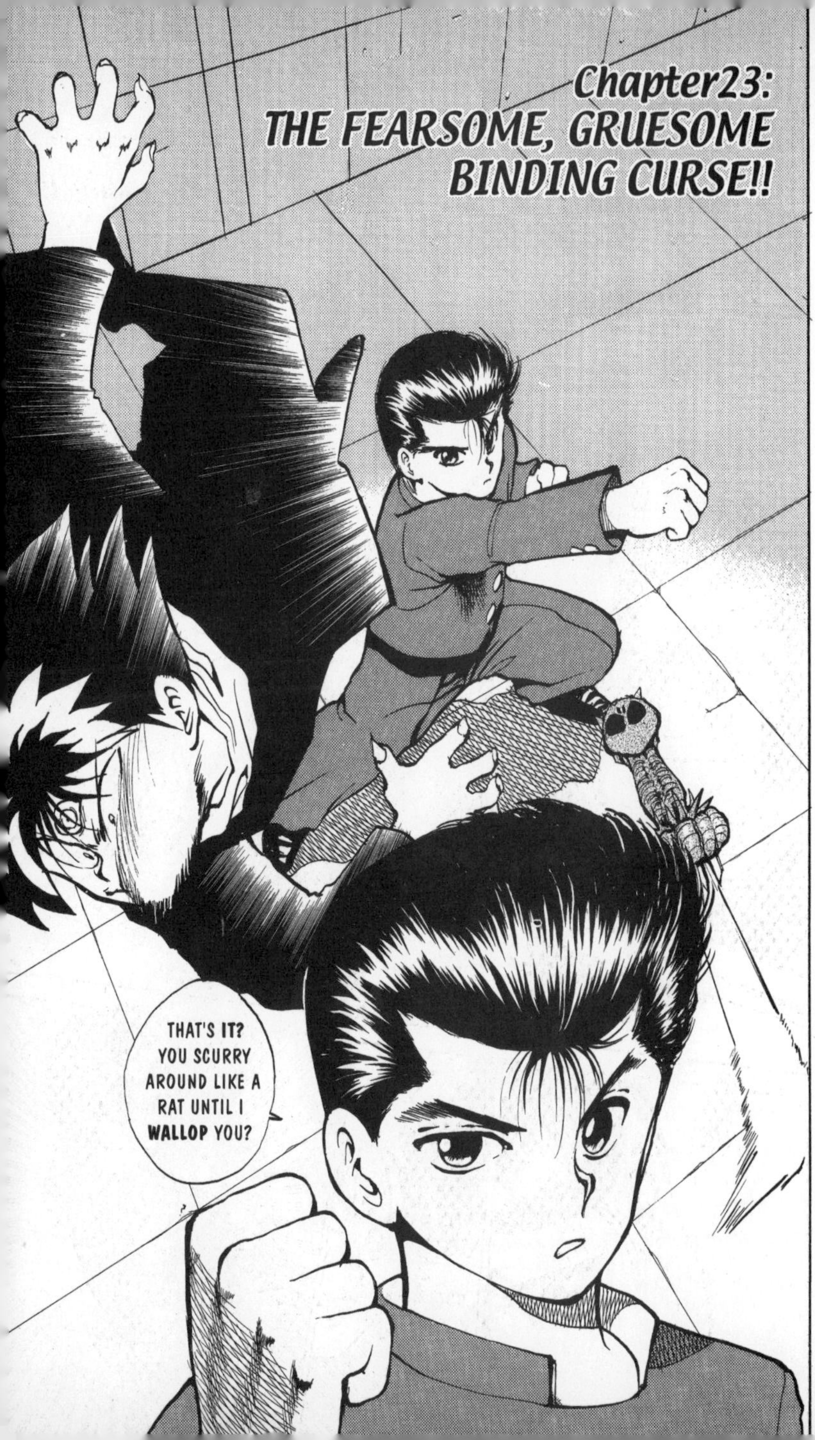
THAT'S IT? YOU SCURRY AROUND LIKE A RAT UNTIL I **WALLOP** YOU?

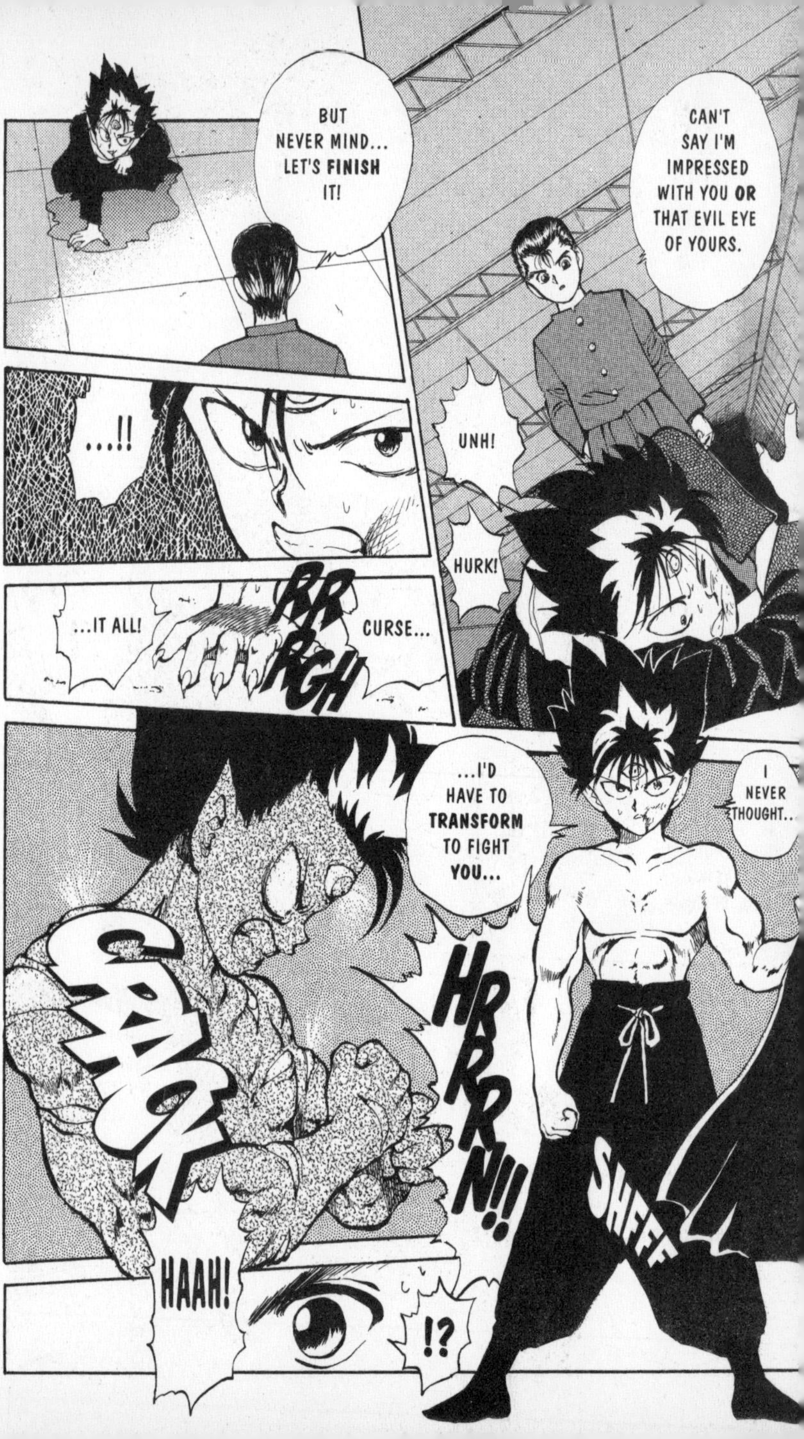
CAN'T SAY I'M IMPRESSED WITH YOU OR THAT EVIL EYE OF YOURS.
BUT NEVER MIND... LET'S FINISH IT!
UNH!
HURK!
...!!
CURSE...
RRRGH
...IT ALL!
I NEVER THOUGHT...
...I'D HAVE TO TRANSFORM TO FIGHT YOU...
HRRRRN!!
SHFFF
CRACK
!?
HAAH!

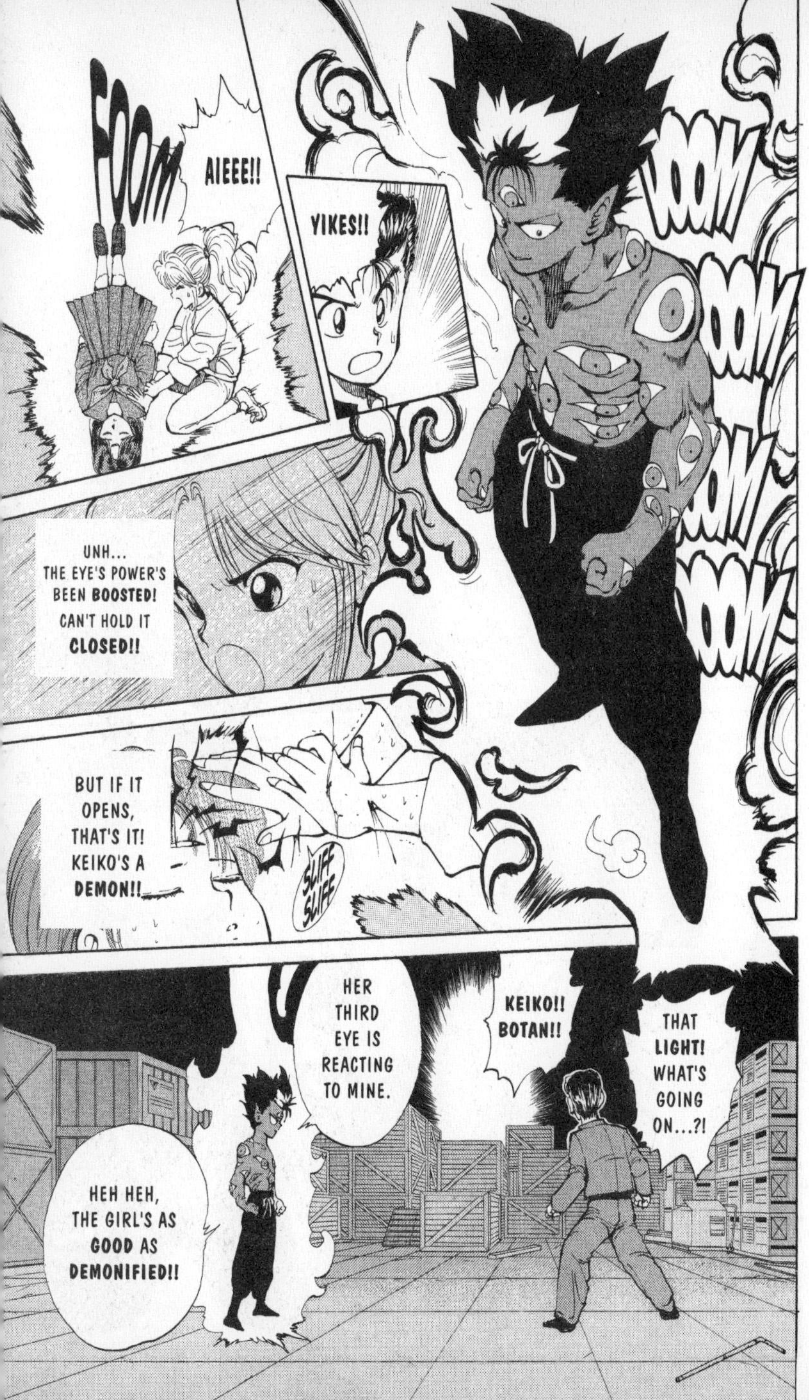
VOOM VOOM VOOM VOOM VOOM
YIKES!!
AIEEE!!
FOOM
UNH... THE EYE'S POWER'S BEEN **BOOSTED!** CAN'T HOLD IT **CLOSED!!**
BUT IF IT OPENS, THAT'S IT! KEIKO'S A **DEMON!!**
SLIFF SLIFF
THAT **LIGHT!** WHAT'S GOING ON...?!
KEIKO!! BOTAN!!
HER THIRD EYE IS REACTING TO MINE.
HEH HEH, THE GIRL'S AS **GOOD** AS **DEMONIFIED!!**

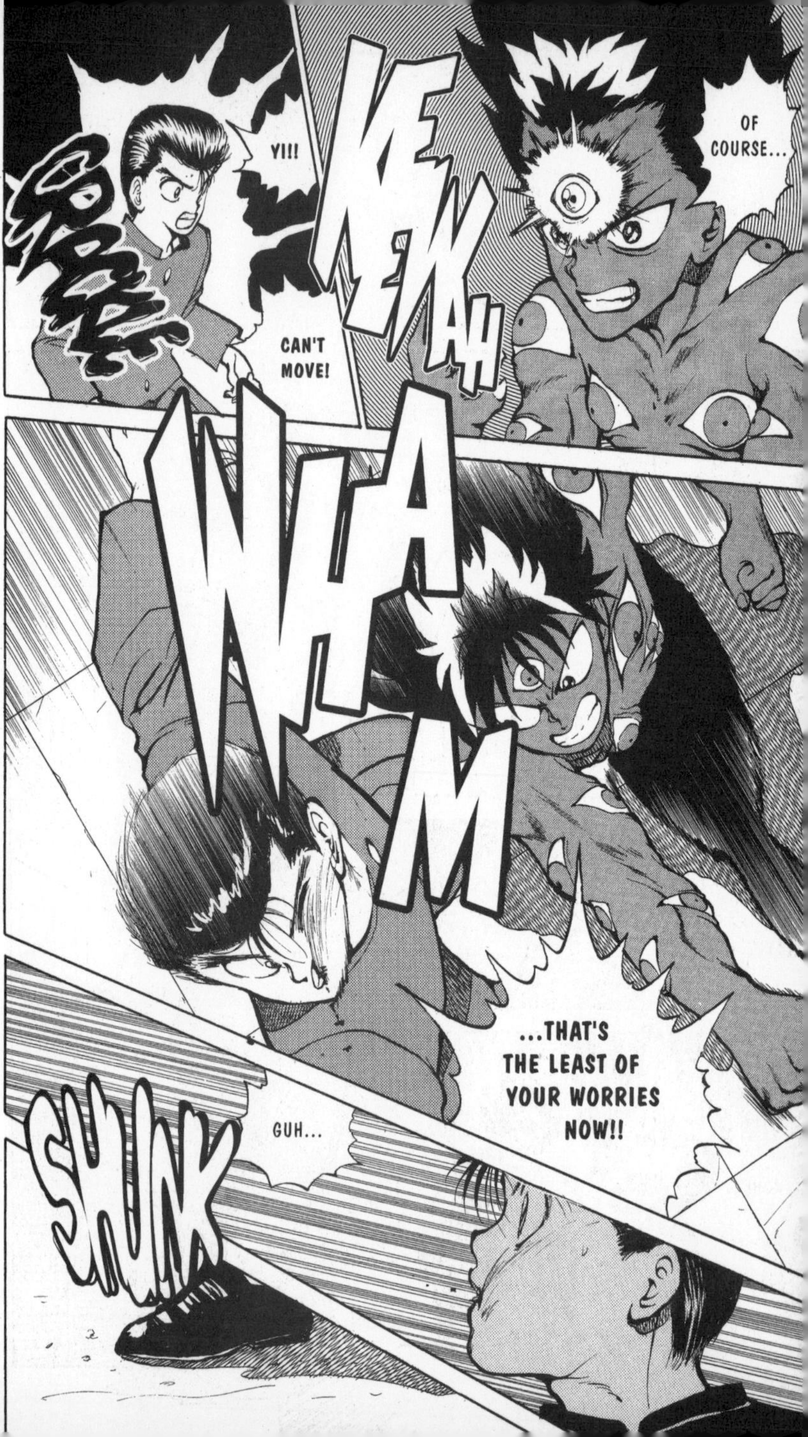
OF COURSE...
YI!!
CAN'T MOVE!
WHAM
...THAT'S THE LEAST OF YOUR WORRIES NOW!!
GUH...
SHUNK

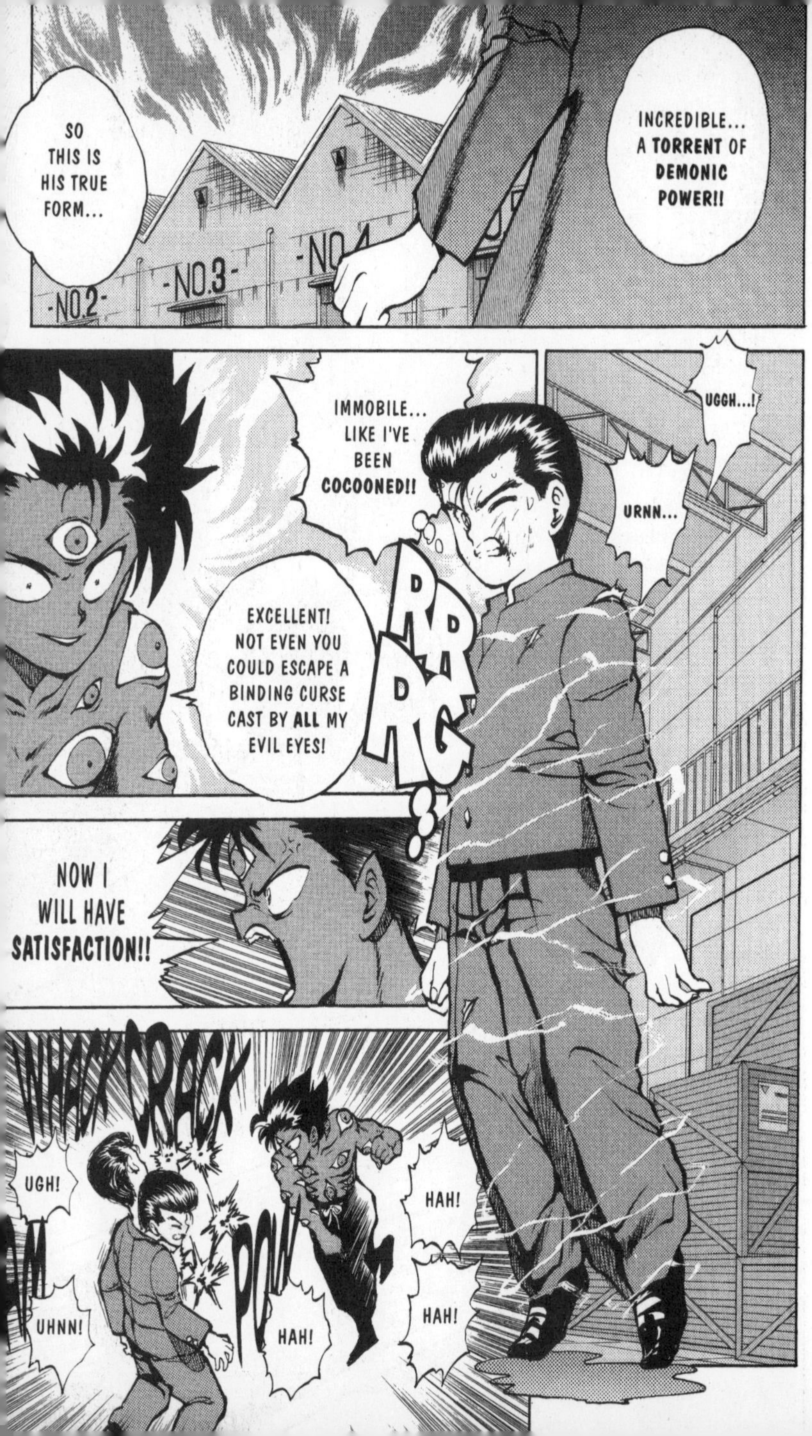
INCREDIBLE... A TORRENT OF DEMONIC POWER!!
SO THIS IS HIS TRUE FORM...
-NO.4-
-NO.3-
-NO.2-
UGGH...!
URNN...
IMMOBILE... LIKE I'VE BEEN COCOONED!!
EXCELLENT! NOT EVEN YOU COULD ESCAPE A BINDING CURSE CAST BY ALL MY EVIL EYES!
NOW I WILL HAVE SATISFACTION!!
WHACK CRACK
HAH!
HAH!
POW
HAH!
UGH!
UHNN!

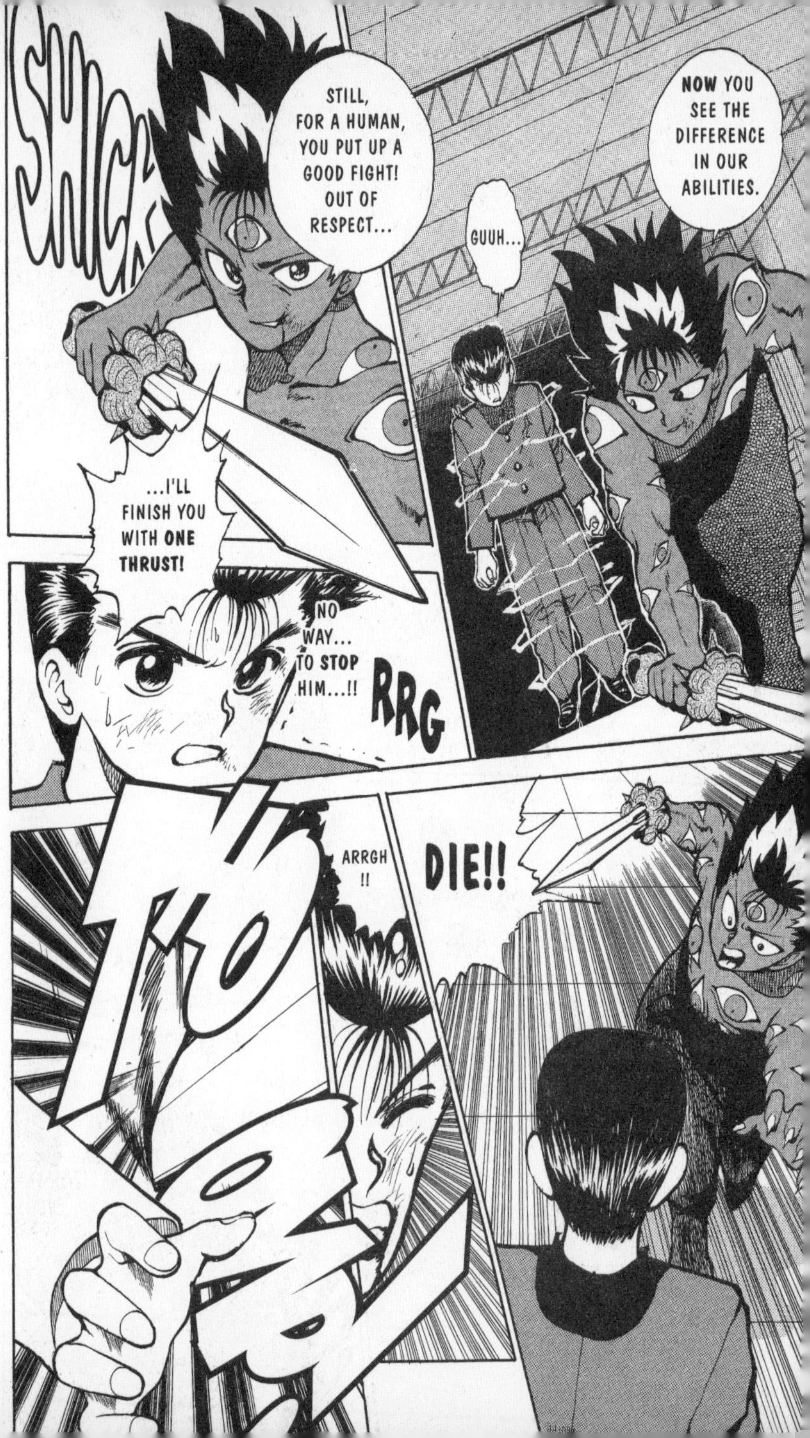
NOW YOU SEE THE DIFFERENCE IN OUR ABILITIES.
GUUH...
SHICK
STILL, FOR A HUMAN, YOU PUT UP A GOOD FIGHT! OUT OF RESPECT...
...I'LL FINISH YOU WITH ONE THRUST!
NO WAY... TO STOP HIM...!!
RRG
DIE!!
ARRGH !!

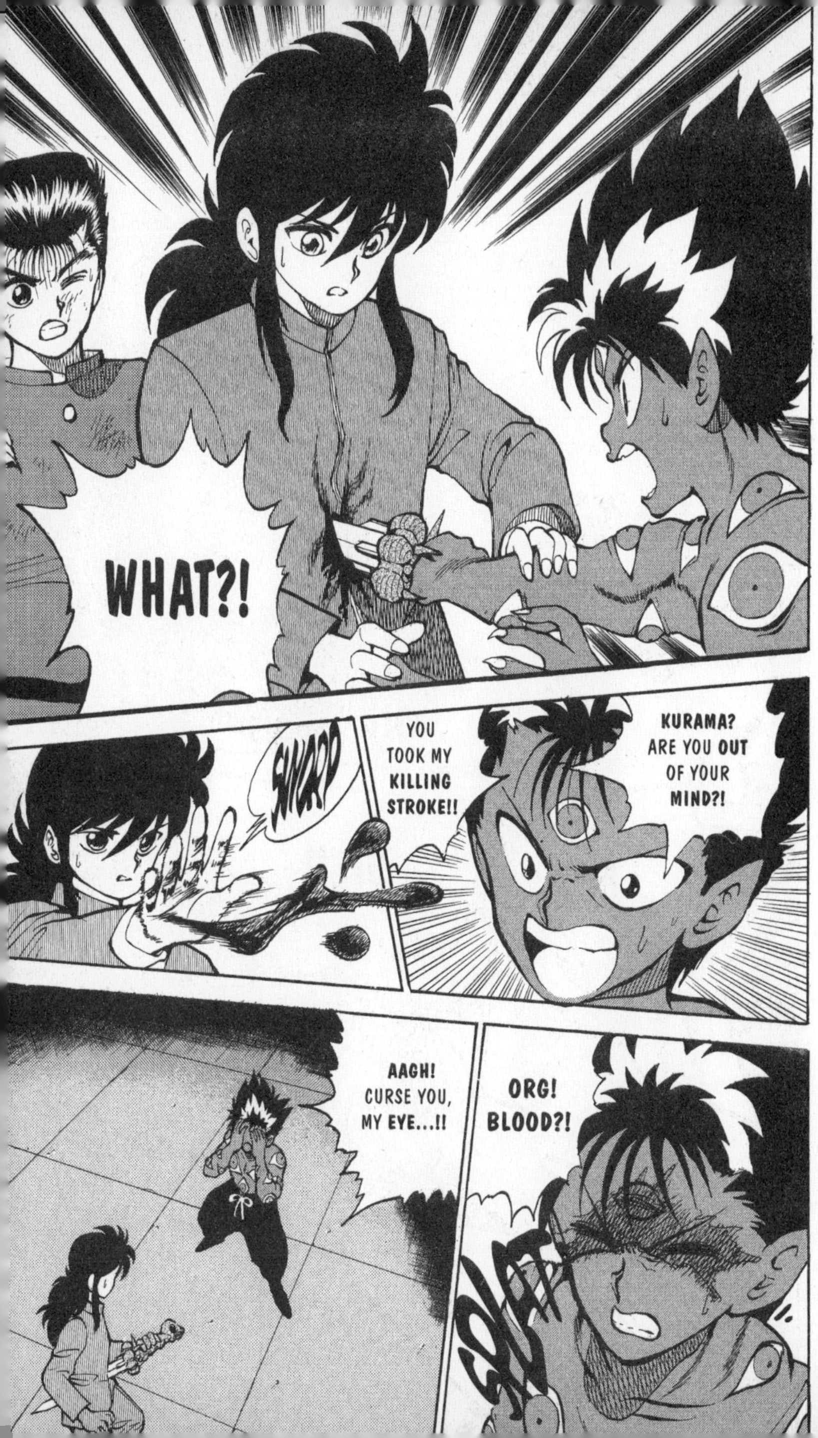
WHAT?!
KURAMA? ARE YOU OUT OF YOUR MIND?!
YOU TOOK MY KILLING STROKE!!
ORG! BLOOD?!
AAGH! CURSE YOU, MY EYE...!!

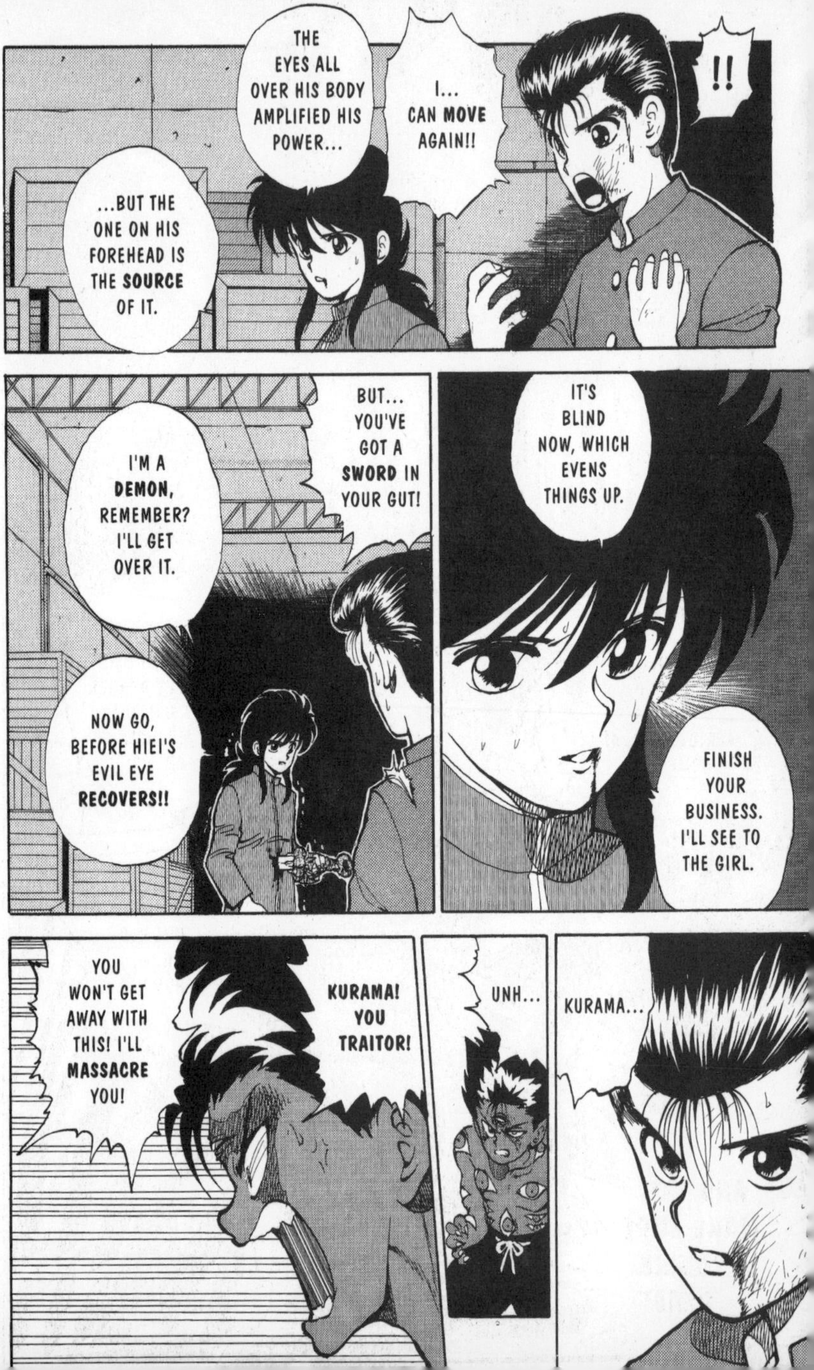
!!
I... CAN MOVE AGAIN!!
THE EYES ALL OVER HIS BODY AMPLIFIED HIS POWER...
...BUT THE ONE ON HIS FOREHEAD IS THE SOURCE OF IT.
IT'S BLIND NOW, WHICH EVENS THINGS UP.
FINISH YOUR BUSINESS. I'LL SEE TO THE GIRL.
BUT... YOU'VE GOT A SWORD IN YOUR GUT!
I'M A DEMON, REMEMBER? I'LL GET OVER IT.
NOW GO, BEFORE HIEI'S EVIL EYE RECOVERS!!
KURAMA...
UNH...
KURAMA! YOU TRAITOR!
YOU WON'T GET AWAY WITH THIS! I'LL MASSACRE YOU!

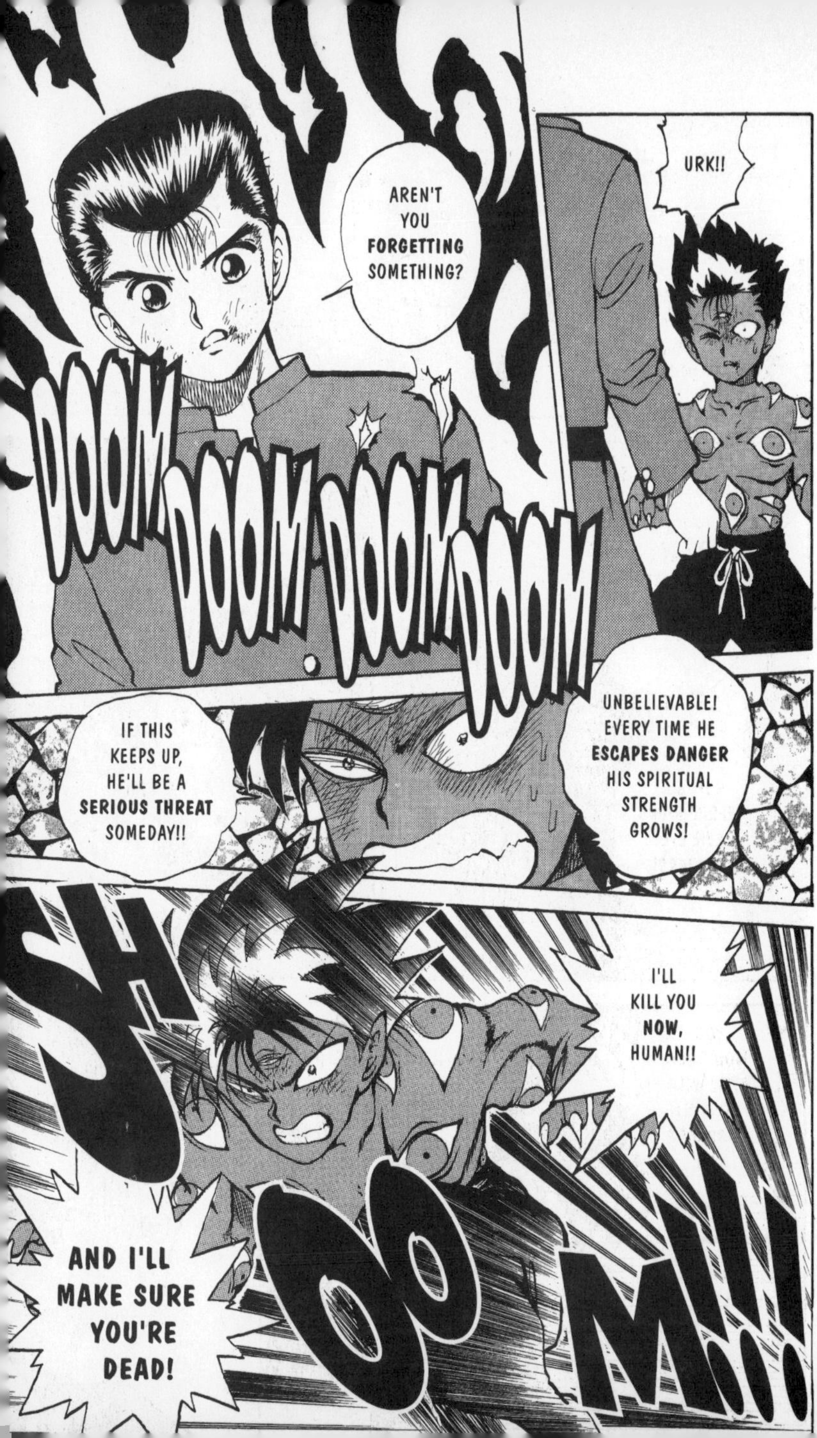
URK!!
AREN'T YOU FORGETTING SOMETHING?
DOOM DOOM DOOM DOOM
UNBELIEVABLE! EVERY TIME HE ESCAPES DANGER HIS SPIRITUAL STRENGTH GROWS!
IF THIS KEEPS UP, HE'LL BE A SERIOUS THREAT SOMEDAY!!
I'LL KILL YOU NOW, HUMAN!!
AND I'LL MAKE SURE YOU'RE DEAD!
OOM!!

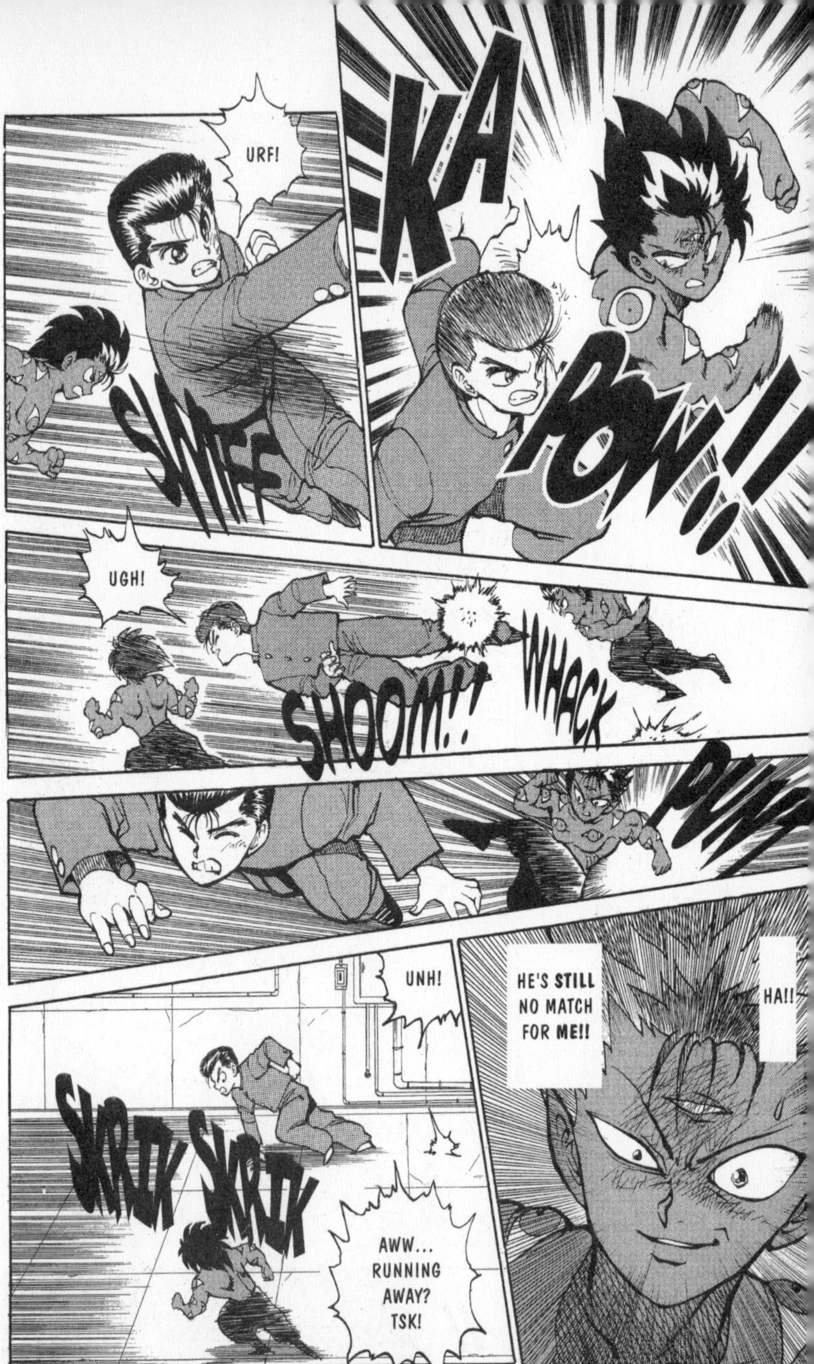
KA
POW!!
URF!
SWIFF
WHACK
UGH!
SHOOM!!
HA!!
HE'S STILL NO MATCH FOR ME!!
UNH!
SKRIK SKRIK
AWW... RUNNING AWAY? TSK!

READ THIS WAY

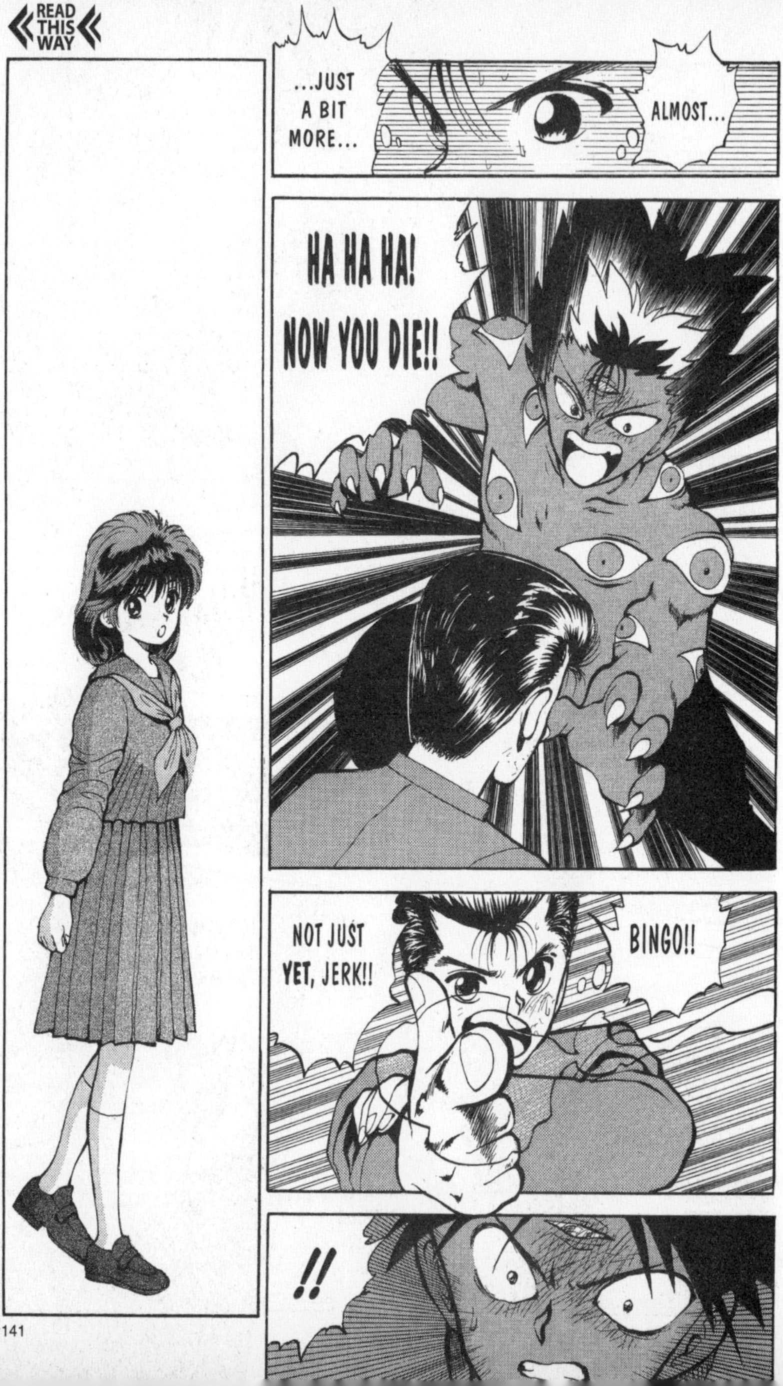
ALMOST...
...JUST A BIT MORE...
HA HA HA! NOW YOU DIE!!
BINGO!!
NOT JUST YET, JERK!!
!!

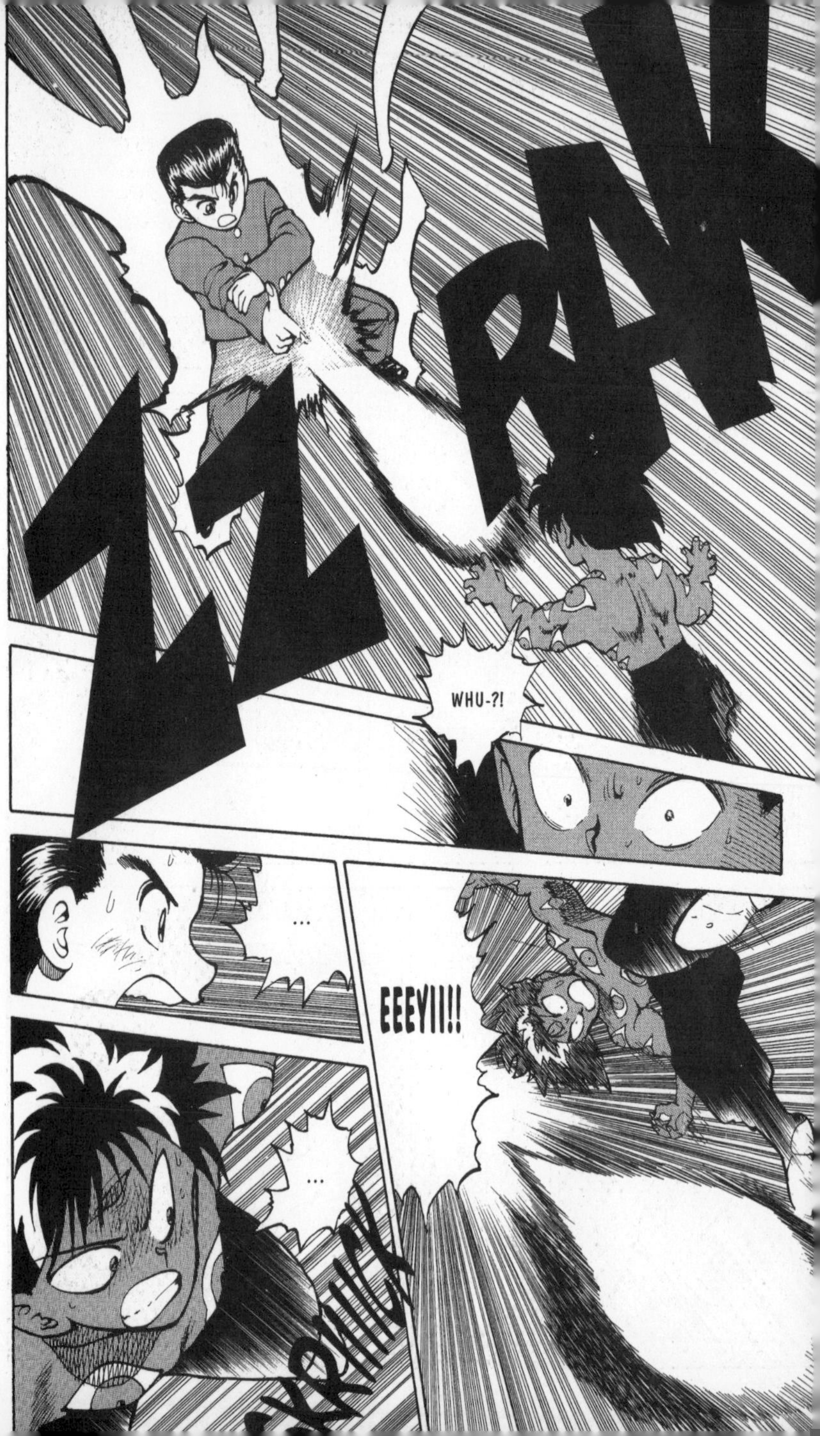
ZZZ-RAK
WHU-?!
EEEYIII!!
...
...
KRUNCK

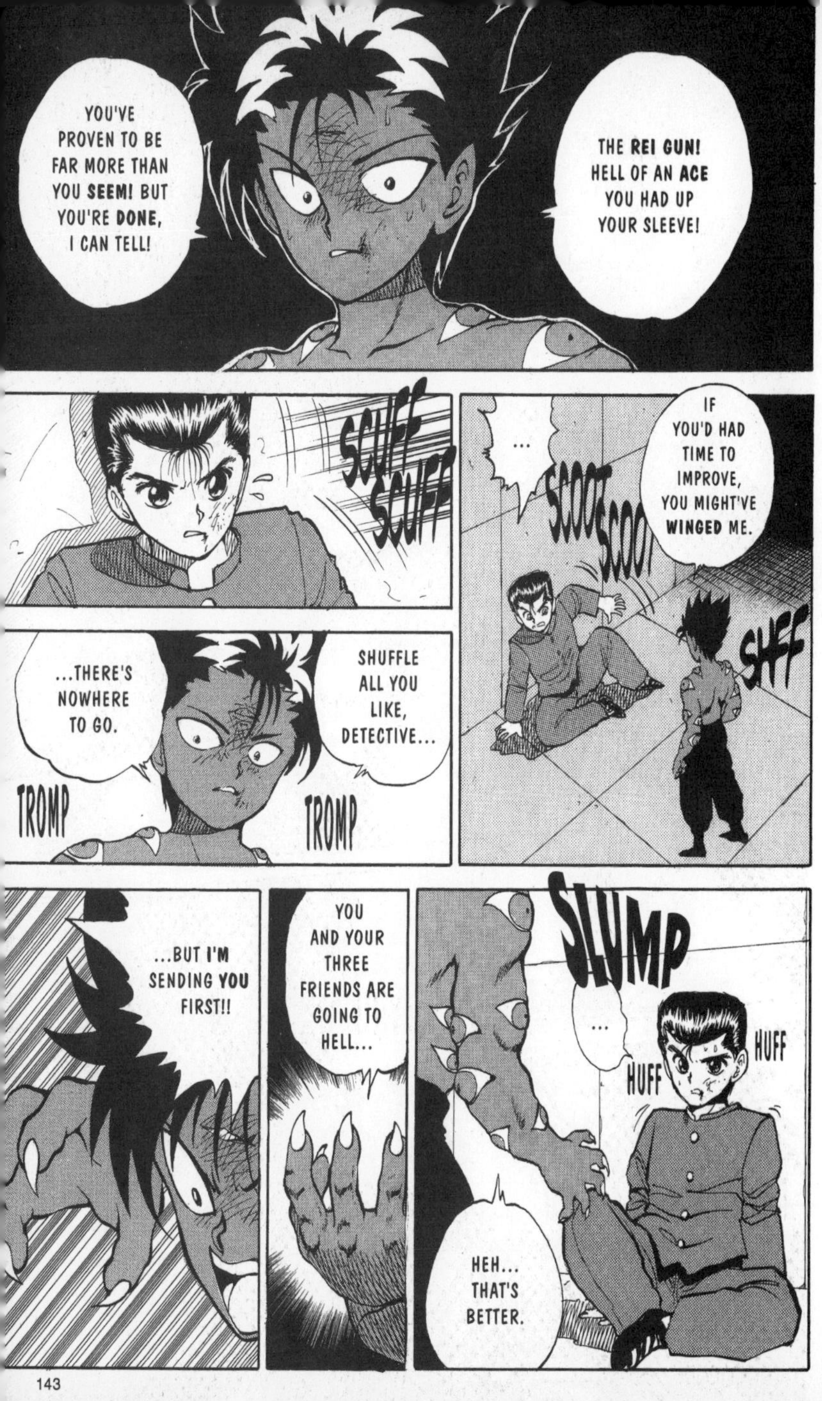
THE REI GUN! HELL OF AN ACE YOU HAD UP YOUR SLEEVE!
YOU'VE PROVEN TO BE FAR MORE THAN YOU SEEM! BUT YOU'RE DONE, I CAN TELL!
IF YOU'D HAD TIME TO IMPROVE, YOU MIGHT'VE WINGED ME.
...
SCOOT SCOOT
SHFF
SCUFF SCUFF
SHUFFLE ALL YOU LIKE, DETECTIVE...
...THERE'S NOWHERE TO GO.
TROMP
TROMP
SLUMP
HUFF
HUFF
...
HEH... THAT'S BETTER.
YOU AND YOUR THREE FRIENDS ARE GOING TO HELL...
...BUT I'M SENDING YOU FIRST!!

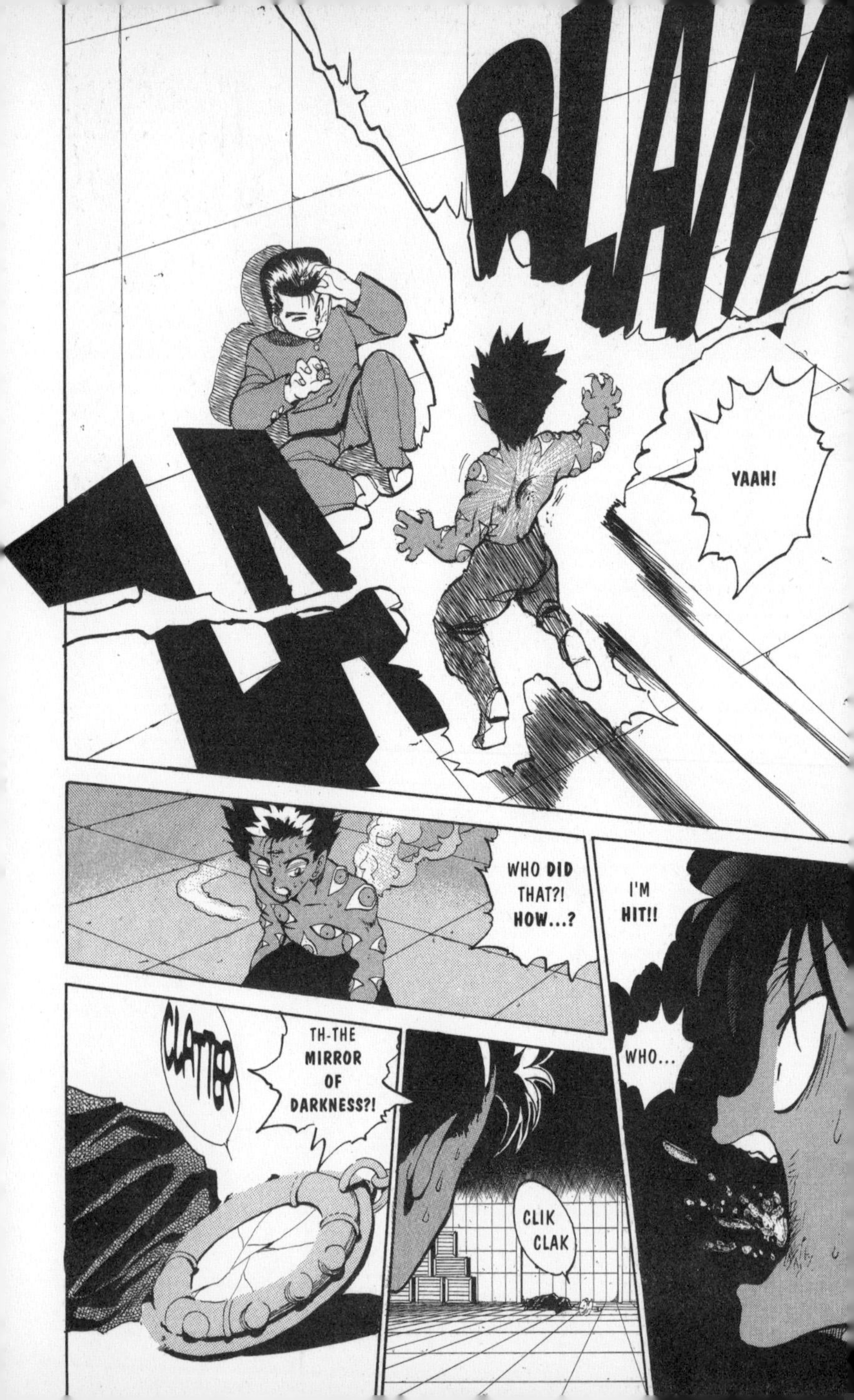
BLAM
YAAH!
I'M HIT!!
WHO...
WHO DID THAT?! HOW...?
CLIK CLAK
TH-THE MIRROR OF DARKNESS?!
CLATTER

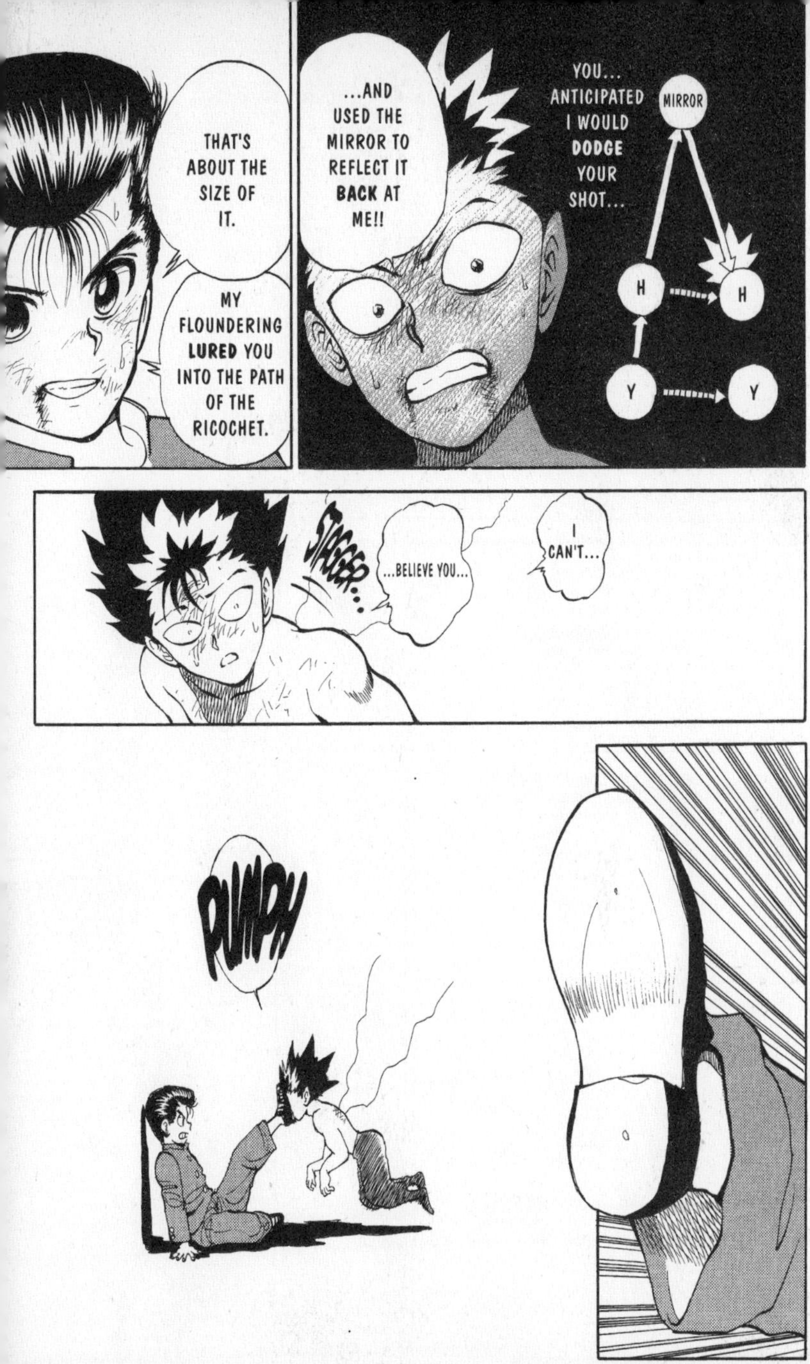
YOU... ANTICIPATED I WOULD DODGE YOUR SHOT...
MIRROR
H
H
Y
Y
...AND USED THE MIRROR TO REFLECT IT BACK AT ME!!
THAT'S ABOUT THE SIZE OF IT.
MY FLOUNDERING LURED YOU INTO THE PATH OF THE RICOCHET.
I CAN'T...
...BELIEVE YOU...
STAGGER...
PUMPH

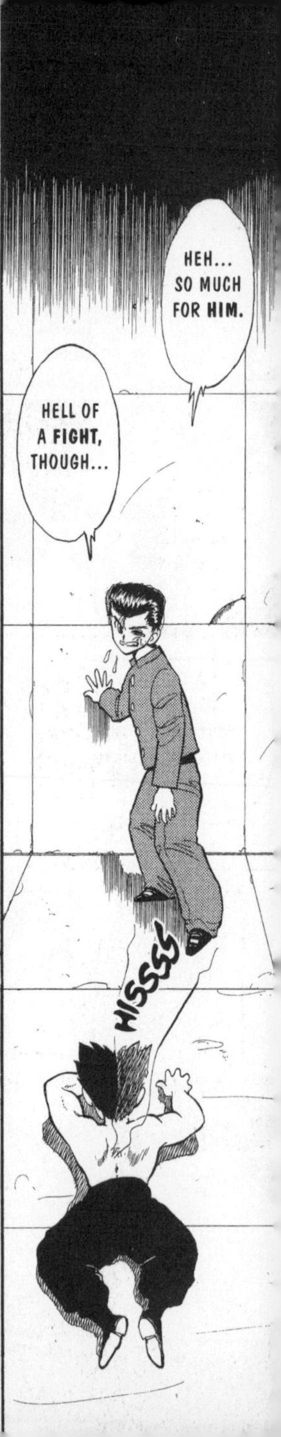
HEH... SO MUCH FOR HIM.
HELL OF A FIGHT, THOUGH...
HISSSS
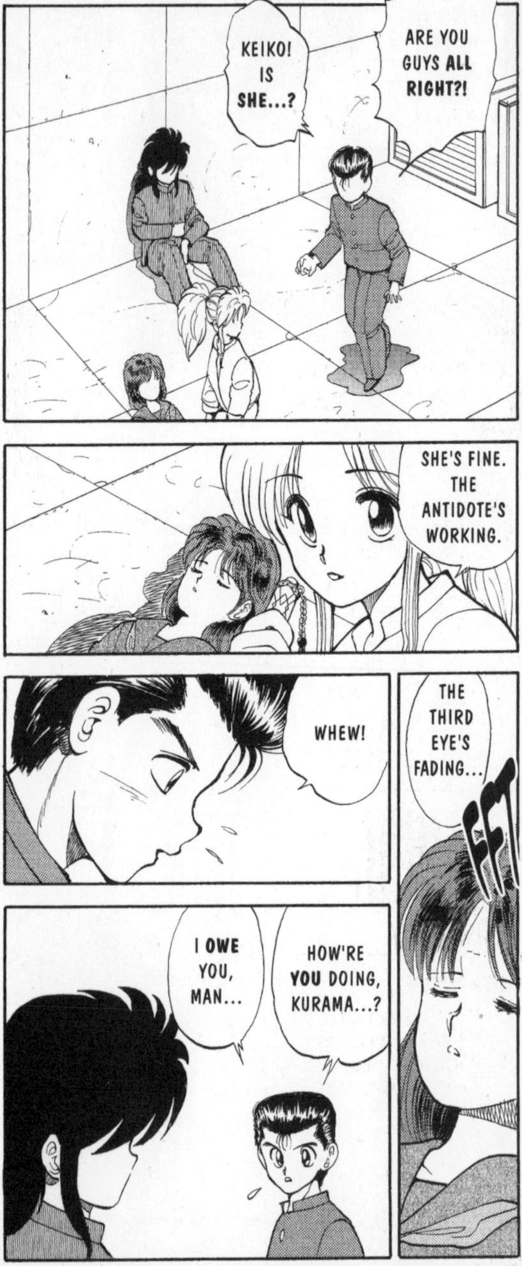
ARE YOU GUYS ALL RIGHT?!
KEIKO! IS SHE...?
SHE'S FINE. THE ANTIDOTE'S WORKING.
THE THIRD EYE'S FADING...
FFT
WHEW!
HOW'RE YOU DOING, KURAMA...?
I OWE YOU, MAN...

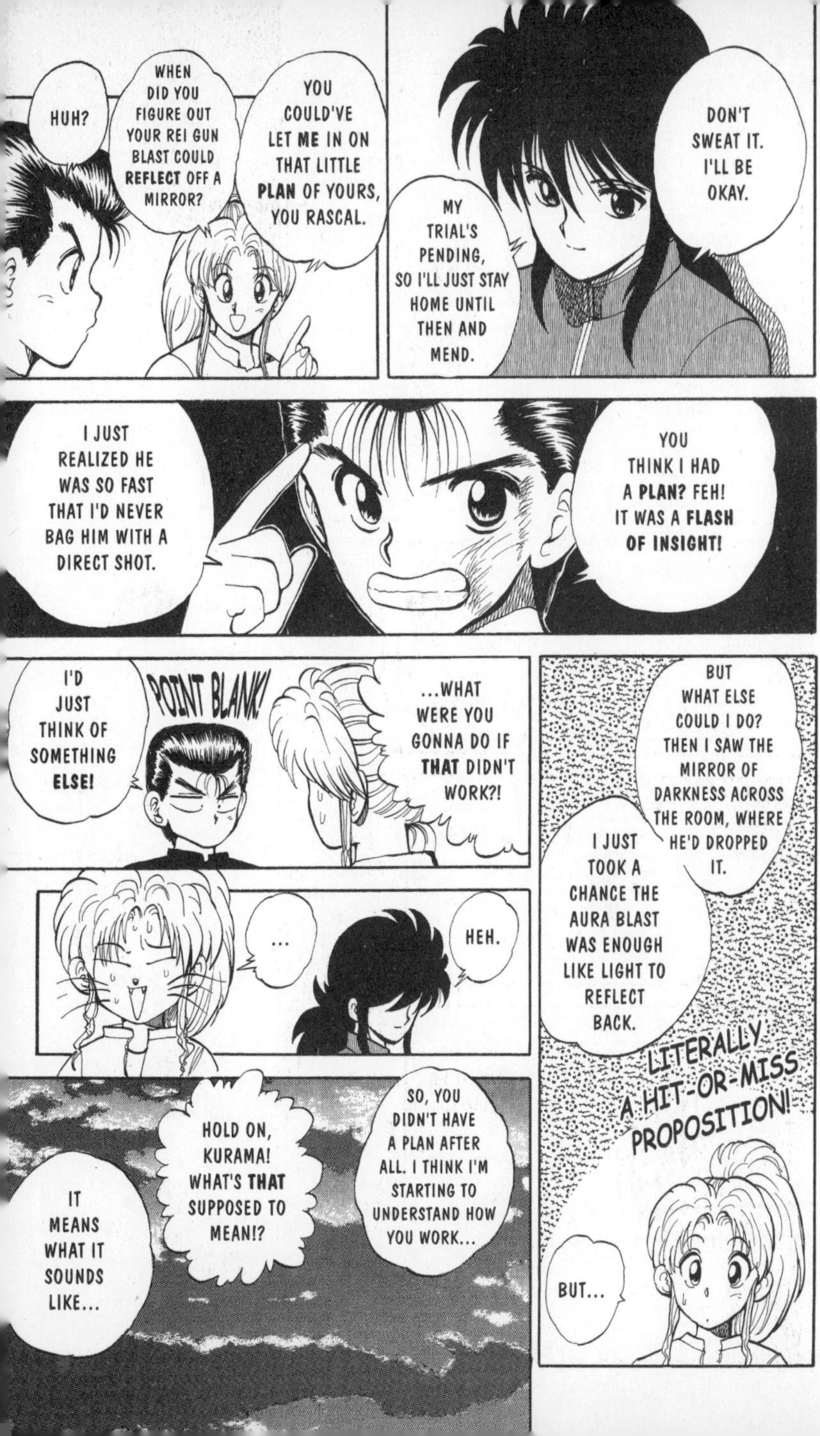
DON'T SWEAT IT. I'LL BE OKAY.
MY TRIAL'S PENDING, SO I'LL JUST STAY HOME UNTIL THEN AND MEND.
YOU COULD'VE LET ME IN ON THAT LITTLE PLAN OF YOURS, YOU RASCAL.
WHEN DID YOU FIGURE OUT YOUR REI GUN BLAST COULD REFLECT OFF A MIRROR?
HUH?
YOU THINK I HAD A PLAN? FEH! IT WAS A FLASH OF INSIGHT!
I JUST REALIZED HE WAS SO FAST THAT I'D NEVER BAG HIM WITH A DIRECT SHOT.
BUT WHAT ELSE COULD I DO? THEN I SAW THE MIRROR OF DARKNESS ACROSS THE ROOM, WHERE HE'D DROPPED IT.
I JUST TOOK A CHANCE THE AURA BLAST WAS ENOUGH LIKE LIGHT TO REFLECT BACK.
LITERALLY A HIT-OR-MISS PROPOSITION!
BUT...
...WHAT WERE YOU GONNA DO IF THAT DIDN'T WORK?!
POINT BLANK!
I'D JUST THINK OF SOMETHING ELSE!
HEH.
...
SO, YOU DIDN'T HAVE A PLAN AFTER ALL. I THINK I'M STARTING TO UNDERSTAND HOW YOU WORK...
HOLD ON, KURAMA! WHAT'S THAT SUPPOSED TO MEAN!?
IT MEANS WHAT IT SOUNDS LIKE...

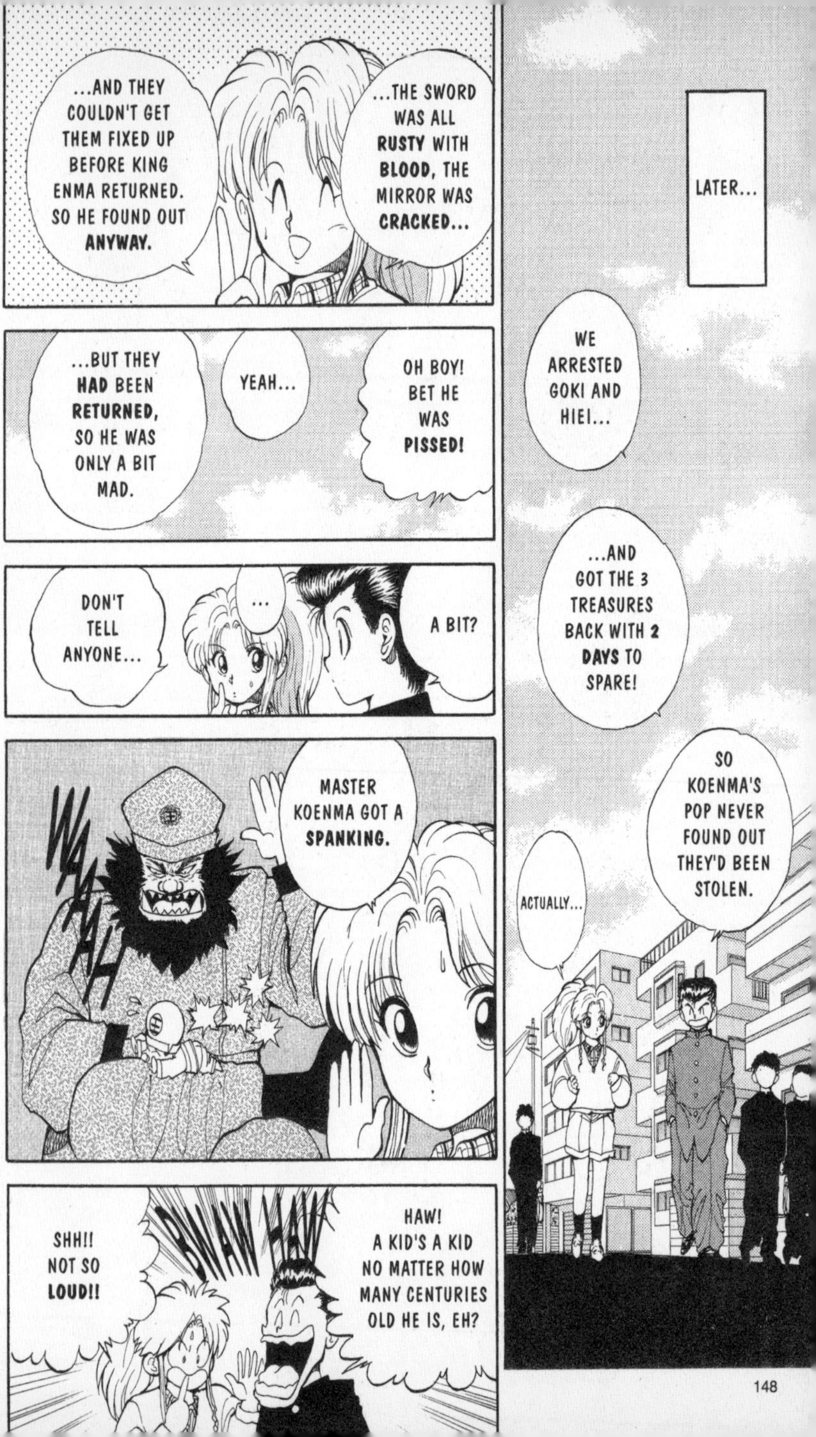
LATER...
WE ARRESTED GOKI AND HIEI...
...AND GOT THE 3 TREASURES BACK WITH 2 DAYS TO SPARE!
SO KOENMA'S POP NEVER FOUND OUT THEY'D BEEN STOLEN.
ACTUALLY...
...THE SWORD WAS ALL RUSTY WITH BLOOD, THE MIRROR WAS CRACKED...
...AND THEY COULDN'T GET THEM FIXED UP BEFORE KING ENMA RETURNED. SO HE FOUND OUT ANYWAY.
OH BOY! BET HE WAS PISSED!
YEAH...
...BUT THEY HAD BEEN RETURNED, SO HE WAS ONLY A BIT MAD.
A BIT?
...
DON'T TELL ANYONE...
MASTER KOENMA GOT A SPANKING.
WAAAAH
HAW! A KID'S A KID NO MATTER HOW MANY CENTURIES OLD HE IS, EH?
BWAH HAW
SHH!! NOT SO LOUD!!

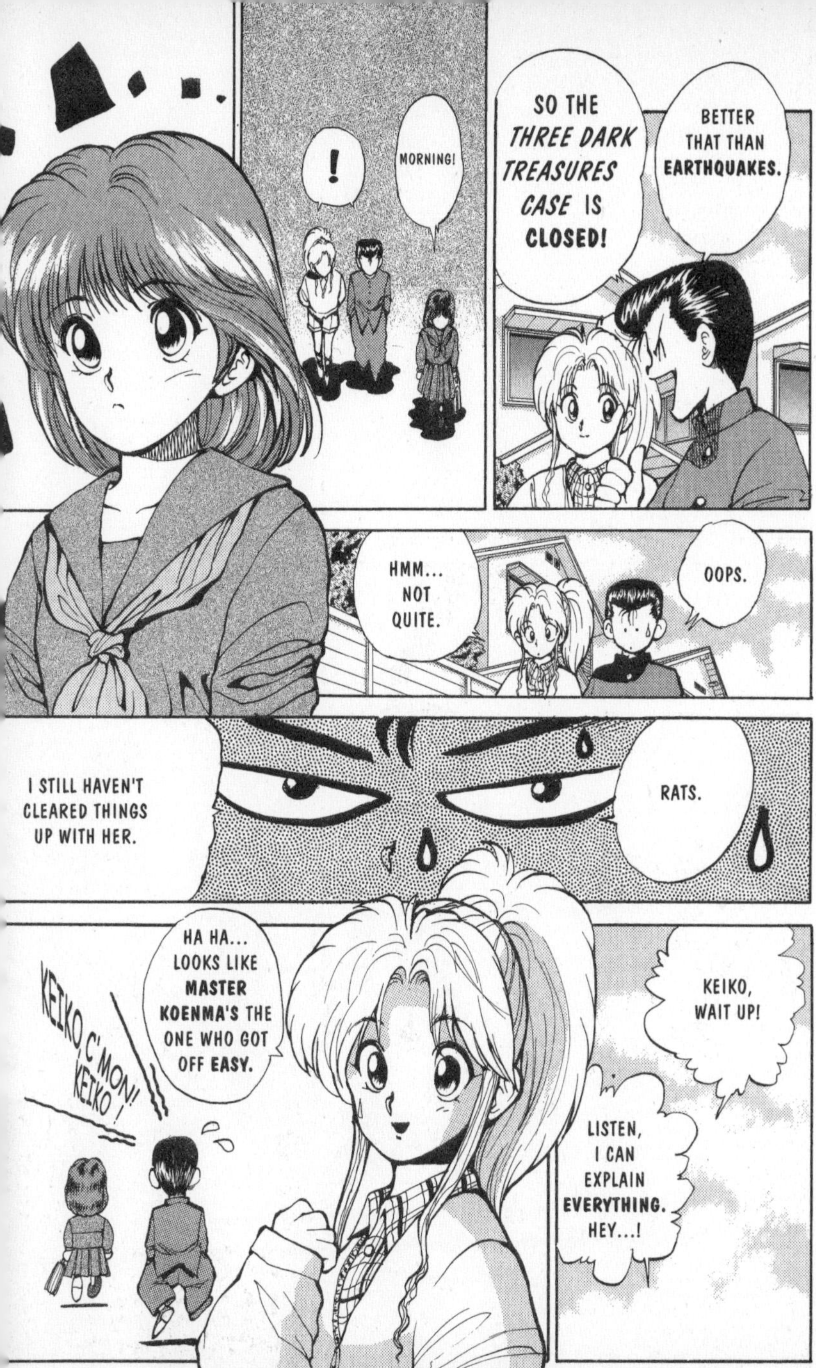
SO THE THREE DARK TREASURES CASE IS CLOSED!
BETTER THAN THAN EARTHQUAKES.
OOPS.
HMM... NOT QUITE.
MORNING!
!
RATS.
I STILL HAVEN'T CLEARED THINGS UP WITH HER.
KEIKO, WAIT UP!
LISTEN, I CAN EXPLAIN EVERYTHING. HEY...!
HA HA... LOOKS LIKE MASTER KOENMA'S THE ONE WHO GOT OFF EASY.
KEIKO, C'MON! KEIKO!

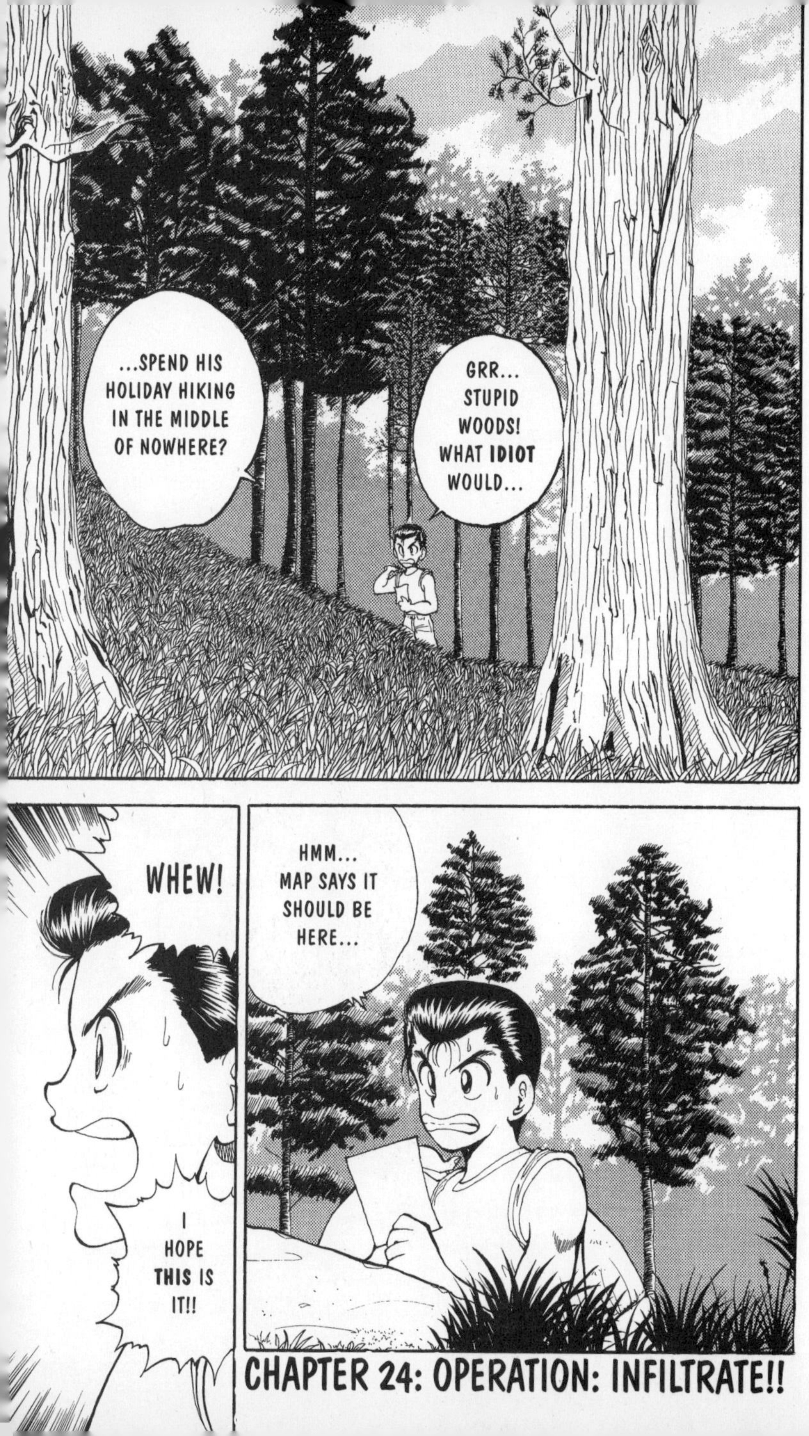
GRR... STUPID WOODS! WHAT IDIOT WOULD...
...SPEND HIS HOLIDAY HIKING IN THE MIDDLE OF NOWHERE?
HMM... MAP SAYS IT SHOULD BE HERE...
WHEW!
I HOPE THIS IS IT!!

CHAPTER 24: OPERATION: INFILTRATE!!

Chapter 24: OPERATION: INFILTRATE!!

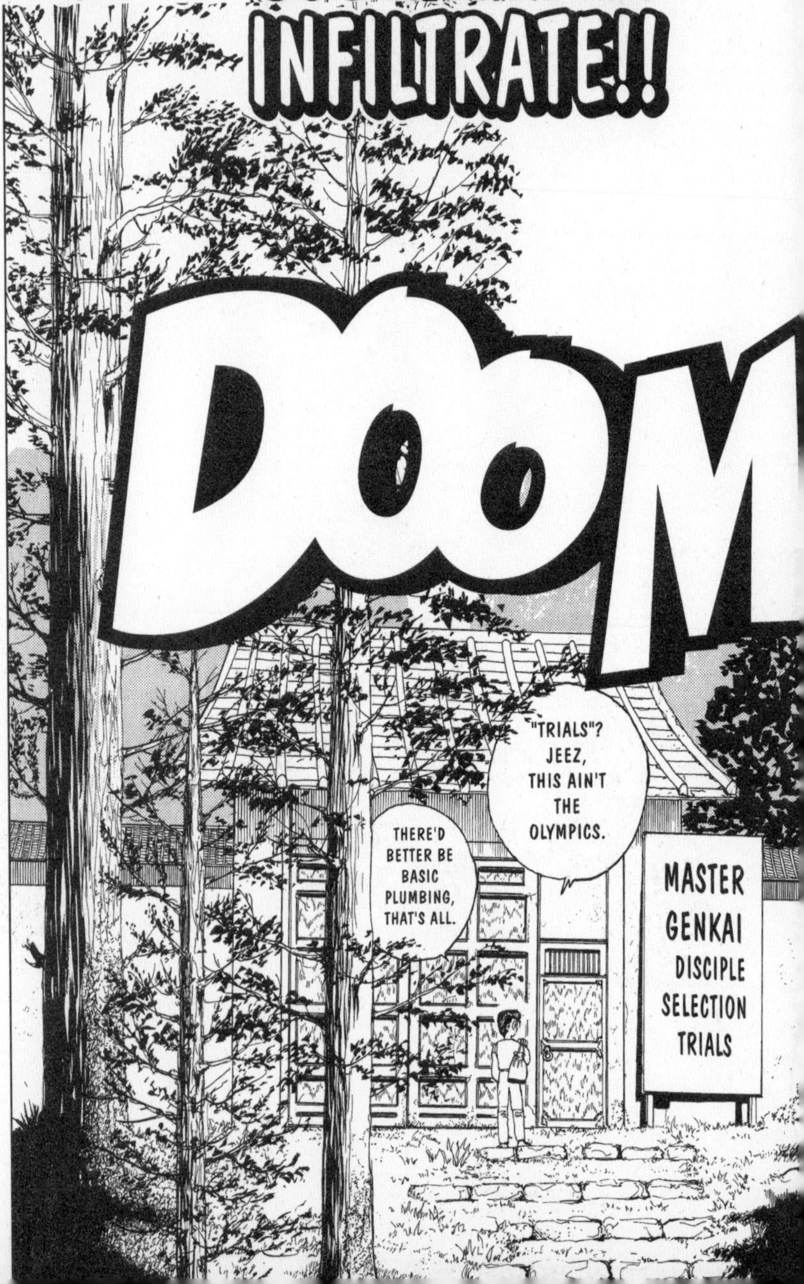
DOOM
"TRIALS"? JEEZ, THIS AIN'T THE OLYMPICS.
MASTER GENKAI DISCIPLE SELECTION TRIALS
THERE'D BETTER BE BASIC PLUMBING, THAT'S ALL.

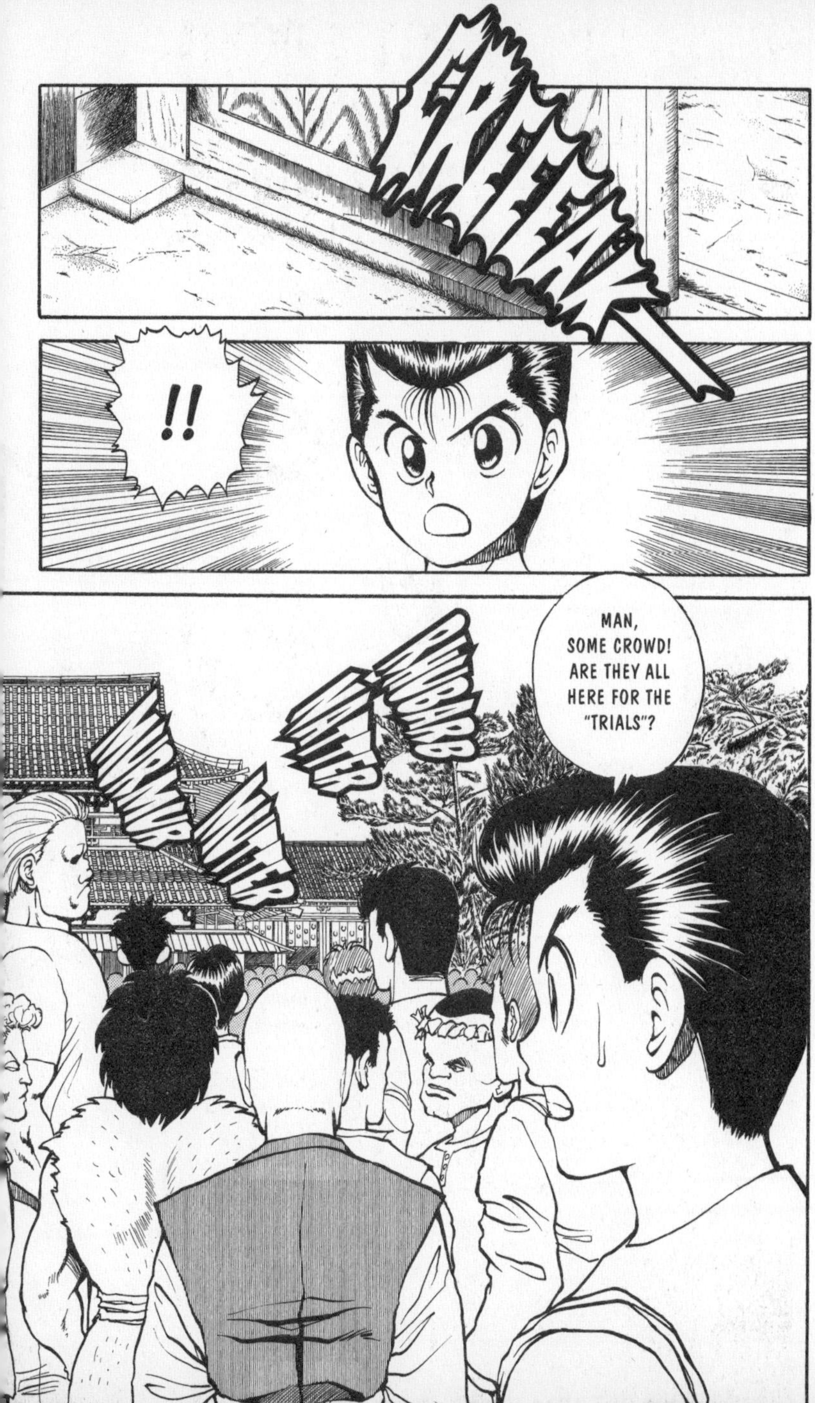
CREEEAK
!!
MAN, SOME CROWD! ARE THEY ALL HERE FOR THE "TRIALS"?
RHUBARB
MUTTER
MURMUR
MUTTER

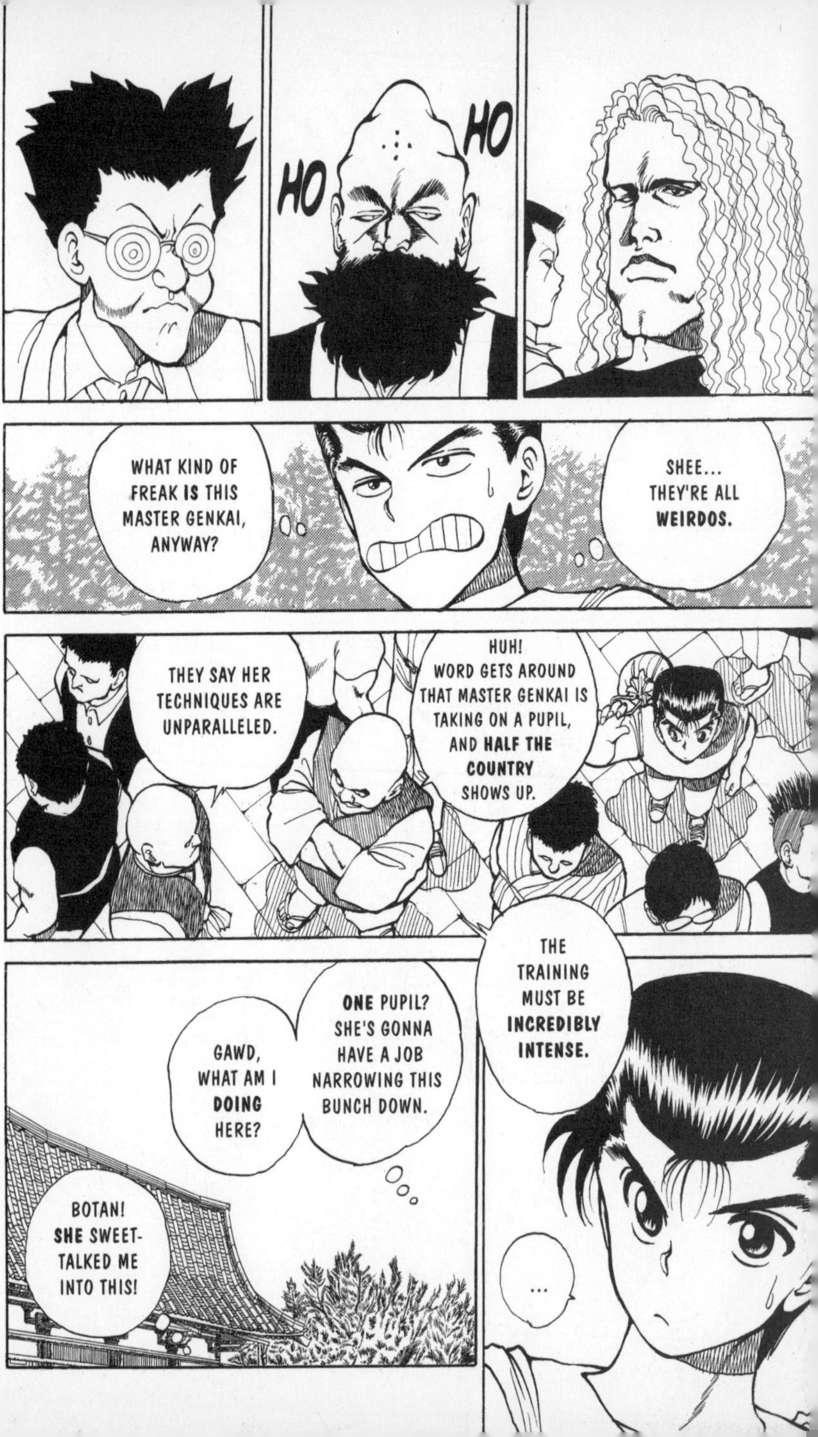
HO
HO
SHEE... THEY'RE ALL **WEIRDOS.**
WHAT KIND OF FREAK **IS** THIS MASTER GENKAI, ANYWAY?
HUH! WORD GETS AROUND THAT MASTER GENKAI IS TAKING ON A PUPIL, AND **HALF THE COUNTRY** SHOWS UP.
THEY SAY HER TECHNIQUES ARE UNPARALLELED.
THE TRAINING MUST BE **INCREDIBLY INTENSE.**
...
ONE PUPIL? SHE'S GONNA HAVE A JOB NARROWING THIS BUNCH DOWN.
GAWD, WHAT AM I **DOING** HERE?
BOTAN! **SHE** SWEET-TALKED ME INTO THIS!

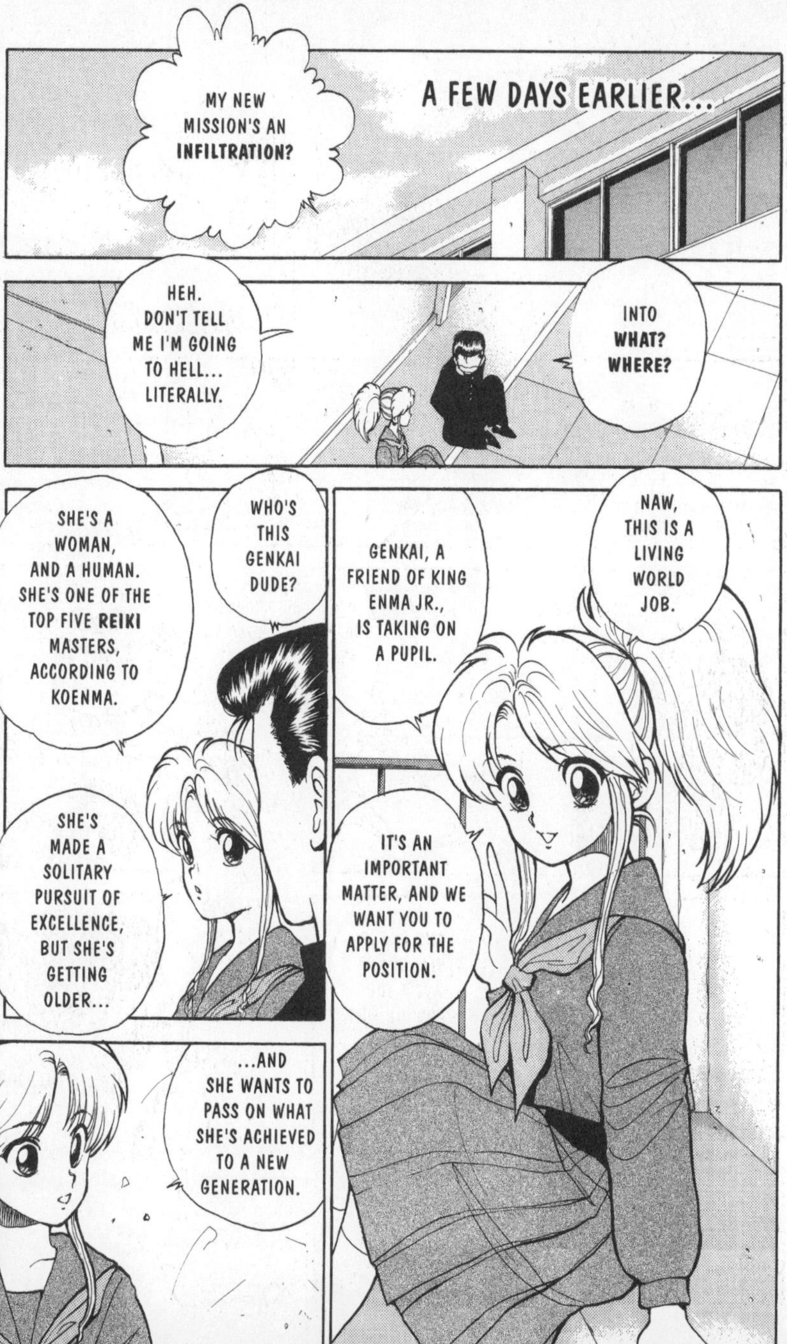
A FEW DAYS EARLIER...
MY NEW MISSION'S AN **INFILTRATION?**
INTO **WHAT? WHERE?**
HEH. DON'T TELL ME I'M GOING TO HELL... LITERALLY.
NAW, THIS IS A LIVING WORLD JOB.
GENKAI, A FRIEND OF KING ENMA JR., IS TAKING ON A PUPIL.
IT'S AN IMPORTANT MATTER, AND WE WANT YOU TO APPLY FOR THE POSITION.
WHO'S THIS GENKAI DUDE?
SHE'S A WOMAN, AND A HUMAN. SHE'S ONE OF THE TOP FIVE **REIKI** MASTERS, ACCORDING TO KOENMA.
SHE'S MADE A SOLITARY PURSUIT OF EXCELLENCE, BUT SHE'S GETTING OLDER...
...AND SHE WANTS TO PASS ON WHAT SHE'S ACHIEVED TO A NEW GENERATION.

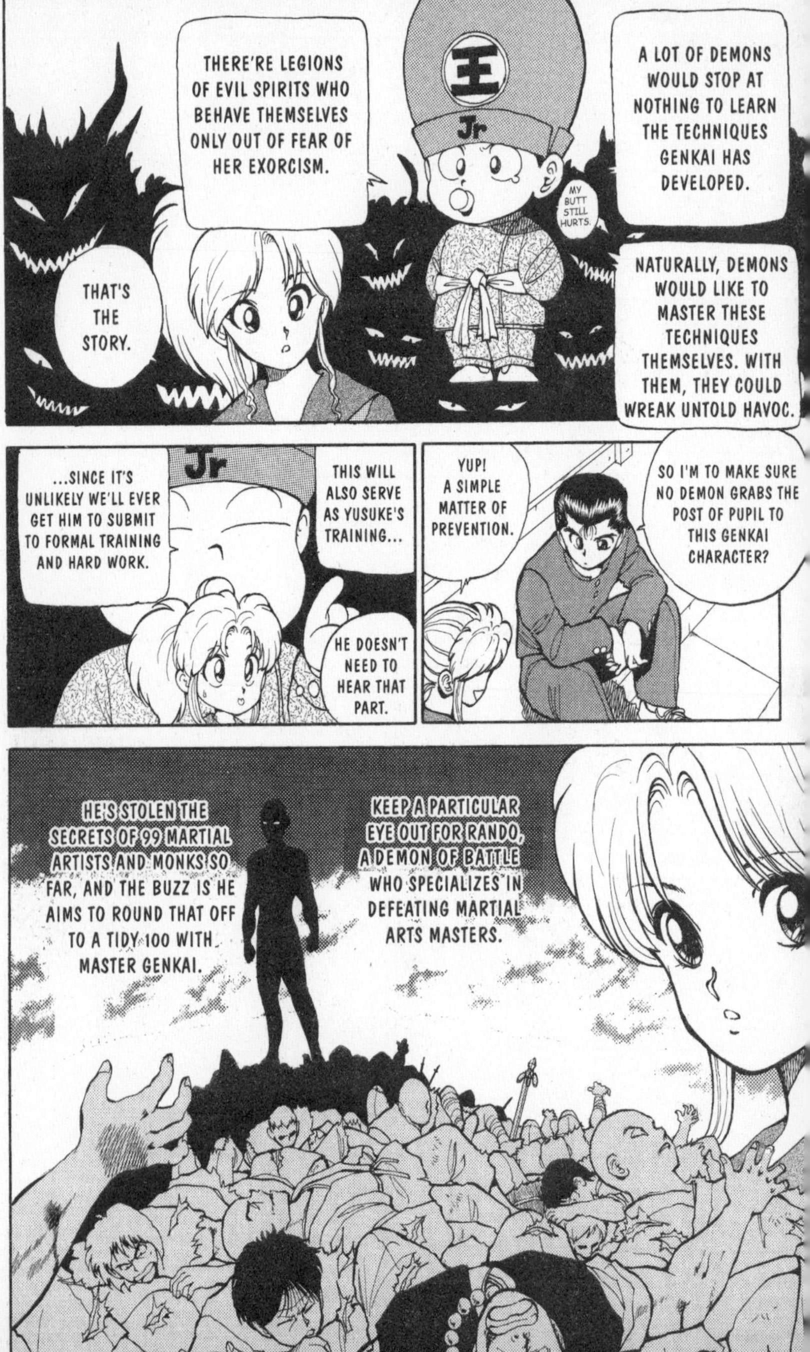
A LOT OF DEMONS WOULD STOP AT NOTHING TO LEARN THE TECHNIQUES GENKAI HAS DEVELOPED.
NATURALLY, DEMONS WOULD LIKE TO MASTER THESE TECHNIQUES THEMSELVES. WITH THEM, THEY COULD WREAK UNTOLD HAVOC.
MY BUTT STILL HURTS.
THERE'RE LEGIONS OF EVIL SPIRITS WHO BEHAVE THEMSELVES ONLY OUT OF FEAR OF HER EXORCISM.
THAT'S THE STORY.
SO I'M TO MAKE SURE NO DEMON GRABS THE POST OF PUPIL TO THIS GENKAI CHARACTER?
YUP! A SIMPLE MATTER OF PREVENTION.
THIS WILL ALSO SERVE AS YUSUKE'S TRAINING...
...SINCE IT'S UNLIKELY WE'LL EVER GET HIM TO SUBMIT TO FORMAL TRAINING AND HARD WORK.
HE DOESN'T NEED TO HEAR THAT PART.
KEEP A PARTICULAR EYE OUT FOR RANDO, A DEMON OF BATTLE WHO SPECIALIZES IN DEFEATING MARTIAL ARTS MASTERS.
HE'S STOLEN THE SECRETS OF 99 MARTIAL ARTISTS AND MONKS SO FAR, AND THE BUZZ IS HE AIMS TO ROUND THAT OFF TO A TIDY 100 WITH MASTER GENKAI.

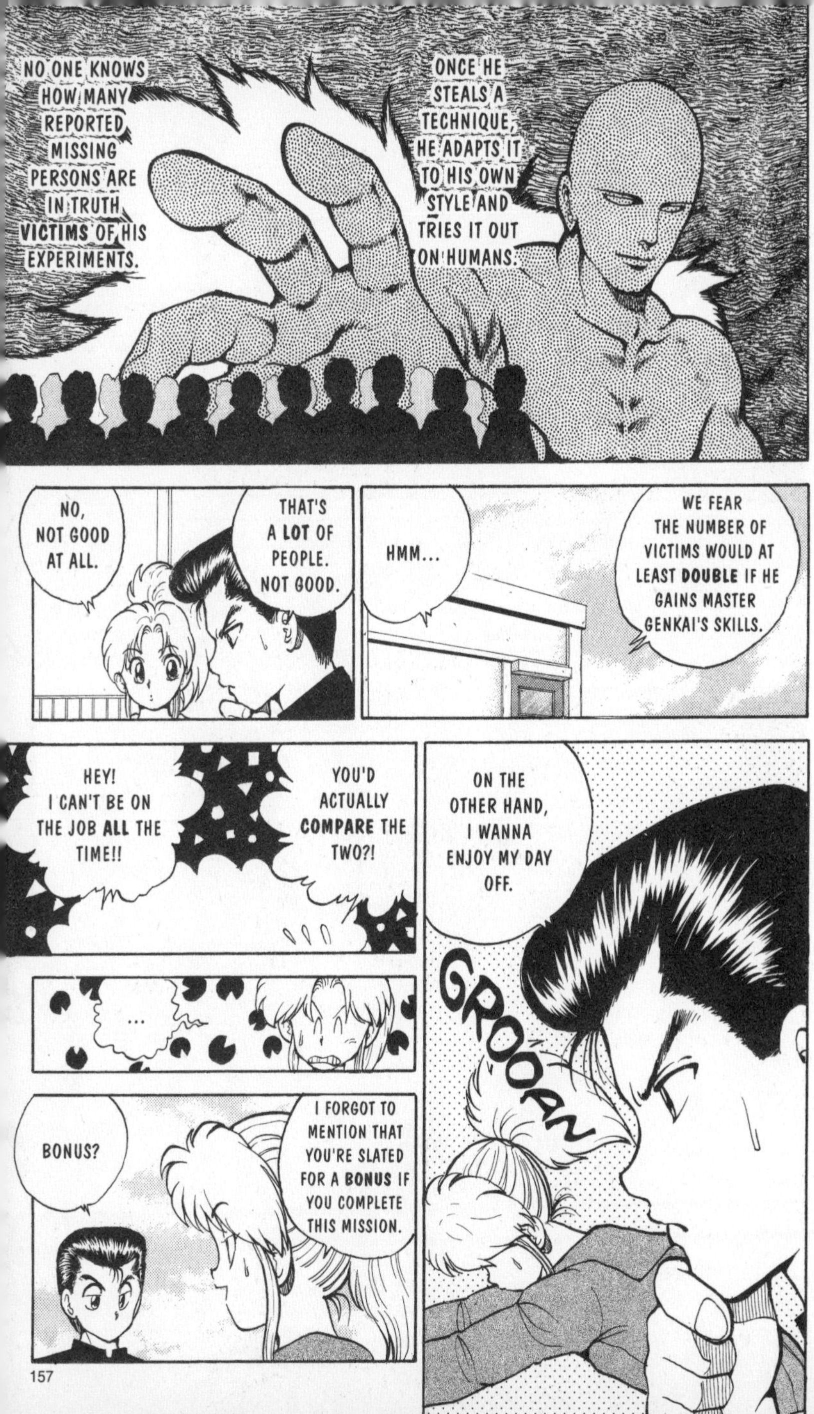
ONCE HE STEALS A TECHNIQUE, HE ADAPTS IT TO HIS OWN STYLE AND TRIES IT OUT ON HUMANS.
NO ONE KNOWS HOW MANY REPORTED MISSING PERSONS ARE IN TRUTH VICTIMS OF HIS EXPERIMENTS.
WE FEAR THE NUMBER OF VICTIMS WOULD AT LEAST DOUBLE IF HE GAINS MASTER GENKAI'S SKILLS.
HMM...
THAT'S A LOT OF PEOPLE. NOT GOOD.
NO, NOT GOOD AT ALL.
ON THE OTHER HAND, I WANNA ENJOY MY DAY OFF.
GROOAN
YOU'D ACTUALLY COMPARE THE TWO?!
HEY! I CAN'T BE ON THE JOB ALL THE TIME!!
...
I FORGOT TO MENTION THAT YOU'RE SLATED FOR A BONUS IF YOU COMPLETE THIS MISSION.
BONUS?

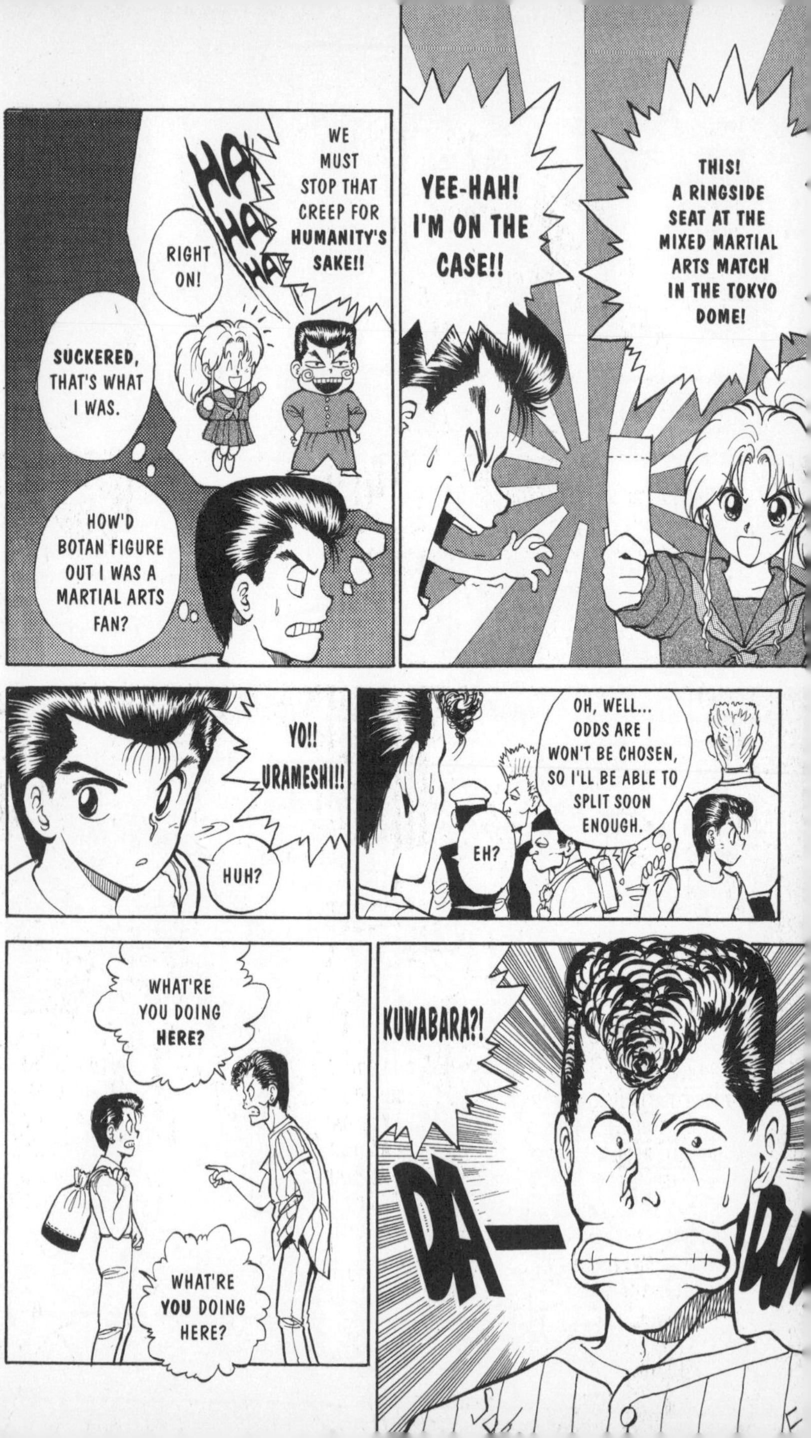
THIS! A RINGSIDE SEAT AT THE MIXED MARTIAL ARTS MATCH IN THE TOKYO DOME!
YEE-HAH! I'M ON THE CASE!!
WE MUST STOP THAT CREEP FOR HUMANITY'S SAKE!!
HA HA HA
RIGHT ON!
SUCKERED, THAT'S WHAT I WAS.
HOW'D BOTAN FIGURE OUT I WAS A MARTIAL ARTS FAN?
OH, WELL... ODDS ARE I WON'T BE CHOSEN, SO I'LL BE ABLE TO SPLIT SOON ENOUGH.
EH?
YO!! URAMESHI!!
HUH?
KUWABARA?!
DA—
WHAT'RE YOU DOING HERE?
WHAT'RE YOU DOING HERE?

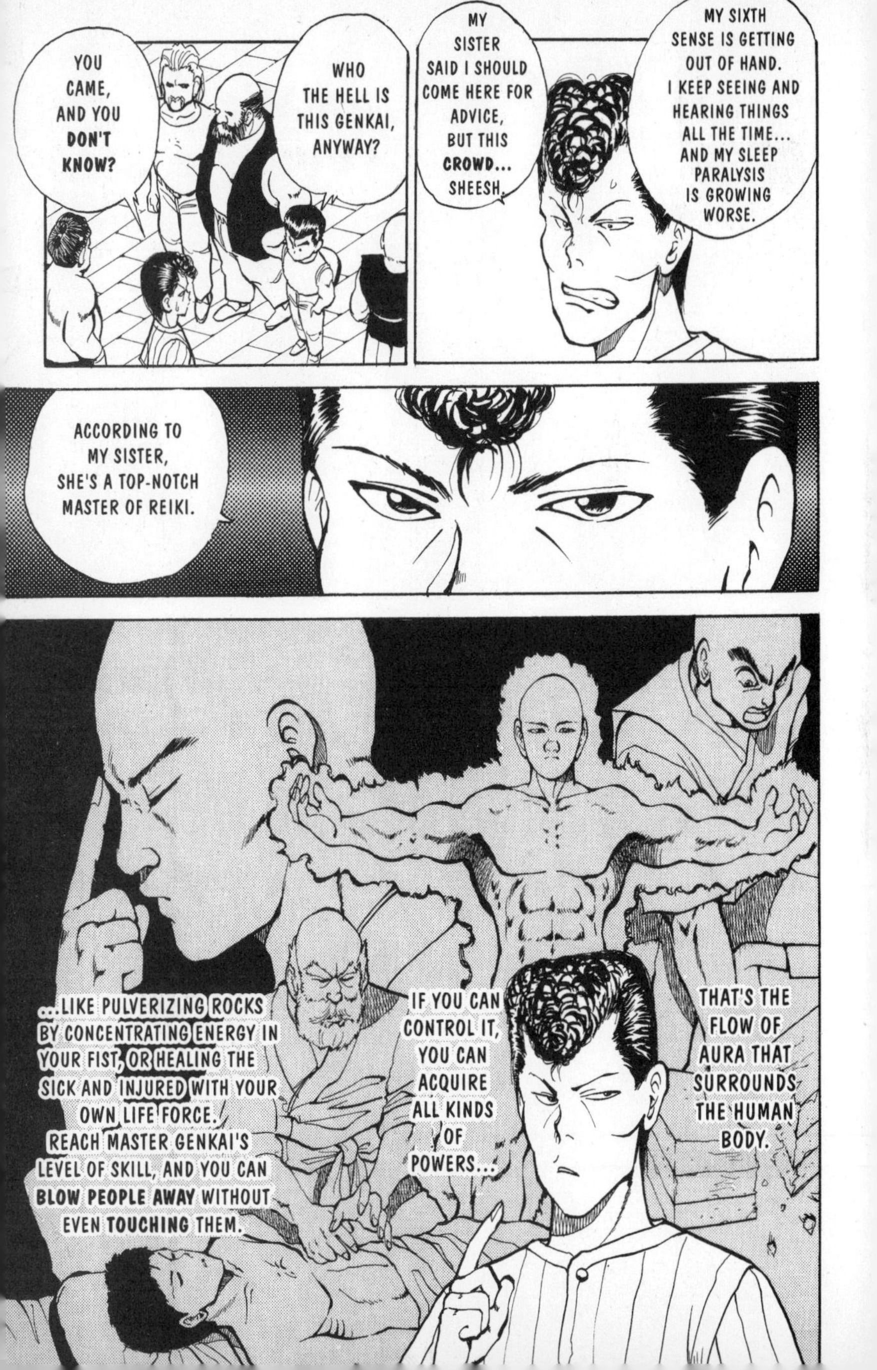
MY SIXTH SENSE IS GETTING OUT OF HAND. I KEEP SEEING AND HEARING THINGS ALL THE TIME... AND MY SLEEP PARALYSIS IS GROWING WORSE.
MY SISTER SAID I SHOULD COME HERE FOR ADVICE, BUT THIS **CROWD...** SHEESH.
WHO THE HELL IS THIS GENKAI, ANYWAY?
YOU CAME, AND YOU **DON'T KNOW?**
ACCORDING TO MY SISTER, SHE'S A TOP-NOTCH MASTER OF REIKI.
THAT'S THE FLOW OF AURA THAT SURROUNDS THE HUMAN BODY.
IF YOU CAN CONTROL IT, YOU CAN ACQUIRE ALL KINDS OF POWERS...
...LIKE PULVERIZING ROCKS BY CONCENTRATING ENERGY IN YOUR FIST, OR HEALING THE SICK AND INJURED WITH YOUR OWN LIFE FORCE. REACH MASTER GENKAI'S LEVEL OF SKILL, AND YOU CAN **BLOW PEOPLE AWAY** WITHOUT EVEN **TOUCHING** THEM.

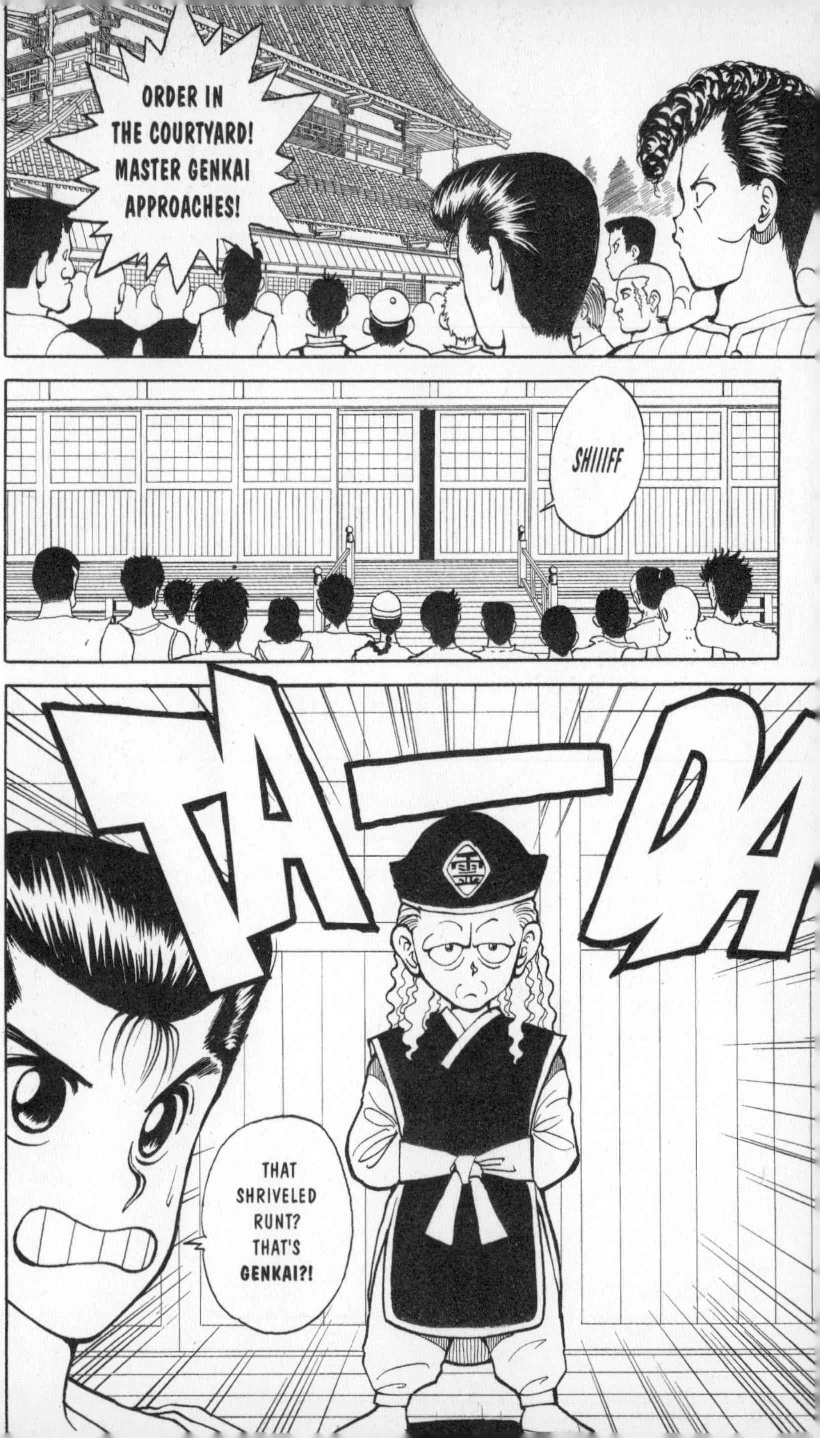
ORDER IN THE COURTYARD! MASTER GENKAI APPROACHES!
SHIIIFF
TA-DA
THAT SHRIVELED RUNT? THAT'S GENKAI?!

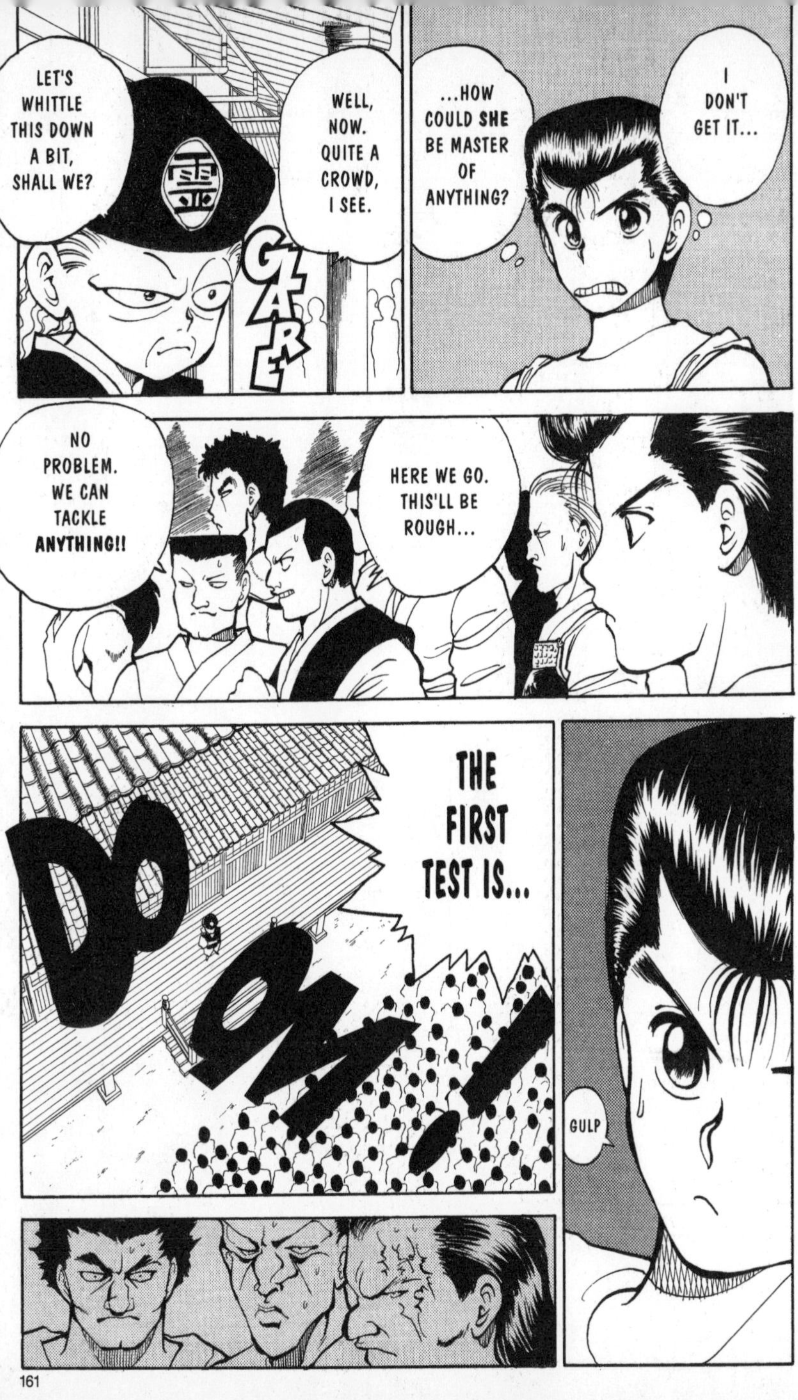
I DON'T GET IT...
...HOW COULD SHE BE MASTER OF ANYTHING?
WELL, NOW. QUITE A CROWD, I SEE.
LET'S WHITTLE THIS DOWN A BIT, SHALL WE?
GLARE
HERE WE GO. THIS'LL BE ROUGH...
NO PROBLEM. WE CAN TACKLE **ANYTHING!!**
GULP
THE FIRST TEST IS...
DOOM!

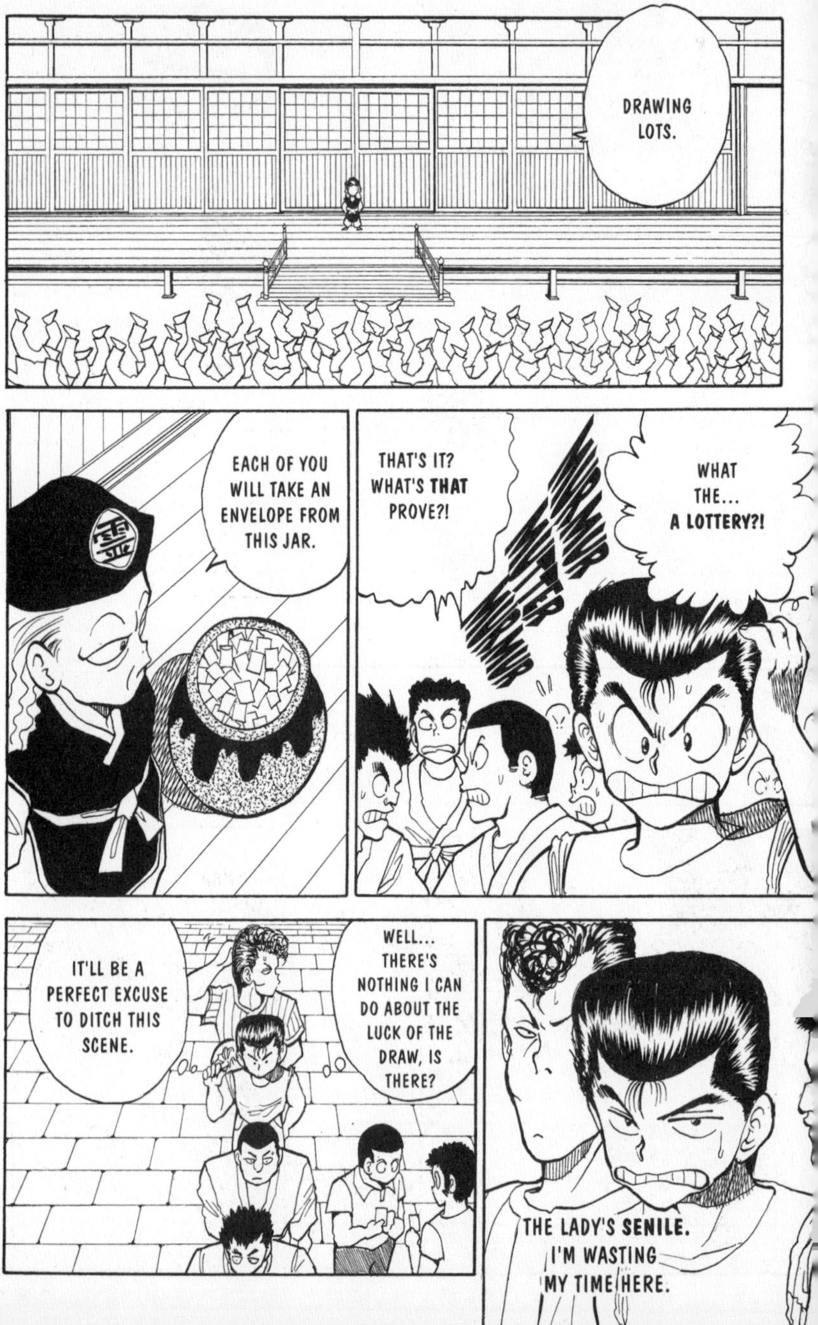
DRAWING LOTS.
WHAT THE... A LOTTERY?!
MURMUR MUTTER MURMUR
THAT'S IT? WHAT'S **THAT** PROVE?!
EACH OF YOU WILL TAKE AN ENVELOPE FROM THIS JAR.
THE LADY'S **SENILE.** I'M WASTING MY TIME HERE.
WELL... THERE'S NOTHING I CAN DO ABOUT THE LUCK OF THE DRAW, IS THERE?
IT'LL BE A PERFECT EXCUSE TO DITCH THIS SCENE.

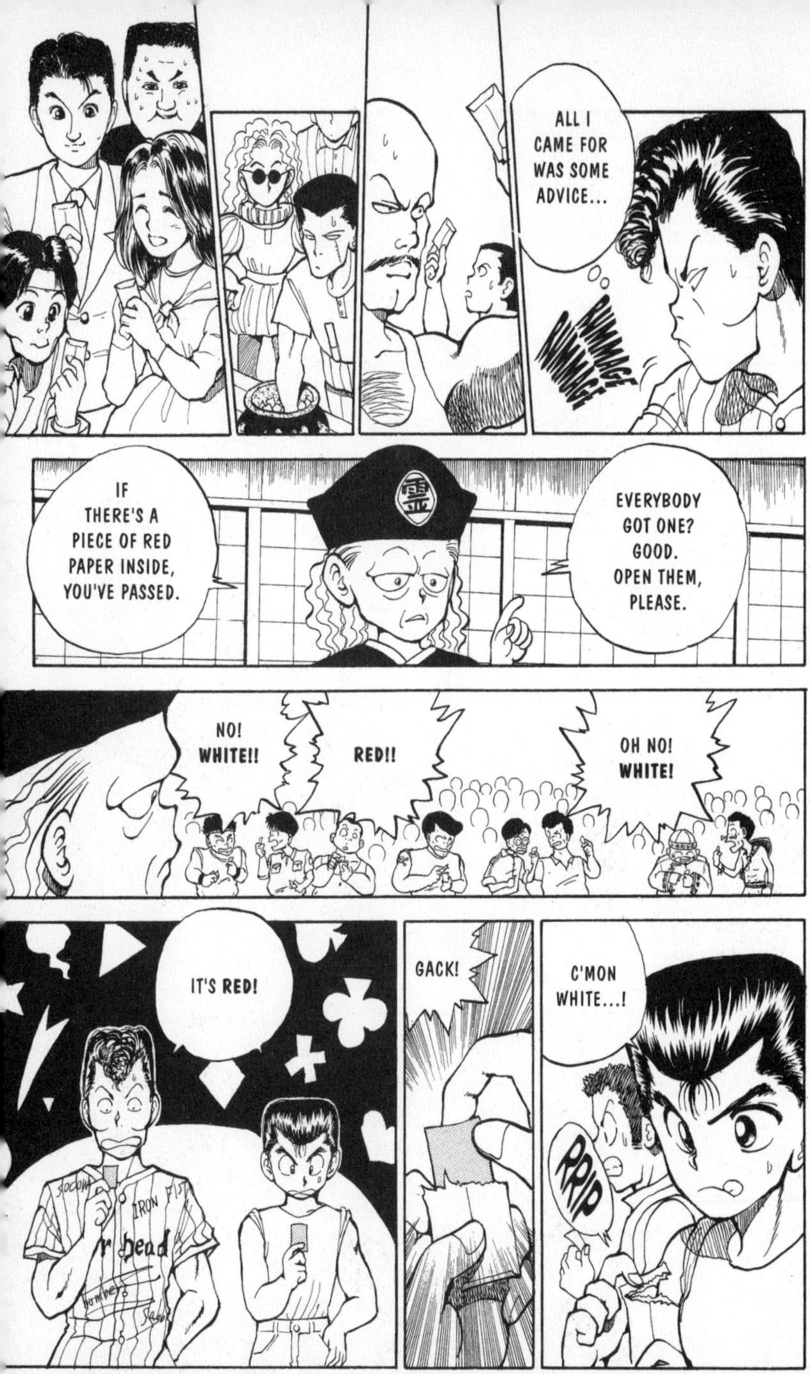
ALL I CAME FOR WAS SOME ADVICE...
RUMMAGE RUMMAGE
EVERYBODY GOT ONE? GOOD. OPEN THEM, PLEASE.
IF THERE'S A PIECE OF RED PAPER INSIDE, YOU'VE PASSED.
OH NO! WHITE!
RED!!
NO! WHITE!!
C'MON WHITE...!
RRIP
GACK!
IT'S RED!

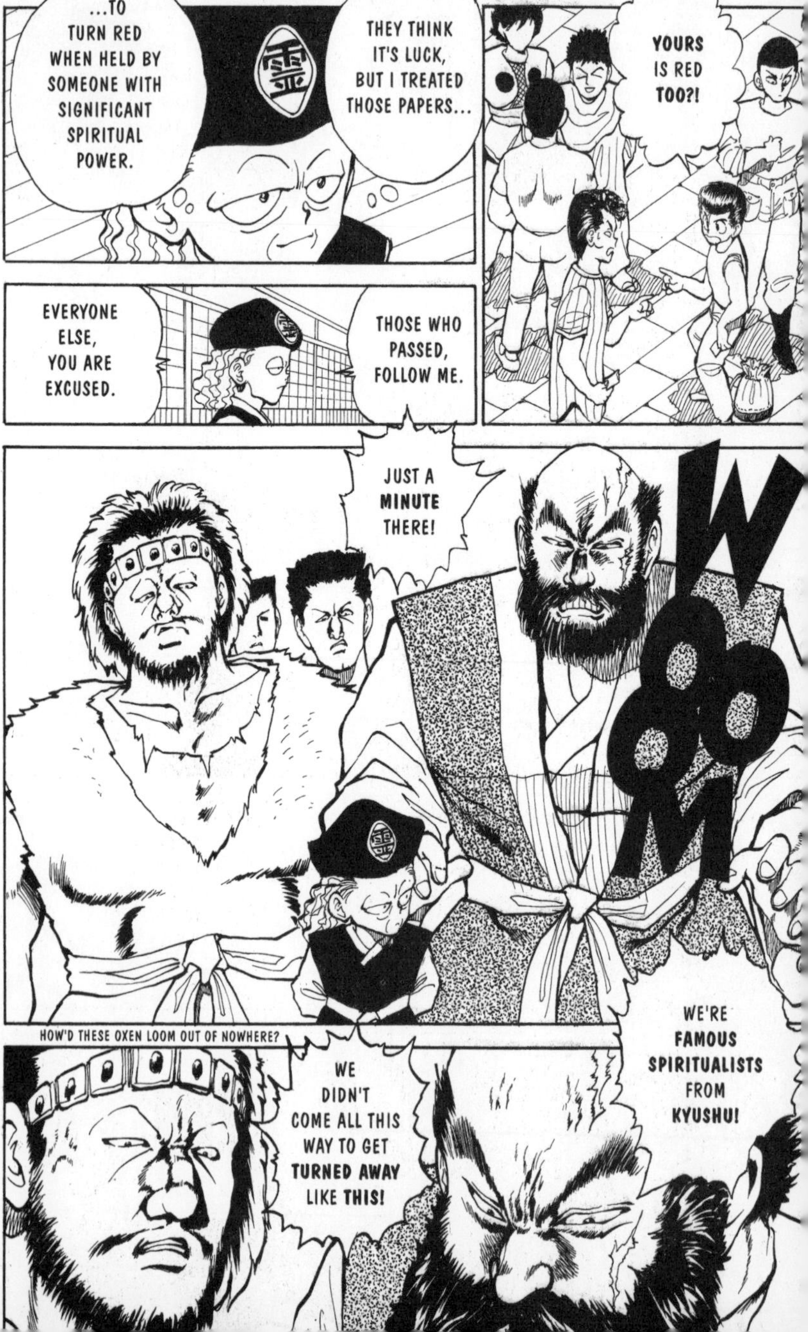
YOURS IS RED TOO?!
THEY THINK IT'S LUCK, BUT I TREATED THOSE PAPERS...
...TO TURN RED WHEN HELD BY SOMEONE WITH SIGNIFICANT SPIRITUAL POWER.
THOSE WHO PASSED, FOLLOW ME.
EVERYONE ELSE, YOU ARE EXCUSED.
JUST A MINUTE THERE!
WOOOOM
HOW'D THESE OXEN LOOM OUT OF NOWHERE?
WE'RE FAMOUS SPIRITUALISTS FROM KYUSHU!
WE DIDN'T COME ALL THIS WAY TO GET TURNED AWAY LIKE THIS!

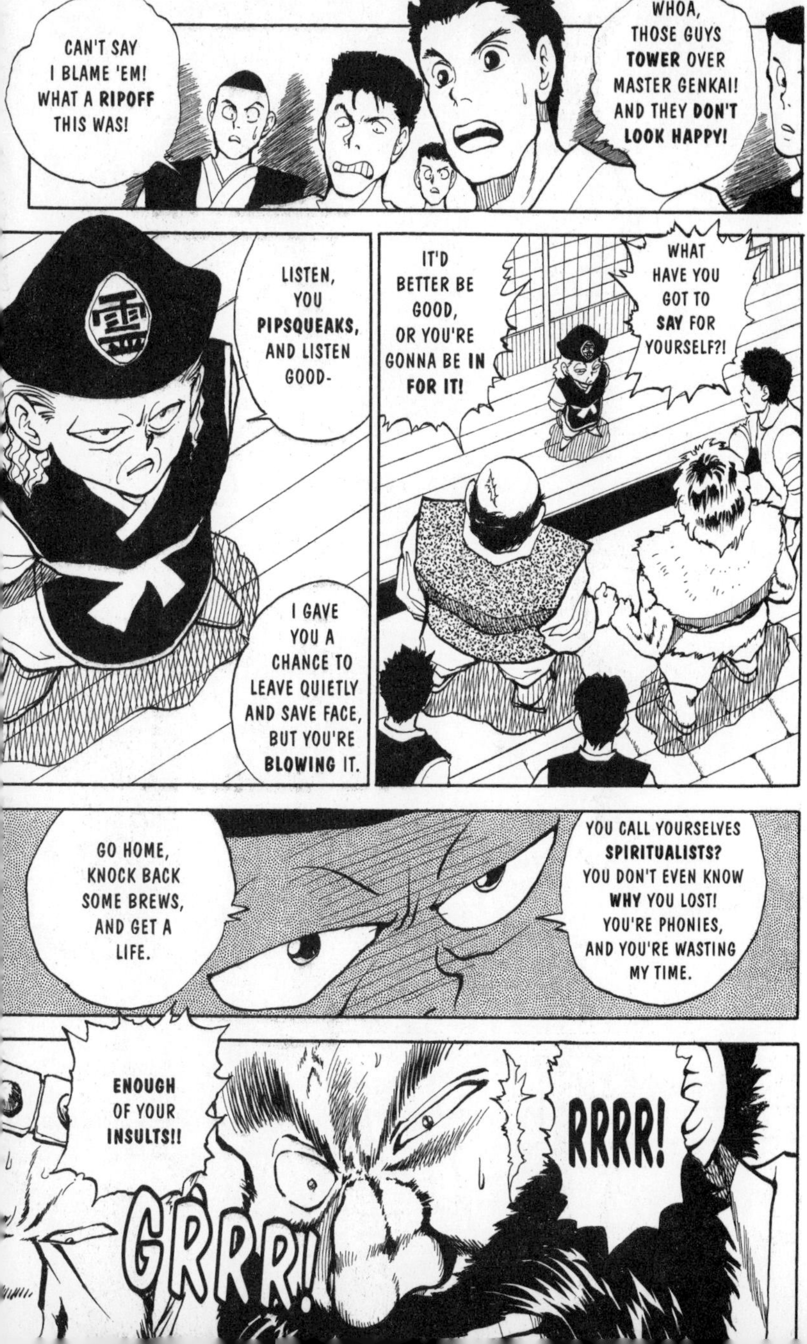
WHOA, THOSE GUYS TOWER OVER MASTER GENKAI! AND THEY DON'T LOOK HAPPY!
CAN'T SAY I BLAME 'EM! WHAT A RIPOFF THIS WAS!
WHAT HAVE YOU GOT TO SAY FOR YOURSELF?!
IT'D BETTER BE GOOD, OR YOU'RE GONNA BE IN FOR IT!
LISTEN, YOU PIPSQUEAKS, AND LISTEN GOOD-
I GAVE YOU A CHANCE TO LEAVE QUIETLY AND SAVE FACE, BUT YOU'RE BLOWING IT.
YOU CALL YOURSELVES SPIRITUALISTS? YOU DON'T EVEN KNOW WHY YOU LOST! YOU'RE PHONIES, AND YOU'RE WASTING MY TIME.
GO HOME, KNOCK BACK SOME BREWS, AND GET A LIFE.
RRRR!
ENOUGH OF YOUR INSULTS!!
GRRR!

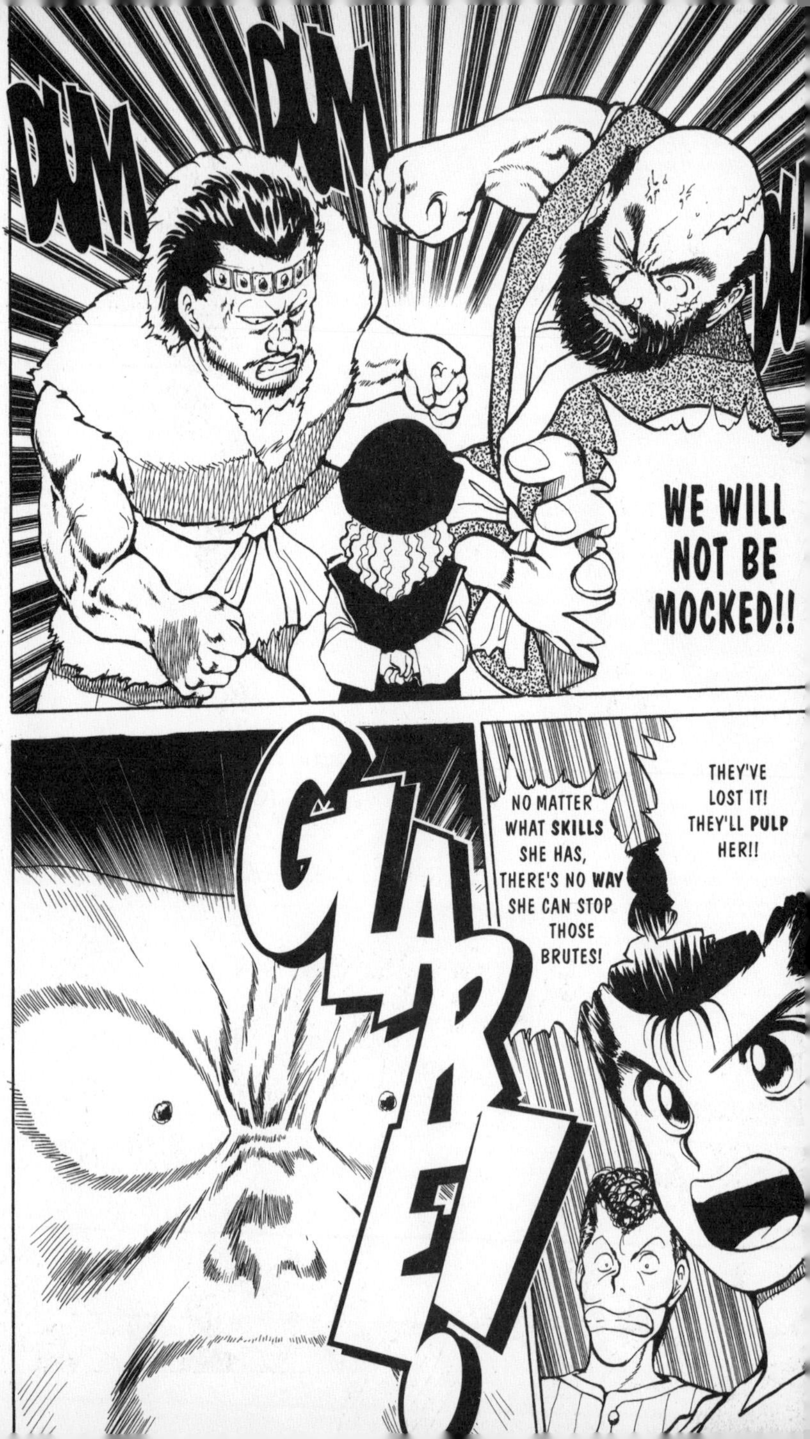
DUM DUM
WE WILL NOT BE MOCKED!!
THEY'VE LOST IT! THEY'LL PULP HER!!
NO MATTER WHAT SKILLS SHE HAS, THERE'S NO WAY SHE CAN STOP THOSE BRUTES!
GLARE!

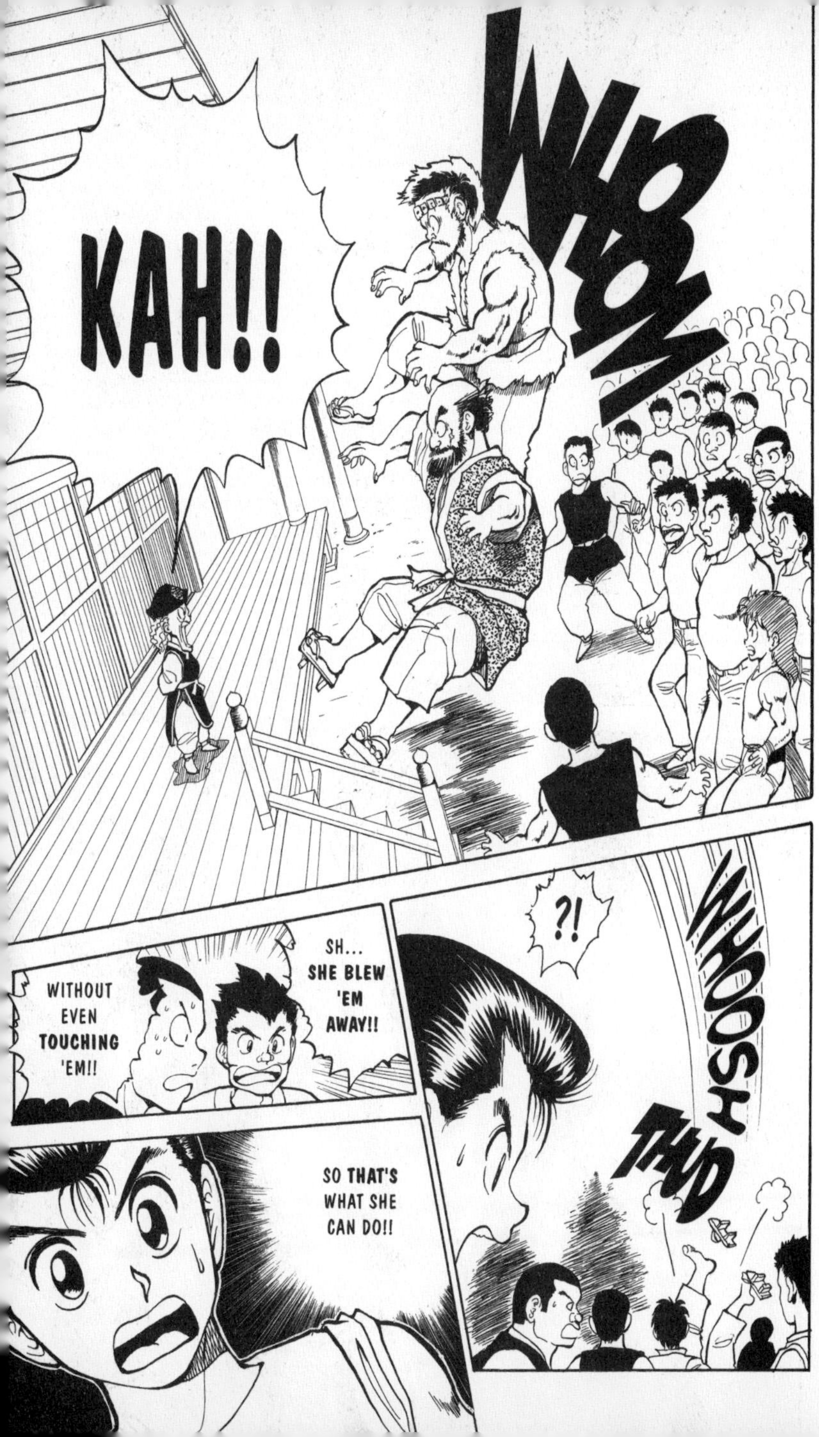
WHOOM
KAH!!
?!
WHOOSH
THUD
SH... SHE BLEW 'EM AWAY!!
WITHOUT EVEN TOUCHING 'EM!!
SO THAT'S WHAT SHE CAN DO!!

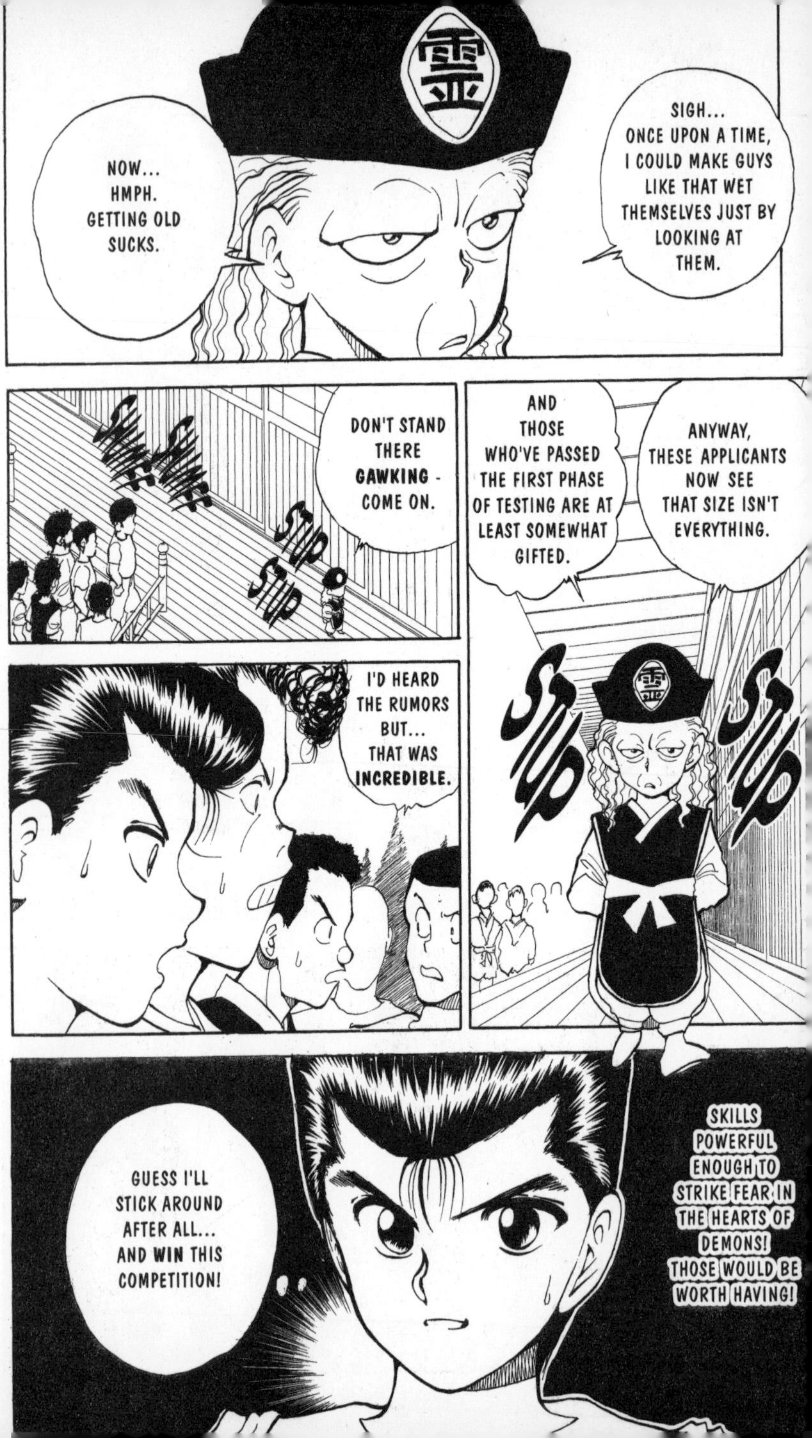
SIGH... ONCE UPON A TIME, I COULD MAKE GUYS LIKE THAT WET THEMSELVES JUST BY LOOKING AT THEM.
NOW... HMPH. GETTING OLD SUCKS.
ANYWAY, THESE APPLICANTS NOW SEE THAT SIZE ISN'T EVERYTHING.
AND THOSE WHO'VE PASSED THE FIRST PHASE OF TESTING ARE AT LEAST SOMEWHAT GIFTED.
STIP STIP
DON'T STAND THERE **GAWKING** - COME ON.
STIP STIP
I'D HEARD THE RUMORS BUT... THAT WAS **INCREDIBLE.**
SKILLS POWERFUL ENOUGH TO STRIKE FEAR IN THE HEARTS OF DEMONS! THOSE WOULD BE WORTH HAVING!
GUESS I'LL STICK AROUND AFTER ALL... AND **WIN** THIS COMPETITION!

READ THIS WAY

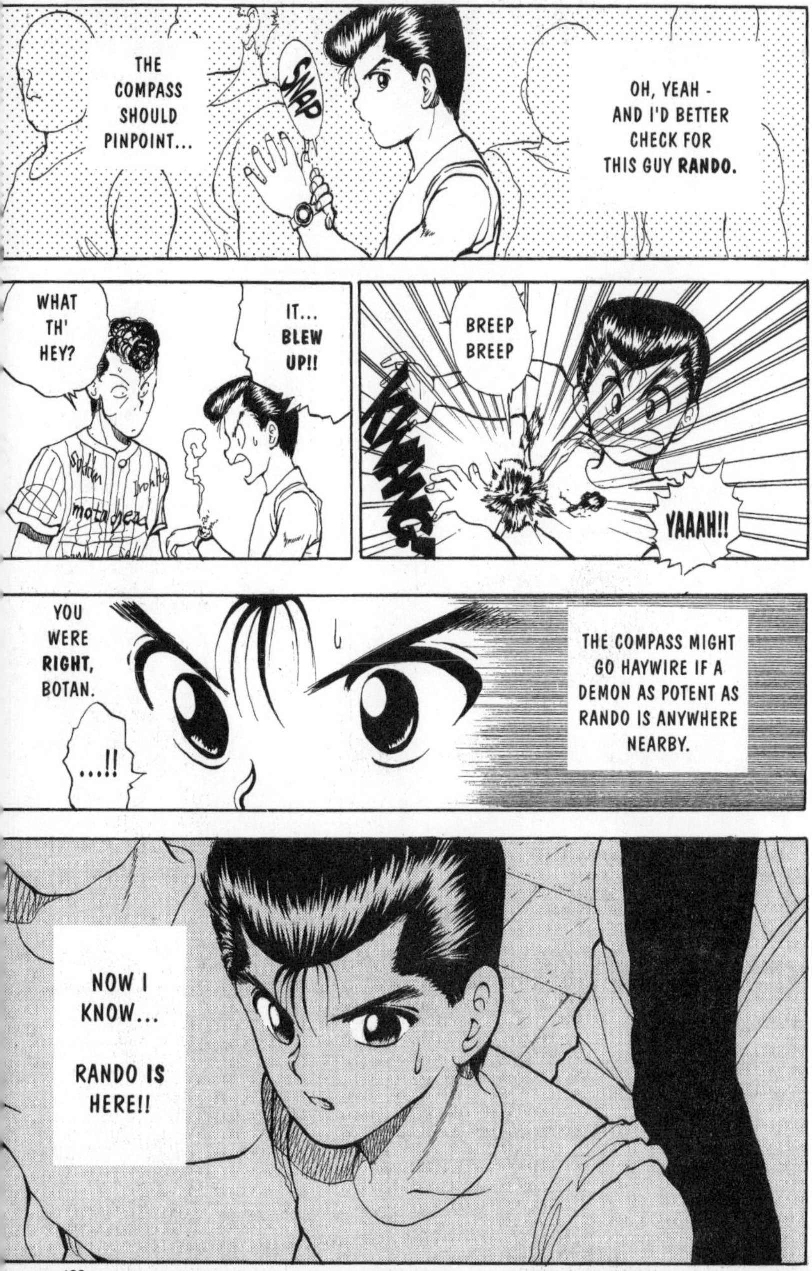
OH, YEAH - AND I'D BETTER CHECK FOR THIS GUY **RANDO.**
SNAP
THE COMPASS SHOULD PINPOINT...
BREEP BREEP
KWANG!
YAAAH!!
IT... **BLEW UP!!**
WHAT TH' HEY?
THE COMPASS MIGHT GO HAYWIRE IF A DEMON AS POTENT AS RANDO IS ANYWHERE NEARBY.
YOU WERE **RIGHT,** BOTAN.
...!!
NOW I KNOW...
RANDO IS HERE!!

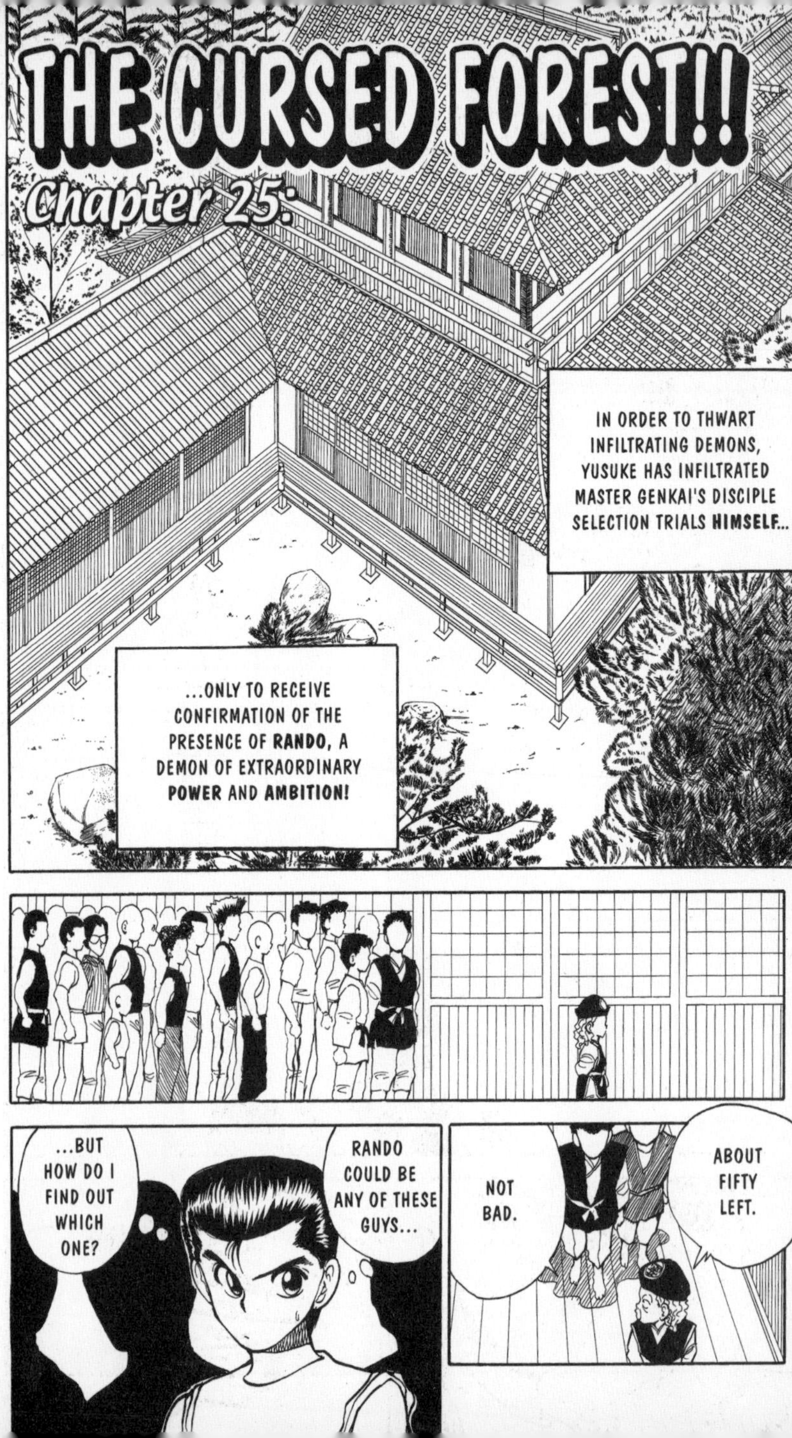
Chapter 25:
THE CURSED FOREST!!
IN ORDER TO THWART INFILTRATING DEMONS, YUSUKE HAS INFILTRATED MASTER GENKAI'S DISCIPLE SELECTION TRIALS HIMSELF...
...ONLY TO RECEIVE CONFIRMATION OF THE PRESENCE OF RANDO, A DEMON OF EXTRAORDINARY POWER AND AMBITION!
ABOUT FIFTY LEFT.
NOT BAD.
RANDO COULD BE ANY OF THESE GUYS...
...BUT HOW DO I FIND OUT WHICH ONE?

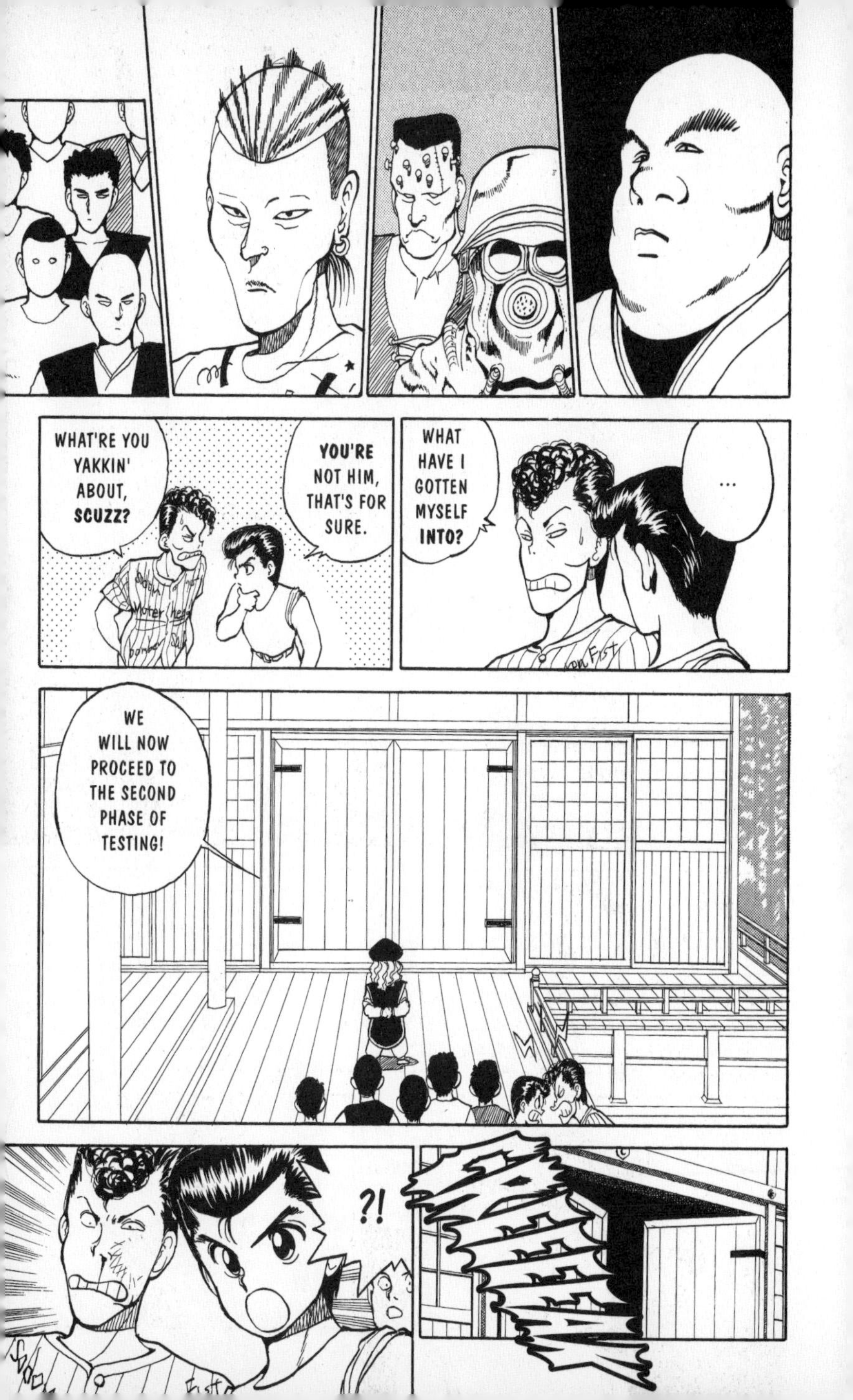
...
WHAT HAVE I GOTTEN MYSELF INTO?
YOU'RE NOT HIM, THAT'S FOR SURE.
WHAT'RE YOU YAKKIN' ABOUT, SCUZZ?
WE WILL NOW PROCEED TO THE SECOND PHASE OF TESTING!
?!

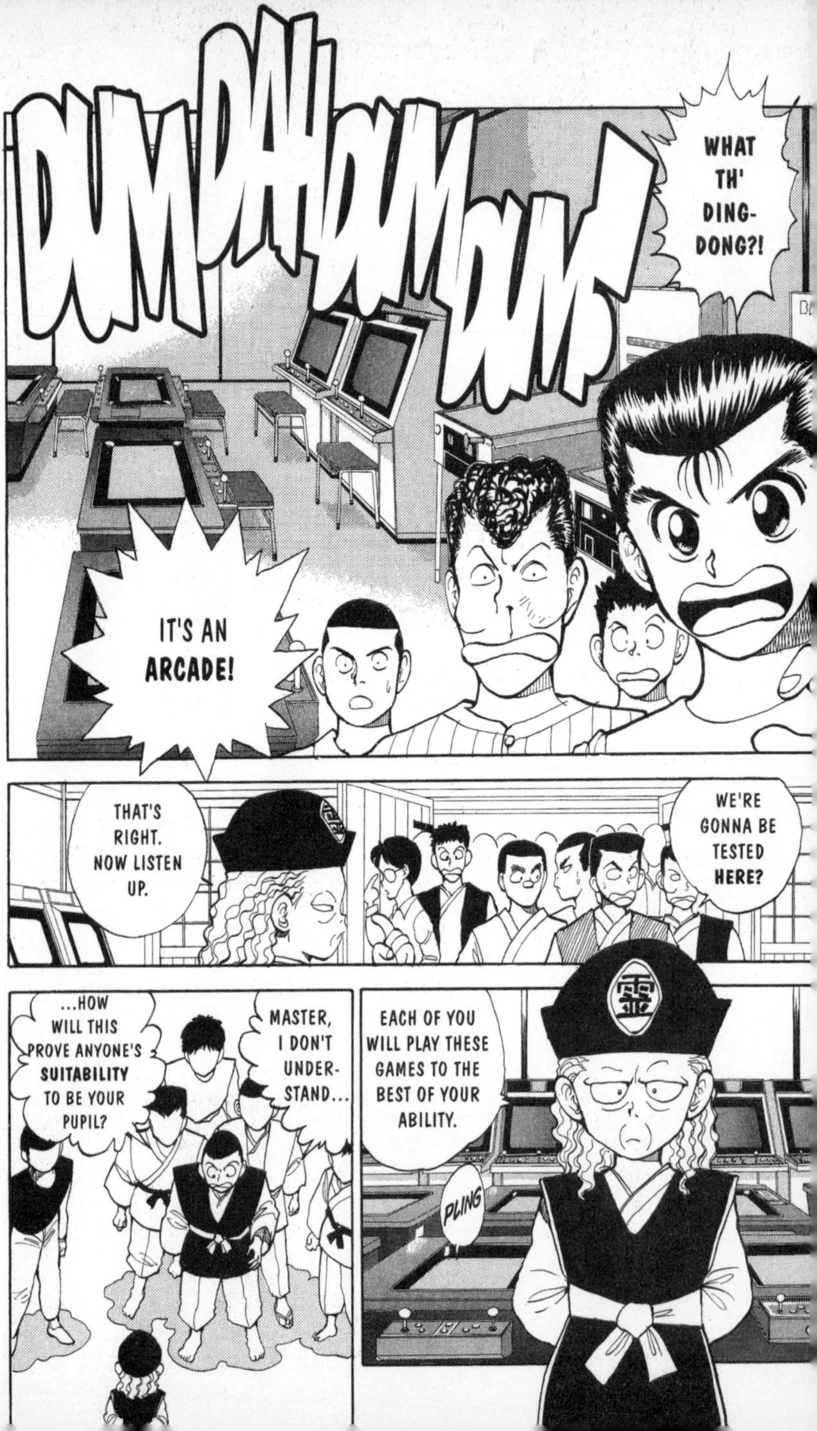
WHAT TH' DING-DONG?!
DUM DAH DUM DUM DUM!
IT'S AN ARCADE!
WE'RE GONNA BE TESTED HERE?
THAT'S RIGHT. NOW LISTEN UP.
EACH OF YOU WILL PLAY THESE GAMES TO THE BEST OF YOUR ABILITY.
PLING
MASTER, I DON'T UNDER-STAND...
...HOW WILL THIS PROVE ANYONE'S SUITABILITY TO BE YOUR PUPIL?

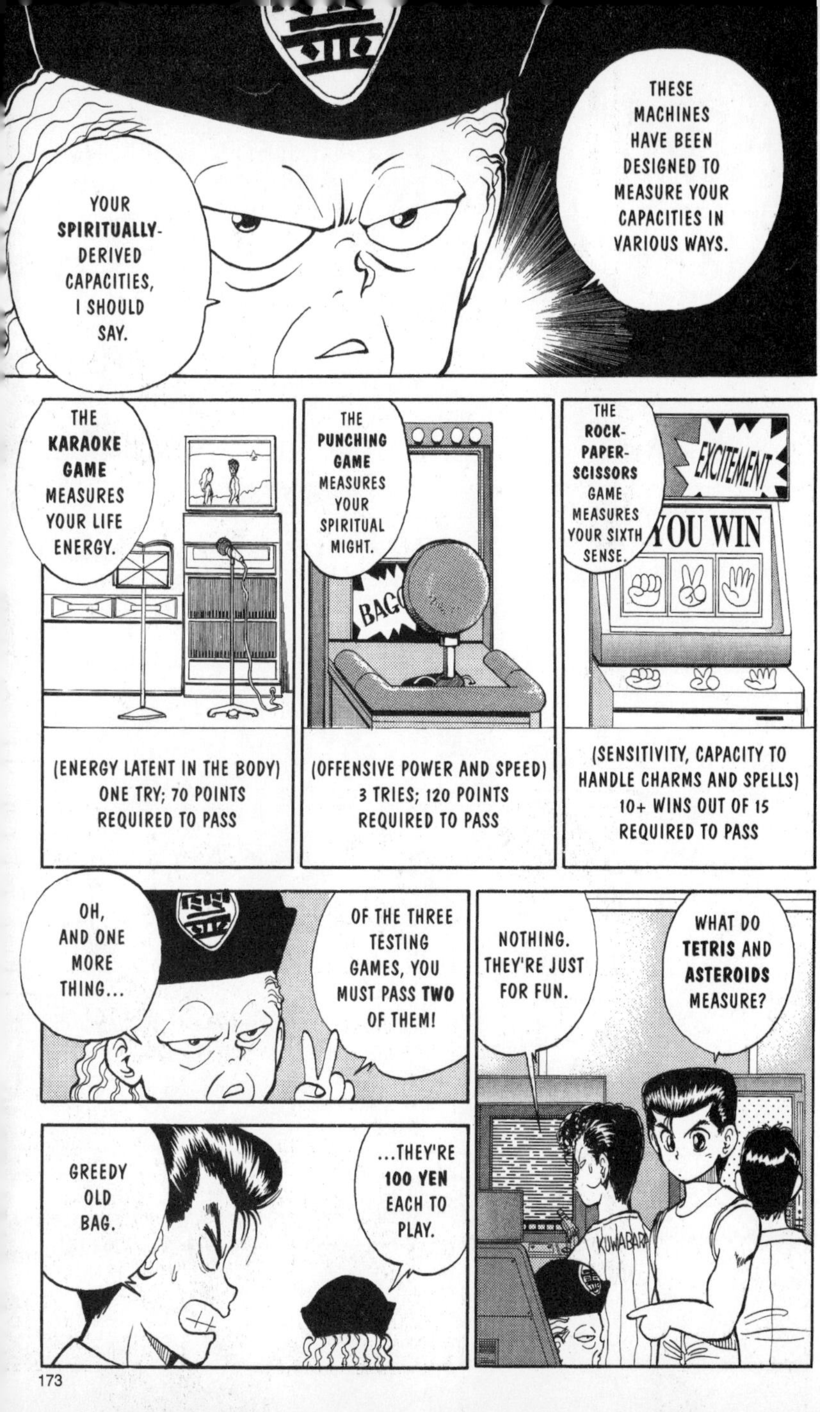
THESE MACHINES HAVE BEEN DESIGNED TO MEASURE YOUR CAPACITIES IN VARIOUS WAYS.
YOUR **SPIRITUALLY-** DERIVED CAPACITIES, I SHOULD SAY.
EXCITEMENT
YOU WIN
THE **ROCK-PAPER-SCISSORS** GAME MEASURES YOUR SIXTH SENSE.
(SENSITIVITY, CAPACITY TO HANDLE CHARMS AND SPELLS) 10+ WINS OUT OF 15 REQUIRED TO PASS
THE **PUNCHING GAME** MEASURES YOUR SPIRITUAL MIGHT.
(OFFENSIVE POWER AND SPEED) 3 TRIES; 120 POINTS REQUIRED TO PASS
THE **KARAOKE GAME** MEASURES YOUR LIFE ENERGY.
(ENERGY LATENT IN THE BODY) ONE TRY; 70 POINTS REQUIRED TO PASS
WHAT DO **TETRIS** AND **ASTEROIDS** MEASURE?
NOTHING. THEY'RE JUST FOR FUN.
KUWABARA
OF THE THREE TESTING GAMES, YOU MUST PASS **TWO** OF THEM!
OH, AND ONE MORE THING...
...THEY'RE **100 YEN** EACH TO PLAY.
GREEDY OLD BAG.

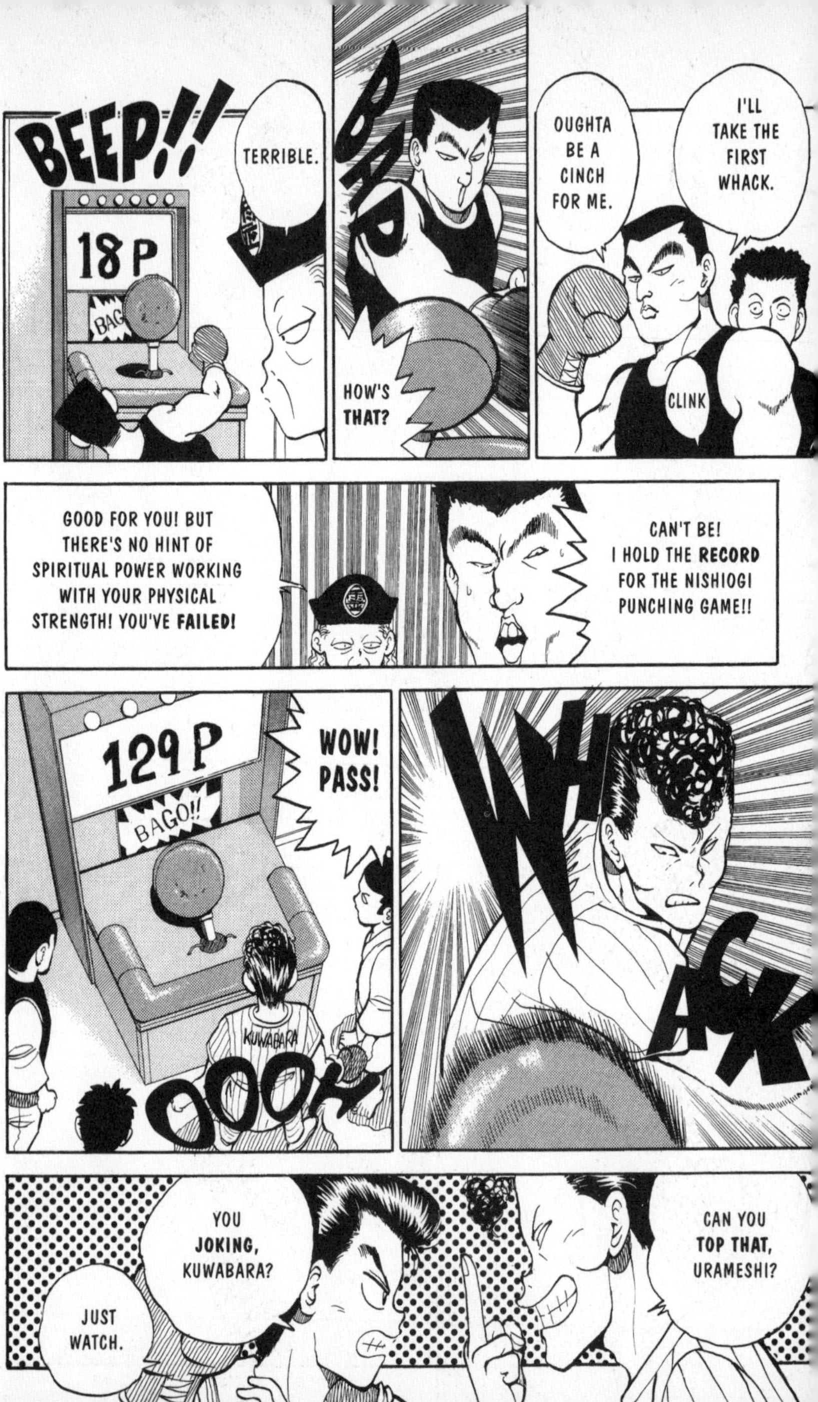
I'LL TAKE THE FIRST WHACK.
OUGHTA BE A CINCH FOR ME.
CLINK
HOW'S **THAT?**
TERRIBLE.
BEEP!!
18 P
BAG
CAN'T BE! I HOLD THE **RECORD** FOR THE NISHIOGI PUNCHING GAME!!
GOOD FOR YOU! BUT THERE'S NO HINT OF SPIRITUAL POWER WORKING WITH YOUR PHYSICAL STRENGTH! YOU'VE **FAILED!**
WHACK
WOW! PASS!
129 P
BAGO!!
KUWABARA
OOOH
CAN YOU **TOP THAT,** URAMESHI?
YOU **JOKING,** KUWABARA?
JUST WATCH.

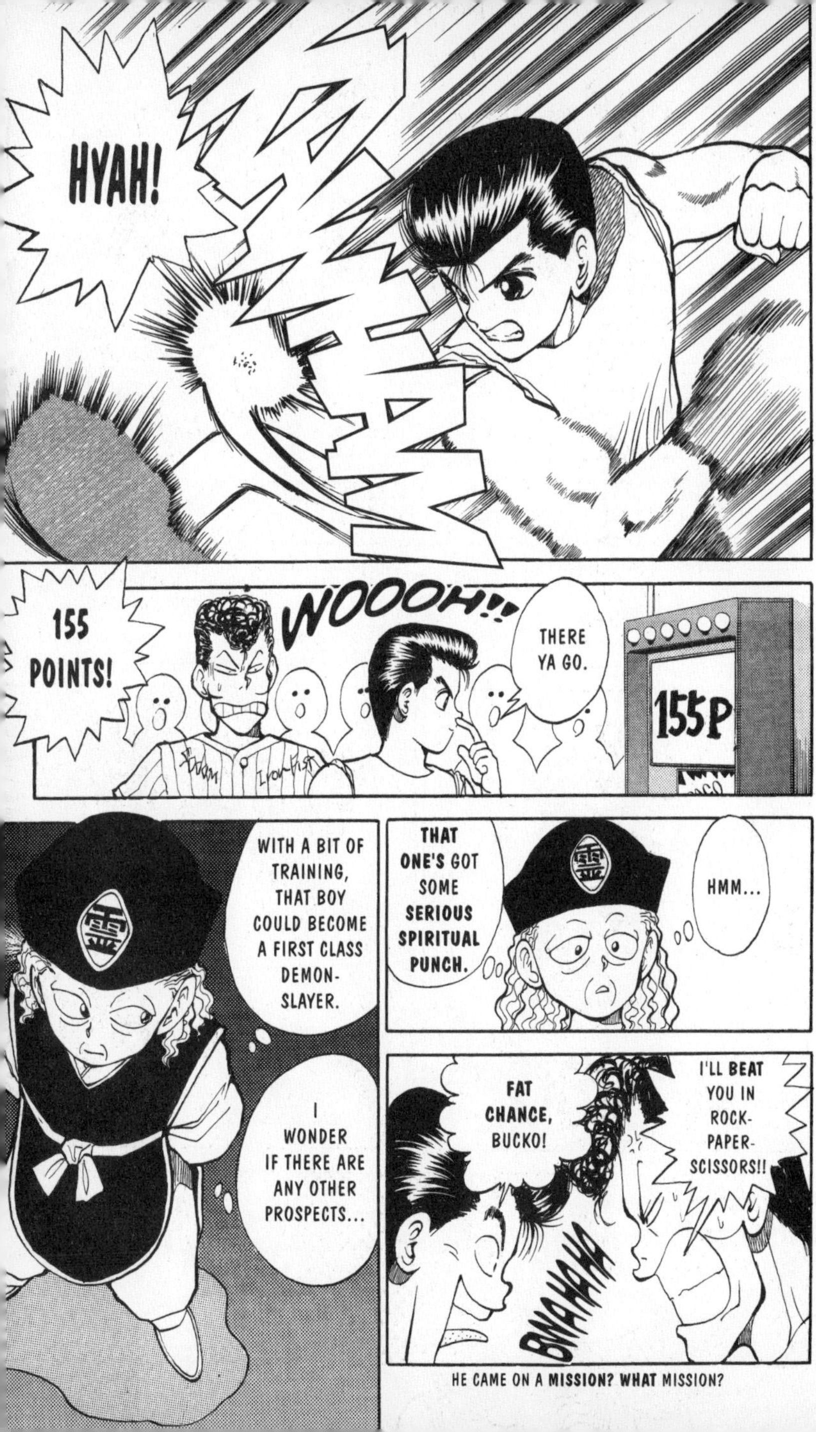
WHAM
HYAH!
155P
THERE YA GO.
WOOOH!!
155 POINTS!
Iron Fist
HMM...
THAT ONE'S GOT SOME SERIOUS SPIRITUAL PUNCH.
I'LL BEAT YOU IN ROCK-PAPER-SCISSORS!!
FAT CHANCE, BUCKO!
BWAHAHA
WITH A BIT OF TRAINING, THAT BOY COULD BECOME A FIRST CLASS DEMON-SLAYER.
I WONDER IF THERE ARE ANY OTHER PROSPECTS...

HE CAME ON A MISSION? WHAT MISSION?

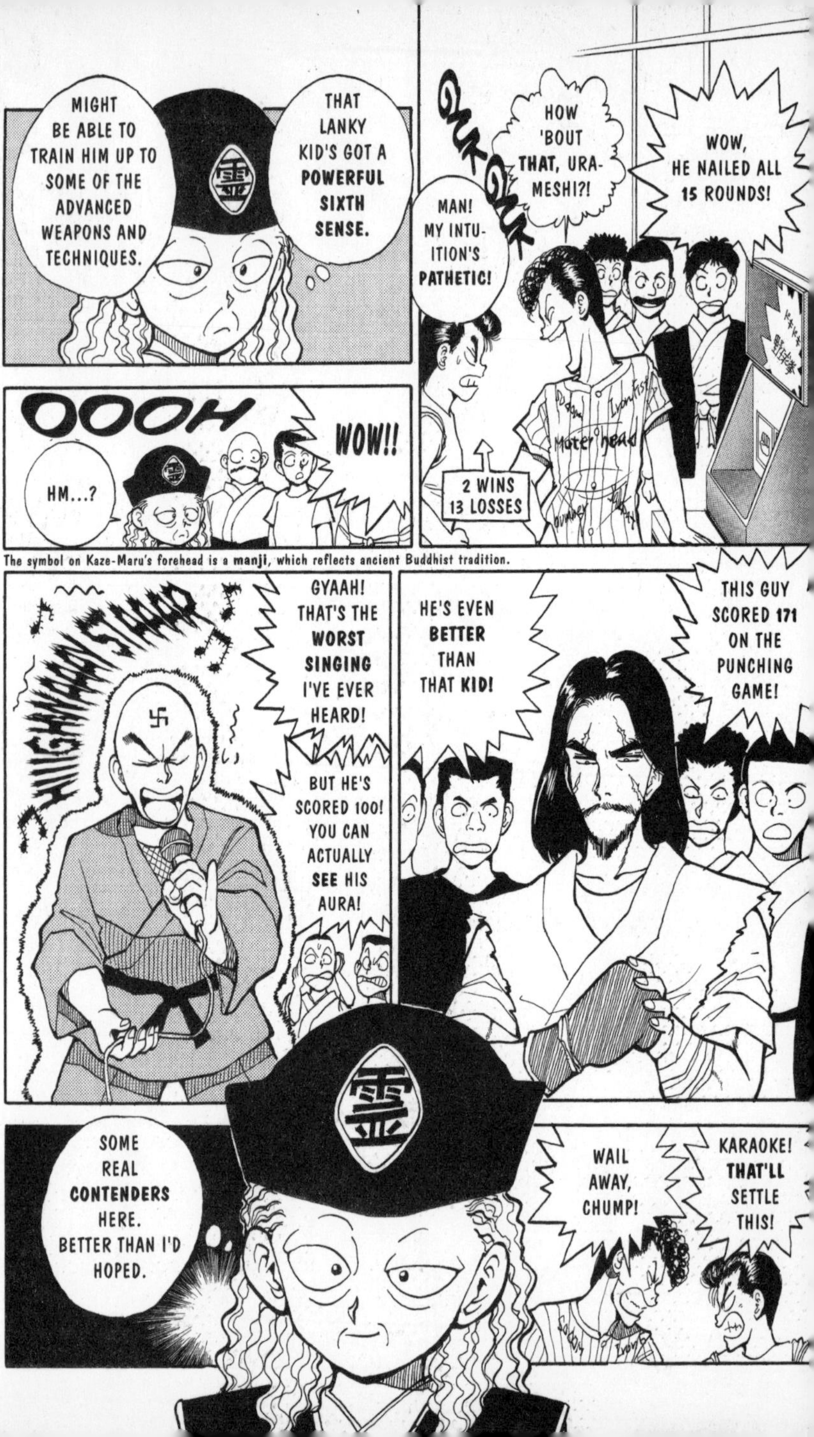
WOW, HE NAILED ALL 15 ROUNDS!
HOW 'BOUT THAT, URA-MESHI?!
MAN! MY INTU-ITION'S PATHETIC!
2 WINS 13 LOSSES
THAT LANKY KID'S GOT A POWERFUL SIXTH SENSE.
MIGHT BE ABLE TO TRAIN HIM UP TO SOME OF THE ADVANCED WEAPONS AND TECHNIQUES.
WOW!!
OOOH
HM...?
THIS GUY SCORED 171 ON THE PUNCHING GAME!
HE'S EVEN BETTER THAN THAT KID!
GYAAH! THAT'S THE WORST SINGING I'VE EVER HEARD!
BUT HE'S SCORED 100! YOU CAN ACTUALLY SEE HIS AURA!
KARAOKE! THAT'LL SETTLE THIS!
WAIL AWAY, CHUMP!
SOME REAL CONTENDERS HERE. BETTER THAN I'D HOPED.

The symbol on Kaze-Maru's forehead is a **manji**, which reflects ancient Buddhist tradition.

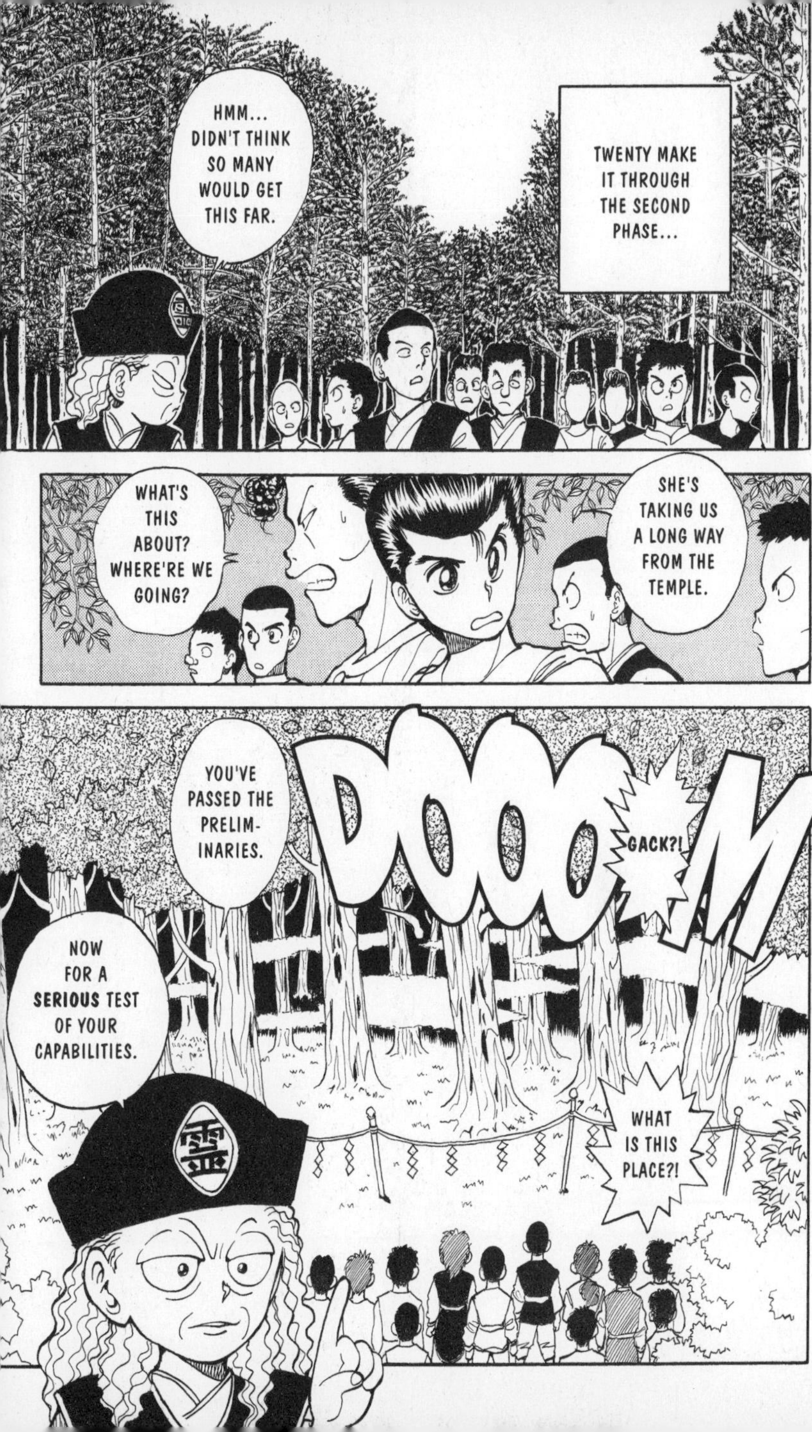

TWENTY MAKE IT THROUGH THE SECOND PHASE...
HMM... DIDN'T THINK SO MANY WOULD GET THIS FAR.
SHE'S TAKING US A LONG WAY FROM THE TEMPLE.
WHAT'S THIS ABOUT? WHERE'RE WE GOING?
DOOOM
GACK?!
YOU'VE PASSED THE PRELIMINARIES.
WHAT IS THIS PLACE?!
NOW FOR A SERIOUS TEST OF YOUR CAPABILITIES.

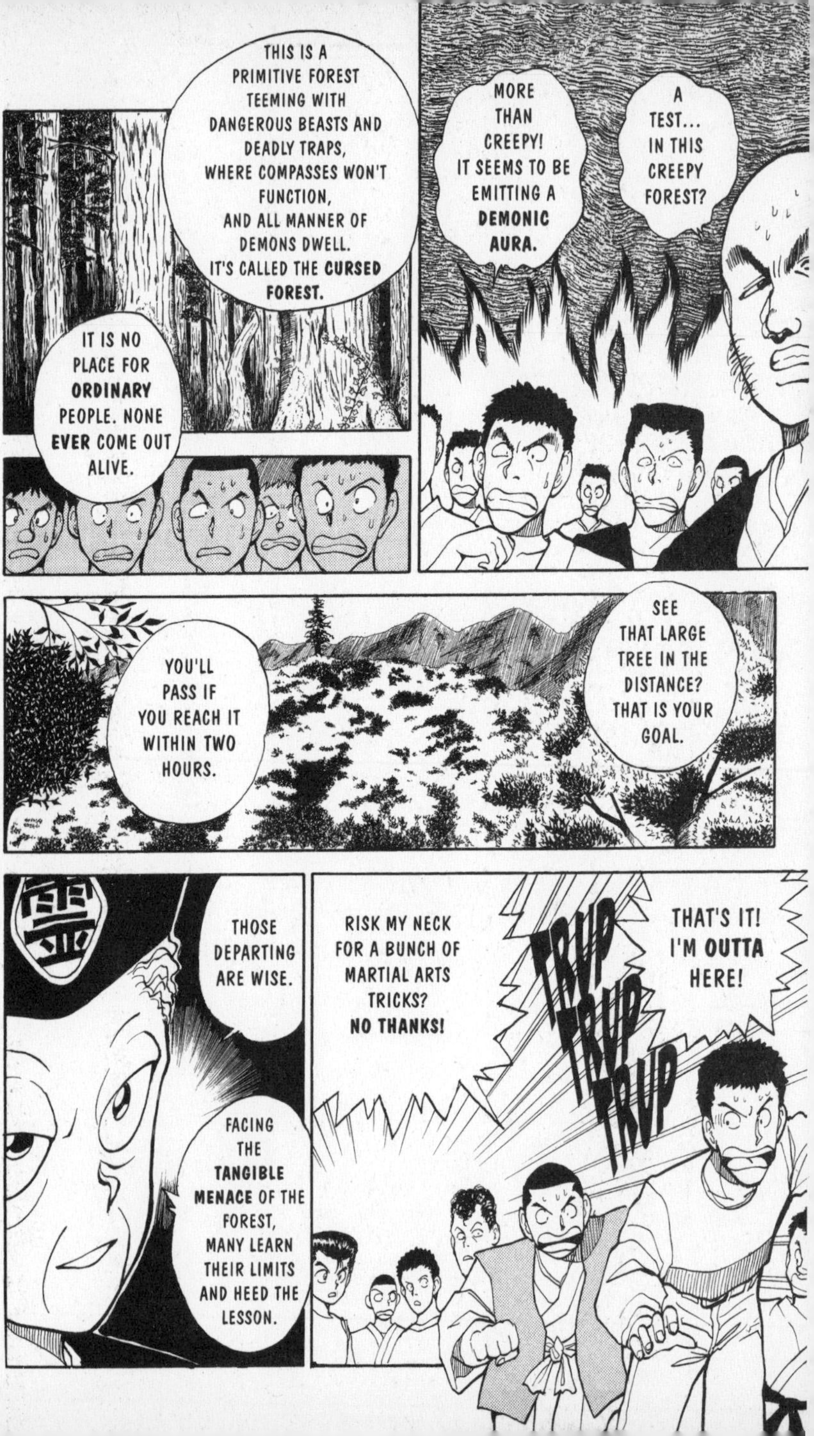
A TEST... IN THIS CREEPY FOREST?
MORE THAN CREEPY! IT SEEMS TO BE EMITTING A DEMONIC AURA.
THIS IS A PRIMITIVE FOREST TEEMING WITH DANGEROUS BEASTS AND DEADLY TRAPS, WHERE COMPASSES WON'T FUNCTION, AND ALL MANNER OF DEMONS DWELL. IT'S CALLED THE CURSED FOREST.
IT IS NO PLACE FOR ORDINARY PEOPLE. NONE EVER COME OUT ALIVE.
SEE THAT LARGE TREE IN THE DISTANCE? THAT IS YOUR GOAL.
YOU'LL PASS IF YOU REACH IT WITHIN TWO HOURS.
THAT'S IT! I'M OUTTA HERE!
TRUP TRUP TRUP
RISK MY NECK FOR A BUNCH OF MARTIAL ARTS TRICKS? NO THANKS!
THOSE DEPARTING ARE WISE.
FACING THE TANGIBLE MENACE OF THE FOREST, MANY LEARN THEIR LIMITS AND HEED THE LESSON.

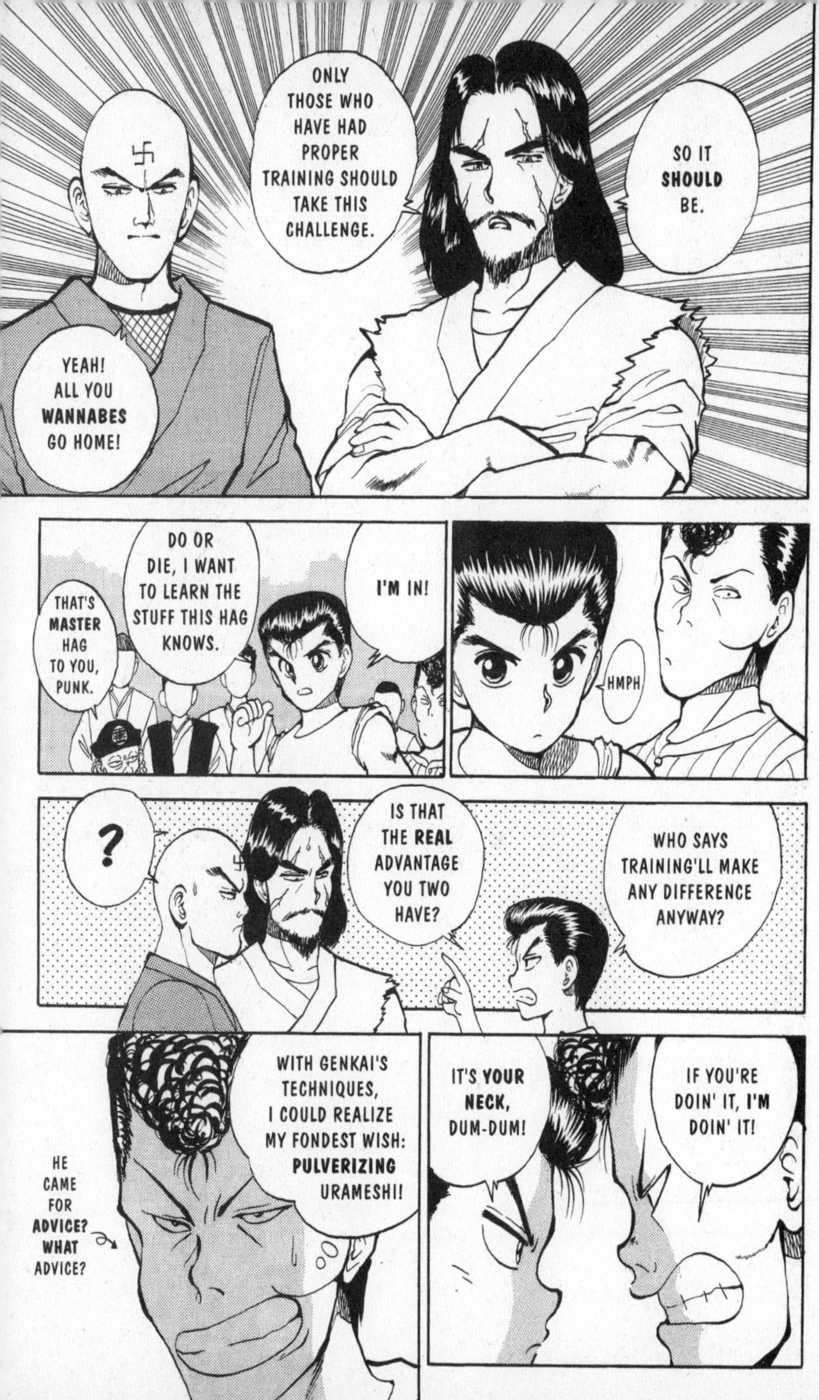
ONLY THOSE WHO HAVE HAD PROPER TRAINING SHOULD TAKE THIS CHALLENGE.
SO IT **SHOULD** BE.
YEAH! ALL YOU **WANNABES** GO HOME!
HMPH
I'M IN!
DO OR DIE, I WANT TO LEARN THE STUFF THIS HAG KNOWS.
THAT'S **MASTER** HAG TO YOU, PUNK.
WHO SAYS TRAINING'LL MAKE ANY DIFFERENCE ANYWAY?
IS THAT THE **REAL** ADVANTAGE YOU TWO HAVE?
?
IF YOU'RE DOIN' IT, **I'M** DOIN' IT!
IT'S **YOUR NECK,** DUM-DUM!
WITH GENKAI'S TECHNIQUES, I COULD REALIZE MY FONDEST WISH: **PULVERIZING** URAMESHI!
HE CAME FOR **ADVICE? WHAT** ADVICE?

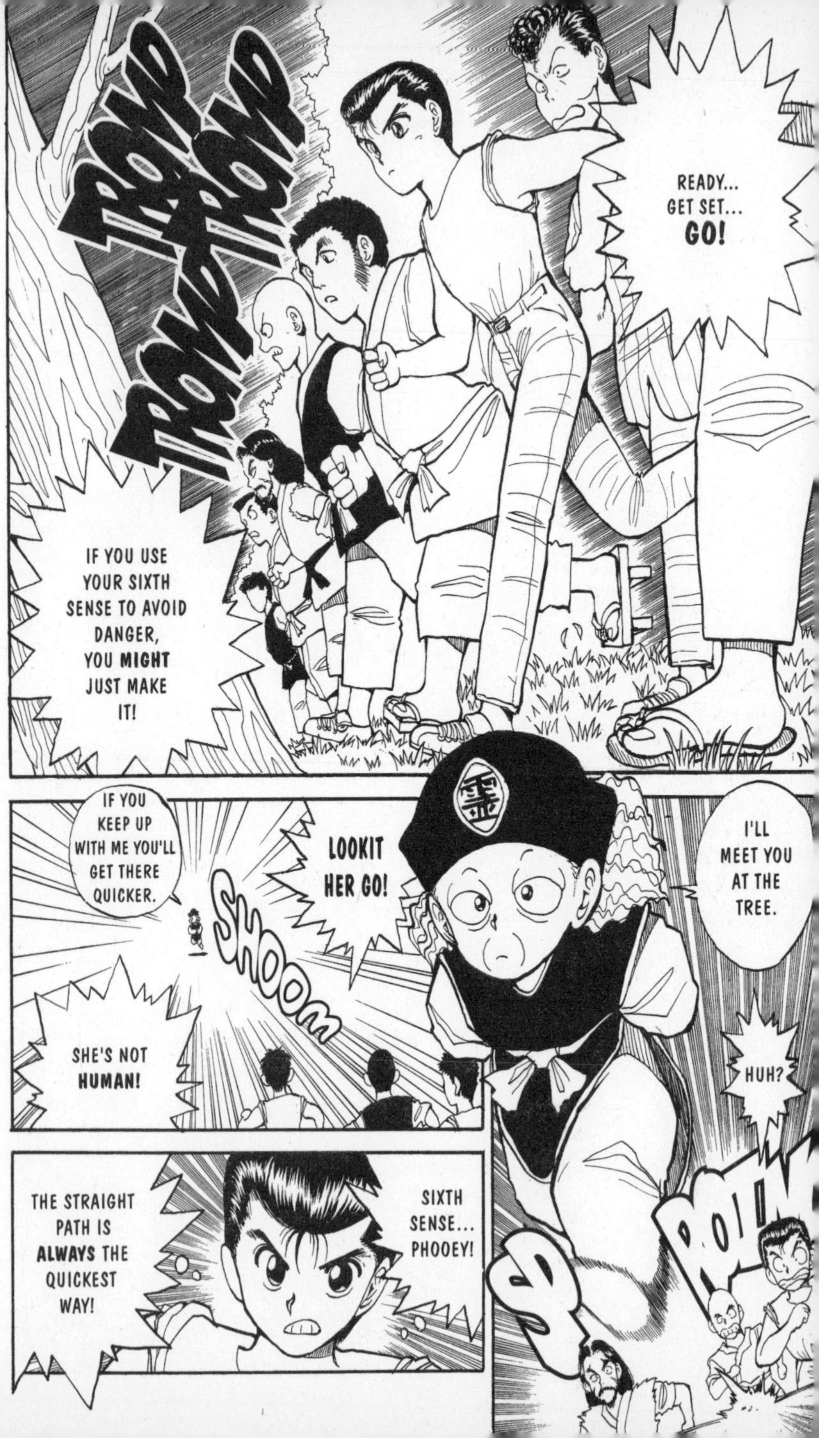
READY... GET SET... **GO!**
IF YOU USE YOUR SIXTH SENSE TO AVOID DANGER, YOU **MIGHT** JUST MAKE IT!
I'LL MEET YOU AT THE TREE.
HUH?
LOOKIT HER GO!
IF YOU KEEP UP WITH ME YOU'LL GET THERE QUICKER.
SHOOOM
SHE'S NOT **HUMAN!**
SIXTH SENSE... PHOOEY!
THE STRAIGHT PATH IS **ALWAYS** THE QUICKEST WAY!

READ THIS WAY

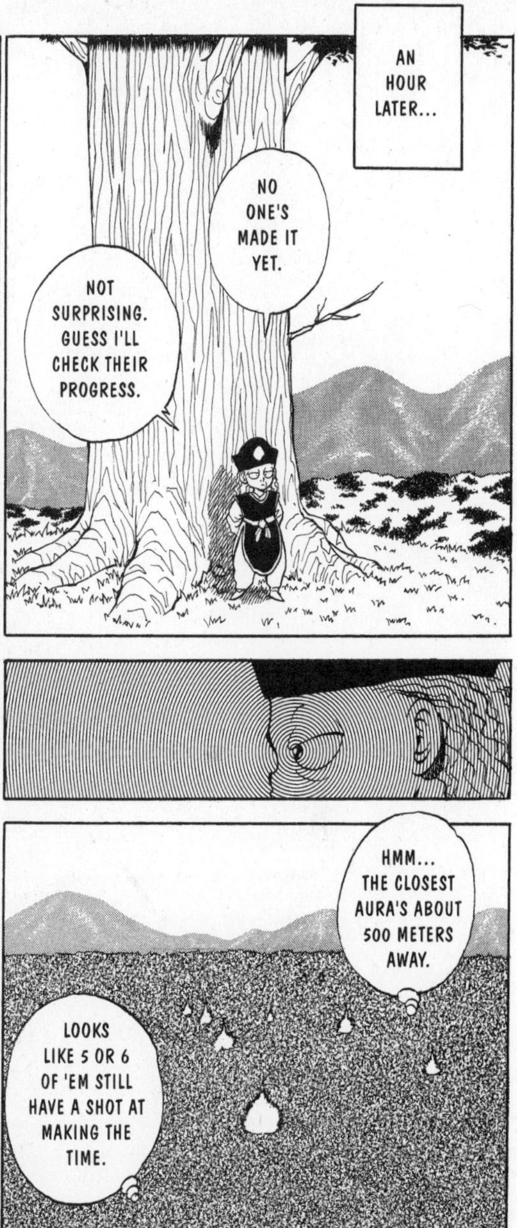
AN HOUR LATER...
NO ONE'S MADE IT YET.
NOT SURPRISING. GUESS I'LL CHECK THEIR PROGRESS.
HMM... THE CLOSEST AURA'S ABOUT 500 METERS AWAY.
LOOKS LIKE 5 OR 6 OF 'EM STILL HAVE A SHOT AT MAKING THE TIME.

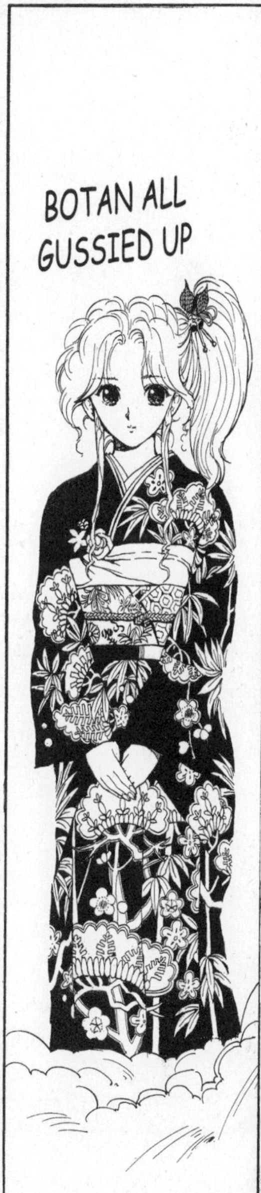
BOTAN ALL GUSSIED UP

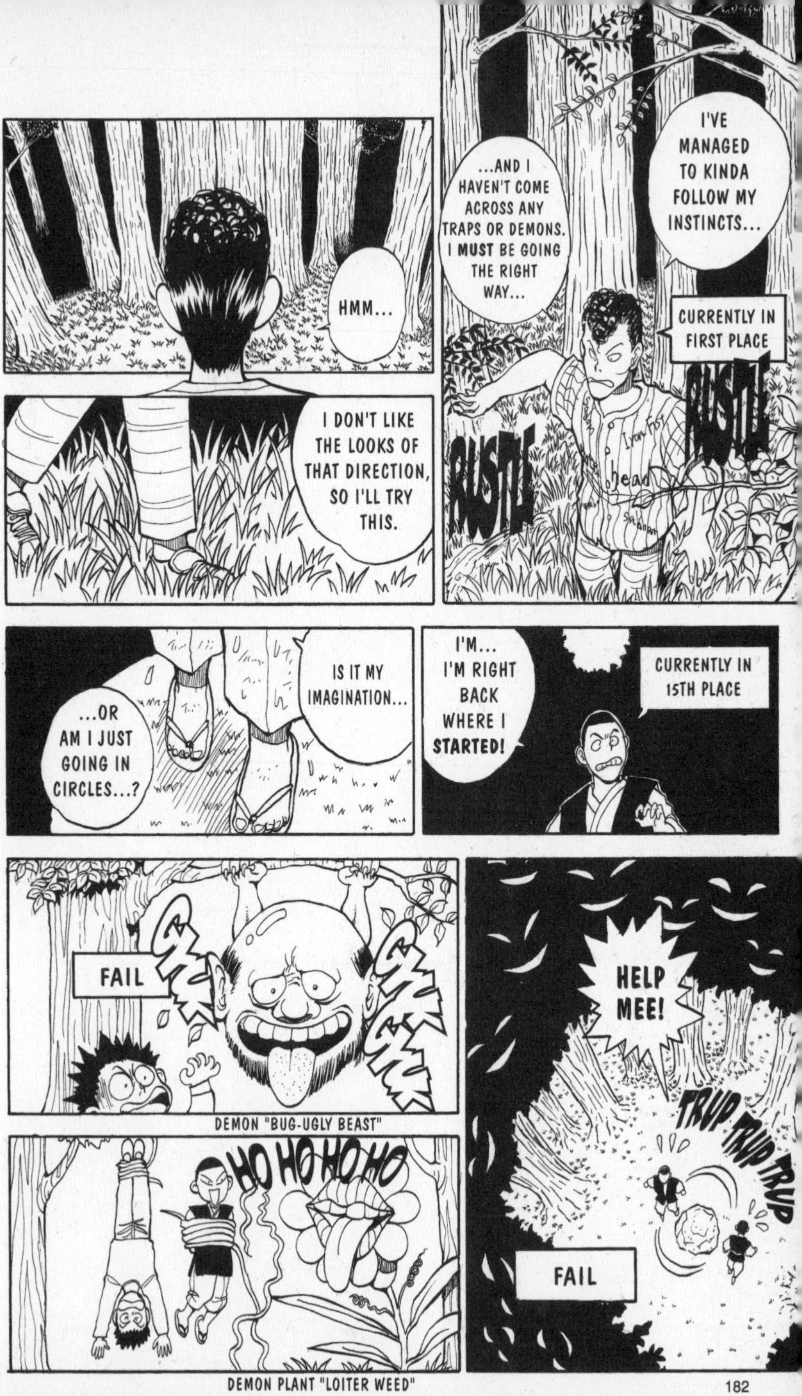
I'VE MANAGED TO KINDA FOLLOW MY INSTINCTS...
...AND I HAVEN'T COME ACROSS ANY TRAPS OR DEMONS. I MUST BE GOING THE RIGHT WAY...
CURRENTLY IN FIRST PLACE
RUSTLE
RUSTLE
HMM...
I DON'T LIKE THE LOOKS OF THAT DIRECTION, SO I'LL TRY THIS.
CURRENTLY IN 15TH PLACE
I'M... I'M RIGHT BACK WHERE I STARTED!
IS IT MY IMAGINATION...
...OR AM I JUST GOING IN CIRCLES...?
HELP MEE!
TRUP TRUP TRUP
FAIL
FAIL
DEMON "BUG-UGLY BEAST"
HO HO HO HO
DEMON PLANT "LOITER WEED"

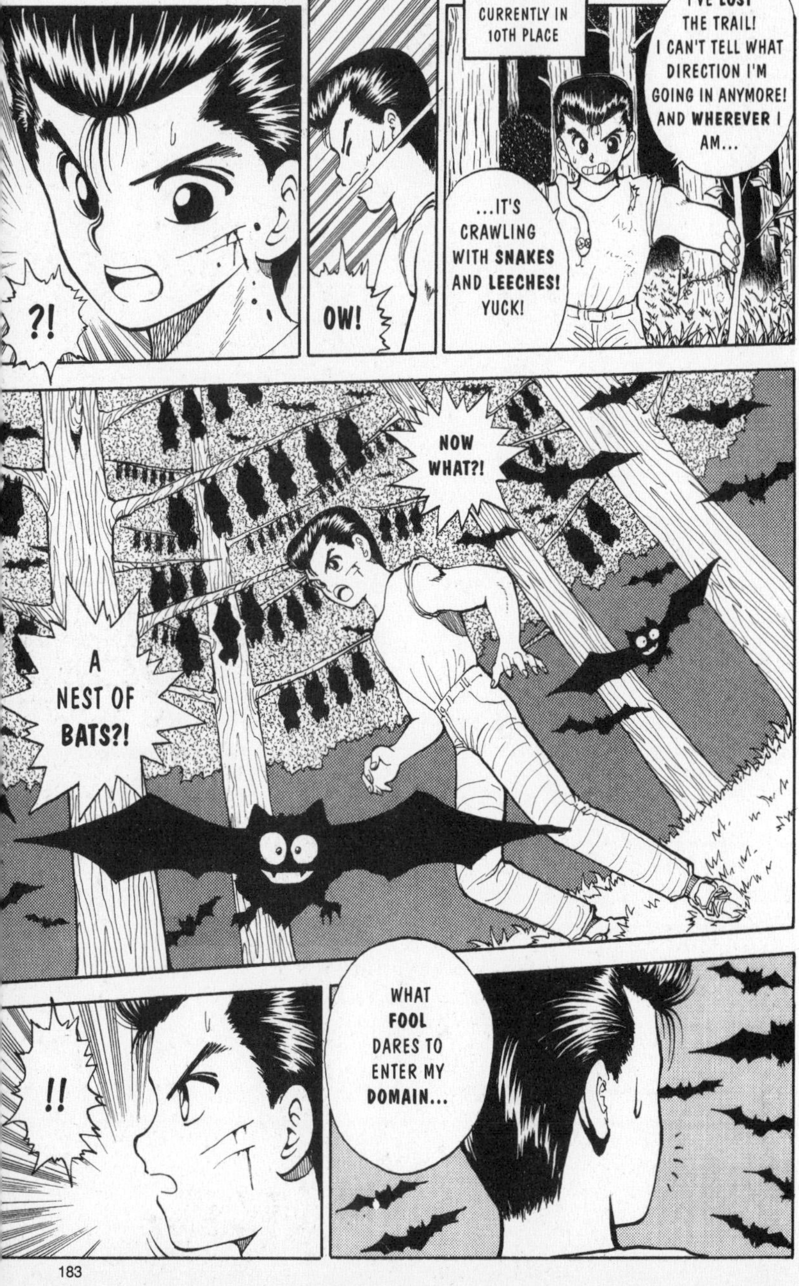
CURRENTLY IN 10TH PLACE
I'VE LOST THE TRAIL! I CAN'T TELL WHAT DIRECTION I'M GOING IN ANYMORE! AND WHEREVER I AM...
...IT'S CRAWLING WITH SNAKES AND LEECHES! YUCK!
OW!
?!
NOW WHAT?!
A NEST OF BATS?!
WHAT FOOL DARES TO ENTER MY DOMAIN...
!!

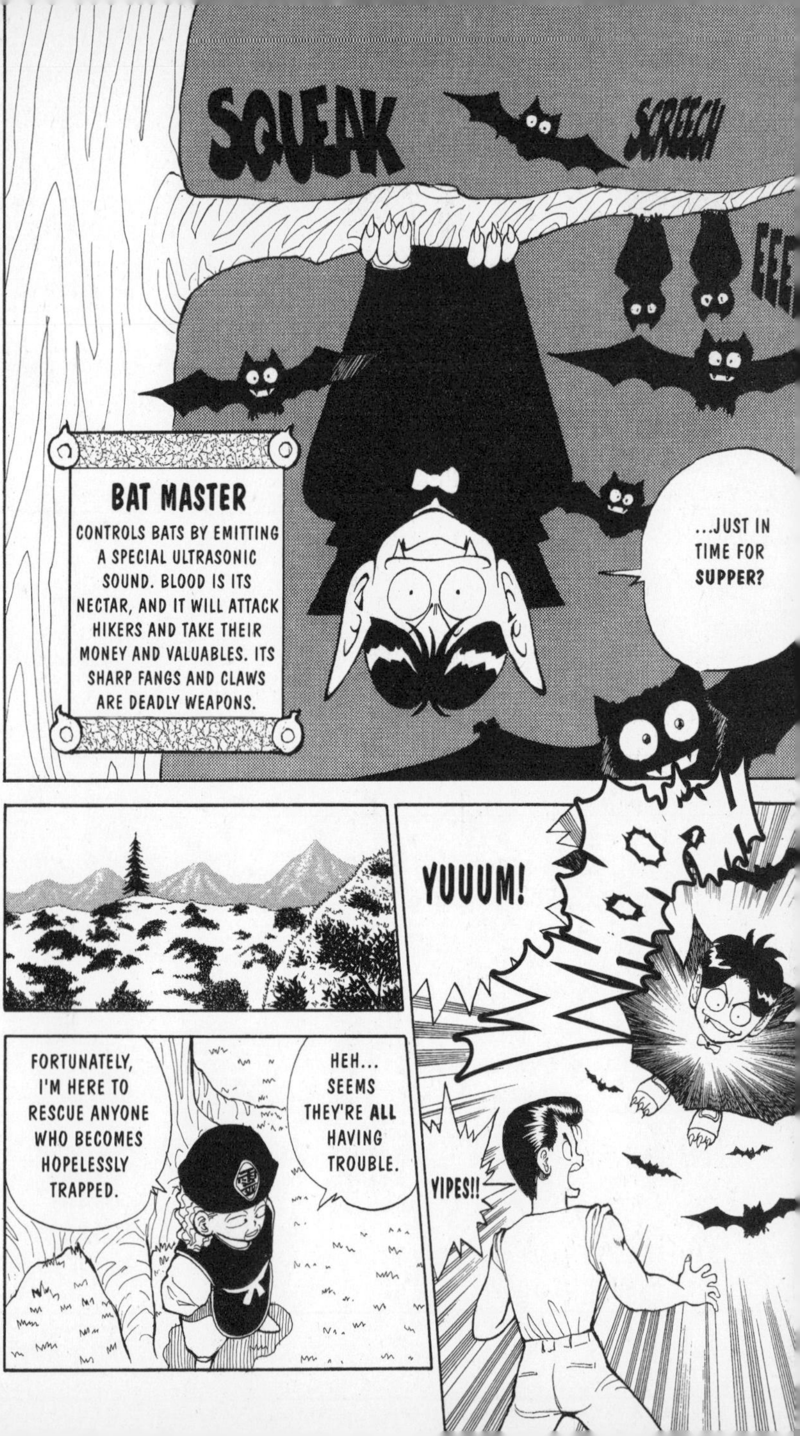
SCREECH
EEE
SQUEAK
...JUST IN TIME FOR **SUPPER?**
BAT MASTER
CONTROLS BATS BY EMITTING A SPECIAL ULTRASONIC SOUND. BLOOD IS ITS NECTAR, AND IT WILL ATTACK HIKERS AND TAKE THEIR MONEY AND VALUABLES. ITS SHARP FANGS AND CLAWS ARE DEADLY WEAPONS.
YUUUM!
YIPES!!
HEH... SEEMS THEY'RE **ALL** HAVING TROUBLE.
FORTUNATELY, I'M HERE TO RESCUE ANYONE WHO BECOMES HOPELESSLY TRAPPED.

READ THIS WAY

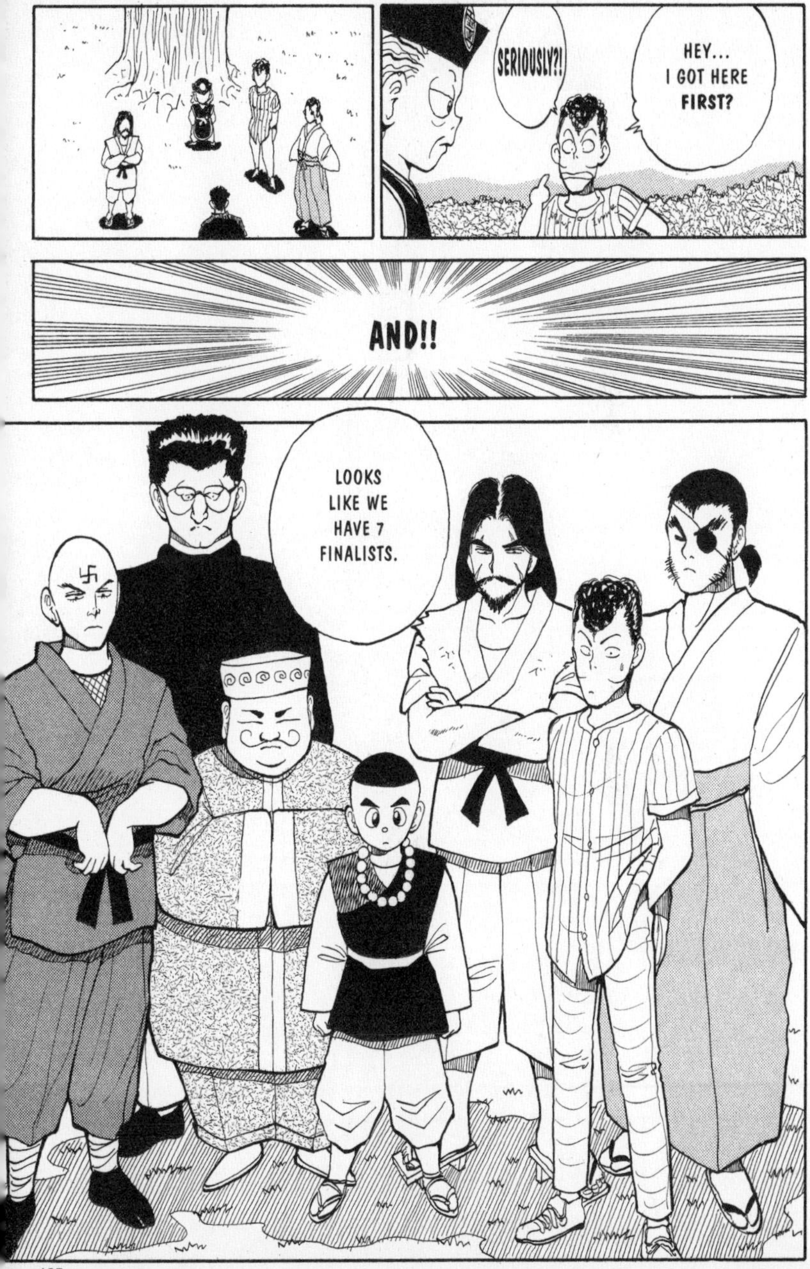
HEY... I GOT HERE FIRST?
SERIOUSLY?!
AND!!
LOOKS LIKE WE HAVE 7 FINALISTS.

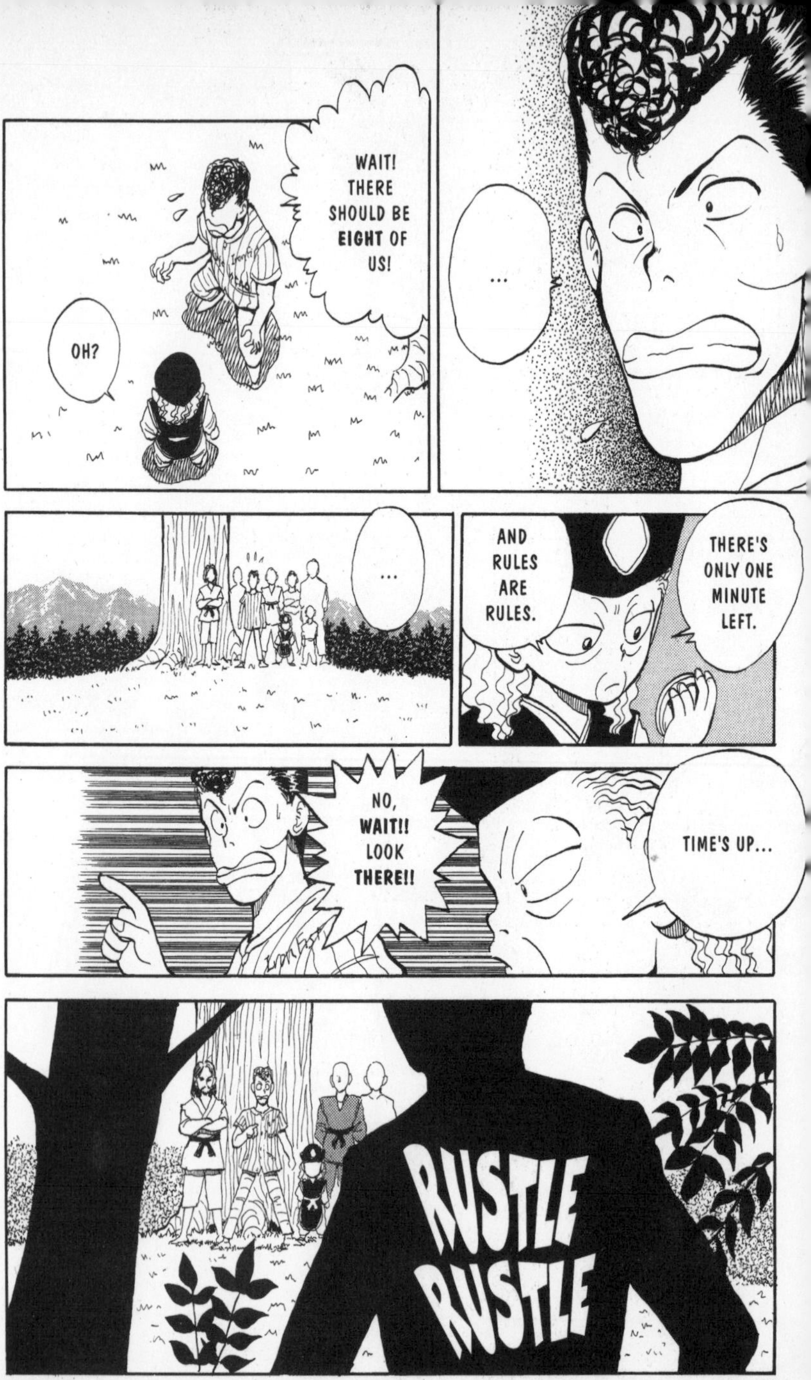
...
WAIT! THERE SHOULD BE EIGHT OF US!
OH?
THERE'S ONLY ONE MINUTE LEFT.
AND RULES ARE RULES.
...
TIME'S UP...
NO, WAIT!! LOOK THERE!!
RUSTLE RUSTLE

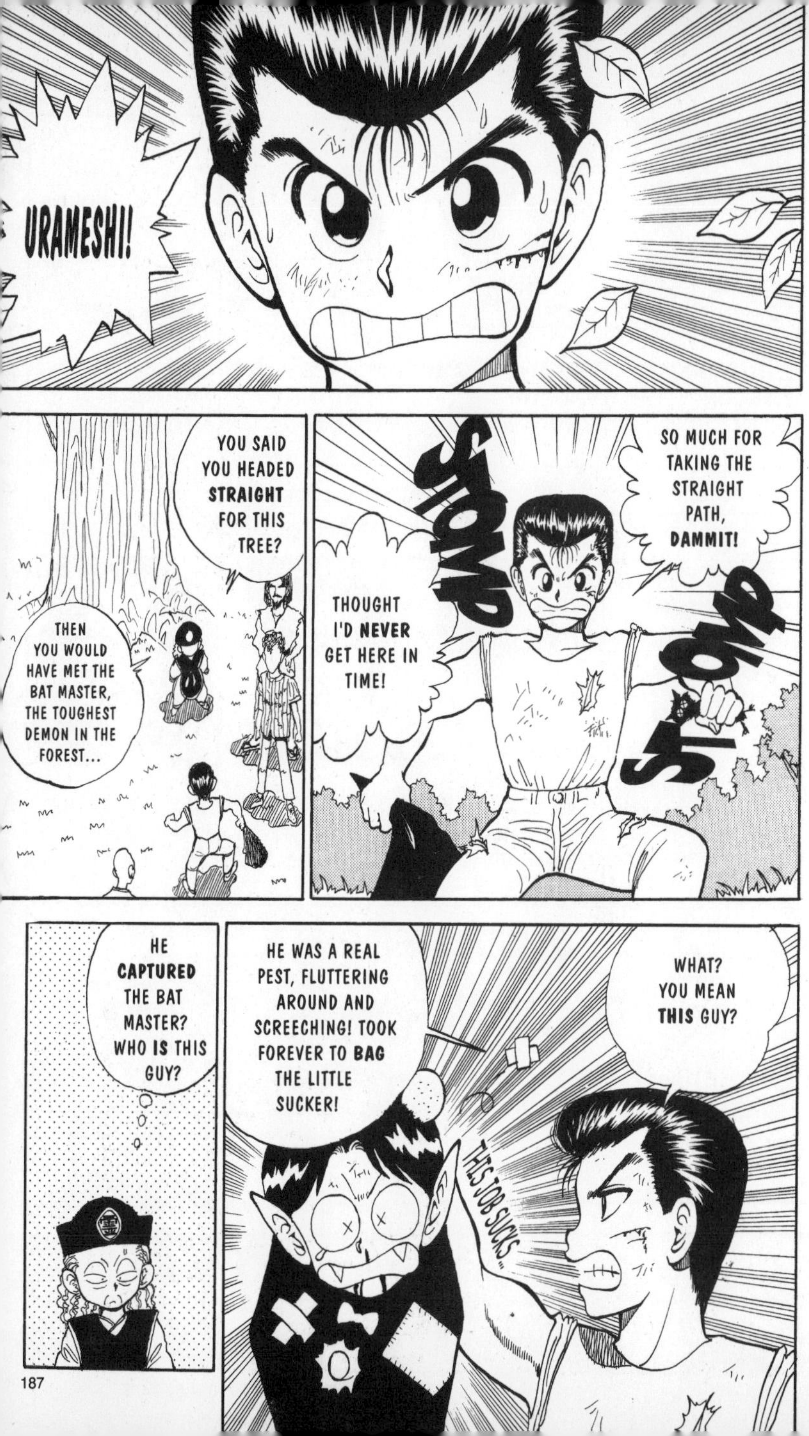
URAMESHI!
SO MUCH FOR TAKING THE STRAIGHT PATH, DAMMIT!
STOMP
STOMP
THOUGHT I'D NEVER GET HERE IN TIME!
YOU SAID YOU HEADED STRAIGHT FOR THIS TREE?
THEN YOU WOULD HAVE MET THE BAT MASTER, THE TOUGHEST DEMON IN THE FOREST...
WHAT? YOU MEAN THIS GUY?
HE WAS A REAL PEST, FLUTTERING AROUND AND SCREECHING! TOOK FOREVER TO BAG THE LITTLE SUCKER!
THIS JOB SUCKS...
HE CAPTURED THE BAT MASTER? WHO IS THIS GUY?

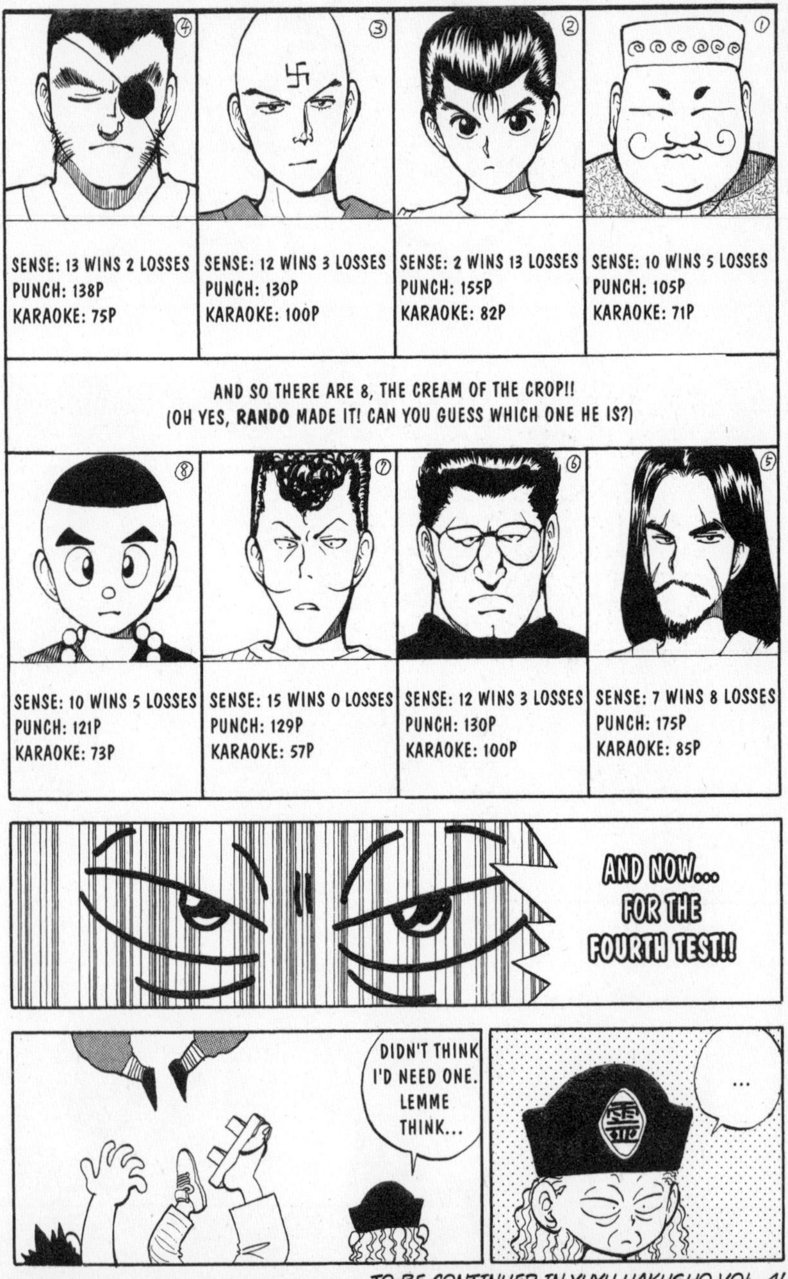
①
SENSE: 10 WINS 5 LOSSES
PUNCH: 105P
KARAOKE: 71P
②
SENSE: 2 WINS 13 LOSSES
PUNCH: 155P
KARAOKE: 82P
③
SENSE: 12 WINS 3 LOSSES
PUNCH: 130P
KARAOKE: 100P
④
SENSE: 13 WINS 2 LOSSES
PUNCH: 138P
KARAOKE: 75P
AND SO THERE ARE 8, THE CREAM OF THE CROP!!
(OH YES, RANDO MADE IT! CAN YOU GUESS WHICH ONE HE IS?)
⑤
SENSE: 7 WINS 8 LOSSES
PUNCH: 175P
KARAOKE: 85P
⑥
SENSE: 12 WINS 3 LOSSES
PUNCH: 130P
KARAOKE: 100P
⑦
SENSE: 15 WINS 0 LOSSES
PUNCH: 129P
KARAOKE: 57P
⑧
SENSE: 10 WINS 5 LOSSES
PUNCH: 121P
KARAOKE: 73P
AND NOW... FOR THE FOURTH TEST!!
...
DIDN'T THINK I'D NEED ONE. LEMME THINK...

TO BE CONTINUED IN YUYU HAKUSHO VOL. 4!

IN THE NEXT VOLUME...

Now that the wheat has been separated from the chaff, the battle to become Genkai's disciple begins in earnest - with a tournament to the death! As he fights for his life, Yusuke realizes there's only one way he can unmask Rando: defeat all other comers and face him in the final battle! But what if Kuwabara - who has no idea he'll be fighting a demon - goes up against Rando first?

COMING JUNE 2004!

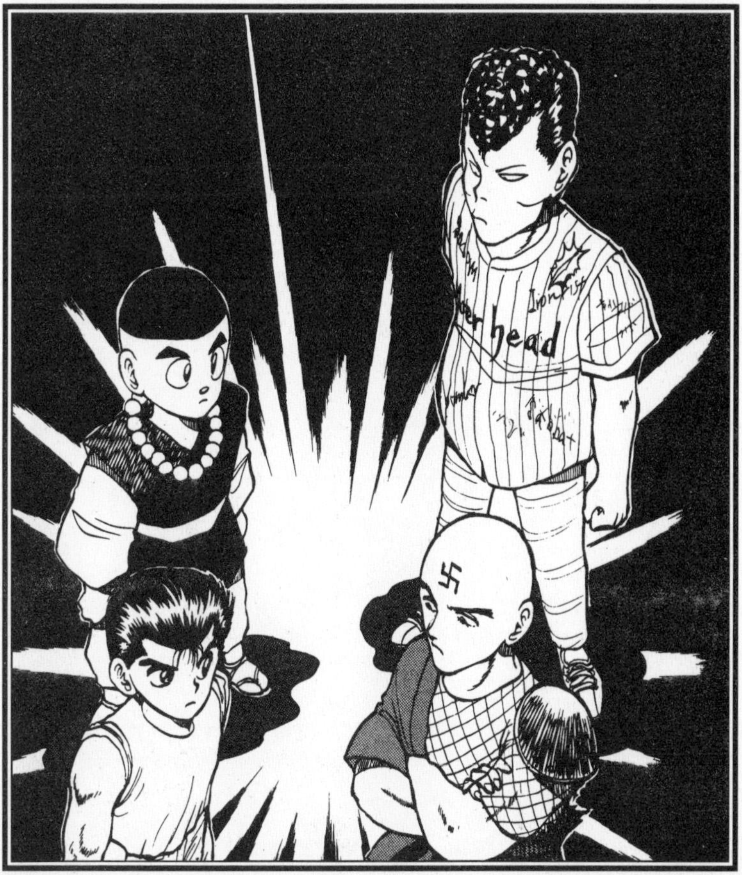

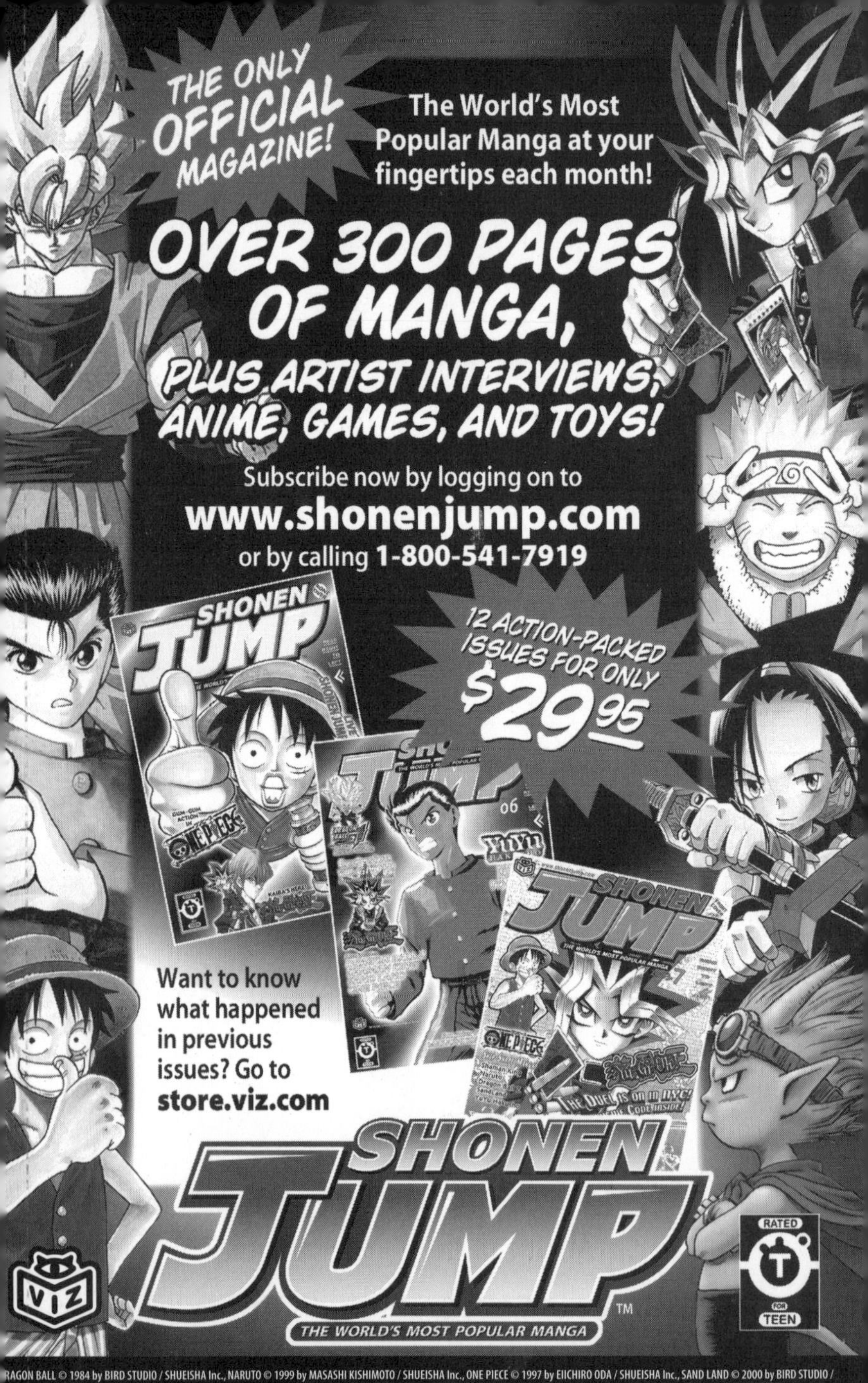

THE ONLY OFFICIAL MAGAZINE!
The World's Most Popular Manga at your fingertips each month!
OVER 300 PAGES OF MANGA,
PLUS ARTIST INTERVIEWS, ANIME, GAMES, AND TOYS!
Subscribe now by logging on to
www.shonenjump.com
or by calling 1-800-541-7919
12 ACTION-PACKED ISSUES FOR ONLY $29.95
Want to know what happened in previous issues? Go to store.viz.com
SHONEN JUMP
THE WORLD'S MOST POPULAR MANGA
VIZ
RATED T FOR TEEN

COMPLETE OUR SURVEY AND LET US KNOW WHAT YOU THINK!

☐ Please check here if you DO NOT wish to receive information or future offers from VIZ

Name: _____

Address: _____

City: _____ **State:** _____ **Zip:** _____

E-mail: _____

☐ Male ☐ Female **Date of Birth** (mm/dd/yyyy): ___/___/___ (Under 13? Parental consent required)

What race/ethnicity do you consider yourself? (please check one)

☐ Asian/Pacific Islander ☐ Black/African American ☐ Hispanic/Latino

☐ Native American/Alaskan Native ☐ White/Caucasian ☐ Other: _____

What VIZ product did you purchase? (check all that apply and indicate title purchased)

☐ DVD/VHS _____

☐ Graphic Novel _____

☐ Magazines _____

☐ Merchandise _____

Reason for purchase: (check all that apply)

☐ Special offer ☐ Favorite title ☐ Gift

☐ Recommendation ☐ Other _____

Where did you make your purchase? (please check one)

☐ Comic store ☐ Bookstore ☐ Mass/Grocery Store

☐ Newsstand ☐ Video/Video Game Store ☐ Other: _____

☐ Online (site: _____)

What other VIZ properties have you purchased/own? _____

_____

How many anime and/or manga titles have you purchased in the last year? How many were VIZ titles? (please check one from each column)

ANIME	MANGA	VIZ
☐ None	☐ None	☐ None
☐ 1-4	☐ 1-4	☐ 1-4
☐ 5-10	☐ 5-10	☐ 5-10
☐ 11+	☐ 11+	☐ 11+

I find the pricing of VIZ products to be: (please check one)

☐ Cheap   ☐ Reasonable   ☐ Expensive

What genre of manga and anime would you like to see from VIZ? (please check two)

☐ Adventure   ☐ Comic Strip   ☐ Science Fiction   ☐ Fighting

☐ Horror   ☐ Romance   ☐ Fantasy   ☐ Sports

What do you think of VIZ's new look?

☐ Love It   ☐ It's OK   ☐ Hate It   ☐ Didn't Notice   ☐ No Opinion

Which do you prefer? (please check one)

☐ Reading right-to-left

☐ Reading left-to-right

Which do you prefer? (please check one)

☐ Sound effects in English

☐ Sound effects in Japanese with English captions

☐ Sound effects in Japanese only with a glossary at the back

THANK YOU! Please send the completed form to:

NJW Research
42 Catharine St.
Poughkeepsie, NY 12601

All information provided will be used for internal purposes only. We promise not to sell or otherwise divulge your information.